D1261577

Intimate Enemies

Intimate Enemies

THE TWO WORLDS
OF THE
Baroness de Pontalba

CHRISTINA VELLA

LOUISIANA STATE UNIVERSITY PRESS
Baton Rouge and London

06 05 04 03   5 4

Designer: Melanie O'Quinn Samaha
Typeface: Galliard
Typesetter: Impressions Book and Journal Services, Inc.
Printer and binder: Thomson-Shore, Inc.

Grateful acknowledgment is made for permission to publish excerpts from unpublished materials in the following collections: Manuscripts, Louisiana Historical Center; Louisiana Supreme Court Records, Earl K. Long Library, University of New Orleans; Special Collections, Howard-Tilton Memorial Library, Tulane University; Louisiana Division, New Orleans Public Library; Archives du Maréchal Ney, Archives Nationales, Paris. The author also wishes to thank Count Adrien Balny d'Avricourt for permission to quote from a letter of Blanche de Pontalba to her son Henri, in the collection of André Maricourt.

LIBRARY OF CONGRESS CATALOGING-IN-PUBLICATION DATA

Vella, Christina, 1942–
    Intimate enemies : the two worlds of the Baroness de Pontalba /
Christina Vella.
        p.   cm.
    Includes bibliographical references (p.   ) and index.
    ISBN 0-8071-2144-4 (cloth : alk. paper)
        1. Pontalba, Micaëla Leonarda Almonester de, baroness, 1795–1874.
    2. Women—Louisiana—New Orleans—Biography.   3. Nobility—
    Louisiana—New Orleans—Biography.   4. New Orleans (La.)—
    Biography. 5. Historic buildings—Louisiana—New Orleans.
    6. Paris (France)—Biography.   7. Historic buildings—France—Paris.
    I. Title.
    F379.N553P668   1997
    976.3'3505'092—dc21
    [B]   96-52688
                                                                              CIP

The paper in this book meets the guidelines for permanence and durability of the Committee on Production Guidelines for Book Longevity of the Council on Library Resources. ∞

To Wendy, Peter Pan, and Tink

with all my love

199

Contents

Illustrations

Acknowledgments

M Y research in France was financed by a generous grant from Elizabeth and the late Paul Selley, awarded by Tulane University, through its former provost, Francis Lawrence. I am grateful for the interest that the Selleys and Dr. Lawrence showed in this work.

I am indebted to all the archivists, librarians, and civilians who dredged up references I would never have thought of and helped me track down elusive details. In particular I want to thank Rose Lambert, formerly of the Louisiana Historical Center, and Wayne Everard of the New Orleans Public Library. I was helped by Frances Batson, Robert V. Bledsoe, Joan G. Caldwell, Patty Eischen, Barbara Everett, W. Burton Harder, Claudia Kheel, John Lawrence, John T. Magill, the late John Mahé, Wilbur E. Meneray, Guillermo Náñez-Falcón, Charles Nolan, Wayne Phillips, Sally Reeves, James Sefcik, and last and most, Marie Windell, God bless her!

In France my husband and I were patiently assisted by archivists M. Aucouturier of the Paris Chambre des Notaires; Mlle. Aujoug and Mlle. Brigitte Lainé at the Archives de Paris; M. Gabion at the Archives Annexe in Villemoison; and Mme. Claudine de Vaulchier at l'Academie d'Architecture, Paris.

For a historian, the best archives are like the most sophisticated computer programs: to really use them for anything more than superficial work, you need someone to help you learn their idiosyncrasies, someone to help you get into them. Though she is not a librarian, my friend Edmée Chanay was that someone, guiding me through the complicated cataloging systems at the Archives Nationales and the Bibliothèque Nationale. Because of the hours she spent with me, our research in Paris was shortened by many days.

Other people did other important favors: Leonard V. Huber and the late Sam Wilson, Jr., shared their topic and their time. Dodi Plateau facilitated my use of pictures in the Historic New Orleans Collection; Mary Edna Sullivan dated pictures for me. Reese Massey and Monica C. Pilman instructed me in the niceties of using the computer; Ralph Lee Woodward, Jr., read a first draft of two chapters long, long ago. Richard E. Greenleaf answered questions about Spain's colonial administration; Thomas Brown and William Sizeler made architectural drawings available; Ted Rowley and Tony Cuevas typed an early version of the manuscript, a very big favor indeed.

Lawrence Powell has been my mentor through two versions of the manuscript; his careful reading—twice—his intelligence, and enthusiasm have meant a great deal to me.

Harry Redman, Jr., pored over Micaela's letters with me and helped me unsnarl her penmanship and atrocious French spelling; he also read the entire manuscript and made suggestions concerning my French translations; Gail Klauder-Vaz reviewed my Spanish translations of Miró's letters. But even these two good friends could not entirely save me from making errors that may remain.

Vaughn Glasgow made the suggestion, years ago: "Why don't you write a biography of the Baroness de Pontalba?" Mazie Roy Doody read the manuscript and contributed her good sense; and Herbert Marks gave his expert attention to the passages concerning nineteenth-century medical treatments. My students at Tulane University unwittingly helped edit this work by perking up at certain topics in French and Louisiana history, and falling asleep at others. My patient editors, John Easterly and Catherine Landry, worked wittingly and wakefully through the whole manuscript.

I deeply appreciate the encouragement and good will I continue to receive from the Pontalba and Visconti descendants. Baron Henri de Pontalba spent a long day talking with me at Mont-l'Évêque, allowing me and my little entourage to tramp around his château and his family history as if it were our own. My children still remember the Baroness Henri de Pontalba's kindness and chocolate yogurt. Countess Paul de Leusse received us graciously and showed us her Pontalba family portraits. Count Adrien Balny d'Avricourt offered me Blanche de Pontalba's important letter, a document I never knew existed until he provided me with a handwritten copy. The late Count Hervé du Périer de Larson gave me unsupervised access to the papers of his ancestor L.-T.-J. Visconti and assisted me in every possible way. Through all of our discussions, none of these lovely people tried to influence my interpretation of personalities or events in the slightest.

My work with the U.S. Department of State in 1995 inspired me to give closer attention than I otherwise might have to certain details regarding the Hôtel Pontalba, now the residence of the ambassador to France. I want to thank Jennifer Loynd and Vivien Woofter of the Curatorial Services Program, Interior Design and Furnishings Division, for their support and enthusiasm for this research. It was fun working with people so dedicated to tracing the accurate history of the Hôtel Pontalba.

Radomír Luža, my teacher and dear friend, deserves his own paragraph in this catalog for his years of dedication and support through every draft of the manuscript. He has advised me in each decision concerning this book and has nudged it along with unnumbered and innumerable efforts.

My little girls, Christie and Robin, have never been thanked for trudging all over France in pursuit of Micaela, nor for spending boring hours in libraries, nor for eating thousands of peanut butter sandwiches while I worked at my desk. I hope someday they will read the book they let me write.

Finally, I want to thank Robert Riehl, the co-author of our children and my partner in all things. He is the unseen presence in every section of this book. He researched, organized, copied, translated, checked, read, discussed, typed, reread, laughed in all the right places, approved—for without his approval, nothing was considered final—so that when I think of any part of this work, I think also of him.

Introduction

THERE is much that is compelling in the story of Micaela Almonester de Pontalba: her strange, troubled marriage which began in New Orleans in 1811; her father-in-law's attempt to kill her and his subsequent suicide; her long struggle to maintain control of her inheritance and her children; her involvement in a prosecution in 1861 that nearly brought down the French government; and her legacy, her graceful architecture in New Orleans and Paris. The plain facts of her existence would be fun to write and probably worthwhile to read, even if we never examined the antecedents of her life or the precincts of history in which the Almonester-Pontalba chronicle took place.

But then, the reader and the writer would miss a great deal. No trim narrative could describe Micaela's two families, the scrappy, acquisitive Almonesters who reared her and the brooding Pontalba tacticians who married her, nor could it explain the jealousy that was gusting between them long before Micaela was born. A straightforward biography might have to sidestep the public events that kept intersecting her private drama: yellow fever epidemics that raged around her in New Orleans, or the Romantic fever in France, or the reconstruction of the streets and social order in Paris during the Second Empire of Napoleon III, or, near the end of her life, the well-mannered invasion of Paris in 1871 by Germans who halted a few yards from her door.

Micaela was not an individual standing alone in time, a stationary hyphen between her birth year and the year of her death. Like each of us, she was in the traffic of a historical period, jostled by some of the passing forces and entangled here and there by people with arresting stories of their own. As we go through her life, we have every reason to gravitate toward personalities and events on the edge of her story. For though Micaela is at the center of this study, the study is not only of her but of European ideas of power, class, money, marriage, and love during her lifetime, and how these were inflected in the piece of Europe that was New Orleans. Micaela's historical value is that she lets us into the dooryards of people she knew on both sides of the

Atlantic, so that we can sort through fragments of their private lives and finally press our faces against the glass of their intriguing century.

This, then, is not a tidy biography, but a book that tends to wander wherever documents uncover curious information which may have touched Micaela only in the most peripheral way. For example, we while away many paragraphs in the court of King Charles IV of Spain, where a relative of the Pontalbas considerately wrote long descriptions about his life as a reluctant courtier. The reader who lacks patience for these meanderings should skip with light conscience over the information concerning Micaela's family, the domestic violence or numbness of her acquaintances, the internecine passions of her friends, the Ney family, the parties of Paris' haut monde, the embezzlements by French bankers, and a dozen other digressions in the biographical narrative. It will take us in all truth three chapters to get to what may be properly termed Micaela's life. Once there, we will sometimes step back to look through her, as it were, to the vivid thoroughfare of history where she lived. The point is not to tell about her life only, but to put together a specific picture of life when she was alive.

Her story begins, therefore, in its desultory fashion, with her father and father-in-law, when Louisiana was a wilderness colony in what Europeans called "the Indies." Frenchmen were its first white settlers. They founded New Orleans in 1718 and haphazardly ruled the Mississippi Valley until 1762, when they ceded the entire colony to Spain as a reward for having joined in a disastrous war against Great Britain.[1] The Spanish came to Louisiana with soldiers, churchmen, bureaucrats (including a notary named Andrés Almonester) and only a premonition of the geographic and psychological distance that would henceforth separate them from other Europeans. Until 1803 they managed Louisiana as best they could for His Catholic and most enlightened Majesty Charles III and his Catholic and dim successor Charles IV, readily intermarrying with the French settlers and their Creole descendants.[*]

Acquiring Louisiana overextended Spain's resources because the huge territory was impossible to defend. But the land at least provided a buffer between the British, already established on the east coast and moving inland, and Spain's far more important possessions to the south.[2] The Spanish

---

*The colonial term *Creole* referred to a person born in the New World whose parents were born overseas, without reference to skin color. Creoles were white (French Creoles, Spanish Creoles) or black or of mixed blood. The term is used here as the contemporaries of Almonester and Pontalba used it, to designate birth in the colonies.

Crown thus resigned itself to supporting its "prize." Eventually, the American Revolution made the New World safer from British expansion, but not from land-hungry frontiersmen who became the new threat to Spain's colonies. It appeared to be only a matter of time before Americans would attempt to seize the Mississippi River. Moreover, although both Spanish and French settlers of Louisiana prospered during the years of Spanish rule, the Crown was steadily losing money on its outpost. Unable to prevent Anglo-American encroachments on the territory, Spain peacefully returned Louisiana to France in 1803. The French kept it only a few weeks, however. Napoleon, freshly blistered from the slave revolt in the French colony of Santo Domingo, abandoned his initial idea of planting a new French empire on the American continent and instead unloaded the entire Louisiana territory, its huge population of slaves, and its nervous slave owners to the United States. In a well-publicized bargain, the colony became a United States territory and was later subdivided into states that entered the Union separately.

Micaela Almonester was born in New Orleans in 1795, while Louisiana was still a Spanish colony, its Iberian population amicably outnumbered by the French settlers. Her father, old and rich by the time of her birth, was famed in the region for his philanthropic building projects; he died when she was two and he was seventy. Her mother was a poor French Creole, famed for marrying her father. Micaela, or Micael,* as her mother called her, was born with the deforming burden of a great fortune and then, at fifteen, married into misery.

The Pontalbas were French Creoles, comfortably rich but not (as Almonester had been) celebrated for their holdings. They looked upon the marriage of Micael and Célestin Delfau de Pontalba as a kind of business merger that would transfer the Almonester wealth into their hands. Célestin's father, Joseph Xavier Delfau, was an obsessive man, morbidly devoted to his only child, although in later years he also developed a genuine attachment to Micael's money. Micael, penny-pinching sometimes, headstrong always, and born with an affinity for architecture, had her own plans for her fortune.

The AP monogram on her Pontalba Buildings unites her maiden and married names; but only in iron were Almonester and Pontalba inseparable. In life Micael and Célestin filed a dozen petitions for separation and divorce

---

*Micaela and her mother used the spelling *Michael,* pronounced so as to rhyme with "knee-high bell." To avoid confusion with our boy's name Michael, I have simplified the spelling.

which, taken together, form a twenty-year narrative of false hopes and aching disappointments. Micael's quarrel with the Pontalbas consumed what should have been her best years, and her father-in-law's hatred disfigured her invisibly, as well as in ways that were all too conspicuous. But her buildings were more permanent than her tribulations. In the spacious arches and dancing galleries of the Pontalba Buildings she captured what eluded her in life: the predictable, the lyrical, the lighthearted. Though she was not beautiful, she must have had beauty in her to turn New Orleans' sober Place d'Armes, with its muddy field and squalid cottages, into an arabesque of iron and color. The Hôtel Pontalba, her home in Paris, is now the official residence of the United States Embassy. Despite its many visitors, it is a private and dignified mansion which to all appearances reflects the comfort of a well-ordered nineteenth-century life, a life of polished marble, seasonal gardens, and protected assets. One could never guess that the woman who planned the lilac trellises and sunny walkways lived with the stain of public humiliation.

Up to now there has been no complete study of Micael or her family. To find her life, it was necessary to search her out piecemeal, through thousands of primary documents. Because written records are the raw lumber of any historical construction, we will take great pains as we go along to describe the documents, those critical scraps that have allowed us to re-create a life and a family. Many are public records still legible in manuscript: letters to officials, minutes of meetings, military service records, communications between the Spanish Crown and colonial administrators, notarial documents showing what the Almonesters and Pontalbas bought, sold, leased, or contracted, and court cases they entered into against tenants, builders, debtors, and each other. To understand Micael's personality and the turbulence that led to her attempted murder, we consulted letters. The court trials for separation of bed and board were also an important resource, for they exposed every sort of behavior, prosaic and profane. To find out what comforts surrounded the Almonesters and Pontalbas, we investigated their estate inventories, those exhaustive household and property listings that were customary in the nineteenth century whenever a person died with many possessions on his soul. Information about L.-T.-J. Visconti, the architect who cracked heads with Micael in Paris, came from private papers. Even with a generous amount of personal material, we have only discovered those family secrets that the Pontalbas or someone else put down on paper, for, as we all know,

the most diligent research can only reveal the fragile evidence which someone, in some generation, saved. The other secrets have evaporated.

Indeed, for most people everything about the Baroness de Pontalba has
been secret up to now. Her name at least is somewhat familiar in New Orleans because her buildings enclose the much visited Jackson Square, as the
Place d'Armes was renamed, forming one of the loveliest architectural compositions in the United States. Almonaster Boulevard* keeps her maiden
name alive. But the name is all many people know of Micaela Almonester de
Pontalba. The tourist guides who celebrate eccentrics have somehow over-
looked her, and perhaps it is just as well. Like all unhappiness, her story is
complicated, and to understand it, one should begin where casual travelers
do not have time to go—to relationships that preceded any of her own involvements, to Spanish colonial New Orleans in the year she was born.

*The spelling of *Almonaster* seems to have been used sometimes by Micael's mother. It
showed up frequently on documents dealing with land tracts in New Orleans, and began to be
used more and more in Micael's later years. After the spelling appeared on the street sign, the
original spelling used by Micael's father, Almonester, was forgotten.

I

New Orleans in 1795

THE town was so small and shabby that, except for its location at the entrance to the Mississippi River, a stranger could not have guessed it was the capital of an enormous Spanish colony.[1] The little houses stretched for about a mile along the levee and went only six blocks deep. The buildings faced the river, for everywhere, in both Europe and America, the main thoroughfares were water. Visitors coming by land entered the city gates at the ramparts and made their way past backyards to the front of town. The gates closed at nine in the evening. Any citizen departing was to leave behind a bondsman who would guarantee his local debts.

Beyond the rampart and surrounding the clump of houses on all sides was swamp, moss-curtained and rippled with alligators, for the town was constructed on stagnant water. A drainage canal had been started in 1795. It was a popular swimming place for society women who, according to Joseph Xavier Delfau de Pontalba, dived "head and all" into whatever water was there until summer droughts turned it into a mudhole.[2] Then as now the center of town was a plaza near the river, but open to the water in those days, for there was no Moonwalk or cement levee wall to obstruct the flooding or the view. This *plaza de armas* (insistently called the Place d'Armes by French residents) was the parade ground for troops guarding the city. It was a treeless field of brown stubble, bordered by a Spanish church and two worthy colonial buildings: the Presbytere, which was destined never to be used as a priest's house, and the Cabildo, or administrative building, which housed the town council. Behind the Cabildo and attached to it were stables and the city jail, "a wretched receptacle of vice and misery," according to an observer.[3] During its deliberations the council, or *cabildo,* could hear prisoners being chastised, and visitors to the council meetings were disturbed by screams issuing sometimes from the jail.

Despite its little triad of church, Presbytere, and Cabildo, the plaza must have been a charmless place. A wooden gallows cast its malign shadow near the spot where Andrew Jackson now presides in bronze; a hangman on the city payroll at fifteen pesos a month eventually requested a raise when execu-

tions tripled—from one to three a year. Two pillories stood a few steps from
the church, a convenience for slave owners who could have their servants
punished there. Pontalba remarked in one of his letters that a pregnant
kitchen slave had stayed away from home a few days: "The pillory will be the
place for her," he wrote.[4] Along the mud street that separated the plaza from
the levee was Ursuline Convent, which served as a school, orphanage, and
abbey; it is still standing below the plaza, its front facing the river as in the
eighteenth century, and its back doors facing the street.

A long colonnade, the market, stretched out from the plaza to the city
limit. The *cabildo* wanted peddlers to be stationed where food could be inspected and a fee collected for a shaded stall; thus, food vendors who traf-
ficked outside the market were threatened with "eight days in jail and a dis-
cretionary fine or lashing if they are slaves."[5] The market contained furs,
food, cloth, and tools, most of which were brought from plantations and
settlements outside town. Almost any morning one could see slave women
hawking sweetmeats left over from some party the previous evening and,
everywhere, reeking butcher stalls—Andrés Almonester estimated that the
market housed at least twenty-five. The slaughterhouse, also reeking, was
just over the levee from the food stalls, on the riverbank.

Everything between this bustling Front Street and the city gates was
"town," a congestion of some six thousand people and perhaps a thousand
houses. Here the crier patrolled all night, watching for fires, calling out the
hour, and giving notice when new laws were decreed or government contracts were let out for bidding. And here, by all accounts, were streets so in-
credibly foul that sometimes even carriages could not get through them.
They were choked with garbage, filthy as sewers, and always wet. Dogs,
pigs, and cows roamed about; their dung was never taken away. Privies
overflowed, even those of the Ursuline nuns, whose waste, according to the
cabildo, "empties directly into the public street."[6] The road itself served as a
toilet when no other was convenient; one of Almonester's slaves unhesitatingly mentioned in court testimony that he woke one night with an intestinal upset and hurried into the street to relieve himself, the same street where
Almonester's daughter, Micaela, grew up.[7]

She never played there, of course, for no one used the street except to get
to somewhere else. Since the area was below sea level, every rain shower
turned the town into a morass. Even in dry weather there were rotted carcasses in the pathways, along with refuse the citizens threw out to be purified
by the air. Wealthy and poor alike lived indoors behind closed shutters and

plain façades that completely sealed in the front of most homes. No one conducted business or met friends in public places.

The highest ground in New Orleans was at the banks of the river. That meant there was no easy way to drain the city. Toward the back of town, the habitable land sank into swamp. Water seeped through the levees, when it did not overflow them, making the soil so soft that people were spared the trouble of having to shoe their horses. There were ditches along every street in town with little bridges at the corners for crossing; but since all the roads held water for most of the year, the ditches and the street were indistinguishable, both full of sodden masses of rubbish anchored in the mud. Travelers who were repelled by the streets in New Orleans had seen waste dumped in other towns; but the wet garbage of New Orleans seemed nastier than dry garbage elsewhere.

The roads of course were worse at night, since the only light came from lamps and candles people carried with them. If pedestrians ventured out after dark, they filed down the plank sidewalk behind a slave who carried a lantern. Eighty lampposts were installed in 1796 under Almonester's supervision; but though the *cabildo* was proud of its newest civic improvement, the lamps scarcely illuminated ten paces. Darkness increased pests: cockroaches, rats, poisonous water moccasins, and the occasional swamp alligator that got into town through the drainage ditch. The whole city was a breeding ground for the most vicious and (though the townspeople did not realize it) lethal nuisance of all, the mosquito. People spent their nights indoors in beds enveloped in insect netting, for in the centuries before drainage and fumigation, mosquitoes owned Louisiana. The architect Benjamin Latrobe observed, "The muskitoes . . . furnish a considerable part of the conversation of every Day & of every Body. . . . they regulate many family arrangements, they prescribe the employment and distribution of time, & most essentially affect the comfort & enjoyment of every individual in the country."[8]

Though everyone knew mosquitoes bred in stagnant water, the town council was too preoccupied with maintaining the levees during rainy seasons to worry about draining streets. Riverfront land had to be protected whether or not it was occupied; therefore, the *cabildo* tried offering levee lots free to anyone who would keep the dikes in good condition. There were few takers. Even though he had an uncle on the council, Pontalba was denied permission to abandon twenty arpents that two other owners had likewise found onerous because of the need to keep up the levee.[9] In spite of everything the *cabildo* tried to do, the dikes were full of cracks and the city was often threatened by flood.

With cypress bogs surrounding the town and stagnant water lying year-round in the streets, it is no wonder that New Orleans became famous in the eighteenth century as a pesthole of malaria and what the inhabitants, including Pontalba, at first described as "putrid fever" or "the sickness." Yellow fever was a mystery plague that did not have a name in Louisiana until after the epidemic of 1796; then it, too, took its place as one of the territory's notorious curses, along with smallpox, which was the major scourge of the times. Governor Miró had introduced quarantining for smallpox in 1787, and it was being used increasingly.[10] Inoculation was also gaining acceptance in spite of the Church's opposition to it. "The Creole youth," an observer commented, "continue to be inoculated before the very eyes of the governor, the bishop, and the Capuchin clergy, who can, if they see fit, excommunicate alike the inoculation, the inoculated, and the inoculator."[11] Pontalba, writing to his wife during the yellow fever epidemic of 1796, was relatively sanguine about his chances of getting "the malady"; but he pleaded with her in one missive after another to have their child inoculated against the infection he was really afraid of, smallpox.[12]

Along with serious epidemics of one sort or another, there were the more commonplace colds, dysentery, "fevers," and something the settlers described as "mange." At least one of the six councilmen was usually incapacitated, according to *cabildo* records, and correspondence of the 1790s leaves the impression that nothing in Louisiana was more normal than illness. "Beside the fatal contagion reigning here now," Pontalba wrote to his wife, "there is an epidemic of gangrenous throat infection carrying away many of the children. Madame Cruzat has lost two of hers, and every day a few are being buried." Disease struck high and low: Governor Carondelet's brother died in the malaria epidemic of 1794. Pontalba, writing to Esteban Miró, described a frantic instance when his Célestin went into convulsions, "his head thrown back, his legs and thighs stiff, eyes turned back in his head. His suffocated breathing made us think he would smother. His mother had just taken a purge an hour before, I had the fever. . . ."[13] Nevertheless, Pontalba threw himself and the baby into a carriage and sped into town. There Dr. Montegut "brought him back to life," though the child suffered "violent fevers" for days. Miró remarked that Pontalba's letters were "full of sickness and the deaths of friends whom I cared for. It made me appreciate having left all that."[14]

No one doubted the benefits of purging to relieve every kind of symptom, along with the ingestion of amazing quantities of quinine. Pontalba described giving a house guest "eight separate doses of quinine yesterday and five today. . . ." Furthermore, he intended "to keep on at that rate for five or six more days." The patient died, however, before the treatment was complete. Only a few years previously Pontalba had reported to Miró the side effects he himself suffered from too much quinine: "unbearable depression," "tightening" of the temples and jaws, "quivering of the extremities, swollen gums, chattering teeth," and "such extreme weakness in the legs that it hurts me to hold myself up."[15] But quinine was what everybody took.

When the 1796 outbreak of yellow fever turned into an epidemic, the frightened citizens followed each preventive vogue: herb tea (promoted by the Baroness de Carondelet), cold baths, cream of tartar, vinegar, camphor and abstemious diets. Every get-together generated its lore of medicaments and precautions. Something the doctors called the "mercurial treatment" passed in and out of fashion. It consisted of dosing a fever victim with mercury so as to produce copious salivation. Three companies of a regiment in New Orleans were killed in 1812, not by the enemy British nor by yellow fever, but by lethal applications of mercury, according to a physician who doubted the benefits of the treatment.[16]

Business was transacted during the winter, for everyone knew that New Orleans was more dangerous in summer. In the hot months (and this became more true as yellow fever returned with increasing severity), theaters and ballrooms closed, *Le Moniteur* reduced its publication, and the streets emptied as residents went to their country houses. "The city is almost deserted," Pontalba wrote to his wife in October, 1796. "My storehouses, which had all been rented, are now left vacant. . . . Clark . . . was so frightened that when the only clerk left to him came to render him an accounting, he would only speak to him from a distance; three people had already died at his house, and his own fright kept him from being able to urinate."

During such times, the recurring issue for the *cabildo* was getting rid of dead bodies that tended to reappear after burial in the marshy cemetery, causing "pestilent exhalations."[17] A particular problem, one complainant told the *cabildo*, was the interment of those persons "who have the misfortune to die in other beliefs than that of our Holy Catholic Religion." The only official cemeteries were managed by the Church, and as these were forbidden to heretics, Protestants were put to rest in a field outside town. They did not rest for long, according to Almonester, who tried to get the *cabildo* to take responsibility for the Protestant graveyard. He reported that "dogs and birds feed on the cadavers, there being uncovered coffins at the edge of the Canal due to the current of the waters."[18]

Notwithstanding the distinctions between dead Catholics and Protestants, the living society of New Orleans—the white segment, that is—was remarkably integrated. According to contemporary estimates, Louisiana's white population in the 1790s was about half French and a quarter Spanish, with Americans, British, and other Europeans making up the rest. The French and Spanish formed a solid, cooperative ruling class. When France first ceded the colony to Spain in 1762, relations had been bitter between the French settlers and their new Spanish masters. Leaders of the French community ejected the first Spanish governor, Antonio de Ulloa, causing the second governor, Alejandro O'Reilly, to arrive with two thousand Spanish troops, a third of the total population of New Orleans and its surrounding area at the time. O'Reilly ended the rebellion by executing five Creoles, members of the city's most prominent French families.

Despite such initial hostility, the French gradually became resigned to the Spanish presence and, as time went on, found less and less reason to wish their colony returned to France. Even when Louisianians learned in 1793 that Spain had declared war on republican France, there were only random incidents of republican agitation among the whites—the singing of jacobin songs in the theater, for example. Governor Carondelet reacted excitedly to the displays of French sympathy that came to his attention; he began banishing people for possessing "diabolical ideas of freedom and equality" or "making remarks against the Spanish government."[19] But in three years he had to get rid of only sixty-eight such troublemakers. Some of these showed up at Carondelet's *residencia*, the official review of his administration, to complain that he had acted against them without cause.

It is easy to see why there was no real outpouring of pro-French sentiment. For one thing, the Creoles were profoundly shaken by what they heard about the revolution raging in France. As they traded horror stories from the continent, they trembled at the thought of mob rule. "Have just learned of your bad news, ours are much worse," Julien Poydras's friend wrote to him from France.[20] "I have heard that de la Lande and Garnier, the former received two bullets in his arms and will be crippled, have been sent to Paris to be guillotined but the executioners were guillotined themselves and they were saved. . . . Keep silent and never speak of what I have written of this revolution in any way." Poydras himself, in the center of the Pointe Coupée revolt, thought he was still better off than his brother in France: "You ask me to return to France. Spare me the pain. I do not need to be coaxed, I am unfortunately too anxious but how can I go to a country where property is not respected; where . . . everyone urges me not to undertake any business as none can be transacted with safety."[21] For another very important thing, slavery had been abolished in republican France; colonial slave owners were afraid of losing everything if Louisiana reverted to French control. Even people who owned no blacks were threatened with ruin if the slaves were freed, because the colony ran on credit—almost every transaction involved a deferred payment of some sort—and the biggest debtors were planters with many slaves. If the slave owners were forced into bankruptcy, they would cause the impoverishment of merchants, shippers, doctors, carpenters—anyone holding their promissory notes or dependent on them for business. The whites in Louisiana were thus not attracted to jacobinism.

However, the French Revolution and the ensuing war between France and Spain caused trade with France to be cut off, exacerbating the colonists' longstanding dissatisfaction with Spanish trade restrictions. This was the real source of Carondelet's headaches, his reason for fearing that the colonists might cooperate with a French or American invasion of Louisiana. In settling Louisiana, the Spanish Crown had the usual mercantile expectations: that the colony would export its raw materials, such as cotton, to the mother country, while Spain would sell its manufactured products, such as clothing, back to the colony. Naturally, the Crown protected its colonial monopoly by trying to control trade between Louisiana and other countries and their colonies.[22] But Spain was never able to supply its American colonies sufficiently. In Louisiana there were chronic shortages of flour, coinage, arms, fortification materials, and other necessities, which could only be remedied by exceptions to the commercial regulations or by illegal trade.

The War of the French Revolution closed Louisiana's legal trade with France and the French West Indies in 1793; Americans were pouring into the region west of the Appalachians and increasing their demand for free access to the Mississippi River. The Americans pressed on the Spanish borderland just as Louisiana was forced to rely more than ever on American contraband goods. Carondelet persuaded the Crown to reduce temporarily the duty on imports from Kentucky, arguing that frontiersmen would seize the Mississippi by force if compelled to pay the usual charge of 15 percent (plus another 6 percent if the cargo was re-exported at New Orleans), and they would be cheered on by the colonists.[23] Despite the Creoles' antagonism toward the Americans, they now were as eager as the Kaintocks for free trade on the river.

Since the Crown could not enforce its commercial regulations, it had no choice but to ignore the flourishing contraband trade on which the colony survived. The government conceded one trading privilege after another during the war with France, privileges which the colonists then retained permanently. Ultimately, the pressure from the United States forced Spain to withdraw from Louisiana; but before that juncture, the colonists were happy enough with the right of free trade. They began prospering again in the last years of the century with export crops that replaced the diminishing indigo and tobacco. In 1795, on a plantation which is now the site of Audubon Park, Étienne de Boré succeeded in granulating sugar. Because of that success, plantations all over the colony revived. In February, 1801, *Le Moniteur* was reporting a yearly export rate of more than a million pounds of sugar, a figure that would quadruple in a few years. And there was cotton, the demand for which was soaring even before Eli Whitney's revolutionary invention of 1793.

By the time Louisiana was returned to France in 1803, there was no longer any danger of the whites rebelling against the Spanish Crown. The French and Spanish oligarchs of the colony ran its internal affairs with a fairly free hand, dividing the lucrative offices among themselves and circulating their wealth within careful limits by intermarriage. Creoles who had been appointed to high offices through the years were handing them down in their families. French nationalism had been placated by a succession of competent and conscientious Spanish governors who did not attempt to change the French character of Louisiana. French remained the language of the colony throughout the Spanish period—even the deliberations of the *cabildo* might lapse into French—and when Spanish was required for a formal proceeding, a translator was generally present. The Spaniards in Louisiana, right up to Governors Gálvez and Miró, married the daughters of Creole planters, served Bordeaux at their official dinners, danced the *galopade*, sedulously gambled their money at *bourré*, and reared children who could not speak a word of Spanish. Almonester and Miró—one Andalusian, the other a Catalan—spoke only French at home, like many other Spaniards in Louisiana. Influenced perhaps by the vogue for French that was sweeping the educated classes in Europe, Almonester allowed himself to be called "Don André"; his wife (who was French anyway) was referred to as "Madame Don André." Before the turn of the century, the French and Spanish had closed ranks against the real threats to their provincial authority: the blacks within the colony and the Americans invading from the outside. For if the Creoles in Louisiana were a privileged class, surrounded by luxuries and catered to by servants, they were not at ease. All of the whites together were outnumbered by people of varying degrees of color—Indians, free Negroes, and slaves—and they never for a moment forgot the insecurity of their position.

Although Indians in the colony included Choctaws, Creeks, Chickasaws, Caddos, Shawnees, Arkansas, Apalaches, and Osages, all very widespread, there was no danger of an Indian attack on New Orleans by 1795. In outlying posts such as Fort Arkansas, a few braves might commit some violence against a trapper or raid an unoccupied country house. For these depredations, Governor Miró advised that it was necessary "to scream at them [the Indian chiefs] . . . and to be satisfied with the repentance which I do not doubt they will demonstrate."[24] The real danger presented by the Indians ranged within and around Louisiana was that they would draw their Spanish allies into risky confrontations with Americans, the mutual enemy. Miró, for one, believed the Americans provoked the Indians in the hope that Spain would come to their aid and provide an excuse for an American invasion of New Orleans via the Mississippi. President George Washington, who was dominated, according to the Spanish view, "by the ambition . . . to see himself again at the head of an army," became notorious in Miró's dispatches for his shifty treatment of the red man. The president was accused of exploding peace conferences by deliberately insulting Indian delegates. It was alleged that on one occasion he "deceived them into signing their mark on some paper, believing it to be a list of presents. . . ." The paper was a treaty by which the Indians agreed to give away their land. The Spanish thus had many willing allies such as a Choctaw chief who "offered to kill any American that would pass through his land."[25]

For thirty years the Spanish tried assiduously to consolidate their control over these Indian neighbors, to create a buffer of alliances with the Indian nations around Louisiana to help protect the nearly unfortified frontier. As a first step, the Spanish tried to monopolize trade with the Indians to keep them dependent upon Spain for their needs. The Crown granted exclusive rights to several individuals to provision the Indians with firearms and food-stuffs. Governor Gálvez found his father-in-law, Gilbert Antoine de St. Maxent, uniquely qualified to perform such services. St. Maxent negotiated with a partner to ship huge cargoes of goods to New Orleans for sale to the Indians. But the policy led to all sorts of complications when the Spanish found that they could not in fact supply the products the Indians had come to like. In desperation, the Spanish governors hired English merchants to bring goods from London for the Indians, transporting them in English ships flying a Spanish flag and accepting colonial produce as payment. Such arrangements were certainly illegal, but Miró, for one, justified them as necessary to keep Americans from entering into the Indian trade.

The dispatches of the governors are heavy with their failures to manipulate the Indians. The Spanish followed the example of their French predecessors in providing gifts to the Indians as part of any attempted negotiation. But even a small conference could prove costly because "the Indian chiefs are not capable of stopping their warriors, women, and children from following them." A Choctaw chief was to meet with Miró accompanied by no more than a hundred persons so that, Miró wrote, "I would be able to shower him with gifts and those who might accompany him." However, the exasperated governor reported, "He at last presented himself with one thousand two hundred persons, telling me that although he had left his village with a little more than one hundred, he had been joined by the rest on his way, and it was impossible to make them return."[26] The townspeople, of course, had little awareness of the importance of the tribes in the eyes of the government. To them, the Indians were just shabby and harmless people living in a few hundred shacks on the outskirts of town, hardly more than a curiosity in the marketplace with their game, baskets, wood, or the few other products they were permitted to sell.

The free people of color, on the other hand, were a pronounced element of Creole life. In 1795 there were only fifteen hundred to two thousand of them in Louisiana, many of whom gravitated to New Orleans because of the scarcity of labor and chance for employment in the city.[27] Usually, free Negroes were of mixed blood, children or grandchildren of white men and slave women. There had always been a shortage of white women in the colony, since neither the French nor the Spanish soldiers had immigrated with their families, and intermating had been widespread. The white masters sometimes freed their slave lovers or their mulatto offspring, if only in their wills; these freed slaves and their descendants found ready work as dress-makers, housekeepers, shoemakers, dancing teachers, shopkeepers, tailors, joiners, carpenters, mechanics, bricklayers, blacksmiths, slave dealers, and, notably, soldiers. If a slave could work outside his master's home and keep his earnings, he could buy himself, that is, buy his freedom. The Spanish Crown encouraged this and other forms of manumission, and slave owners such as Pontalba who found themselves overstaffed might cooperate in letting a slave earn his freedom; but given the imaginable difficulties of a slave procuring several hundred dollars, it is no wonder the overwhelming majority of free blacks or their ancestors had simply been granted freedom by some former master. The Spanish government was always desperate for troops to defend the colony and welcomed every loyal body it could get under arms, white or black. The free Negro battalion, which for most of the Spanish period had black officers and a white commander, fought alongside whites and were part of the strategic forces of every important military expedition.

But although free blacks could and did prosper in Louisiana, perhaps more than in any of the English seaboard colonies, they were at various times subjected to many of the legal restrictions of slaves. They had to be off the streets by nine in the evening; since they could not "be recognized from slaves or savages [runaways]," they were required to carry their certificate of freedom at all times.[28] The firmness with which these rules were enforced depended upon whether rumors were circulating of a planned black uprising, whether New Orleans was being flooded with mulatto refugees from Santo Domingo, and whether the free black found violating a rule was a trusted resident, a known troublemaker, or a stranger. The law prescribed severe penalties for free Negroes who engaged in sexual relations with either whites or slaves; like many other colonial laws, the prohibition was constantly and openly violated. As for the famous quadroon concubines of New Orleans, the government was officially hostile to them: a woman known to have any black ancestry, no matter how remote, was forbidden by law to use a coach in daylight, enter a public room if a white woman was there, or sit in the presence of a white.[29] But again, the zeal of enforcement depended on the individual woman and individual official apprehending her, since at least a few of the quadroons had liaisons with prominent white protectors. Judging from the repeated attempts to regulate every detail of the courtesans' dress (Miró ordered them to stop wearing feathers, curls, jewelry, *mantillas*, or caps), they must have given the city a scattering of glitter.[30]

But however often the whites might lump all blacks together, one curious fact set free people of color apart from slaves. In any showdown between whites and slaves, the free Negroes would side with the whites and keep them from being seriously outnumbered. Under Governors Gálvez and Miró, free black militiamen were used to catch fugitive slaves and to infiltrate and attack a colony of runaways.[31] Governor Carondelet used free people of color as a valuable and voluble source of information about slave conspiracies, coaxing long depositions from them; in return, he tried to keep those found guilty of crimes from being punished by the lash, like slaves. The white citizens, if not the governors, nevertheless viewed the free blacks as a potential threat and distrusted them. Slaves were dangerous, but they were a necessity; no enterprise could begin, no plantation could continue without them. Free Negroes could not be supervised like slaves. Despised by both whites and slaves, and hating both in return, they could be counted on to act only in their self-interest; therefore, the whites reasoned, the fewer of them, the better.

In 1791 a revolution of slaves began in Santo Domingo which culminated, after more than a decade of ferocity on both sides, in the establishment of a black republic in 1803. Throughout the period, free Negro refugees immigrated to New Orleans in successive waves, causing the alarmed *cabildo* to offer one proposal after another for stopping their influx. The whites in Louisiana were slow to realize that the mulatto emigrés had been driven out of Santo Domingo by revolutionary slaves and that, by and large, they were no more sympathetic to slave rebellion than the white refugees also flocking to New Orleans and the Gulf ports. When Americans took over Louisiana, they began abrogating the privileges of free blacks, deactivating the Negro battalion, for example. Even so, in 1811, during Louisiana's most serious slave uprising, near New Orleans, free Negroes volunteered their services against the insurrectionary blacks. At the end of the rebellion, Governor Claiborne reported on the "exactitude and propriety" of the free black militiamen, commending their "zeal for public safety."[32]

Whether they loathed or liked the white people, both Indians and free blacks were comparatively few and peaceable. It was the largest element of the colored population, the slaves, that caused continual anxiety. During the 1780s the major problem had been to keep them from running away. In session after session of the *cabildo*, ideas were proposed for stopping what must have seemed an evacuation of slaves from the houses and plantations around New

Orleans. Not only were the owners required to register their blacks, but until Carondelet interfered with the practice in 1795, any slave found off his owner's property without a note could be punished with twenty-five lashes by any white who met him. No one was allowed to give a slave a horse. No locksmith was to make keys "unless the lock is brought to him by identified persons."[33] Despite the precautions, *cabildo* records of the 1780s are filled with references to *cimarrons,* runaways who were supposed to have gathered in the swamp; the white folklore described horrible deeds reputedly committed by these fugitives when they ventured out of their lairs in search of food or vengeance. Bounties were advertised for anyone who caught a cimarron, and the bounty hunters were not careful with their prey. *Cabildo* meetings constantly touched on the subject of "savage Negroes" who were killed while being recaptured.[34] Nevertheless, there were always slaves willing to brave the odds for a chance at freedom.

One of the first efforts of the Spanish Crown after taking over the colony had been to regulate the treatment of slaves. But the royal government was far away and the local governor could not supervise every planter in the colony. In July, 1792, Pontalba reported to his uncle Miró that many slave owners were defying the requirement that the Negroes have Sundays free, receive one barrel of Indian corn per month and one set of clothing per year. The Spanish Crown sent a stream of edicts ordering the humane treatment of slaves; and the *cabildo* sent back sulky letters explaining "the great injuries which would result if . . . the Royal Order were carried out."[35] The Crown tried to coerce owners into registering slave marriages; it prohibited the separate sale of husbands and wives; it insisted that owners observe the day of rest and support a priest to minister to the spiritual needs of the slaves. The observance of Sundays and holidays, the masters protested, was impractical during harvesttime. The expense of a chaplain for the slaves was prohibitive. As for slave marriages, the Creoles dismissed the idea by pointing out that "only the Spanish allow marriage, with the other colonists it is not the custom."

By the 1790s the preoccupation with runaways had given way to a graver fear of revolt which obsessed the whole colony. Long before any significant slave rebellion erupted, the *cabildo* had prohibited any merchant from storing more than fifty pounds of gunpowder "in order to avoid such ammunition to fall into the hands of the negroes."[36] Slaves were forbidden by law to buy liquor or possess weapons, even sticks. Yet despite all the restraints placed on slaves by the masters and on masters by the king, the letters and judicial records of the period reveal frequent, random violence between the owners and the owned. The French Revolution exacerbated the chronic tension. The main fear concerning republican ideas was not that they would infect the citizens but that they would incite the slaves. Carondelet believed that white jacobin agitators from outside the colony were behind the increasing slave unrest. Panic-stricken whites fleeing to New Orleans from Santo Domingo added their voices to the general apprehension and conservatism of the town. Because of the Santo Domingo revolution, Carondelet in 1792 banned the importation of slaves from either Jamaica or the French Caribbean colonies where Negroes might be contaminated with revolutionary ideas. The *cabildo* considered recommending further restrictions, such as admitting only blacks who were "entirely illiterate."[37]

The Spanish Crown's laws and policies regarding slavery in the Mississippi Valley and Gulf Coast were more humane during the colonial period than those of the French, British, or later, the Americans. But nothing in Louisiana was as routinely disregarded as law, and the governors, whose responsibility it was to curb slave masters, often had their hands full with more pressing business. In 1791 and 1792 two minor slave uprisings occurred in Louisiana, and one potentially serious conspiracy was uncovered in April, 1795. This rebellion was to have begun on the indigo plantation of Julien Poydras in Pointe Coupée, some 150 miles from New Orleans. All of the slaves in the area reportedly knew of the plans for a revolt, and several hundred were directly involved, or so the authorities believed, when the plot was aborted. Twenty-five slaves were killed while the militia was making arrests. In addition, Carondelet in his dispatches took credit for "the prompt and exemplary punishment of fifty-four"; or as Poydras reckoned the loss of life, "They hung 20,000 piasters worth of my negroes." Several were left hanging near churches in the area. Three whites arrested among the ringleaders were sentenced to leave the colony.[38]

For weeks after the revolt was crushed, the *cabildo* solicited information from citizens regarding possible culprits, conversations overheard, gossip picked up from house servants, and the like. Among the scraps of evidence turned over to the council was a "Patriotic Song" supposedly used to rally the slaves. "When we get to be republicans," the song promised, "we shall punish all those scoundrels." The intended victims included "the swine governor," who was to be guillotined, and the treasurer of the colony, who would be "hanged in the rampart." Pontalba, commandant of the troops reinforcing the local militia, had earned special treatment. "We shall not hang

Pontalba," went the last verse of the song, "he shall be whipped in the street/ And we shall keep him to make a spy out of him."[39]

In *cabildo* meetings, no rumor or remark about revolt was deemed too trivial for lengthy discussion. Carondelet's dispatches to Cuba were replete with frantic pleading for troops, along with various schemes for forestalling a black revolution. The governor had fortifications constructed at the corners of the town, ostensibly to protect against attack from outside the colony, and he had a wall fifteen feet high built around the frightened inhabitants of the city. As we know, the terrible rebellion did not materialize; it is perhaps easy now to believe that the white community was hysterical and that Carondelet's anxious letters to his superiors reflected his paranoia. But Carondelet had seen the countryside around New Orleans, where whites lived in isolation, each surrounded by as many as a hundred slaves whose grievances were fierce. Except for their own guns, the planters and farmers had no protection; there were hardly enough troops in the area to safeguard the town. Carondelet's superior, las Casas, even warned the governor that the best way to deal with jacobin agitators of the slaves was to let them alone as far as possible, "to avoid a confrontation that will reveal how desperately weak we are."[40]

Whatever policing measures existed in the colony were intended primarily to police the slaves. In the countryside Carondelet appointed a planter every nine miles to serve as justice of the peace, to keep an eye on the levees and the Negroes and report to him if either appeared to be at the breaking point. "This Easter Sunday had been chosen by the blacks to get rid of all the whites," Pontalba wrote in 1796, when a new plot surfaced at Pointe Coupée. His relief is palpable when he later reassures his wife that no attack occurred. "This Easter day . . . is finally over."[41]

Rumors of rebellion were constantly in the air, and the events at Pointe Coupée and Santo Domingo haunted the whites. "I can recall when our position in this colony was ever so critical," Pontalba wrote to his wife a year after Pointe Coupée, "when we used to go to bed only if armed to the teeth. Often then, I would go to sleep with the most sinister thoughts creeping into mind, taking heed of the dreadful calamities of Saint Domingue, and of the germs of insurrection only too widespread among our own slaves. I often thought, when going to bed, of the means I would use to save you and my son, and of the tactics I would pursue if we were attacked."[42] Pontalba's wife must have had her own sinister fears; when she was a young girl, her father had been murdered by one of his slaves.

Carondelet's nightmare of revolution ultimately came true, but not while he was in Louisiana. In 1803, after the governor had left New Orleans to become president of the Audiencia of Quito, in present-day Ecuador, a furious Indian revolt began in Guamote. The 400 soldiers whom Carondelet sent to put down the rebels found the road to the town strewn with the hands, legs, arms, and heads of the Spanish victims.[43]

Not until 1811 did Louisiana have a serious slave insurrection, sometimes called the largest slave uprising in U.S. history. On the night of January 8, slaves numbering between 180 and 500 gathered on the levee at the border between St. Charles and St. John the Baptist Parishes, thirty-six miles above New Orleans.[44] Fortified by taffia and armed with cane knives, sabers, and a few guns, the slaves first attacked the plantation of Manuel André, a colonel of the militia, and murdered his son. Then, led by a mulatto slave, they began moving toward New Orleans, burning two houses and pillaging along the way. At the Trepagnier plantation they hacked François Trepagnier to death with a hatchet. But André and Trepagnier were the only whites killed. The other planters in the area were saved by loyal slaves who ran ahead of the rebels and urged the families to flee to the woods. The Labranches, Bernoudys, Fortiers, and Charbonnets thus escaped the mob, Jacques Charbonnet carrying his elderly mother on his shoulders. Though wounded, Colonel André gathered a citizen militia and dispatched an alarm to the governor. On January 9, Claiborne sent an army detachment and two companies of volunteer militia (including free men of color "under a respectable Citizen Major Dubourg"), whose instructions were to "meet the Brigands and arrest them in their murdering career." In the rout that ensued, twenty-one slaves died in the fighting and forty-five others were apparently executed summarily.

The leaders of the insurrection were rounded up within a few days and tried by a judge and a planter tribunal. Claiborne counseled the six men to be merciful "for the sake of humanity" and expressed his willingness to grant any pardons the tribunal recommended. Of twenty-two slaves interrogated, eighteen were found guilty of a capital offense. They were sentenced to be shot "without torture," their heads displayed on pikes along the river. The eighty-four slaves killed in the uprising and its aftermath, together with twenty others who took the opportunity to run away, represented a hard loss for their owners, according to the accounting made after the revolt. Most of the slaves killed had been young—about thirty years of age—intelligent, and experienced cane workers, each worth on average a thousand dollars.

In Louisiana, as in all the Indies, such exigencies as slave rebellions had to be dealt with by local people. Since the Crown was too far away to provide

assistance in a crisis, the system for administering the colonies was critical if
frontier towns such as New Orleans were to survive. The governor was
under the jurisdiction and, invariably, the close supervision of the captain-
general of Cuba. We tend to think of colonial governors as earlier versions of
the modern official, but their position was actually that of commander of a
military post who had, in addition to the primary responsibility of defending
the colony, the secondary concern of governing its inhabitants. Perhaps 90
percent of the governor's correspondence with his superiors dealt with military matters: service records of officers, justifications for new appointments,
Indian policy, defense strategy, and the like. In military expeditions out from
the capital, the governor might lead his troops like any other commander.
Just as every military officer does, the governor turned over to his superior,
the captain-general in Havana, the most important messages of his subordinates, as well as every significant letter, rumor, conversation, or transaction
that caught his attention.

These dispatches of the Louisiana governors are refreshingly candid, especially the confidential correspondence to Cuba. The governors frankly disclosed what was in their minds as they made particular decisions; which
rivalries and winds of malice influenced their actions; and which contingencies or developments they were watching out for. The letters are never those
of a groveling subaltern to his superior; they are rather like advisories from
one soldier to another. Like any sincere missives, the dispatches reflected the
personalities of the individual governors. Young Gálvez (he was twenty-nine
when he became governor in 1777) was open and emotional in his letters.
Miró was blunt, self-assured, and cynical. Carondelet tended to fret, or as
A. P. Nasatir expressed it, "He got excited and wrote at length and with
great patience."[45] Obviously, the governors made self-justifying comments
to the captains-general, but even more, they confided in them, unburdening
themselves of all sorts of observations. This is particularly true in the case of
Carondelet, whose superior was his wife's half-brother. Luis de las Casas, in
turn, addressed Carondelet in the tone of an experienced man dealing with a
kid brother, though the "kid" had been in the service of the Crown for
twenty-nine years when he took his post in Louisiana. All of the dispatches
make it clear that the governors expected to receive orders regarding anything that mattered. Since their most trifling decisions were subject to review sooner or later, the governors welcomed orders and advice. As Spanish
administrators, it was their right not to bear total responsibility for any mistakes, and to enjoy the protection of the long, legalistic chain of command.

Just as his subordinates usually had to go through the governor to reach the captain-general, the governor generally had to go through the captain-general in addressing the Crown. The captain-general sent back a reply and perhaps certain orders to Louisiana, and then forwarded the governor's communication to the Minister of the Indies in Spain, together with his own remarks or recommendations concerning the matter at hand.[46] Several weeks were required to send a message to Cuba and receive a reply. The journey from Cuba across the Atlantic to Spain took another three or four months. The Crown, appreciating the irreversibility of its decisions, took its time in sending a reply which in turn required several months to cross the ocean. Meanwhile, the governor or the captain-general could issue directives that had the effect of law—until somebody got around to reviewing them.

Bernardo de Gálvez was governor from 1777 to 1782, a popular hero, since he wrested East and West Florida from the English in several military campaigns. Esteban Miró was acting governor from 1782 to 1785, and governor in his own right until 1791. He developed both firm friends and loyal enemies; his protracted tenure and his position as both governor and intendant gave him the prestige to brush aside the carping of a hostile *cabildo*. Miró was followed as governor at the end of 1791 by the energetic Baron de Carondelet, a Walloon from the southern Netherlands.[47] Although Miró called his successor "prejudiced and two-faced" (presumably meaning prejudiced against Spaniards), the Creoles thought they had in Carondelet a governor who understood them—he was intensely Catholic, French-speaking, and anti-American—and they showed him more courtesy than his abler predecessor had received.[48] Carondelet was succeeded in 1797 by Manuel Gayoso de Lemos, who arrived in New Orleans with an English education and long military service. Honest and enlightened, Gayoso showed ability in dealing with the Americans who were beginning to pour into the colony. He liked women and liquor, but only his susceptibility to yellow fever proved fatal. He died in 1799.[49] The courteous and officious Marqués de Casa Calvo was appointed acting civil governor, and Nicolás Vidal acting military governor, until the arrival of Juan Manuel de Salcedo in 1801. This last Spanish governor, though notoriously ineffective and decrepit during his two years in office, did not formally die until some time after completing his term, long after Louisiana had become a United States territory.[50]

The governor was assisted, at least theoretically, by the town council, the *cabildo*, whose members were also the judges for New Orleans courts. The

cabildo could be an irritation to the governor, or it could be a help in reinforcing his decisions. In any case, the governor was not bound by the *cabildo*,
which was an advisory council. He himself appointed the members, called
regidores, from among local landowners who offered to buy any vacant position (although every governor after O'Reilly was stuck with those councilmen he inherited from previous administrations). Once purchased, the office
of *regidor* was held for life, and brought an annual salary of six hundred
pesos, which was about the yearly income of a government warehouse
keeper. Since a Spanish bureaucratic office was a form of property, the *regidor*
could pass his position on to his heirs, as Almonester did when he named his
brother-in-law Pierre de la Ronde to succeed him as *cabildo* magistrate.

For most of the Spanish period, there were four *regidores* in New Orleans
with lifetime tenure and two councilmen whose appointments lasted for one
year. Almonester was a permanent *regidor*; Pontalba was a one-year commissioner for 1795. In 1797 the council was enlarged to six *regidores* and two "jun-
ior judges," as the one-year councilmen are conventionally designated in
English. Council members could hold outside offices along with their *cabildo*
membership. In addition, it was customary for councilmen to take on several
positions within the *cabildo*, none of them necessarily time-consuming. In
1791 Almonester was appointed Royal Ensign (or Royal Herald), a coveted
position that involved little more than carrying the royal banner in parades
and swearing in other government officials. He paid twelve hundred pesos
for this post, which brought in return an annual salary of only one hundred
pesos and the envy of his fellow commissioners, for with no monarch physically present in Louisiana, the royal banner received the cheers, pledges, and
reverence that would ordinarily be directed to the king.

Like all the institutions of the Spanish Crown, the *cabildo* was unstinting
with the time and ink it expended when it gathered each week "to discuss
matters relative to the welfare of the Community." Meetings frequently
lasted for hours and touched on a range of civic concerns: slave and flood
control, the shortages of coin, wholesome meat and flour. After the Good
Friday conflagration, fire prevention and repairs to the damaged public
buildings were incessant topics of discussion.

The fire of 1788, called the Great Fire, started on a windy night on
Chartres Street when the altar candles in the army paymaster's home ignited
some lace curtains. Within a few hours 856 houses—four-fifths of the popu-
lated section of the city—were reduced to hills of ashes, and all the commercial buildings in town except three were destroyed, together with their mer-

chandise.[51] Rebuilding had to be financed by the citizens; consequently, Al-monester advanced funds for a new Cabildo and jail, donated the money for rebuilding the Presbytere and St. Louis Church, and gave some of his rental property for public use. The restoration of the city was still going on when another fire broke out in 1794, causing two and a half million dollars in dam-age.[52] The St. Louis Cathedral, just rebuilt and about to be dedicated, was somehow spared, but the fire consumed surrounding buildings. Again Al-monester came forth with financing and donations. Again the government published ordinances, just as it had in 1789, insisting that new construction must be built of brick or brick-between-posts, with cement covering the posts; roofs were to be flat, made of tile or brick. All these fire ordinances were ignored, judging from the repetition year after year of the council's "strong resolution" to enforce them. Brick buildings deteriorated quickly because of the poor quality of the bricks available in Louisiana, and they were expensive. Pontalba, for one, complained that they needed hundreds of hinges and a prodigious amount of iron in addition to bricks and mortar. Builders, therefore, continued putting up cypress houses with steep French roofs, while the *cabildo* reiterated building regulations and tried to think up new schemes for protecting the town. Years after the Good Friday con-flagration, the city fathers were still debating the benefits of having a fire watchman on the roof of the Cabildo. Samuel Wilson noted that "the prob-lem of providing access to the roof of the building occupied the council for several months."[53]

Administering the city jail was another of the responsibilities the *cabildo* discharged with unhurried thoughtfulness. Any improvement to the jail might require discussion for many sessions, even while the roof no longer sheltered prisoners from the rain.[54] There was no intentional irony in pro-tracting these deliberations; it was simply that the individual prisoners were by and large slaves, and troublesome slaves at that, whereas the jail was an official building representing the authority of the Crown and was not to be carelessly tampered with. The *cabildo* was obliged to make careful inspec-tions of the prison and its records on one hand, and to uphold barbaric sen-tences on the other. The slaves convicted in 1771 of shooting J.-B. LeBreton, Louise de Pontalba's father, were dragged to their execution from the tail of a horse; their heads and hands were cut off and exposed on the gibbet; other slaves implicated in the murder received two hundred lashes and had their ears "cut off close."[55] But justice was sporadic. Prisoners might be allowed to escape. And, since executions usually required a series of authorizations that could take years to arrive, men under the death sentence sometimes died from age or disease, or were murdered by other prisoners before official justice could get to them. Exceptions were made for blacks convicted of murdering whites; their swift executions were thought to provide cautionary examples. In 1792, according to *cabildo* records, the city jailor resigned when his pay was reduced to one peso a day, out of which sum he was expected to feed the inmates. His further obligations, if anyone had bothered to look them up, were "to keep the prison clean and healthy, to supply it with water for the use of the prisoners, to visit them in the evening, to prevent them from gambling or disputing, to treat them well, and to avoid insulting or offending them."[56] The hangman was fired in 1798 when it was found that he gave liquor to the inmates and let several of them go; he was replaced by a black prisoner convicted of robbery who was set free so that he could become the new executioner.[57]

The minutes of the *cabildo* deliberations reflect the utter earnestness and self-importance with which the commissioners entered into each discussion. The translation seems atrocious—until one reads the original garbled Spanish, with its verbless sentences and word-salad summaries. The WPA translation, it turns out, is a generally faithful rendering of what the *cabildo* notary reported as he tried to follow the exchanges of garrulous *regidores* unaware that their Illustrious Body emitted but a meek light in the vast Spanish imperial galaxy. John Lynch's observations about the *cabildo* of the Rio de la Plata are certainly true of the municipal council of New Orleans: "Its *actas capitulares*, barbarously written, are full of the most humdrum routine such as prison inspection and license granting. . . . Any fundamental work, such as reconstruction of the town reservoir, would take years to accomplish."[58]

The citizens of New Orleans nevertheless respected the *cabildo* even as they disregarded the laws it helped the Crown to promulgate. "May God protect your lives many years," wrote a typical correspondent to the *cabildo*, using the rhetorical style that was customary even in this alligator-ridden outpost.[59] The writer closed his letter by "Kissing the hands of your Lordships" and signed himself, "Your most passionately fond and courteous servant." The commissioners set an example of dignity. They were supremely pompous, too, of course. With their magistrates' wands and sense of lofty purpose, one would not have guessed that they sweltered like everyone else in the heat and stench of the drainage ditches and slaughterhouses they had to visit. Despite the considerable work and modest pay, there was keen competition for membership in the Illustrious Body. This was certainly because *cabildo* members had access to other posts, such as collector of fines, which yielded fees or percentages. But with or without fees, commissioners had a sober view of the duties as well as the prestige of their positions. They were part of the only government most people in New Orleans knew, the only nobility they would ever see. They therefore imitated and exaggerated what they thought were fashions at the Bourbon court (though by the time fashion news crossed the Atlantic, the styles had sometimes changed), and they displayed all the vanity befitting the king's representatives to the people. They were required by law to carry their wands of office at all times; probably this was one law they obeyed, and proudly.

Every communication from the Throne produced some little excitement. In the absence of the king, commissioners bowed to documents bearing the royal seal and tried to bring themselves closer to the distant Spanish court by sharing in its celebrations. For such events as the birth of a royal baby, the Cabildo was decorated and illuminated; and for a royal funeral, council members marched out with high seriousness to a chapel so elaborately draped that the *cabildo* scribe required several pages to describe it adequately.[60] Charles III had been dead four months when word reached New Orleans in April, 1789, but his death was nevertheless news to the *cabildo*. When the town crier was sent forth with the important tidings, he was accompanied by two councilmen and two mace-bearers. The funeral Mass lasted until midday; the *regidores*, "at their own expense," wore strict mourning for six months.

Despite their isolation from the Spanish court, the colonists were not exempt from what one observer of the period called "the universal hunger for noble status."[61] In the colonies as in Spain, many a trifling hidalgo emptied his purse to have his standing as a petty nobleman confirmed, a process that required payment of a large sum and the dredging up of qualified ancestors for a genealogical record. The petitioner was charged more if he had to go back four or five generations to establish his status, but that did not thwart the ambitions of poor men willing to make themselves poorer in order to enter the ranks of the nobility. The Crown finally tried to escape the burden of petitions by refusing to consider any concession of *hidalguía* except in cases where "personal merits should be united in services" to the empire.[62] The "services" meant benefactions of the sort which would compensate the Crown for the revenue it gave up each time it recognized a nobleman, since the nobility paid no taxes and enjoyed a number of other financial exemptions. The size of the benefaction had to be commensurate with the economic privileges the noble would enjoy. The kings Charles III and Charles IV further extended the idea of services in exchange for titles so that men who were already members of the nobility could join in the scramble for rewards. The Crown created new honors or revived old distinctions to bestow on individuals such as Almonester who spared the royal treasury by supporting public institutions which the king might otherwise be obliged to pay for. Men of means throughout the Indies began to compete for royal recognition of their generous deeds. In New Orleans, all of the *cabildo* members zealously pursued titles and what we would call today ornamental offices, heartened by the expectation that they would win distinctions (heritable, to be sure) through large benefactions to the state. Anyone who received a royal reward minutely insisted on its privileges.

But ranks and titles were not all these donations were about. The aristocrats of course approved of a class system for a secure social order; they did not believe in equality and they would have resented any scheme for systematically sharing wealth. But they understood noblesse oblige. Poverty was a condition, not a sin, and it was the responsibility of the rich to ameliorate it, if not to cure it. There was a vague and widely diffused sentiment, a kindly feeling toward mankind that was closer to philanthropy than democracy. Wealthy people enjoyed their privileges as they had always done; but they worked too for the economic betterment of their inferiors, without going so far as to arrive at the notion of equality before the law.

Piety did not spur most benefactors because people were not severely religious. The Church encouraged philanthropy, and the clergy prominently participated in public events at which community leaders were recognized; but convention more than religion seemed to govern the behavior of the town and its wealthy chiefs. The three places of worship in New Orleans in the 1790s were all built by Almonester—two small chapels and St. Louis Church, designated a cathedral in 1795. These facilities would have been inadequate if most of the people in the city had attended Mass.[63] According to visitors, only the women went in numbers, and only to stay for about fifteen minutes of the service. In 1790 the Crown had made a half-hearted attempt to establish the Inquisition in Louisiana through Father Antonio de Sedella (called Père Antoine). Miró temporarily expelled Sedella, writing to his superiors, "When I read the communication of that Capuchin, I shuddered. . . ."[64] Miró convinced the government that the mere mention of the Inquisition in Louisiana would be sufficient to check immigration, and the Crown dropped the whole project.

On the other hand, the clergy was not without influence over certain diversions. Rumors reached Carondelet in 1795 that his subordinate, Gayoso, then governor of Natchez and on a mission in the West, was about to jilt his fiancée, his deceased wife's sister, for a paramour he had met on his journey. "Reflect on what you are doing," Carondelet wrote to Gayoso, "if you are having any affair of this kind there, because our bishop takes such matters very seriously and would certainly make you regret it if, having solicited a license to marry Wats' daughter, with whom it is sure you have lived publicly in Natchez, you were intimate with another in the same manner."[65] At forty-five, Gayoso was sage enough to heed a friendly warning; he went through with the marriage, taking his seventeen-year-old sister-in-law as his third wife.

In New Orleans, as in European cities, the shops, markets, and taverns remained open on Sunday, a custom that shocked visitors from the United States. Bars were always prosperous. According to the 1791 census, there were half as many tavern keepers as there were merchants of all kinds.[66] But though visitors from the puritanical northern states gave the city something of a reputation for corruption and sin, New Orleans throughout the eighteenth century was not the sort of place where vice could flourish. For one thing, most of its people worked too hard. There was an aristocracy, but the planters, smugglers, and shippers who composed it were too busy making money to qualify as a leisure class. Pontalba, for one, managed his wife's indigo plantation with its sixty slaves until indigo declined as an export crop; he ran a distillery; he was constantly engaged in building rental stores; he imported textiles and domestic supplies for resale—all this along with his duties as an officer of the militia with 1,084 men under his command. Most of his relatives were likewise engaged in several pursuits at a time. By 1792 Almonester was probably the richest man in Louisiana and also one of the most overworked. "If his occupations continue like this," Pontalba remarked to Miró, "he [Almonester] will go crazy; he never has any leisure on feasts and Sundays; he barely has time to swallow a morsel at meals, and is often at the Government at midnight. Monsieur de Carondelet keeps him constantly busy and you know he is naturally lazy, you can guess what state he is in."[67] Almonester's brother-in-law Prieto was a warehouse keeper, and not wealthy. Pontalba noted that he, too, gave himself "to the devil;" he was "at the store from morning till night."

Money was not as visible in town as it was on the kingly plantations. New Orleans looked poor and was years away from being able to manufacture its own clothes or supply its domestic needs. Despite the marked increase in the volume of trade after 1795, the townspeople continued for years to be deprived of ever so many items of convenience. People either produced household necessities themselves, or they worked continually training their slaves to do so. Resourceful people even turned their extra house servants into dressmakers and shoemakers, always in demand because of the terrible quality of imported clothes. What could not be made or purchased in town had to be imported, of course, and that might be the most time-consuming procedure of all, especially before the river was opened. Pontalba's letters matter-of-factly record months of waiting for seeds or tools or glass jars; shipments of wrong items at wrong prices; bookkeeping mistakes that had to be righted. Procuring the simplest things could require endless effort, tedious even for a man such as Pontalba who loved commerce and close accounting. "There is no waffle iron for sale," he wrote to Miró in April, 1792. "I am told that Anthony the blacksmith can make one, I shall give him an order immediately, giving him Madame Laronde's iron as a model, on the condition that we can try it out before accepting it. The worst that can happen is to have to order one from Bordeaux, which I would not receive before September. . . . We are trying to arrange starlings' feathers on paper with gum arabic to send you; this year we have not been able to procure over 100."

Food continued to be one of the many things in short supply, even after the opening of the river, because it was so difficult to store. After several shipments of flour had been spoiled in 1796, the *cabildo* assigned Almonester, its expert in construction affairs, to build a warehouse that rats could not get into. Meat was the mainstay of all classes. Almonester called it "a staple commodity . . . especially in this city where no one can live without this food."[68] Although cattle had to be driven in from Opelousas, more than a hundred miles from New Orleans, Almonester noted that "It is a daily occurrence that many homes buy 3 pounds of beef for one *real*, which has also been witnessed by this exponent, he being one who buys it at this price, during any time of the year. . . ." As one traveler observed, "Little bits of bread are served with great pieces of meat; the amount the children eat would frighten a European."[69] He might have noted that bread flour was an imported luxury, whereas meat was a local product, more or less. Vegetables and fruits, with the exception of oranges and strawberries, were hard to find in the markets; but some people such as Pontalba had backyard gardens to round out their diets. When chewing quinine bark gave Pontalba a voracious appetite, he tried to satisfy it by grazing on "a plateful of sorrel, after first removing from it all of the hard boiled eggs, a turkey leg, some beans, a bunch of asparagus, three heads of lettuce, a salad of wintercress, then some quince jelly, some waffles, marzipans and three slices of bread." In spite of all this, he reported, "I managed to leave the table still hungry."[70] Governor Miró remarked in 1787 that when it came to food, the Creoles were not great savers. "They make their well-being depend upon the enjoyment of a good table," he complained, noting that "a governor who did not do likewise would be despised."[71] Consequently, it was costing him eight thousand pesos a year to live—twice as much as his salary.

The well-to-do worked hard, but they were energetic spenders, too. The foodstuffs that dented Creole fortunes and caused Miró to go into debt were not grocery staples but imported luxuries lavishly spread on carved oak tables: olive oil, brandied fruits, anchovies and invariably, coffee, which the Creoles served in spectacular quantities. People ate remarkable amounts of chocolate, considering that it was expensive and hard to come by. Soon after the turn of the century, New Orleans was receiving 34,000 pounds of raisins each year, a staggering quantity even if a great deal was re-exported.[72] Creoles loved sweets. Pontalba described a formal dinner with "many courses" and "many spices," which was nevertheless followed by desserts "seemingly without end." Cakes were served at every party; the guests divided up the leftovers and brought them home in their lanterns, which might not be needed for light because many parties broke up after dawn. The pastries so generously distributed were not cheap; flour was of course in short supply, and even sugar was brought into Louisiana up to the end of the colonial period.[73]

Wine and liquor were expensive; sugar was thirty cents per pound toward the end of the century, compared with meat, which was less than ten cents. The Spanish Crown kept the price of sugar high in order to encourage local producers to export sugar and import Spanish wines. Claret and liquor were imported in great quantities but not necessarily from Spain; five hundred gallons of whiskey came from Natchez alone in 1794, illegally sent downriver from the North, and imports came from other places as well. Moreover, Orleanians must have been prodigious home brewers—they imported 100,140 empty bottles in 1802.[74]

Despite the significant expense, wealthy people seemed happy to spend much of their money entertaining. Everyone who could afford to gave balls, lively affairs with elaborate decorations, games, dancing and feasting. The earnest young American governor, W. C. C. Claiborne, thought they were an unmitigated nuisance. "I fear you will suppose I am wanting in respect in calling to your attention the Balls of New Orleans," he wrote to the secretary of state, "but I assure you Sir, that they occupy most of the Public mind."[75] In addition to gala parties in private homes, public balls of three types were held on Sundays and Thursdays: one for whites, one for blacks, and one for children, all with inexpensive admission.[76] Women of all classes attended, walking barefoot through the mud, the wealthy ladies accompanied by slaves who carried the gowns and shoes their mistresses would put on at the hall. Young mothers brought their babies and nursed them in between the dances, for public balls like private parties lasted far into the night. Any important event might be celebrated by several public and private balls. The ceding of Louisiana to France in 1803 inspired two official balls with the same five hundred guests for both, involving tea, dancing, gambling, dinner, an all-night buffet, and a final meal of forty or fifty dishes.

The balls surrounding the cession of Louisiana were no doubt exceptional, as was the event that prompted them. But exuberant festivities must have been somewhat routine—inventories of the estates of rich Creoles reveal that many of them had fortunes invested in table settings. St. Maxent owned fifty dozen napkins with matching tablecloths, and thirty dozen more napkins of damask, enough to accommodate any fastidious army of invasion that he might be obliged to feed. At his death St. Maxent left one hundred dozen pieces of china, porcelain and crystal, and three thousand bottles of wines and liquors. His furniture could not be listed in detail, according to the officials making the inventory, because to check it piece by piece would be "to immortalize the task."[77]

It is easy to see why New Orleanians cherished their dances and spared no extravagance on them. Without these parties, the town would have been a dull place indeed, offering only the mildest pastimes. Young people with time on their hands could promenade on the levee in front of the Place d'Armes, skirting the garbage and curiously eyeing the quadroons walking there with their mothers. Women might drive out at dark in one-horse carriages, each accompanied by an elegantly dressed Negro boy or girl. But weather and mosquitoes placed limits on these entertainments.

For both men and women the cheapest diversion in the city was gossiping. In the large compendium of disregarded laws, no regulation was more futile than Carondelet's requirement that anyone having news of importance must first tell it to his local syndic, who would either permit or forbid him to divulge it.[78] "I can assure you," Pontalba warned Miró after the governor had left New Orleans, "that when you write any confidential information and instruct me to tell even one person, the next day the whole town is full of it, it is the news of the day, and hereafter you may depend on it; to share your letters with anyone, whomever it may be, is to publish them. . . . You have friends, but they are not secretive. All you wrote in confidence was advertised."[79] Pontalba himself had an encyclopedic store of up-to-date gossip; he hoarded it like small change and circulated it abroad with his letters. He was especially prompt in reporting to Miró anything Almonester told him "in strictest confidence" with instructions "not to tell Miró." He lived, after all, in a society where print was occasional, mail was a semimonthly event at best, and even the town crier traveled only on the sidewalks. One was almost duty-bound to share what little information one had with everyone else.

For people with time to squander in New Orleans, there was always gambling, prohibited in the harshest terms by the Spanish government and openly enjoyed by people of every rank. Pontalba gambled with the Baroness de Carondelet, if only for matchsticks, every time he visited "at the Government," and card tables were set up everywhere at formal balls given by the officials.[80] "No person of whatever rank or quality or condition," was permitted to hold "in his house, in another's, or in the faubourgs" of the city, "games of cards or dice," according to governors' proclamations repeated through the end of the Spanish regime. Yet in 1802, when gambling was still forbidden, New Orleans imported 54,000 packs of playing cards, more than four packs for every man, woman, child, and visitor in the city.[81] However, before attaching too much significance to this colonial recreation, we should note that not only in New Orleans were people mad for card games. As governor of Louisiana, Miró had warned in 1786 that "nothing will stop me from punishing those who are found gambling or those who consent to allow it in their homes." But scarcely had he arrived in Madrid than he described participating in a daily round of card parties that lasted from four in the afternoon until one every morning. When he developed a serious fever, he attributed it to getting overheated while gambling.[82]

At each gathering (and this was also true of Miró's parties in Spain), the same people turned up. Everyone dressed to the teeth for every soirée, the women in richly embroidered dresses trimmed with lace, taffeta, and gold sequins. Since the company was always the same, the costume had to be always different. People required many outfits. Most gowns were probably made at home, judging from the purchase orders of traveling salesmen and the imports of cloth goods, which show that women bought quilted satins and velvets by the yard. A dress ordered from abroad might arrive in pieces so that it could be fitted to an individual. A traveler remarked that New Orleans women had a penchant for going barefoot at home. If they did, it is not because they lacked shoes: there were sixteen shoemakers in the city in 1791, all thriving despite large quantities of footwear imported into the colony.[83]

It is a little surprising to find that men loved splendid shirts and jackets, considering they spent long, humid hours in them as they bustled around town. Inventories listed dozens of velvet and silk suits in black, crimson, and scarlet—and mirrors in every room. Men wore wigs and hair powder until the first years of the nineteenth century, so that along with the flour, shoes, and needles imported in 1802 were 111 hair pieces.[84] Almonester appears to be handsomely bewigged in a 1797 portrait, though it is hard to imagine him wearing any of his portrait attire while he presided over the endless sessions of summer court. Like many wealthy men, Almonester had his own wig-maker, a versatile slave named Jasmin whom he leased out.[85] Although the citizens of New Orleans were not mindful of the hygiene of their streets, they must have been fastidious in their personal grooming: 322,500 pounds of soap were imported from the United States in 1803, according to *Le Moniteur*. We cannot be certain how much found its way to local bodies and how much was re-exported abroad. Probably a great deal more soap was made at home.

The cultural and educational level of these dandies is difficult to assess. The plantation homes in the colony are evidence of the fortunes lavished on architecture; but nobody, apparently, spent much on paintings.[86] St. Maxent, for example, with too much furniture to inventory, had only one painting, valued at ten pesos. As for music, people must have heard a great deal of it at the many dance parties; however, a census of 1791 listed only "3 violinists" and "1 musician" living in New Orleans.[87] Theater was probably the third most popular sedentary diversion enjoyed by all classes, after gambling and solemn High Mass. The theater was located on St. Peter Street, a long, narrow building with one tier of boxes for whites and an upper tier for people of color. Although the scenery was badly deteriorated, subscriptions to the little theater were quite expensive—about the equivalent of two hundred dollars—and sold quickly. Judging from some of Pontalba's remarks, the performances must have been as primitive as the sets. When one actor who was the habitual target of the audience's mockery made his appearance on stage, "people kept on applauding with both their hands and feet, until they made such a noise that I could not hear a word he said."[88]

Pontalba had some familiarity with many of the plays produced, and although he was not an addicted reader, he mentions books now and then. Most Louisianians certainly cared less for reading than for getting together with friends, judging from the rarity of books in the estates of men who owned almost everything else, but then, many wealthy people even now possess relatively few books. St. Maxent owned 4,700 volumes, too many to read in one lifetime, apparently, since at his death they were still new.[89] Jean Baptiste Prévost owned half as many books as napkins, about 150 volumes. And Jean Baptiste Castillon, Madame Almonester's second husband who had no qualities, from all accounts, had books to sell—some eight or nine hundred volumes which he advertised as "a precious collection, rare in this country."[90] Finding no one in New Orleans in 1803 who sold books exclusively, the curmudgeonly Berquin-Duvallon thought it was because "a bookseller would perish of hunger there in the midst of his books, unless these taught the fascinated reader the art of doubling his capital in a year's time."[91]

Some outsiders disparaged the overall level of education in the colony, but their observations should not be accepted uncritically. New Orleans' newspaper in 1795, *Le Moniteur de la Louisiane,* appeared weekly. Printed on four sheets in French (with some information repeated in English), it was a good paper for its place and time. In addition to articles on foreign affairs, *Le Moniteur* published decrees and government regulations, indemnities for escaped slaves, announcements of arriving shipments, and local agricultural news. Berquin-Duvallon estimated that the paper never had more than twenty-four subscribers; even the high-priced theater did better.[92] But if subscriptions were so few, which is doubtful, readers must have been plentiful or the paper would not have attracted advertisers.

In 1803 Thomas Jefferson averred that no more than two hundred people in all of Louisiana could read and write well. Pontalba's wife Louise, called "Ton-Ton," was apparently one of those who found writing extremely laborious, due, Pontalba thought, "to the little practice" she had.[93] Literacy was supposed to be so rare in the countryside that, according to Amos Stoddard, "a person who could read and write was considered as a kind of prodigy among them."[94] Yet there were hundreds of notaries, merchants, military commanders, clergymen, and government workers scattered over the colony who were hardly illiterate. And country courthouses up and down the Mississippi Valley are even now full of records dating from the colonial period, documents written in French or English by "prodigies" quite confident with words and paper.

To encourage literacy, the Spanish Crown exempted printers from military service, provided a noncirculating library of about two hundred books in several languages, sold some books to the public at cost, and established a free public school. The French would not use the Spanish school—only a handful of poor children appeared for the reading and writing classes. The Ursuline Convent had about seventy girls boarding and one hundred day students, with tuition set according to the family's ability to pay. Besides the tutors who went from home to home, there were also French private schools in New Orleans, some with boarding accommodations; their collective enrollment was about four hundred boys and girls. A typical advertisement for such a school listed the elective offerings: French, English, Italian, writing, spelling, elocution, history, something called "chronology," mythology, sewing, needlework, pianoforte, arithmetic, geography, embroidery, artificial flower- and basket-making, and "if the parents desire it," singing and dancing.[95] There were no compulsory courses, and no Spanish.

New Orleans was above all a town for men on the make. Throughout the colonial period, during the rise and fall of indigo and tobacco, money grew on trees: lumber employed three thousand workers in 1793 in mills along the Mississippi River. Lumber exports—boards, shingles, boxes, casks for sugar, pitch, tar, and construction materials—were exchanged for Caribbean slaves. But the sanctioned trading of all commodities, whether lumber, tobacco, or slaves, was only the tip of the mast. The colonists wanted legal trade to continue with the French islands in great part because it made possible an enormous volume of illegal trade with the English and Americans. When ships from both New Orleans and the United States legally entered a port of the French West Indies such as Cap Français, a Spanish vessel could simply load up with American shoes, iron, hemp, nails, seeds, or flour, along with its recorded cargo of West Indian slaves, wine, and liquor, paying for the whole shipment with Spanish piasters that could be exchanged in the West Indian port city.

There were a dozen systems for smuggling. American or British merchants could send goods destined for New Orleans through French Santo Domingo or Spanish Cuba in ships which carried papers attesting that the vessel was owned by a Spaniard, generally a resident in New Orleans acting as the alleged owner. An in-law of Governor Miró, J. B. Macarty, was up to his powdered wig in such semilegal, quasilegal, and illegal schemes for circumventing the rules, as were many merchants. The captain of the ship *Mathilde* left Havana for New Orleans in 1785, but made a stopover in Philadelphia. When accused of smuggling American goods from Philadelphia into Louisiana, he explained to a Spanish court that bad weather had forced him off course.[96] There must have been a great deal of bad weather in the Gulf of Mexico. The Spanish minister to the United States, Diego de Gardoquí, noted while in the North that several ships from New Orleans which were cleared for Santo Domingo had been forced by storms to stop in New York.[97] By the 1790s, direct smuggling between the United States and New Orleans was largely ignored by the Spanish authorities; even war between France and Spain did not stop the flourishing contraband traffic.

Trade, most of it illicit, was what kept the city going. New Orleans produced virtually nothing that was sent through its port. Only services were to be found in the city; but the city was the only place to find them. Every exported pound of Natchez cotton or Les Allemands sugar, every imported drop of rum or quinine had to go through New Orleans to be stored, taxed, inspected, weighed, contracted, notarized, packaged, and accounted for. And what kept trade alive was the interdependence of the city merchant and the country farmer. It is misleading to refer to a "planter class" with respect to New Orleans, or to make rigid distinctions between the supposedly aristocratic planters and the mercantile traders who found markets for their crops. Planter wealth, as often as not, had its origin in trade and business. Macarty, for example, who was related to both Miró and Pontalba, was a merchant, owned a sawmill, purchased American goods on commission for planters, collected debts from planters, and supplied implements to them. Yet, since he eventually invested part of his fortune in a plantation with many slaves, he is generally considered one of Louisiana's great planter barons. The planters were not a closed caste, for in Louisiana's economy, there was little specialization in business or occupations. People did whatever made money, and it was commonplace for men such as St. Maxent to earn fortunes from commissions when they acted as agents in New Orleans for overseas purchasers. St. Maxent eventually owned 167 slaves and three plantations. But he did not acquire his wealth by sitting on one of his verandas.

Almonester was an exception to the trader-shipper-planter type, having gained his fortune through building and real estate. From the day of its founding, the colony had steadily increased in population. There were never enough houses in New Orleans. New construction was going on constantly, but more was always needed because of recurring fires and hurricanes. So Almonester prospered without ever handling crops or merchandise.

The 1795 Pinckney's Treaty, allowing Americans free access to the Mississippi River, came adventitiously just as cotton and sugar were about to become the great export crops of Louisiana.[98] The colony now had products for overseas export and a consumer market near New Orleans for imports. Americans, having pushed into the Ohio Valley a few years before, created an agricultural hinterland, with surpluses they wanted to send to world markets. The Mississippi was the only north-south artery accessible to American farmers, who at last had the right to deposit goods at New Orleans until they could be re-exported.

The opening of the Mississippi to Americans transformed the port, ex-posing it to the interior of the continent. As always, everything came through New Orleans: the traffic—taxes, storage, services—was the city's wealth. Thus began the wholesale invasion of American traders who poured down the river in flatboats with their coonskin caps, Kentucky rifles, and contempt for the Old World formality they found in New Orleans. Pontalba foresaw that American trade on the Mississippi would change Louisiana. Along with a burgeoning of population, he predicted that "property will double in value, and our city will resemble Philadelphia in the diversity of nations who will live here."[99] But Creoles, including Pontalba, glimpsed the new order and hated it, even while they welcomed the opportunity to get richer. They realized instinctively that they would not absorb the Americans as they had the Spaniards and that New Orleans would become an American outpost. Pontalba remarked that one of Philippe de Marigny's sons, after making "a slight attempt" to educate himself in the North, had brought back with him "the vices of the country, and the boorish manners of the Ameri-cans; he goes around with a pronounced stoop, chews continually, swears at the least provocation, and seems to be bored with everything he sees as well as whatever is told him."[100]

By the time Louisiana was sold to the United States in 1803, New Orleans was becoming the headquarters of officials, merchants, and planters who lived in the city only in the intervals when they conducted business. Tran-sients swelled the population in the winter months, returning to their homes during the season of heat and pestilence. Bankers, credit and sales agents, shippers, hunters and trappers from upriver, stevedores, clergymen, sailors from ships docked at the river, prostitutes, and shopkeepers of all sorts turned the city into a frontier station for five months. The boomtown condi-tions intensified every year. Governor Claiborne complained in 1804 that the town was full of "adventurers," "vagabonds," and *"various characters,"* who, he feared, comprised "the materials for a mob."[101] The Creoles now wit-nessed the growth of every kind of business, more commercial traffic, more crime, and especially more contact and conflict with the people whom they indiscriminately referred to as "Kaintocks." By 1809, even the public bath stayed open twelve hours a day and offered rooms for transients.[102] New Orleans was still the sort of place where a horse found astray might occasion a newspaper advertisement, but the character of the town had changed irrevocably. After the turn of the century it was a place where people came, not to start a new life or settle into the conventions of a provincial outpost, but to make money quickly and leave.

Almonester died in 1798, the year after Pontalba emigrated to Europe, never to return. The peaceful town they had known, with its regulated atmosphere and predictability, began to vanish too. Within a few years, New Orleans belonged to a new generation and a culture they would not have recognized.

II

Almonester

DON Andrés Almonester attended the weekly meeting of the *cabildo* as usual the day his first daughter was born. There is no evidence that his colleagues congratulated him on becoming a father at sixty-seven, or that he himself took any particular notice of Micaël's birth. But then, Almonester had other events on his mind. With or without a baby, November 6, 1795, should have been one of the finest days of his life.

He waited until the end of a report by Joseph Delfau de Pontalba on sanitary conditions in the slaughterhouse. Then, as the tedious council session was about to close, Almonester produced two documents bearing the unmistakable royal seal: edicts from the king. The first paper confirmed Almonester as the sole authority of the Charity Hospital of St. Charles and its chapel, both of which he had built as a gift to the city in 1785. The administration of the hospital "which had so unjustly been taken from him by the *cabildo*," according to the edict, was now returned to Almonester with the privilege "to appoint, at his will, all the employees of the Church and Hospital." As long as he lived, Don Andrés would "not be asked to render any accounting of the administration. . . ." In the hospital's church, Almonester was to occupy the first seat, inferior only to the place occupied by the governor. The second edict concerned St. Louis Cathedral, another of Almonester's benefactions, where the king granted him "ownership of a special pew erected over the main entrance. . . ."[1]

Almonester was thus vindicated completely in his bitter ten-year quarrel with the *cabildo*. After the edicts were copied into the record, Almonester's fellow councillors, Nicolas Forstall, Michel Fortier and the rest, affixed their signatures to the *cabildo* minutes (with what sullenness we can only imagine), and dismissed the meeting without another recorded word. The king had distinguished Almonester as a favored courtier and warned the governor, the council, and everyone else to let him alone. Such a communication from the Throne was at least as momentous to a Spanish functionary as having a baby.

But if Almonester was too preoccupied to make a public announcement of Micaël's birth, we can be sure that the town nevertheless took note that

one of its preeminent officials and his thirty-seven-year-old wife were beginning a family after eight childless years. The children (in 1797, six months before Almonester's death, a second daughter was born) came after Almonester had long since made his will, at the end of an exertive life that had
already accommodated many surprises.

Andrés Almonester y Roxas was born in Spain in 1728 near Seville, in a village of thirteen streets and two parish churches.[2] His mother died when he
was nine, leaving him and his three sisters to be brought up by a stepmother.
The poverty in his province of Andalusia was so widespread that once while
he lived there the entire rural population considered emigrating en masse.[3]
However, Almonester's father had sufficient means to send his son to the
local school. In later life Almonester made much of his family's membership
in the nobility, although it was well known that half the starvelings in Spain
could claim noble rank. The father left a will naming Andrés as its executor,
indicating that by the time Almonester reached maturity, if not before, the
family had acquired disposable wealth. It even appears that Almonester had
some connection in Madrid, for he moved to the capital around 1760 and
won an appointment as royal notary in the court of one of Spain's most intelligent monarchs, Charles III.

   Madrid at the time of Almonester's arrival was a cramped, filthy metropolis where pigs infested the winding streets and 150,000 citizens threw their
slops into the roads and alleys. Over the fierce resistance of his subjects, the
king launched a campaign to demolish slum houses. Public lighting was provided during the winter. Animals and sewage were banned from the streets,
despite the protests of resident doctors that the polluted air of the city was
beneficial to health.[4] The transformation of his native capital was not lost on
Almonester. A decade later he and all the incoming Spaniards met similar
foul conditions in New Orleans, and they tried to clean up the town by similar reforms. A generation after the lights were turned on in Madrid, Almonester supervised the installation and maintenance of streetlamps for the
treacherous thoroughfares of New Orleans, and petitioned the governor to
destroy squalid shacks which blighted the riverfront.[5]

   In Spain Almonester married Maria Martínez, a girl from a village near his
childhood home, and had a son who died at birth. He married possibly for
love, certainly not for money, since he tells us in his will, "We both came on
equal terms to that marriage, without fortune or dowry. . . ." Apparently, this
first wife died in Spain, for he states firmly, "I have no responsibilities arising

from that marriage . . . for which cause I owe nothing and have nothing to assign to any person."[6] Perhaps they were first separated when he left Andalusia to seek his fortune in Madrid.

It was while he was still in Spain where housing shortages were critical that Almonester must have developed an interest in construction. Perhaps he was drawn into building through his involvement in real estate transfers, appraisals, or some ramification of his work as a notary. Building was a lucrative business both in Spain, where the middle class lived in ugly cottages and the poor often lived in caves, and in Louisiana, where the lack of laborers caused an ever-worsening shortage of housing as the population grew. Although no one in New Orleans was living in caves, contractors were wanted for all kinds of buildings. Storehouses were needed everywhere, since most of what was used in the colony had to be imported, and whatever was imported had to be stored, usually at government expense. By the time Spain took over Louisiana, conditions were ideal for an enterprising man with an eye for real estate to make a fortune.

We do not know why Almonester decided to emigrate to the Indies in 1769. At forty-one he was no longer young, and having had a notarial practice for some years, was probably doing well enough in Madrid. For whatever reasons, he came alone in 1769, part of the entourage of soldiers and bureaucrats sent in the wake of the colony's second Spanish governor, Alejandro O'Reilly. He had been appointed to a notarial post in New Orleans before he left Spain.[7]

How did Almonester then make the money that he gave away so generously in the New World? To start with, the new office, Notary Public of War and Royal Finance, was a particularly remunerative position in the colonies, even though it had to be purchased from the Crown and thus involved a cash investment. Notaries were required for every sort of transaction. To sell a slave, for example, the owner was obliged to have his title to the slave confirmed, obtain a permit to sell, and finally have the Negro appraised, all procedures requiring the services of a notary. Any evidence presented in court required the authentication of a notary. Almonester was obliged, for example, to go himself to examine the corpse of Juan Baptiste Cézaire LeBreton in June, 1771, to certify that he had been shot. He had to examine the musket balls taken from LeBreton's body and compare them with ammunition taken from one of the victim's slaves. His presence was required when LeBreton's slaves were tortured to exact confessions, and he had the unpleasant duty of certifying that the horrible punishments to which the convicted slaves were condemned had been carried out.[8] Hundreds of documents sent to the captain-general in Cuba every few months had to be inspected and signed by a notary. In addition to the modest government salary of five hundred pesos a year, Almonester was paid by his clients according to fixed rates—so much per line for each act witnessed, so much per line for each document drafted. The documents remain in notarial archives exactly as they were written, their sheets as strong as stiffened fabric, all loosely bound on open shelves. The sixteen volumes are organized by date, so that we can see the acts of sale, loans, wills, contracts, and so on, that Almonester notarized on any particular day, a collection as authentic and mundane as old bones. From their quantity we can judge that he made more than a comfortable living in New Orleans as a *scribano real*. By 1779, ten years after taking up his post, he was petitioning the king to allow him to name a successor to the position.[9]

Like all Spanish notaries in the colonies, Almonester was eager to buy land with his leftover earnings. His first investments were his best: the property on both sides of the *plaza de armas,* which later generations would know as the site of the Pontalba Buildings. The lots were owned by members of the *cabildo* who had bought them when they were first taken out of the public domain in the 1770s and offered for sale to anyone who would agree to build on them. They were mostly vacant and inexpensive, since the church and public buildings then on the square were humble structures.[10] As quickly as he could, Almonester bought one lot after another from the original purchasers. By about 1782 he owned all the land on both sides of what would become, because of his donations there, the city's central plaza and the basis of his real estate fortune.

He started his empire by building rental houses and stores on this ground and on other property he acquired all over the city.[11] In a frenzy of construction in the 1770s and 1780s, he concentrated on buildings that could produce revenue. Shortages of supplies did not much affect him, for lumber was the one plentiful material in Louisiana; it grew reliably on his own plantation. He could ignore the chronic scarcity of labor, too, because he trained his slaves in various trades. Almonester owned at least one brickyard worked by his blacks, and Pontalba estimated that he had more than one hundred slaves before his second marriage, including, according to Pontalba, "masons, joiners, carpenters, blacksmiths, sawyers, locksmiths, brickmasters. . . ."[12] From time to time he rented out his skilled workers, since a slave carpenter or mason could be let out for about the same monthly amount as a small house. Probably he was able to export his leftover provisions to Cuba, which for much of the Spanish period depended on Louisiana for building supplies. Everything imported to New Orleans had to be stored; therefore, warehouses were always needed. In a country as desperate as Louisiana for both construction and construction workers, Almonester's investments in land and slaves were bound to provide a smart profit. Within about fifteen years he was able to turn a notary's robust income into a fortune, with shops, warehouses, and houses from which he collected rents.

We know nothing about Almonester's social pleasures during his bachelor years in New Orleans, except that he lived modestly and worked too hard building rental houses and taking on public duties to have much of what we would call a "private" life. During his lifetime there were mulattoes christened with the surname Almonester in New Orleans. Though it is exciting to come across the names in the sacramental registers, we cannot say with certainty that these were or were not Almonester's children. It seems likely that they were foundlings named in his honor, like Maria Antonia Almonester, who was born a few months after his death and abandoned to the orphanage at Charity Hospital.[13] In 1778 Almonester was living with his secretary on the Quay, an unhandsome strip of service buildings on the river, in the only residence he kept for himself in town. No servants lived with the two men.[14] The man who became his most steadfast friend in New Orleans, Father Antonio de Sedella, arrived in 1781; Almonester was also comradely with the de la Rondes and the Monteguts. Since he had no blood relatives in Louisiana, he was cut off from the most important personal and social connection one could have in the colonies—family.

But if we have no certain knowledge of Almonester's character or recreations, we can find odds and ends of information about business relationships that overlapped his friendships, such as his connection with St. Maxent. Gilbert Antoine de St. Maxent had been one of the plutocrats of the colony when Almonester was still an up-and-coming arriviste. However, when St. Maxent was charged with contraband shipping in 1784, his funds and merchandise were placed under embargo for three years, with Almonester as their custodian. St. Maxent and Almonester remained close friends throughout the period; Almonester even lent him money.[15] St. Maxent was damaged by the trial, though he was finally cleared of the charges. Almonester, whose fortune meanwhile increased from his own enterprises, stepped into his place as Louisiana's foremost citizen and patron of public projects.

Although the men's financial positions had changed, their friendship continued as before.

As might be expected in an isolated Spanish anthill, there was busy wrangling within the leadership of New Orleans. So long as Esteban Miró was governor, he was the ultimate target of most discontent, and the political combinations that were made and unmade around him were transilient. During those years, 1780 to about 1791, Almonester showed a curious talent for remaining neutral during the feuds of his companions—curious, because he was too outspoken to have been tactful or even two-faced. Yet time and time again, we find him being a solid friend to two ardent enemies. Almonester was Miró's strong ally in the *cabildo*; but he was friendly toward people who, if they were not Miró's sworn enemies, were certainly not his supporters: St. Maxent, for example, whom Miró prosecuted, and St. Maxent's nephew, Gilberto Guillemard, whom Miró called "a fawning little snipe."[16] Then there was Sedella. Father Antonio had been appointed commissioner of the Holy Inquisition in 1787; in 1790, in response to various pressures mounting against him, he began demanding his prerogatives as an Inquisition official, including his right to a squad of soldiers. Miró responded by having the friar arrested and deported.[17] Miró gathered a dossier of information against Sedella which he forwarded to his superiors, along with his explanation of his actions. Sedella in turn gathered a dossier in his own defense, including a testimonial letter from Almonester. Almonester was openly in the middle between his two firmest friends. Eventually the Crown's plans for a colonial Inquisition were dropped, and Sedella was allowed to return. He resumed his friar's work, spending the rest of his life in New Orleans as a brother to mankind, if not to Miró. Father Antonio baptized Almonester's first daughter and was godfather to his second; meanwhile, Almonester remained friends with Miró. He extended courtesies to another of Sedella's serious enemies, Father Patrick Walsh, or "Don Patricio," as the Spanish referred to him. Blunt-spoken Spaniard though he was, Almonester could somehow stand in the crossfire of other people's wars without getting hit.

As a businessman Almonester let out goods on credit, as everyone did in the colony, and as soon as he began to accumulate money, he lent a good deal of it to individuals. Like many others who acquire wealth late in life, he found himself involved in a number of eleemosynary projects within the space of a few years. Or perhaps that is to impute too much inadvertancy to his charity; in any case, around 1787 he decided to perpetuate his newly prominent name by making public benefactions. He set aside 400,000 pesos for a charity fund, a substantial commitment when we consider that at the time, the assets of the colony's governor amounted to only 4,000 pesos.[18]

Why did Almonester at the age of sixty turn with such deliberation to a life of philanthropy? Probably because the Crown required donations in exchange for titles. Moreover, when he first became involved in public charities, Almonester had neither children nor family in the New World to whom he could leave his assets; he had no reason not to dedicate his fortune to buildings that would last beyond his lifetime. And most likely, since he was in many ways a typical man of the Enlightenment, Almonester wanted to improve the quality of life in his adopted home. As a protégé of a reform-minded king, he realized that the resources of one man, properly managed, could change the lives of many.

The Charity Hospital of St. Charles was the first and longest deferred of Almonester's projects. It was the humanitarian achievement of his life and the one that best reflects his genuine kindliness; but it embroiled him in controversy with the *cabildo* from 1782 until his death, and kept his widow in litigation for several years longer. To appreciate the viciousness that buffeted Almonester as he tried to establish and run his hospital, we must understand certain power stresses in the colony. The *cabildo* was not the governor's cabinet, but rather the center of whatever recalcitrance he might encounter in his administration. Alliances were formed within the *cabildo* on the basis of support or opposition to the governor, just as members of our Congress adjust their political positions according to whether or not they wish to cooperate with the president in office. The governor and *regidores* were not members of registered parties, but they were the disciples of rival ministers and court cliques in Spain. The *cabildo*, moreover, was itself a little political aquarium where, in plain sight but rarely noticed, the biggest fish randomly and continually nipped at each other and the governor, so as to control as much of the fishbowl as possible. The aggression heated up whenever a few crumbs were being sprinkled.

The Charity Hospital was exactly the kind of project that could incite the *regidores* to jealous secretions, since it involved money, commissions, contracts, jobs to be awarded, decisions that affected the whole colony, and it had the potential of attracting a dribble of royal attention. There had been a charity hospital in Louisiana as far back as 1737, poorly maintained by public donations but under the supervision of the Superior Council, the French municipal commission. Spanish rule supplanted the French government following the 1762 transfer of Louisiana, and the *cabildo* was set up to replace the Superior Council; but to the surprise of the commissioners, some of whom had been on the French council, the hospital was taken out of their hands. In keeping with Spanish colonial administration of all such facilities, the charity hospital was placed under the direct supervision of the vicar general of Louisiana and the governor. The members of the *cabildo* never got over being deprived of "their" hospital and resented every expression of the governor's authority over the institution. They continued to try first one strategem and then another for regaining control over the hospital; all the schemes were quashed, first by Governor Gálvez and then by Miró.[19] The tug-of-war over the hospital came to a forced truce when the building was unroofed and practically destroyed by the hurricanes of 1778 and 1779; the city hospital became six beds in a makeshift room. Though the *cabildo* did absolutely nothing to restore the facility for three years, the members were outraged when Miró, without consulting them, accepted Almonester's offer to rebuild the hospital and maintain it at his own expense.

Almonester had placed himself in the middle of a nasty fight. He was now the main obstacle to any schemes the *cabildo* members had for regaining authority over the hospital, and he became the target of their wrath. In their view, he was a commissioner just as they were, but he was to have exclusive control over an institution from which they had been shut out. Never mind that he alone was to pay for the hospital and support it. In a meeting on December 13, 1782, the council accused a "certain person" of using the hurricane disaster to seize control of the facility. The councilmen raised ridiculous objections to Almonester's plans for the rebuilding, such as protesting that he should not be allowed to take bricks from the ruins still on the ground. Defended by Miró, Almonester proceeded with the project, taking the precaution, however, of petitioning the king for the right to serve as the hospital's patron and director.[20]

The new Charity Hospital of St. Charles opened in 1785. It contained four wards, a church, a chapel, an attendant's room, a pharmacy, and a vegetable garden on the grounds. Almonester also provided for an orphanage on the site for foundlings who might be delivered to the staff "at any hour of the day or night, and that they [the staff members] should not contrive to investigate, nor ask questions of the person who leaves, or delivers them."[21] The attendants were to care for the orphans, according to Almonester's directions, "with much tenderness."

Almonester wrote a detailed constitution for the institution, basing it on the government's rules for hospital administration in the Indies. The superintendant appointed by the patron, Almonester, had to oversee the staff, supplies, and funds. In addition, he was charged with making sure that the utensils were handled with "the greatest care and cleanliness"; that the food was well seasoned "with salt, saffron, and cinnamon"; that the servants "prayed with their rosaries"; and that "lavender or incense" was sprayed after the regular emptying of chamber pots.[22] No two people were to sleep in the same bed, "even though they say they are relatives, friends, or countrymen," and the lights of the wards were to be kept burning all night. Surgeons and doctors were required to visit patients twice a day. By the time he wrote the constitution, Almonester was so accustomed to being criticized that he protected himself in advance from the possible antagonism of the doctors. They were cautioned not to "prescribe a medicine, or food that is not found in this country, the lack of which the doctors usually take advantage when they are disgusted with the administrator for personal reasons and wish to make it evident they do not furnish the necessary food or drugs."

The "ordinary ration" of food, subject to prescribed changes by the physician for individual patients, consisted of a pound of beef per day, an ounce each of bacon and chickpeas, fourteen ounces of bread, and one half-ounce of lard, with many variations allowed, including eggs, milk, wine, meatballs, chicken, vermicelli, and chocolate. Patients were to be kept in the hospital for three days after being pronounced cured by the physician, "so that they may convalesce with the full ration of bread, meat, and wine." This was to be a rare example of a hospital where the patients stayed longer than necessary in order to savor the food. Inventories of the hospital's supplies made in 1794 and 1801 showed a surprising abundance of equipment—everything from mosquito bars to new linen mattress covers, tools for the yard, undergarments, and, just as Almonester specified, enough bed slippers and nightcaps for each patient.[23]

Almonester's constitution and hospital records are long, fascinating documents of pretechnological medicine. Since there was, in fact, no medicine to speak of, his instructions to the doctors are preoccupied with what we would consider nursing care. In all of the constitutions for royal hospitals, the instructions are fairly uniform, though the hospitals, no doubt, were not; but the administrators all had at least learned to appreciate the abstract satisfaction of completing a minute record. Not only were patients classified according to the kind and degree of their illnesses, but the condition of the hospital utensils, down to the spoons, was recorded as "good," "medium," or "useless."

In addition to donating the initial cost of the building, 114,000 pesos, Almonester made several proposals for maintaining the hospital after his death. The *cabildo* made strenuous objections to three of the plans but accepted the fourth one after much wrangling.[24] The hospital was free to indigents only; people of means were supposed to pay fifteen pesos a month. But in the rare instances when someone was ejected from the hospital, there were immediate complaints about Almonester to the governor. Miró noted that "people falsely believe that he should bear all expenses and no one pays his hospitalization bills." After the fire of 1788 destroyed two of the hospital buildings, Almonester had to go into his personal funds to support the facility. "Continuing the charitable spirit," Miró wrote, "he admits all the poor patients who present themselves, at times numbering 70, so that the disbursements which he makes annually are considerable."[25]

The Charity Hospital caused Almonester many headaches; but other donations such as the Lepers' Hospital which he proposed in 1785 were not so controversial. During his residence in the colony Almonester had seen that every few years an outbreak of what was presumed to be leprosy sent the population and the *cabildo* into alarmed conferences about how to protect the town from the disease. In April, 1785, there were again rumors that lepers had entered the city. These people could not be admitted to Charity Hospital because horror of the disease would keep other patients away; but to deny the lepers hospital care, Almonester believed, was inhumane. In the midst of the council's commiserations on a possible epidemic, Almonester sent a letter to the *cabildo* stating "that he has built a hospital for the lepers with four separate divisions, large enough to lodge many white families with other separate quarters for colored people, all at his expense . . . which he graciously offers to your Lordships so that the lepers may be kept together." The San Lázaro Lepers' Hospital was situated on part of Almonester's large farm on Bayou Road, "about two gunshots" from the city. The donation, described to Thomas Jefferson as "a large hospice for lepers," included a canal that Almonester built as a bathing facility for the patients and a long roadway (known as "Leprous Road") to the remote sanitarium.[26] Some years later Governor Miró wrote that the hospital had "such a good effect that, since the death of the five lepers who were caught, no others have been seen in the province."[27] With that success added to his record, Almonester was more than ever a leper to the *cabildo*.

In 1785 Father Sedella pointed out to Almonester that the Ursuline nuns needed a new chapel for their devotions. Almonester thus built a large, new brick chapel adjacent to the Chartres Street nunnery, remodeled and reroofed the convent, and added a small brick classroom to the school. The French sisters repaid Almonester as best they could: with prayers, Masses, and a general communion. At Almonester's behest they changed the chapel's name from Our Lady of Victories to Our Lady of Consolation. He received privileges as the chapel's patron, an honor he also expected to enjoy when he built the church of the Charity Hospital. Among other emoluments, this meant that he was given a seat in the Ursuline sanctuary second only to the governor, a happy arrangement so long as Miró was the governor. But Carondelet, who replaced Miró in 1791, was more jealous of his distinctions, particularly those due to him by the clergy; he had Almonester's seat taken away. It was restored by the king himself in 1794 when he ordered not only that "Don Almonester be given possession of his seat," but that it was to be "covered with a cushion but without a *priedieu*. To this seat are attached all the privileges, the incense, the kiss of peace, and the candle, in the same way that it is observed for the Governor-General."[28] None of this endeared Almonester to Carondelet.

Almonester picked his donations carefully. The Spanish public school had been a favorite project of King Charles III until it was destroyed by the fire of 1788. In the aftermath of the fire, Almonester came forth with a building suitable for a classroom and teacher's residence. Though the school had never been well attended, Governor Miró eagerly accepted Almonester's "small edifice," offered "free of charge, and as long as it should be wanted."[29] Almonester fostered French as well as Spanish projects, having come from a part of Spain where French was used extensively. As a notary public he had to be knowledgeable in both languages, and as a judge he tried cases in either tongue. It is certain that he spoke French tolerably at least, since on March 20, 1787, he married a French Creole, Louise de la Ronde, who spoke no Spanish at all.

"Louison," or Loweezy, as Joseph de Pontalba derisively nicknamed her in his letters, was twenty-nine when she married the fifty-nine-year-old Almonester, whom she had apparently been close to for a long time. She had no dowry, Almonester ungallantly informs us in his will, so five years before their marriage he gave her a house next to the Government House on Levée Street, "that she might have an establishment." It was a fourteen-room establishment worth 70,000 pesos.[30] She did, however, bring something to the union: a family that Almonester liked. Louison's mother had been married to Louis Xavier de Lino de Chalmet, the father of her first three children. After his death, she married Pierre Denis de la Ronde with whom she had three more. Louison was the eldest of the second brood. Her father died early and we find her in 1778 living with her twice-widowed mother and younger brothers on Conti, a street that also housed two laundresses, some army officers, and several seamen, according to a gossipy city directory of the period.[31]

Almonester did his best to rescue the family from its modest circumstances; his gifts and favors to the horde of Louison's relatives almost qualify as another public benefaction. Several of the official positions he purchased were later passed on to Louison's little brother Pierre. After a few years of wearing Almonester's various hats, Pierre de la Ronde had accumulated enough profits to build a magnificent plantation home. A few sticks of it are still standing in Chalmette, Louisiana, fenced in and commemorated with a plaque, obstructing the heavy industrial traffic at an intersection. The plantation's live oak trees remain unimpaired and impressive a little distance away; they have given rise to a legend about Almonester's brother-in-law. The fifty-seven Packenham Oaks, as they are called, were planted by Pierre after his travels in Europe, where he had an encounter with Catherine the Great; the Russian empress told him that of her fifty-seven lovers, fifty-six had been better than he. Whereupon de la Ronde withdrew to Louisiana and put his remaining energy into raising trees.[32]

The family must have approved of Louison's marriage, for several of the relatives served as godparents of Almonester's children. He once reminded his colleagues in the *cabildo* that he had made legacies to the city even though he was "not without family" to whom he might have left his worldly goods, a reference not to his own kinsmen in Spain, but to Louison's relatives.[33] He remembered all of the de la Ronde sisters, brothers, nieces, and nephews in his will, leaving each a token legacy, and he bequeathed to his mother-in-law ten pesos a month "to aid her necessities as long as she shall live"—probably a decent little pension, considering that for fifteen a month, one could stay in the hospital. Clearly, Almonester and his in-laws got on.

It is less clear whether Almonester lived amicably with his wife. But they did live well. They were served by forty-four house slaves in their residence at the corner of the plaza on St. Peter Street, where there was a constant and more or less furtive traffic of black men coming to visit the women servants. Joseph Montegut, the doctor contracted to maintain the health of this platoon, once itemized his services in a bill to Almonester, probably in the early 1790s: dressing an abcessed tooth, setting compound fractures, pulling teeth, delivering a child, treating tetanus, and combating a "putrid fever."[34] The time when Almonester would live in shabby bachelor's quarters without a personal servant was past.

As a reward for his early philanthropies, Almonester was made a commissioner of the *cabildo* for the year 1789 and was appointed *regidor perpetuo,* or permanent commissioner, the following year. The office of *regidor*, according to one writer, was "always lucrative because in practice, no Spanish official ever failed to find some source of revenue in his office."[35] If there was a turning point in his later life, it was probably not his marriage but rather this appointment to the *cabildo,* which made him one of the handful of governing officials in the city. In the bickering villadom of the *cabildo* Almonester would always remain "a mere notary," as Carondelet referred to him in a dispatch.[36] But to the hundreds of people who now encountered him as a judge or inspector or the man to whom they could bring a complaint, he was a personage deserving of some respect. He stopped piling up wealth for its own sake; in fact, according to his wife, during these years he "set his mind upon squandering our entire estate" on charitable endeavors.[37] He began seeking the titles and positions that were ardently pursued by all the commissioners—perquisites that were by no means empty honors under the Spanish Crown. He became involved in three more building donations: the St. Louis Cathedral, the Presbytere, and the Cabildo. And he placed himself under a staggering load of official duties for the rest of his life.

Because of the meticulous record-keeping of the *cabildo* and his immense work within that body, we know a great deal about Almonester after 1789—not the hard-driving entrepreneur of his earlier years, but the public servant he became from the age of sixty-one until his death at seventy. The *cabildo* minutes give us a rough outline of what he was doing every working day. Like all the commissioners, Almonester served as both magistrate and city councilman. As a judge, he was obligated to "hear mildly those who may present themselves" and to decide various kinds of civil cases.[38] First, there were complaints involving sums under twenty pesos. Since there were no written proceedings, we cannot be certain how much of his time was taken up by them. Next came the regular civil cases which were presumably the magistrate's major burden. The overwhelming majority of these were uncontested debt claims against the estate of a deceased person. Each case was painstakingly transcribed on heavy paper, folded so that the sheets resemble modern manila folders. The court scribe did not quote verbatim but related the testimony: "Plaintiff says that he went several times to request the payment, but that. . . ." Most cases fit entirely on one folder, with writing on all four sides. Other cases required two or even three folders. The yellowed paper is still wonderfully sturdy and flexible, but the ink on some of the pages has permeated the paper to the other side, where there is also writing, so that a number of the cases are now unreadable, despite the efforts of curators to preserve and protect them. As with many old documents, the handwriting often defies all effort and patience, having been illegible since the moment it was written two centuries ago. Thanks to the work of WPA translators, there are loose-leaf binders containing typed summaries of those cases that had been preserved up to the 1930s, when the summarizing began. A researcher can therefore scan virtually all of the Spanish court records in a matter of hours, even though the original manuscripts of the cases may now be lost or too deteriorated to read.

The summaries show us that most cases were not adversarial proceedings in the modern sense: a nail supplier might sue for payment of a bill and present a signed invoice as evidence; the builder then acknowledged his signature on the bill and was condemned to pay. It was usual for the defendant to offer no resistance to a debt claim. Matters that we might expect to be expedited by a bureau of permits or a police report—selling a slave, for example, or proving that something had been stolen—required a court appearance before a judge. During Miró's tenure, Almonester and the governor seem to have been stuck with hearing most of the cases tried in the summer, a heroic discharge of duty in New Orleans, where nothing moves in July except sweat. Occasionally, a trial was interesting: a free Negress charged a mulatress with assault because she "attacked her with a paddle and bit her thumb."[39] The injury prevented the complainant from working as a seamstress. Two witnesses saw the fight, but as they "did not speak French they ignored the trouble and did not see which was the attacker." We can imagine the stifling tedium of these proceedings as each statement was read, usually in two languages, each piece of written evidence laboriously described or copied word for word for the court record. Trials could proceed only as rapidly as a perspiring court notary could write. Many of the litigants were illiterate; some of the officials, including Almonester, were partially deaf.

There were compensations for the monotony. A scale of fees was used for every court procedure, even for a magistrate's signature: the litigant paid more for a full name than for a simple surname or a cipher; he paid additionally for a rubric and still more for flourishes, if the judge was in the mood to earn a little extra money. Large signatures cost more than small ones, because the litigant paid for the paper as well; many a fancifully embellished name covered half a page. Almonester's usual signature was unselfishly small.

The judicial records, exhaustive as they are, represent only half of Almonester's responsibilities as a *regidor*. For in addition to his court hearings, there were all of his duties in the *cabildo*, starting with the long Friday meetings where work was parceled out for the week. Besides overseeing his big construction projects for the city—the Cathedral, Presbytere, and Cabildo—Almonester was charged with building a storage facility for fire engines and with restoring it when it was later damaged by a hurricane. The sidewalk on the levee was damaged by floods; Almonester was appointed to take charge of the repairs. The roof and foundation of the market needed some replacement. Almonester would see to the renovation and present a report to the council. He was "unanimously commissioned" to award the six-year contract for repairing the city bridges after the 1794 fire—bidding was announced by the public crier and edicts were posted "at the customary places."[40] The bridges located at every street corner needed continual repair; Almonester thus found himself occupied with bridge inspection throughout his nine years as commissioner.

Among the six *regidores* of the *cabildo*, two were chosen each year as annual commissioners, a post to which Almonester was elected many times. His most important work in that position was auditing the accounts of the city treasury and serving as the appeal magistrate in cases originally adjudicated by the governor. Annual commissioners also answered letters addressed to the *cabildo* and handled its official correspondence, including its messages to the Crown—no small privilege when we consider how anxious the *regidores* were to have their individual names before the eyes of the king; and they represented the council in ceremonial duties, as when Almonester was assigned to go "a short distance" from the city to greet the new governor, Carondelet, and escort him to town.[41] They were supposed to take precedence over the other four judges in deliberations; what this meant in practice was that the two led *cabildo* processions and did more work than anyone else. Money issues were as a matter of course handed over to Almonester, who was "unanimously commissioned" to find funds for everything.

He ran the "lighting department" for the city, ordering and inspecting supplies, processing a chimney tax to pay for the lamps, supervising chimney inspectors who assessed the tax, and reporting his interminable dealings with one Francisco Merieult, who charged the city for fish oil and delivered water.[42]

The Friday *cabildo* meetings were strikingly similar to present-day city council deliberations: monotonous, unintentionally funny, fractious, and protracted by procedural formalities. A frequent topic was the shortage of coin in Louisiana caused by the colony's chronic trade deficit. Some question regarding the treatment of slaves came up continually as the *cabildo* tried to create a sense of public security in an atmosphere of Negrophobia. Carondelet was criticized for hearing the slaves' complaints. The council lengthily discussed whether literate blacks should be admitted to the colony; whether slaves ought to be permitted to attend dances with free Negroes; and how best to resist the Crown's attempts to protect the slaves. The judges also handled minor matters: here we find a citizen petitioning to be appointed hangman at a salary of two *reales* a day. Another is soliciting the position of public crier, as the present crier is ill. The night watchman is rewarded for reporting a fire.[43] Even the meeting place of the council could be a topic of some discussion. After the Cabildo was destroyed in the fire of 1788, the *regidores* appointed Almonester to rent a comfortable place for them. They were not satisfied with one house he found, nor with other quarters he offered within his own residence on the square. But another apartment in his house, unconnected with the rest of the building, they judged "more decent" for meetings and rented it for three years while the new Cabildo was being constructed.[44]

But though they accepted his work, his money, and his rooms, the *cabildo* members were uninhibited in showing that they had little fondness for their landlord. We do not know all the reasons why they picked on Almonester, since we are limited to public records for our information, and most animosities arise from private, unacknowledged feelings. The first explanation that offers itself—Almonester's "hard disposition," as Carondelet once termed it—probably had little to do with the way the commissioners tried to obstruct his projects.[45] In the first place, the society in which Almonester lived did not set a great store on personality; a man's relatives, political connections, financial resources, health, piety, and honesty were all considered more crucial to getting on in the world than an affable manner. An individual could get only so far on his disposition, whether hard or soft; a good family was worth incomparably more.

In the second place, Almonester does not seem to have been more vain, immodest, or peremptory than anyone else in the Illustrious Body. As we look at the *cabildo* minutes, we see him insisting that each of his contributions is recorded, since he is after the appreciation of higher authorities who are dependent on documents for their information. He criticized, fairly often, proposals the others were willing to go along with, a habit that must have vexed them. Some of these objections are obviously for the record, as in a courtroom, and not for the purpose of explaining himself to his colleagues. Some are entirely justified, as when he strenuously protested making the city's meat supply a monopoly and awarding that contract to another council member.[46] All of his explanations to his fellow officials seem reasonable, as any argument might when removed from the context of personal jealousies and previous incidents. During the slave rebellion at Pointe Coupée in 1795, the *cabildo* wanted to bypass Governor Carondelet, who they contended was not moving quickly enough to crush the revolt; the *cabildo* proposed appointing its own committee to arrest "all the mischievous slaves who are suspected."[47] Almonester thanked the councilmen for their zeal on behalf of the public welfare, maybe or maybe not sarcastically, but he argued against the *cabildo* arrogating such authority to itself. He was outvoted, and the vigilantes were elected. When the king after many requests agreed to enlarge the *cabildo* with two additional members, Almonester certainly had every reason to contest the appointment of army captains who would not be able to attend the meetings. "The King's intention," he argued, "was to lighten the burdens which had for many years been carried out by only four lifetime commissioners . . . who are old and in ill health."[48] Almonester was outvoted and his workload remained the same as before.

The old man's diligent attention to detail was undoubtedly a nuisance to his fellow councilmen. Like many people of his time, he loved statistics and precise numbers, particularly if they could be used to foil his enemies. He examined the accounts of the city treasurer (one of his critics in the council) and found "not the least objection," except that he refused to reimburse the treasurer for ink and paper since a 5 percent surcharge had already been awarded for overhead.[49] Prolix, fussy, and rambling, he was the Polonius of many a fatiguing session, but he was not malicious; and there is nothing in the *cabildo* records to show that his idiosyncrasies were the cause of the vile attacks that were made on him in his last years.

Almonester's quarrels were political, not personal. For years he was rarely criticized or even questioned about his performance of *cabildo* duties, although he submitted reports, financial accounts, and trial judgments by the hundred that might have supplied fault-finders. His colleagues consistently reelected him annual commissioner, the one office within their control. Only when the controversy simmered over patronage of Charity Hospital was Almonester attacked on all fronts. Almonester was Miró's man, and the relationship between the *regidores* and Miró was so contentious that they drummed up a long indictment against the governor which they pursued even after he had left Louisiana. Almonester had made it possible for Miró to ignore the archons of the colony by building a hospital that they were not to control and that made both Almonester and Miró look good in the eyes of the government. The hospital was run like all the royal hospitals in the Indies were supposed to be run; it was a credit to the empire, but the Crown did not have to support it. For that offense, Almonester would always be an outsider, no matter how much of his money the *cabildo* accepted.

Almonester was courteous, almost courtly, in debate; but he could fight tenaciously. When backed into a corner he let it be known that he was always ready to appeal over the heads of the commissioners to the king. It must have galled the self-important councilmen to be reminded that he alone among them could get the ear of the monarch. Not only was Almonester Miró's ally, but as time went on it became apparent that he had "found grace" near the throne, as Charles IV stated his position.[50]

Was it solely because of his benefactions in New Orleans that Almonester was so strongly defended by the king? He had no one speaking for him at court, his only relative there being a nephew with whom he had no communication. It is possible but unlikely that he performed some service to the Crown before he left Spain, something which distinguished him not only in the eyes of Charles III, who might be expected to recognize merit, but which also won him the favor of the befuddled and undiscerning Charles IV. The younger king had never laid royal eyes on Almonester, but he was as steadfast as his father in backing him. Near the time that Miró in Spain was chortling to Pontalba that Charles IV "seemed to nod in my direction," Almonester was being singled out in the king's edicts as one "who has become very dear to Our person."[51] After Almonester's death Charles IV sided with his widow in her disputes with the *cabildo*, even though the king presumably knew nothing about her except that she had been married to Almonester.

The kingly solicitude does not seem so mysterious if we realize that in a monarchy which had no obligations or mythology about sharing authority, it cost the king nothing to anger the *cabildo*. Churches, hospitals, and schools were considered more valuable to the government than the good will of any municipal council. To the colonial ministers who had to read through the disputes, the back-and-forth between the governors and the *cabildo* over Charity Hospital was an old and wearisome story. Almonester's offer to take the problem off their hands came as a relief and a budgetary boon, as were the other buildings he undertook. The royal authorities knew that a chorus of complaints would harry any progressive enterprise in New Orleans—Gálvez and Miró had told them so—and they were prepared to defend Almonester and discount his attackers as long as he was willing to persevere in spite of them.

Almonester was willing, for aside from everything else, he was ambitious for something more durable than popularity. Titles and recognition from the Crown were the normal rewards for outstanding public donations, just as tax exemptions are today. He had every reason to hope for such honors, and it would have been eccentric for a philanthropist not to seek them. Titles were investments that could be sold, let, bequeathed, used for tax advantage or collateral, or traded to other individuals in return for favors (although, to be sure, every "renunciation" required royal confirmation and the payment of hefty fees). Distinctions were not won effortlessly, however, even by a philanthropist in the king's favor. One had to file formal petitions, follow these up with inquiries and reminders, lobby friends one might have at court, hint at possible future services to the Crown.[52]

The first of these honors to come to Almonester was a position that he bought, but a laurel nonetheless, since he won the right to purchase it over a field of competitors. In 1790, after a flurry of correspondence to the Crown, he was named Royal Ensign (Herald); the edict appointing him also approved his installation as lifetime commissioner. For the two positions he paid the equivalent of more than fifteen thousand dollars, plus half a year's income tax, perhaps six hundred dollars, plus an 18 percent surcharge for transportation of the money to Spain.[53] One of the duties of the Royal Ensign was to receive the oath of office from other magistrates, a privilege Almonester guarded peevishly and for which he was paid double the nominal salary of a *regidor*. But more important, the Royal Ensign carried the royal banner and therefore marched at the head of all processions, generally with an escort of "distinguished persons" who called for him at his house.

Carrying the banner was not simply a matter of colonial etiquette; the symbols of the monarchy were revered and fussed over in the Indies more than they would have been if a king had been physically present to receive displays of affection. Spanish subjects in Louisiana bowed to the regal portraits and to edicts bearing the royal seal as if the king were eucharistically present in these objects, and they cherished the idea of the monarchy with a spiritual, almost secretive reverence. Governor Gálvez wrote of making a patriotic speech to rouse his militia and of accomplishing the task "without exposing the name of Our Sovereign."[54] Subjects were required by law, though they needed no compulsion, to bow to the royal standard wherever it appeared, and involuntarily, to the Royal Ensign holding the flag as well.

Almonester's next honor was a military appointment. In 1789 St. Maxent retired as colonel of the Militia of the White Battalion guarding New Orleans, recommending Almonester for the post. The command brought another burden of paper work. Almonester's battalion consisted of five companies, a total of five or six hundred men. He had to review the service sheets of each officer and handle petitions for retirement, pensions, appointments, promotions, rewards, and special permissions, forwarding them with his recommendations to the governor-general. Recommending an officer for promotion required a long epistle detailing the man's experience and qualifications. Where the militia was to be reorganized or where a vacancy near the top ranks caused each officer below to be advanced one step, Almonester had to write a recommendation for each man he wanted to move. In addition to one-page service sheets that had to be filled out on each soldier, there were service records, several pages each, that had to be kept up to date. Then there were the summary sheets detailing the battalion's enrollments, shortages, discharges, promotions, and so forth, and the tabulations of each soldier's age, time served, and seniority, computed by years, months, and days.[55]

How Almonester got through the alpine stacks of minutiae we may guess from the complaints of Governor Carondelet, who remarked that Don Andrés had brought him his work on the militias but that he "could not make head or tail of it." Carondelet had him do it all over again. Nevertheless, Carondelet's successor Governor Gayoso found Almonester a valuable assistant. Filling out Almonester's own service sheet, dated a few months before his death, Gayoso commented on his "robust health" and noted, perhaps with more assurance, his "inestimable usefulness because of his philanthropic spirit."[56]

Almonester applied for all of his honors within a period of a few years between 1787 and about 1791, after building the Charity Hospital, the hospital
for lepers, the Spanish school, and the Ursuline chapel. He had already accumulated his philanthropic fund and was apparently prepared to devote the
rest of his life to public charities in return for what the Spanish delicately referred to as "some grace." The Good Friday fire of 1788 gave him the opportunity he may have been waiting for to make another spectacular contribution to the city. The day after the fire, Almonester offered to replace the
ruined wooden church with a larger one of brick and wood and to rebuild
the priest's house next to it; both were to be outright gifts. Normally, these
buildings would have been financed by the king or by voluntary donations
from the parishioners. A new Cabildo, which was not royal property but a
city project—a city hall, in fact—was not in Almonester's original plan, but
he agreed to advance funds for it also (with small hope of being repaid)
when it became clear that the city had no money for such an undertaking.

Almonester started on the church first, "pursuing it with such vigor," according to Governor Miró, that "three years from now, as work cannot be
carried on in the cold season, it will be entirely completed." After an initial
burst of activity, however, Almonester stopped construction, causing his colleagues in the *cabildo* to resolve "to send a simple message . . . asking him to
kindly state plainly whether he has decided to reconstruct the said Parish
church or not." After some in-fighting and mutual recriminations between
Almonester and the council's attorney general, Michel Fortier, Almonester
resumed the work. "He promised me that he would continue it to completion," wrote Miró, "despite the flood which caused a break in the levee of the
river on his lands, entailing the loss of his harvests, washing away his fences,
and destroying a large brick kiln which cannot be rebuilt for another month
when the waters recede."[57] But Almonester's bad luck was not all that was
holding him up. Miró reminded his superiors that long before the fire, in
1786, King Charles III had expressed his gratitude for Almonester's many
benefactions by instructing him to "ask for whatever favor he most desired."
What Almonester desired was a title of Castile granted for extraordinary services to the Crown.

The Royal Order of Charles III to which Almonester aspired had been
created by the king to encourage philanthropy and reward the liberality of
his subjects without incurring any cost to the Crown. Knights of Charles III
enjoyed privileges that were worth having—exemption from taxes and criminal prosecution, for example—and that could be passed on to heirs and

even to servants. The Crown at first encouraged petitions for the honor. Each applicant paid large sums to have his lineage confirmed as a prerequisite to membership in the order. Several Orleanians besides Almonester coveted the title, including at least one of his detractors on the council.[58] But after Charles IV assumed the throne in 1788, he gave notice that titles of Castile would thenceforth be harder to procure. Almonester's erratic progress in constructing the church was no doubt due in part to his discouragement when his reward was not forthcoming. Miró made it clear that Almonester "did not set any conditions in promising to contruct the church and rectory, much less that of a title," but that Almonester had every right to expect this reward in the light of all the donations he had previously made. Miró brought up the matter of Almonester's title in many other dispatches, pointing out that Almonester had already spent over 100,000 pesos in charitable works and would probably spend as great a sum on the projected buildings.[59] In fact, Almonester ended by putting out 114,000 pesos on the cathedral, 40,000 on the Presbytere, and 30,000 on the Cabildo; the last sum was reimbursed to his estate.

Almonester meanwhile had been occupied not only with the constructions on the plaza but with the administration of Charity Hospital, his pet project. Throughout the 1780s the *cabildo* had continued to nurse its grievance against Miró for depriving it of control of the institution. Even while Miró was still governor, the royal treasurer, Joseph de Orué, together with a group in the *cabildo* whom Miró referred to as "the cabal," conspired to ruin Miró's reputation with his superiors. However, so long as Miró ran the colony, there was little his opponents could do about the hospital except to criticize Almonester from the sidelines for the way he was running a facility that he built and supported. With Miró protecting him and interceding for him with the Crown, Almonester was able to turn his deaf ear to the barbs. His rights to the patronage of the hospital were as clear as if he had located it in his own parlor and fed the sick from his own kitchen; Miró made sure the authorities understood that.

But at the end of 1791 Miró's long tenure ended in Louisiana; he left for Spain to hang around the court, uneasily awaiting the outcome of his *residencia* and his next assignment. His shield gone, Almonester became the main target of the malediction of the *cabildo*. The campaign against him became one part of the ugly crusade to discredit Miró. The former governor was charged by the cabal with having embezzled Crown funds; specifically,

Miró was accused of scheming with an American adventurer, James Wilkinson, to make a personal profit of two thousand dollars a year on the purchase of Kentucky tobacco. Miró was gone, however. With each passing month the quarrel with him must have seemed to the *cabildo* more and more like shadow boxing, especially after the verdict in the case was rendered and Miró was found innocent. Whereas Almonester was very much present, sharp as life at every Friday *cabildo* meeting, and always rousable for another round.

Now, however, Almonester faced his attackers alone, for the new governor, Carondelet, sided with the *cabildo*. Ignoring Almonester's privileges as the hospital's patron, Carondelet named a manager for the institution who remained in charge for two years. Almonester was deprived of all authority. Almonester, who had himself gone to the market to purchase the patients' food for six years, was now a trespasser in Charity Hospital. Carondelet's motives for this outrage appear fairly simple and ignoble: he wanted the support of the *cabildo* to carry out several projects he had in mind for the colony; he was as irritated as a second husband by Miró's successes; and he disliked Almonester. Six months after first meeting Almonester, Carondelet concluded that he had no capability as an officer and did not apply himself to military matters. The governor reported to the captain-general of Cuba that despite his many public works, Almonester had failed to win the good will of the citizens and "they would sooner stop attending Mass than enter the Church he is constructing."[60] Considering that the people were already using Almonester's other churches and that they thronged to the St. Louis Church from the day of its completion, this was a foolish assertion. He went on to write that the animosity began four years previously in the aftermath of the Great Fire. During the housing shortage which followed the fire of 1788, Almonester, according to Carondelet, "suddenly raised the rent of his clients. He took advantage of his unfortunate public in order to increase his capital." Nevertheless, Carondelet continued with some petulance, the king had ignored Carondelet's dispraises and granted Almonester his promotion to colonel of the militia.

Although his letter has the ring of sincerity, Carondelet did not arrive in the city until three years after the time he was describing and did not know firsthand what had happened after the fire. It is most unlikely that Almonester would have retained Miró's support if he had publicly shown such callousness. During the crisis, Miró was acclaimed for prohibiting merchants from raising prices on all sorts of provisions. He would have been sorely embarrassed if, in the midst of all his exhortations to the business community, Almonester had increased his rents.

However, another, later accusation against Almonester deserves more consideration. It was a practice of the Spanish government to award land grants with the stipulation that the property had not been previously awarded, even during the French period. In 1795 J. B. Macarty, a relative of the Pontalbas and of Miró, was granted some land by Carondelet, part of which already belonged to Almonester and part of which was the property of the widow Chalon.[61] Almonester sued Macarty, defending both his title and that of the Chalon widow; Carondelet was forced to revoke the grant. Years later, in 1836, Micael tried to sell the land and was confronted by the Chalon heirs, who claimed that Almonester had concealed the documents, titles, and surveys of the land that he took from their mother and that he had deliberately tried to keep the heirs ignorant of their claim to part of the tract. Almonester was by this time too dead to defend himself, assuming he would have had a defense; his daughter eventually effected a compromise with the Chalon heirs by dividing the disputed property with them.

In 1795 Carondelet naturally knew nothing of the future Chalon dispute, and in any case, his dislike of Almonester went deeper than a reaction formed by gossip and rumor over someone's business dealings. Carondelet's distaste was the prejudice of a lifelong army officer and seigneur against a nouveau riche bureaucrat who had been catapulted to high military rank. In recommending Almonester for colonel of the militia, Miró had written, "I consider him quite worthy. . . . in the eyes of the public, he is very meritorious." Referring to Almonester as "the major and senior magistrate of this city," Miró wrote, "The captains have not any particular qualities, faculties, or the necessary decorum to hold that position. Therefore, in all justice, they have no right to complain, if we show a preference to . . . Almonester."[62] Nevertheless, Carondelet noted dryly on Almonester's service sheet: "This official, who advanced from notary public to Colonel, is in no way suitable for his position." Almonester was hated by his men, according to Carondelet; they were accustomed, he wrote, to being commanded by a more "distinguished" personage.[63] The governor refused to punish deserters from Almonester's battalion because "there could not be found sufficient jails to hold them all." However, when Almonester tried to get recognition and rewards for the men in his corps who had served with Gálvez in winning Pensacola from the British, Carondelet withheld his approval. One of Carondelet's first dispatches mentioning Almonester advised retiring him with his rank of colonel without pay, which the governor thought would leave him "better rewarded than he could ever hope to expect." Since this suggestion was disregarded, Carondelet had to content himself with disparaging Almonester to his superiors in Cuba whenever the opportunity presented itself. He called attention to Almonester's "advanced age" in his reports and praised men whom Almonester criticized. He instructed his second-in-command, Francisco Bouligny, not to hesitate to burn down Almonester's houses if they obstructed the defense of the Mississippi. Especially, Carondelet opposed Almonester's petition requesting a promotion to brigadier, Carondelet's own rank.[64]

It was no doubt dispiriting for a military careerist such as Carondelet or, for that matter, Pontalba (who was still a captain) to witness Almonester's rise in the royal service. "It is apparent that neither Don Andrés nor his aide understands one word when it comes to troops, discipline, or the maneuvering of a corps," Carondelet wrote in 1794, probably in all truth, since competence was not a prerequisite to gaining rank; Bouligny put forward his thirteen-year-old son for a command post.[65] But there was still that other reason why Carondelet did not hesitate to rob Almonester of his patronage. He was irked that Almonester, as benefactor of the Ursuline Chapel, the church and chapel of Charity Hospital, and St. Louis Cathedral, would enjoy ecclesiastical privileges that Carondelet believed should be granted only to the official royal vice-patron: himself.

The prospect of sharing his ecclesiastical prerogatives was no trivial matter to Carondelet, and we must not discount it as the cause of his hostility to Almonester. One does not have to read far in Carondelet's official correspondence to find, along with conscientious anxiety for the general welfare, examples of the governor's impressive pettiness. According to a series of dispatches to his captain-general las Casas, Carondelet presided over a shoving match between the colonel of the Fixed Regiment, Francisco Bouligny, and the lieutenant governor, Nicolás Vidal, concerning who was to sit next to the governor during public celebrations.[66] Following the incident, which Carondelet characterized as "extraordinary," the governor forwarded long briefs from the shovers—one of Vidal's ran to ten single-spaced pages in typescript. In a letter that Carondelet forwarded to Cuba, Vidal recounted being further slighted at a public Mass at which, despite his being the ranking official present, he was handed a smaller candle than Bouligny, a complaint he intended "to take to the feet of the King." The case got no further than the hand of las Casas, who replied to Carondelet with some annoyance that the matter was too silly for his or Carondelet's consideration, "my pen refusing to be employed in cases of this nature." He added that he preferred not to know "if in the parlors of the governors there are floor bricks marked for certain persons." The church historian Roger Baudier has commented that candles and seating stations were serious matters to Carondelet, who was "a stickler for form and demanded the observance of all ceremonials connected with or due to his dignity as Governor of His Catholic Majesty, especially Church ceremonies that were seen and noted by the public."[67] Baudier cited an instance where Carondelet reported a hapless assistant curate to the bishop in Cuba for failing to offer him a candle during the Mass, as called for in the rubrics. We can be sure that the candle and kiss of peace that the king ordered bestowed on Almonester each Sunday, "in the same way that it is observed for the Governor-General," gave Carondelet no peace at all.

Almonester appealed to the king to restore his patronage of Charity Hospital after Cardondelet took it away, and while waiting for a reply, did no more work on the church. "He is entirely disgusted with being beneficent," reported Pontalba to Miró in April, 1792; ". . . he has not laid a brick on it since your departure." Apparently Almonester never placed Carondelet among his enemies, which attests either to Almonester's ingenuousness or Carondelet's subtlety. Almonester praised the governor on several occasions in the council and, according to Pontalba, said "that he regrets this trouble [regarding the hospital] on account of the Baron who is an excellent man." Charles IV, however, was not convinced of Carondelet's excellence; he vindicated Almonester in a royal *cédula* which reprimanded both the governor and the *cabildo* for interfering with the Charity Hospital's founder.[68] In the face of defeat, Carondelet dug in his heels. Though the king commanded that Almonester's patronage be immediately restored, Carondelet mulishly refused to withdraw the physician he had appointed to the hospital so that Almonester could install a staff of his own choosing. Almonester was forced to appeal yet again to the king, who replied (two years later) with two unequivocal edicts. The monarch noted that Almonester had been handicapped by the local despots "to such an extent, that anyone would have desisted doing any charitable or beneficial work for the public good."[69] He had suffered severe damage to one of his factories, a gunpowder plant, and had been made a defendant in several court cases arising from the explosion, which was presumably the work of an arsonist. (It seems that Almonester's hand was critically injured in the explosion, although this was not mentioned in the edict.) The king thus ordered the *cabildo* to restore "all privileges of honor which are due him, including his special pew in the church." Carondelet was specifically warned to "distinguish, assist and attend in a very special way, the said Almonester in everything he might justly require, without giving him cause to complain, for he has endeared himself to my Royal Person. . . ." These were the edicts that Almonester set before his enemies at the Friday council meeting on November 6, 1795, the day his first daughter was born.

Despite all his hardships, Almonester had completed the church the previous year. Having been miraculously spared by the fire that destroyed the center of the city on December 5, 1794, the church was dedicated three weeks after the blaze in an elaborate Christmas ceremony. Almonester's cathedral was to undergo several transformations in succeeding years. A central bell tower designed by Benjamin Latrobe was added to it in 1819, just before Latrobe succumbed to yellow fever; in 1850 the entire edifice was remodeled by J. N. B. de Pouilly to its present design. Except for their roofs, the Presbytere and the Cabildo look much the same today as they did in Almonester's plans.[70]

Almonester received his coveted reward from the king while he was still working on the priest's house and the Cabildo. On September 8, 1796, he was invested in his cathedral as Knight of the Royal Order of Charles III. After the church ceremony and a reception at home a few steps away, Almonester sent up a balloon over the plaza to the accompaniment of fireworks. Then the guests, numbering in the hundreds, stuffed themselves with sweets and finished the celebration by gambling until ten. "He asserts that the King relieved him from furnishing the usual proofs," wrote Pontalba, as if he doubted it, "but that he insisted on doing it, and that he was able to prove to three centuries of noble rank."[71] Probably Almonester was glad to go to the expense of furnishing "the proofs." Anything to show the other members of the *cabildo* that he was as good as they were. Almonester had his eye on at least one more reward. "The minute he obtains one thing, he wishes for another," wrote Pontalba. "His mind is now occupied with the rank of brigadier, and he can speak of nothing else." For indeed, soon after his investiture as knight, Almonester resuscitated his application for the grade of brigadier of the Royal *Exercitos*.[72] His petition was among the items of unfinished business he left when he died.

The cathedral was completed, but so long as the Presbytere and Cabildo were under construction, the council had a resource of fresh issues for its attacks. Almonester was no doubt less humble after winning his title, perhaps expecting the "honors and preeminences" promised by the award. Certainly no one liked him better, now that he was "that famous knight and nobleman," as Pontalba sarcastically referred to him. As his health declined, he became more crotchety and as unhesitant as ever to take on the *cabildo* in any controversy. Almonester's arrangement with the council was that he alone would pay for the Presbytere. He would advance money for the Cabildo and supervise its construction so that it matched the Presbytere in design. The council would repay Almonester with whatever surplus remained in its treasury at the end of each year until the loan for the Cabildo was amortized. Since there had rarely been any surplus at all in the treasury, Almonester must have considered the loan just another of his donations. So, apparently, did some members of the council who opined that the architect Guillemard, when he wanted an advance for his plan of the Cabildo, "should not be paid with city funds and that said payment is entirely up to the Royal Ensign."[73]

The *cabildo* complained about the prices Almonester paid for nails, about the quality of his shingles on the jail (which was part of the Cabildo), about the pace of the work, about his having been permitted to use old bricks belonging to the city for his construction of the cathedral. In the recriminatory atmosphere of the council, the aging and irascible man was sometimes uncertain as to whether conspiracies were being hatched against him during his absences or whether, "being a Spaniard and deaf," as he put it, his enemies were insulting him in his very presence without his fully realizing it.[74] Quick to anger, he was quick to repent. After a particularly heated quarrel he left the *cabildo* chambers (which were still located in his own house) and refused to return. But at the next meeting a contrite Almonester offered that he "would not dare insult this *cabildo* in the terms recorded" and had not intended his leavetaking to be a gesture of defiance.[75] He even refused a reimbursement payment on the Cabildo which the council, in its own act of contrition, offered him.

Thanks to one of the momentary truces between Almonester and his colleagues, we have a portrait of the great benefactor bought by the council in professed gratitude for his donations.[76] Attributed to José de Sálazar and dated 1796, the painting shows him magna cum laude, his *cabildo* walking stick, his colonel's sword, and the insignia of his knighthood all part of his array. His posture reveals his restless energy. His hand, disfigured for several years, is hidden. He has the look of a man who has paused briefly and is anxious for the artist to release him from his pose so that he can get on with his projects. They are listed beside him on a scroll, next to his family's coat of arms.

Almonester did not live to win the rank of brigadier or to see the completion of either the Presbytere or the Cabildo. He had suffered several severe illnesses beginning in 1794 when, "apprehending that death is natural, its hour uncertain, and that my own is destined to arrive," he thought it timely to draw up a will.[77] The affliction to his hand prevented him from signing the document. He was still going about his council duties when he died four years later on April 25, 1798, so quickly that there was no time to administer the last sacraments. Only a few days previously he had delivered an exhaustive report on the chimney tax in a *cabildo* meeting which lasted for hours.

Almonester's will relinquished his *cabildo* offices to his brother-in-law. Having provided for in-laws, relatives in Spain, and ten of the poorest girls in the city, Almonester further instructed that alms be furnished for two hundred poor people who were to be present at his funeral. The alms were to be paid by the executors only after they made sure the mourners were actually at the burial, "in order that presence may not be falsely pretended on the part of some." He ordered that only three Masses be said for his soul, although it was not unusual for wealthy Spaniards to order more than a thousand such requiems. He wanted to be laid out in his military insignia and, in a coda to his will, requested burial in the cemetery behind Charity Hospital. King Charles IV later overruled this gesture of humility and had his remains moved to a tomb in St. Louis Cathedral.[78]

The councilmen may have regretted no longer having Almonester to abuse, but they suppressed any show of grief about it. They were concerned about his unfinished donations, however. Two days after his death the *cabildo* decided it would wait a decent interval (five days) before calling on his widow to persuade her to complete the building of the Cabildo and Presbytere. The administration of the Lepers' Hospital was turned over to one of Almonester's chief tormentors in the council, the city treasurer Juan de Castañedo, who took one and a half percent of the hospital's revenues in return for his management, discontinued all medical and household care for the patients, and allowed the hospital to lapse into a "deplorable" condition, according to an inspection made in 1800.[79]

No one replaced Almonester as the workhorse of the *cabildo*—certainly not the heir to his positions, his wife's brother Pierre de la Ronde, whose only contribution to municipal management for two years was to have a wagon added to the garbage collection.[80] Presumably Almonester was mourned by his widow, although with her babies, her kinspeople, her servants, and the distraction of the building projects she was soon to undertake, Louison was hardly bereft of companionship after his death. Almonester's succession records have been lost; but we know that he left behind one plantation, a great deal of uncultivated acreage, two factories, over twenty rental houses and stores on the Place d'Armes, his own residence, and probably a large number of properties scattered over the city, all Louison's responsibility.

Almonester also left behind two daughters, one of whom would live to enjoy, perhaps, his reputation as a philanthropist. Being an Almonester must have provided Micael with at least some gratifying associations in New Orleans. In her letters she was homesick for years after leaving the city, painstakingly naming each relative to whom she wanted to send regards. She possessed no picture of her father after she left Louisiana, but there is no evidence that she longed for one.[81] Whether she had been well or sickly growing up on the busy, unkempt plaza, comely or plain, loved or neglected, we can only conjecture. We do know that because of her father, from the moment she was born—and it may have been the only thing about her that Célestin de Pontalba understood with certainty on their wedding day—she was very pleasantly rich.

III

Pontalba

On March 24, 1796, Joseph Xavier de Pontalba sat at his desk and began his daily letter.[1]

> Yesterday I put in the mail what I had written you so far, *amie*, so as to take advantage of the courier leaving today. I still cannot get used to having to write to you; it was not for this that we gave ourselves to each other; it was more to mutually assuage the sorrows of our lives through sharing them, and to enjoy the sweetness it might offer. Since your departure I have become insensible to pleasure, and the burden of my sorrows has never seemed more unbearable. No, *amie*, no more separation for us, may this be our last one. . . . Since your absence I have sought pleasures without ever being able to find them; nothing can distract me. . . . I see you this moment in your uncomfortable cabin . . . addressing prayers to Heaven for the happiness of your *ami*, it being inseparable from your own; and I also see our little darling interrupting you, often perhaps, to speak a little about his dear papa. . . .
>
> Thirty-one days have elapsed since you left La Balize; thirty-one days of fatigue and sufferings; if you have at least been able to keep in good health, and if our little darling has not met with any accident, and if in fourteen or fifteen days you make port, more than half my sorrows will have been done away with.
>
> All this bad weather has put our levees in a very bad state . . . the water from the river is topping the levees everywhere; the flat lands are all under water, and it will be necessary for the planters next year to increase the height of their levees by one foot.
>
> Good night, your *ami* embraces you tenderly; he feels more than ever as if he were dying with the passing of each day.

Xavier, as he was called, wrote each day to his wife, Jeanne Louise ("Ton-Ton") de Pontalba, during a separation of nearly two years in 1796 and 1797. Ton-Ton was close to her aunt Céleste, who left New Orleans with her husband when Miró's governorship ended. In Spain the ex-governor died in 1795 and the widowed aunt fell ill. The Pontalbas decided to move permanently to Europe to join her. Madame de Pontalba went first, taking their five-year-old son Célestin, temporarily leaving her husband in New Orleans to sell belongings and settle their affairs.

During his wife's absence Pontalba kept a letter journal which he turned over to a courier every few months when there was a ship leaving for Spain. For the first ten or twelve weeks he was sunk in paralyzing depression, unable to describe anything in his letters to his wife except his misery and the household's reaction to her leaving. In time, however, he began reporting details of his building projects (he was erecting some rental houses on his New Orleans property so as to furnish himself with an income after the planned move to Europe). He wrote about the gossip around town, the yellow fever epidemic that struck during the summer after his wife's departure, and the affairs of his wife's numerous relatives. He never got adjusted to the separation, however, and his letters were always those of a heartsick man.

If Almonester exists for us as a bustling public figure whose official papers admit only hints about his private life, Pontalba, in contrast, hardly seems to have lived at all except in an interior world of melancholy dreams and fears which he recorded painstakingly. It is somehow disorienting to learn that he bought roof supplies, was sued in court, or lost at gambling, so difficult is it to picture him anywhere but at his writing desk, floundering month after month in despair. There are other striking differences between the two fathers. Almonester, though he lived in New Orleans thirty years and never showed any serious intention of leaving, remained a transplanted Spaniard, uncertain of the precise mores of his surroundings. There is something of the self-made man in his impatience and enthusiasm for the practical business of life in the New World, something of the nouveau riche in his efforts to do palpable things with his money and time, as if good fortune in life were a surprise that should be prolonged. Pontalba, on the other hand, was a thorough Creole, born in the New World and at ease in his native land, receiving the deference of his neighbors not because of any egregious wealth but because of his aristocratic attitudes and his network of relatives reaching to every corner of Louisiana society. "The gentleman Joseph Pontalba entered the chambers," wrote the *cabildo* scribe when Pontalba appeared before the council on some business; and a gentleman he always seems: elderly (though he was only forty-two when we come to know him in the letters to his wife), dignified, reflective, and unremittingly morose. Almonester passed out of his child's surroundings when she was three, leaving her to cope with his reputation, property, and money. Pontalba hovered over his son, rarely living apart from him, until Célestin was forty-three and had lost the emotional resources for an independent life. Nor was it only Célestin he dominated; he preoccupied Micael from the time she was sixteen until she was a middle-aged woman with grown sons. Far more than Almonester, Pontalba was the father from whom she had to break free.

Joseph Xavier Delfau de Pontalba was born in 1754 in New Orleans. His father had been a French soldier in Canada who came to New Orleans with the Sieur de Bienville, the city's founder; he had a "too obvious" taste for business, which his military superiors noted and excused.[2] Pontalba's mother was a French Creole, the daughter of the royal engineer. The most striking thing about Xavier de Pontalba's childhood is that there was little of it. His parents divested themselves of him when he was four, sending him to France to school.[3] His father died when he was six. All his life he hungered for attention and closeness. He entered the French navy and worked up through the officer ranks in the French provinces and Caribbean colonies. His finances were apparently up and down; his health was all down, according to army reports that repeatedly remarked on his "sickliness."[4] Practically all that we know of Pontalba's youth is the information in his military records, mainly terse comments on routine forms, with nothing much revealed either for or against him. In 1783 he was allowed to retire from the French service without a pension, so that at thirty years of age, he settled down to manage his family's indigo plantation near New Orleans. Finding Louisiana part of the Spanish crown under the governorship of Esteban Miró, he joined the Spanish army with the understanding that he would hold his same captain's rank.

   In October, 1789, he married into the Miró family. Ton-Ton LeBreton was more a daughter than a niece to Miró's wife, that Céleste de Macarty who was popular among her fellow Creoles because of her lively parties and her ignorance of Spanish ways. Pontalba became a constant visitor to the Government House and Miró, as the head of the family, began guiding his career.[5] Miró was the most powerful man in his clan in a society where an individual could get nowhere alone; the governor was expected to live up to his patriarchal responsibilities by advancing his relatives. Miró thus procured a command for Pontalba as head of the militia of the German Coast, raising him over two men in line for promotion and attempting (unsuccessfully) to give him a nominal advance in rank to lieutenant colonel—modest favors in the eighteenth-century world of energetic nepotism. However, since the Spanish government was more generous with titles than with money, Miró made no attempt to increase his nephew's salary, which remained that of a captain.

The German Coast, called Les Allemands, started about five miles from New Orleans; it consisted of a stretch of about fifty miles on both sides of the river, an uninterrupted line of farms without a single village in the whole territory. Most of the men were trappers, ready fighters in case of war but too spread out to be "susceptible" to training, as Miró himself admitted.[6] Miró wanted Pontalba to inspect the Les Allemands militia every two or three months on six consecutive Sundays. Besides teaching the men to make column formation and march in unison, Pontalba was obligated "to get acquainted with every individual, particularly finding out the number of persons who compose each family, as well as their fortunes, so that in case any part of this militia is needed, we may be able to choose those more capable and less needed for the cultivation of the land." In proposing him for the command, Miró referred to Pontalba's "suave disposition" and his personality which would be attractive to the one thousand men under his supervision. It was not a post of vaulting significance (the Crown had considered leaving the commandantcy permanently vacant). But presumably Miró was doing what he could for his nephew.

Pontalba fitted himself easily (or so it seems from his later correspondence with Miró) into both his military post and the position of admiring son-in-law. Even before his marriage we find him acting as agent for various Macarty kinfolk, conducting their business and bringing lawsuits to collect debts owed to them, court actions in which Miró himself sometimes presided as judge.[7] In 1791 the Pontalbas had a son whom they named after Céleste, Joseph Célestin Delfau—the adored "Tin-Tin" of Pontalba's letters. The parents retired somewhat from society. "We live almost like hermits on the plantation," Pontalba wrote. Madame de Pontalba became, as her husband noted with a tinge of pride, "a slave to her son," while Pontalba continued as the de facto attorney and caretaker of a tribe of Madame de Miró's relatives. Until his death, Miró remained Pontalba's closest friend and his one confidant. When the governor was relieved of his duties and obliged to move to Spain, the two men maintained a three-year correspondence. Pontalba completed a letter in French every few days, dispatching a three-months' packet at once. Miró, writing in Spanish, also kept a letter diary in which he described each detail of his efforts to get another position in the king's service.

Pontalba's letters to Miró are neither as literary nor as self-absorbed as his missives to his wife. They deal in voluminous detail with military matters

and more generally with aspects of his life outside the army, such as his management of a taffia still in which Miró had some monetary interest. On both
sides the correspondence reveals Pontalba as very much Miró's protégé. The
governor's affairs were unsettled when he departed from New Orleans, and
he left it to Pontalba to take care of everything from debts to orphaned relatives. Pontalba took up all tasks eagerly. "Jonchère spoke to me about the Negroes he rented to M. Soubise," Pontalba wrote in a typical communication.
"I took the opportunity to make him write a draft of 204 piasters which he
owes you . . . payable in September on the rental of the Negroes he has
taken. . . . I will manage somehow to make him pay 3,000 piasters in interest.
This year . . . he won't be able to give us anything on the principal."[8]
Madame de Miró's godchild, Feliciane, is settled with the Ursuline nuns,
thanks to Pontalba. Pontalba informs Miró that "Farges, the bad debtor, has
left your house and I re-rented it . . . to someone named Renaud, a shop-
keeper who already rents two of your small houses." Pontalba sells Miró's saddles (after letting them out on trial), sues his delinquent tenants, leases out his
slaves, and works diligently to keep Miró's accounts straight.

Miró took his nephew's efforts for granted. He did not offer gratitude,
nor did he hesitate to have Pontalba attend to the smallest details, such as
checking the price of a few napkins that were among the household goods
Pontalba auctioned off for him. In one letter he charged Pontalba with communicating his greetings to fifty-two individuals and, "especially," all of the
officers in Miró's old regiment. Pontalba devoted hours and days to satisfying Miró's continual requests for items of local color with which the ex-
governor hoped to ease his own progress toward a promotion. "Send me 4
dozen bottles of *tobaco rape* registered to Don Miguel Antonio de Herrera,"
Miró instructs him; ". . . it would be a splendid gift for the Minister of War
and other gentlemen, if it is good, which you must take pains to assure."
Through Pontalba's shopping, Miró was able to treat his acquaintances at
the Spanish court to buffalo tongue and bottles of "high quality" bear
grease. Back in Louisiana, it fell to Pontalba to repay various obligations
Miró incurred. "Ton-Ton succeeded in exchanging the 12 pairs of white
gloves for the Herrera girls," Pontalba explains: "the first were ugly, so they
have received others which are very fine."[9] At Miró's behest he distributes
duck, strawberries, wine, and pomade.

For his part, Pontalba expected Miró to push his promotion from captain
to colonel. "If you could obtain it for me," he writes Miró in one of a dozen
pleas on the subject, "you will have made my career." He observes that if

Miró loves him and his wife "half as much as we cherish you, you will try to advance me within a few years . . . to some regiment where I will no longer have to be apart from you." Being with Miró, he explains, is necessary to his happiness; "the time we will spend near you and my aunt will be more precious than all the rest of my life."[10]

His most insistent request is that Miró find a place for him as his secretary. When Miró mentions that he might be sent on a short mission to the United States, Pontalba cannot contain his excitement. "I shall begin studying English. . . . I would bring my wife and Célestin, and I assure you that we would spend a pleasant year in Philadelphia and your business would in no way suffer from it, I shall put it in good order before leaving here. . . . I beg you not to fail to bring me into the party, in any capacity whatever." Within a few letters, Pontalba has made plans to turn his business affairs and the rum still over to a manager and has decided which slaves will serve as cook, chambermaid, babysitter, and coachman in Philadelphia: "Since receiving your letter, I have been studying English four hours a day. . . ."[11]

Miró, addressing Pontalba as "Dear Pontalba," "My Very Esteemed Pontalba," or most frequently, "Dear Nephew," counsels him to be patient and gently breaks the news that he does not really want the post in Philadelphia. Pontalba manfully accepts the confession and remains entirely at the service of the Mirós, as he constantly reminds them. Does their friend Herrera need a favor? "Assure him that I shall feel flattered to be of use to him in any way whatever, that I expect him to call on me with the same freedom he used toward you; he may be certain that every commission will be a new pleasure to me, I shall give it special attention so as to renew his good will toward me. . . . All those here whom I believe to be your friends have excited my interest in them to a degree of which I did not believe myself capable. . . . I meet them with pleasure, I seek them out, I linger with them, I leave them with regret."[12]

When he was not assuring the Mirós of his devotion, submitting information about some business he was handling for them, or describing changes in the local militia, Pontalba wrote about sick people in the town, especially the victims of the "putrid fevers" that swept the colony every few months. His brighter news usually consisted of a few words about Tin-Tin; he proudly reported in one letter that Tin-Tin had four teeth, in another that he had weaned, or that he was beginning to resemble Madame de Miró.[13]

A great part of the correspondence dealt with the accusations made against Miró by *cabildo* members. Pontalba reported the progress of these "calumnies," along with bits of gossip and information about the lawsuits he instituted on Miró's behalf against members of the cabal. He passed along evidence as to which of Miró's former associates had proved themselves true friends, cautioning Miró, "Do not say it was I who told you." When Miró complains that Almonester has failed to write, Pontalba reassures him that the Spaniard always "greeted with joy all good news that comes from you; he should have written to you, I have no excuse to plead on that score; he always postponed sending you the papers you were expecting when he could have done so," Pontalba reminds him, but then adds, "He exerted himself zealously in procuring them for me, and has, I am persuaded, compromised himself by sending you the indices intended for the Secretary's office. Excuse this laziness, pity his slavery,"—Pontalba does not state what it is Almonester is enslaved to—"but never impugn his friendship for you. He is abhorred by the Cabal—that is a great point in his favor."[14]

Pontalba gives relatively little information about himself in the letters, and even less about his wife, except to remark that she corresponds infrequently because writing is hard work for her. In this, as in all his correspondence, Pontalba shows that he had abnormal difficulty separating from people he loved, as if with each disengagement he relived his childhood exile from home. Receiving Miró's first letters, he explains, was like experiencing "a second separation." It seemed "that I was accompanying you on board with my aunt and that we were repeating our goodbyes there. . . . I want to slide over there and occupy myself only with my wife and our reunion. . . ." Months after Miró's departure Pontalba rises from a sickbed to assure him that "fever will not prevent me from repeating our goodbyes to you. . . . We will all be reunited to embrace our dear and good aunt . . . to enfold her . . . and to love you both with all our hearts. Goodbye my dear uncle and best friend; consider us a family which has given itself to you for life."[15] His attachment to Miró shows the obsessive character of all of Pontalba's close relationships: "There is no interest, happiness, or peace in life so long as there is any question of proving our devotion to you; if you need us to go from one end of the world to the other, say the word and rest assured you will be obeyed, with sorrow to be sure when it means going away from you, with rapture when it means coming closer."

Miró responded with fatherly restraint to these effusions. He expressed "great satisfaction in seeing the fervor with which you sustain our friendship." But he was too preoccupied to make more than passing inquiries about the couple he called "our first, best, and favorite friends." He was strenuously trying to get himself appointed field marshal and consultant on Louisiana to the Spanish minister of war. To that end he wrote a long monograph summarizing the historical and practical reasons for setting the boundaries of Louisiana according to his recommendations. Probably it was a meaningless document to anyone thousands of miles away from the rivers and surveyor's measurements he described in detail. The essay must have been almost as hard to write as it is to read; but Miró willingly applied himself. Unemployed in Spain, he tells Pontalba, he works harder than he ever did when filling multiple posts in Louisiana.

His days, as he describes them to Pontalba, are separated by card games. Every afternoon at four he is expected to be among the courtiers who gamble with the minister of war. Céleste comes to fetch him at six-fifteen for the opera, but he leaves each performance promptly at eight forty-five in order to return to the minister in time for the game which starts each night at ten and breaks up around midnight. He complains that it is too cold to get up in the morning before nine-thirty or ten; he has to gulp down breakfast so as to arrive at court in time to watch the king eat at eleven forty-five. Afternoons he spends visiting one minister or another, trying to figure out how he can profit from various introductions. "I know very well that if I continue making up to him, I will leave here as a field marshal," he writes, referring to Hore, in the ministry of war. "But," he adds, "I abhor both him and his wife to whom I have given 12 dozen buffalo skins, 2 dozen tongues, and 5 thousand thrush plumes."[16]

Miró follows the court when it repairs to the country, prepares to pay a large fee to accede to higher office, and dogs Hore with his essay on Louisiana ("my work," he calls it) until a cornered minister confesses that "this Louisiana makes me tired."[17] Miró, who is incapable of summarizing a conversation, reports to Pontalba every word bearing on his advancement, even to the shrugs and nods he elicits from the king's councillors. The promotion to field marshal "would give pleasure to my Céleste," he avers, "which is all that I desire." Even his brother Pablo is fitted into Miró's ambitions when he agrees to accompany Céleste on her rounds of calls. Since Pablo is "a grandee of the first class," Miró notes, in an oft-repeated refrain, his visits "can in time be useful to us." It takes a while for Miró to appreciate the vicious stupidity of the royal court into which he and Céleste have been dropped. His first comments about the queen, for example, refer to María Luisa as if she were a normal monarch and not the flagrant mistress of a former bodyguard. Through the royal wardrobe mistress, Céleste gets permission to visit the queen in her room ("a concession not easily obtained," Miró reminds Pontalba with no hint of irony) and is honored by an invitation to kiss the sweaty hand of the king when he wanders in, shirtless, on a hot day.[18] The two or three conversations which ensue between Céleste and the queen are clearly Miró's finest hour. When Céleste is received in a group of women, Miró reports, twitching with pride, that the queen talks mainly to her. He cannot resist asking Pontalba to write him the reactions of his friends when they hear that Céleste was presented at court. "These visits, although short and of little substance, can help in the future," he observes.

Like all officials in the Indies, Miró had spent his career making obeisances to pieces of paper that bore the royal seal and witnessing the competition among government dignitaries for such privileges as touching the king's picture. To be actually in the royal presence, receive a word or two from the monarch without the intermediary offices of the scribe, hear fresh gossip without an intervening lapse of several months—these were heady experiences, and it is understandable that Miró's excitement sometimes seeped through his general tone of grievance and ennui. Miró quickly learned the tactics necessary to attract the king's attention. The Count of Aranda, whom he took as his model, was dependably among those present when the king took his meals before the court. Consequently, "both the King and Queen single him out in public, saying, 'How are you, Aranda? How is your wife? It is very cold today,' and similar small talk."[19] Aranda had in fact fallen from power in 1792, before Pontalba received the letter, ousted by Manuel Godoy, the queen's lover and the king's master, who would become prime minister at the age of twenty-five. But at the moment Miró was writing, Godoy's powers over the court were being consolidated and his war with France was still ahead of him; he had not yet become the "Prince of Peace."

Miró is plainspoken, with rarely an indulgent word for anyone in these letters. Nevertheless, he shows himself to be a tender husband who is not embarrassed to praise "my Céleste." On arriving at Cadiz, he reported to the Pontalbas the "good news" that Céleste was "so plump her corset cannot be fastened on three notches. . . . She is bright and as cheerful as I could desire; I take satisfaction in seeing that my constant attention and affection make her happy."[20] At court he saw no one nearly as beautiful, he wrote, for she had become robust and healthy-looking "without losing the delicacy of her figure."

It is difficult to judge from the Miró-Pontalba correspondence how much influence Miró exerted on the younger man. Although only ten years separated them in age, Pontalba seemed willing to take on Miró as a surrogate father. While pressing his affections on him, Pontalba addresses him deferentially and is grateful for his trust. Miró's letters, though far less solicitous than Pontalba's, reflect the ease and candor one uses with contemporaries. Pontalba dates and numbers his letters, sometimes even noting the time of day and whether he is writing from his indigo plantation, the still, or the tobacco warehouse that served as an army barracks on the German Coast. Miró, scrawling twenty or thirty pages over a period of weeks, never bothers to separate the entries in his letter journal and sometimes omits the exact date. He knocks off the letters so carelessly that he tends to repeat himself, even to six or seven verbatim pages. Miró was an Iberian with a precise sense of caste. As a man of consequence, he expected most people to be at his service.[21] Pontalba, on the other hand, was comfortable with friends who could use him; the person in need was his favored companion. Again and again Pontalba offers testimony that he liked being indispensable to one or another friend. The more he could serve Miró in particular, the happier they both seemed.

The two men had in common a certain calculating preoccupation with money. Miró complained about the cost of everything—sending letters, traveling with the court. His concern with money is that of a man trying to avoid the nuisance and anxiety of debt. Pontalba, however, rarely seems to resent his expenses and is not especially mindful of the possessions and influence wealth can buy. It is the accounting, collecting, and disbursing of funds that fascinates him. The money he saves or the profit he realizes in some business manuever is his way of measuring his resourcefulness. He could write about it ebulliently and endlessly.

It is interesting to note that Pontalba, the eager disciple, was sufficiently his own man to ignore Miró's disparagement of the new governor. He was not on intimate terms with Carondelet, but he refrained from criticizing him. "Though we neglect the Government so badly," Pontalba wrote, referring to the Government House, Carondelet's official residence, "we constantly receive courtesies from them. The Baron continually invites me to dine . . . but I do not remain so as not to abandon my recluse; on rare occasions when my wife presents herself, the Baroness seems to distinguish her among all others."[22] One courtesy Carondelet withheld, however, was recommending Pontalba for a promotion from captain to lieutenant colonel. He kept giving excuses which, in Miró's view, "only an enemy" would offer. "That angers me," Miró wrote to Pontalba, "but what makes it worse is that

you seem satisfied." When Pontalba submitted a plan for reorganizing the
militia, the governor delayed reading it for three months; eventually he
adopted many of the proposals for forming additional regiments, but without placing Pontalba at the head of any of the new formations. Miró despaired of convincing Pontalba that Carondelet was sabotaging his chances
for advancement. "Let us not speak of this any more," he finally wrote, "because it really makes me furious."[23] Carondelet, in his turn, slyly disparaged
Miró to his superiors in Cuba, but his praise of Pontalba was often generous.[24] Despite his slow advance in the army (his salary remained that of a captain for more than ten years), Pontalba was earnest about his military career.
He loved writing to Miró about events within the militia, even down to details of a reorganization or the trim on new uniforms. He once attributed the
death of a sergeant in his regiment not to the malignant fever diagnosed by
the doctors but to the man's being excluded from a list of promotions.[25]

Pontalba continued to "seem satisfied" with his position under Carondelet, enjoying the comfortable life of an import agent and property holder
and the prestige of an officer. He constantly wrote to Miró about getting an
army promotion, but meanwhile, his life went on. In 1793 he raffled some of
his houses and gave one thousand pesos of the profits to Charity Hospital;
this was not a donation to Almonester but to the *cabildo* which had taken the
hospital away from him and was trying to run it without his largesse.[26] No
friend of Almonester would have made the gift. In 1795 Pontalba served on
the *cabildo* as a one-year councilman. He does not appear to have been particularly active in the council; however, he did report once on sanitation conditions in the butcheries, a presentation he made to the *cabildo* just a few
minutes before Almonester jubilantly informed his colleagues that the king
had made him the hospital's indisputable patron.[27] Most of the time Pontalba gardened, attended to Miró's business, genially gossiped with the
neighbors, and played with his son.

In September, 1795, the Pontalbas received the information that Miró had
died three months before. Pontalba's pain at this news can perhaps be measured by his eloquent silence; he rarely mentioned Miró again in his personal
letters. All of his filial devotion seemed to shift to Miró's widow. When
Madame de Miró decided she would stay on in Europe, the Pontalbas made
plans to join her. Ton-Ton and Tin-Tin would go at once (accompanied by a
male cousin and a maid). Pontalba would follow as soon as he could settle
his affairs and those of the late Miró and apply for a leave of absence. The
plan meant that Pontalba would be apart from his wife and child for nearly

two years, from February, 1796, until late in 1797 when they were reunited in Paris.[28]

"Where is *mon amie* just now? Where is my Tin-Tin?" Pontalba wrote on the day after their departure. "What a dreadful moment it was, *mon amie*, when I saw the ship disappear before my eyes, rapidly carrying away everything that my hopes depended on. . . . I spent the night without closing an eye. I often envisioned you during the same night as being afflicted with the same sorrows as my own. I seemed to be hearing you calling for me and moaning over my absence. I could see our pretty little Tin-Tin crying with you, asking for his dear papa."[29]

Again and again during his long months of grief, Pontalba imagines his wife enduring some misery, "a prey to suffering in the cabin where I left you; made the victim of seasickness." When he thinks of her on the ship, he imagines "seeing you and your son tossed about in your narrow prison, the port holes closed, enjoying neither daylight or air, and without me at your side to alleviate your trying situation. Thoughts of possible accidents are forever crowding my mind." He feels as if a weight on his chest is smothering him; his legs collapse under him. "A dark and depressing gloom seems to weigh over me, and if it keeps on that way I do not know what will become of me."[30] Pontalba recalled previous depressions; now again the "most sinister thoughts" haunted him—of a trunk falling on Tin-Tin in the cabin, or his wife overboard "in the midst of the boundless seas." He begged her not to deprive him of details of the journey. "Tell me if you have been ill or felt tired, or if your son has been, if you have lacked anything . . . especially if you have met with bad weather, if you have ever been in danger. . . . Have you and your son been put to any inconvenience . . . did he have any falls? . . . Did you have him sleep with you? Did he bother you much? In short, do not keep me in ignorance of anything."[31] He was tormented for weeks by a nightmare in which a passenger who was blind in one eye threw boiling water in Tin-Tin's eyes. "The water had eaten the flesh down to the bone, and he had completely lost his sight. May this abominable dream not be an omen of some terrible misfortune." So relieved was he to learn of their safe arrival in Europe that he celebrated by giving the slaves "plenty to eat" and releasing one who had been in shackles eight days.[32]

In view of the suffering the separation caused him, one wonders why Pontalba ever consented to let his family go. Perhaps he regarded his sacrifice for Madame de Miró as his last service to his dead friend. In all of his correspondence, Miró had discussed Céleste as if she were a fragile goddess who had to be shielded from every discomfort. His chief complaint about life at the Spanish court had been that he was compelled to leave Céleste all day with nothing to occupy her. He had resented their obligatory travels with the court because the trips deprived Céleste of the Madrid opera. Thus, after Miró's death, Pontalba sedulously took up the duty of bringing happiness to the widow whom he described as "a model of her sex," "the adorable woman worthy of all sacrifices." Madame de Miró was to choose their future residence. "If she prefers Europe let me know of the province," he instructed his wife. "I need not admonish you to yield in everything that might give her pleasure, but please do it in such a manner that she will think she is merely following what your own taste decides, while you will be giving way entirely to hers." One might suppose that Madame de Miró, as Pontalba always referred to her, was a surrogate mother as much to him as to his wife, but the fact was that Céleste, fifteen years younger than Miró, was five years younger than Pontalba. Nevertheless, Pontalba averred that Madame de Miró was one of "the three persons who alone make life worth living for me."[33]

In fact, Pontalba began assuming so many tasks for Madame de Miró's sisters and nieces that as months wore on he had no time for his melancholy and had to give it up somewhat. He undertook huge projects for them— building rental houses for one, taking over plantation accounts for another. It becomes clear from his letters that Pontalba spent more than half his time tending other people's business. Madame de Miró's ten brothers and sisters married Jonchères, d'Aunoys, Fazendes, and Lecomptes.[34] Pontalba was a willing agent for all these kinspeople, and he relished the position of mentor and protector. "Poor Mademoiselle [Jeanne] Macarty would be having great trouble with Lafon had I not taken charge of her work myself; the walls of her houses are already up two feet, but I have to spend several hours there every day." Pontalba eventually instituted a lawsuit against Lafon on behalf of Mademoiselle de Macarty. "Her confidence in me is so great she no longer occupies herself with any of her affairs, and so I have made them my own," Pontalba wrote happily.[35] "LeBreton left this morning. . . . I will arrange to get him out of the bad business he is now busy with."[36] Barthélemy LeBreton was Ton-Ton's brother who spent hours on Pontalba's front gallery, relieving his host's loneliness. Pontalba had no apparent contact with his own brother and two sisters who lived in France.

One of Pontalba's continuing diversions was following the escapades of Madame de Miró's brother, Jean Baptiste de Macarty. Although middle-aged (he was born in 1750) and the father of grown sons, Macarty was given to mad infatuations with the wives and sisters of various relatives. His pursuit of Eulalie LeBreton Robin, the wife of Pontalba's brother-in-law, landed him in jail. Carondelet, who decided Macarty had "an alien mind," would not release him unless he promised to stay away from the LeBreton and Robin women.[37] Since Macarty refused to make this pledge, he stayed in prison for nearly a year, until dysentery weakened his ardor.

Macarty's next obsession was another relative, Eulalie Fazende, who wanted nothing to do with him. On one occasion he broke down the door of a room where she had retreated to get away from him. Another time, according to Pontalba's account, "having tormented that young lady and her family for many days, and seeing himself getting nowhere, he stole into her bedroom before daybreak, got into her bed, and, at the outcries she made, her mother, who was sleeping in an adjoining bedroom, proceeded to get up and summon help; during the tussle that took place between the young lady and Macarty, the mosquito bar fell on them, her mother failed to drag him away, and her brothers, who had come running down, found him still there." Pontalba was of the opinion that Macarty wanted to ruin Eulalie's reputation so that no one else would have her and she would be forced to accept him. "They now keep themselves barricaded at Fazende's and they always keep a servant playing the part of a sentinel to pass along word of his arrival." When, in desperation, the Fazende brothers "are about to engage in acts of violence" against Macarty, "he throws himself on them, embraces them, and begs them to intercede for him." Pontalba must have been surprised to learn that these methods eventually worked; several years after the bedroom incident, Mademoiselle Fazende became Macarty's wife.[38]

Pontalba's chief occupation during his wife's absence, and the source of his later sufficiency, was building rental houses and stores on his various properties. He expected to get a 10 percent return on his investments, a sound enough scheme on the face of it, although we have no way of knowing the actual revenues that his houses yielded. Some of his constructions were fairly rude, without even glass windowpanes, but he also built what he called "the finest large building in the province," which was more than 240 feet across.[39] One of his projects got him into an altercation with Almonester. In 1795 Pontalba bought an unfinished house for one of Madame de Miró's sisters; he contracted with Almonester to furnish all that was missing and to erect a balcony floored with tiles. Almonester wanted to put wood under the tiles; Pontalba demanded a flooring of iron, at an added cost of one thousand piasters. Threatening a lawsuit, Pontalba collected depositions from witnesses who heard the two men strike the bargain. Almonester pleasantly insisted that Pontalba go to court, so as to be proved wrong. By the time Almonester was invested as Knight of the Order of Charles III in September, 1796, the matter was sufficiently resolved that Pontalba accepted an invitation to the church celebration, though declining to go to the home of "the trickiest of all men."[40]

Pontalba appears to have been a knowledgeable builder who never hesitated to argue with contractors or supervene their decisions. A thousand inconveniences impeded his constructions: the expensiveness of iron needed for hinges and of tile used in roofs; a shortage of bricks, which led him to give up the brick-between-posts construction, ordered by the governor, in favor of sod-covered posts with shell and tar roofing. He had to wait for logs to arrive in the city and, after purchasing them, measured them himself before letting his sawyers make them into lumber. The hot weather kept him from supervising his workmen in June; the rains stopped construction in September; and in October, breaks in the levee required that he give up his laborers for repairs.[41]

By far the misfortune that most affected Pontalba's building, as well as all other activity in the city, was the yellow fever epidemic that raged throughout the summer and fall of 1796. At the height of the epidemic New Orleans was cut off from receiving many supplies, since in all ports in North America, ships from Louisiana were quarantined. Pontalba referred to the disease as "the sickness" or "putrid fevers," usually—he did not at first agree with the doctors in town that the scourge was the yellow fever pestilence of Philadelphia. According to Pontalba, the townspeople believed the fever had been brought by a ship from the North whose crew had completely perished. The owner had taken on another crew when he reached port, but all the members of this crew died also before the ship could sail. He found still another crew and set out for Havana, but got only as far as La Balize because every one of the third group died on the way.

Like many Creoles, Pontalba seems to have been immune to the plague, which particularly attacked newcomers. The year seemed especially fatal to virgins, he noted. "I do not remember if I have already told you that Mademoiselle La Chaise has come back to life; it was being said that she had been left covered with spots, as is usual with this malady, and also dead and buried. Now all this is said to have been false, it being said, instead, that she had suffered agonies for three days . . . that she was vomiting blood from up above as well as down below, being finally left alone by the doctors, the monks, and even those who were taking care of her. . . ."[42] The doctors, Pontalba pointed out, routinely condemned their patients "so as to receive greater credit when any of them pull through or in order to acquire the reputation of being infallible should these die." Throughout October Pontalba thought the fever was moderating, but in every letter he reported two or three more who had succumbed very quickly. "A few are still dying every day," he wrote. "Almost all of the English masons and carpenters are dead, the few remaining are being sought after by everybody, and they are paid extravagant wages."[43]

Pontalba grieved pathetically over one of the victims, a young man named de Coigne who arrived in town hoping to find a rich wife. Pontalba took him in and for several months expressed delight in having a companion in the house. De Coigne had a few mild attacks of some kind of fever which Pontalba nursed with the standard treatments: purgative, tea, cream of tartar, and almost lethal doses of quinine. But after one such bout, Pontalba was writing, "You know well the sensitiveness of your *ami*, and you can judge how much my heart is oppressed when I tell you that I have just closed the eyes of my unfortunate friend, de Coigne, he having died but a while ago."[44]

Pontalba repeated to his wife the accepted explanation of the time for the cause of yellow fever, that as the flooded earth dried out, fevers arose from its "fetid exhalations." Following this idea, the citizens did whatever they could think of to dissipate the fogs hanging over the city and push the bad air out by stirring up the atmosphere. Everywhere, he reported, the townsfolk were burning animal skins, horns, hoofs, and tar against the dampness, and many carried "bits of garlic on their persons." People were badly frightened, even though the doctors and monks, according to Pontalba, kept secret the true number of deaths. Pontalba protected himself from contagion by sprinkling vinegar around the house. He soaked the slaves in it. "I always have camphor on me," he assured his wife, "and also much vinegar."[45]

People who could afford to leave left the city, if only to sleep at one or another plantation across the river and return each morning—even the governor reluctantly stayed away at night. This makes sense when we consider that mosquitoes, unsuspected carriers of the disease, were worse at night. Several times Pontalba joined some of his friends "on the other side" during the height of the epidemic. There the companions tried to shake their preoccupation with "the fevers," giving themselves up to play like truant children.

At one house party the men found that their breeches, shoes, and coats had been stolen by the women; they had to return to the city in their nightshirts. Even Pontalba was drawn into some elaborate horseplay that, until he caught himself, he seems to have relished. The ladies, he reported to his wife, "found pleasure in knotting my bedsheets together, in throwing water at me. . . ." In retaliation, he explained,

> I smudged their bedclothes with lamp black, so that they became smeared all over with it; I inserted an apothecary drug, one with a subtle scent into their pillows; I squirted water at them with a syringe. . . . I dropped bits of wood down their chimneys at night, made holes in the chamber pots . . . They were all thirsting for revenge then; as for me, after I had managed to get the best of them, all of these things only bored me . . . since all such pranks, *mon amie*, cannot fill the void of my days, being only amusing for a time.[46]

When the arrival of cold weather ended the epidemic, Pontalba resumed his customary mild diversions: gambling and gossiping at the get-togethers arranged by the Baroness de Carondelet. "I go everywhere, but everywhere this ennui goes with me. There was a party given at the Government House. . . . I went to assuage my pains, I gambled, I lost, and I was bored. . . ."[47] Though there was gambling at every soirée, the betting does not appear to have been intense, judging from Pontalba's accounts of the distractions that were tolerated at the gaming tables and the small sums at stake.

Pontalba supported the theater by purchasing subscriptions for his wife's aunts, and he occasionally attended himself. The acting was bad and the leading actress homely, he complained after one production; and besides, he was sunk in melancholy. He reported, nevertheless, that there was hot competition for the theater's best seats. Madame Almonester suggested changing boxes with him; she would pay him sixty piasters, since his was better placed. "I have asked her 100," Pontalba commented to his wife, "so as to be able later on to give up her present box and my share to Chalmette for 132 piasters, and in that way help him to gain 100 piasters at the expense of Louison."[48]

Although he seems surrounded by friends most of the time, Pontalba stated that he was constantly declining invitations. "The company of people bores me," he complained (understandably, since the same six or seven people invariably made up the company). "I am as much bored as I am boresome, always absorbed in my sad reflections."[49] There was, however, Almonester's grand celebration which Pontalba attended. "We went to a reception, *mon amie*, given by that famous Knight of the Order of Charles III, Don Andrés Almonester."[50] The ceremony followed the usual routine, according to Pontalba. Almonester was enveloped in the great robe of the order, its train carried by three "lackeys," as Pontalba termed the bearers, all dressed in red. Almonester walked "in that state" a few steps from the church to his house—the one at the corner of St. Peter Street, overlooking the public square—followed by an immense crowd. At his drawing room door he took his station, still in the robe, and to Pontalba's profound distaste, "proceeded to affectionately kiss on both cheeks all those who came up to him, to the number of over 300." Pontalba was not among those kissed; he preferred to keep his distance from the man who would use wood to floor his aunt's gallery.

Almonester's wife, who was Pontalba's first cousin, quarreled with him also, although less seriously. Pontalba was present at a card game where one Madame Rivière, "always ready to amuse herself with childish pranks," had attached a hair to one of Madame Almonester's coins.[51] She pulled the coin carefully away from its owner, to the delight of the other players, while Louison absent-mindedly kept putting it back in front of her, wondering what all the mirth was about. Eventually she decided that Pontalba, sitting next to Madame Rivière, was making some joke at her expense. Louison frowned and "mumbled that if things kept on that way she would give back tit for tat." The upshot was that Madame Almonester hardly spoke to her cousin for several weeks.

Pontalba had a great deal more on his mind than the jokes his friends played on one another, although these antics occupied some space in his letters. Aside from supervising several constructions at a time and selling his domestic possessions as he prepared to leave the country, he had a houseful of slaves to dispose of. After the revolts at Santo Domingo and Pointe Coupée in the 1790s, Louisianians tried to reverse their custom of owning many more slaves than they needed. Moreover, each time it was rumored that the colony would be ceded to republican France (where slavery had been abolished) or that the king of Spain would himself declare the slaves free, the price of Negroes plummeted. Slaves worth one thousand piasters were sold for four hundred. The servants were a particular nuisance for Pontalba. He had to get rid of them somehow before quitting the colony, but no one was eager to buy. "I had found a place for Pélagie and her father Antoine," he wrote in a typical complaint, "but Madame André, far from accepting

Pélagie, had sent Antoine back with her . . . so that now I have thirteen people in my kitchen, although I do not eat at the house."[52] He tried to get the slaves to sell themselves, as a last resort, giving one a note together with instructions to "find herself a new master."

Pontalba does not appear to have been a worse (or better) master than his neighbors, even though the slaves at Pointe Coupée had singled him out for particular resentment in their revolution song. Probably none of the slave owners he describes in his letters would satisfy modern notions of humane behavior. Pontalba reported to his uncle that many masters defied Baron de Carondelet's "wise rule" requiring that the Negroes have Sundays free and receive one outfit of clothing per year.[53] Although the uprising at Pointe Coupée was the only organized, large-scale Louisiana slave revolt described by Pontalba, there were continual incidents of slaves being mistreated and retaliating against one or another of his acquaintances. His letters, both to Miró and his wife, describe an appalling level of violence on the plantations at a time when attacks of whites on each other were extremely rare.

He described one episode in which a slave tried to hang himself but was cut down by his master.[54] The slave shot the owner a few days later while the latter was eating dinner, then hanged himself in his cabin. The overseer, gathering all the blacks, told them that those most faithful to their old master must volunteer to cut off the head, arms, and legs of his assassin. Several of them complied with alacrity, according to Pontalba, who nevertheless agreed with the general view that the owner had been a barbaric master who brought his fate on himself.

More often, Pontalba took the master's part, as when he recounted "a very unfortunate incident" involving his friend Guy Dreux. Dreux surprised a black woman servant who was rummaging through his wardrobe. As she began to run away down the stairs, he threw a saber at her and killed her. The woman's son complained to Carondelet, who took depositions from all the witnesses. Pontalba went to see Dreux: "I advised that he arrange the matter with money, if possible; I even opened my purse to him. . . ." He was worried that his friend would be sentenced to several years in a penal colony, especially since many people came forward to allege that he was violent-tempered, "even going so far as to say he ill-treated his first wife shamefully, something I myself, refuse to believe." There seems to be no record of Dreux having been tried or his occupations interrupted on account of the incident.[55]

There were rare but haunting instances in Pontalba's society of blacks sadistically mistreating helpless whites. Marie Glass, a free quadroon married to a white man, tortured to death a young white girl, apparently retarded. After a stomach-turning trial, the records of which should not be sought out by sensitive eyes, Marie Glass was paraded through New Orleans and, in the presence of a large crowd, executed by hanging.[56]

For the most part, Pontalba regarded his own slaves as bothersome children. Sometimes he meted out harsh punishments for venial offenses. Augustin, the "most useful" of his blacks, who "never complains" and whom "no one could replace," is nevertheless whipped because he is repeatedly late when he brings Pontalba his milk at dawn. As a result, Augustin runs away "at a time when I need him most," but one of the slave's relatives returns him to his master. Lucille, having been sent to town to sell milk, sells only half as much as the blacks who accompany her. "For fifteen days she kept doing as badly as all that, only wanting me to take her off that work," Pontalba explains to his wife, "so that I found myself forced to put her in shackles."

Like almost everyone else, he had problems with runaways. Jeannette, one of his most spirited servants, lost the money she had collected from selling food (Pontalba thought she spent it) and, fearing punishment, took off. When she was returned to Pontalba by a neighbor, he decided that "the stocks will be the place for her until I find some way of getting rid of her. Her conduct has much decreased her value and may, perhaps, keep me from being able to sell her. Here is one who at least did not inconvenience me through her absence, which I only noticed through the lesser amount of victuals having to be distributed around. . . . She is now well advanced in her pregnancy, and as soon as she gives birth to her child I will send her the same way I did Claire."[57]

Next to running away, the slaves could cause Pontalba the most trouble by getting sick. Several servants were invariably "*sur le grabat*"—"on the humble bed." "Fiore does the selling for Adélaide," he wrote to his wife; "Jean-Baptiste has the fever; Annette goes about limping, so that I have to be content with only having Lucille to wait on me, but she at least is always well." Pontalba took care of the slaves when they were hurt or ill, as did many of his friends; he matter-of-factly mentions an acquaintance who stays home from a party to tend a servant with dysentery. "Lucille has been added to the number of my patients. She fell from the top of a fig tree like a log, and she feels some pain under one of her breasts, it keeping her in bed, and

I am worried over it. . . . Jeannette is in her tenth month of pregnancy, her belly does not show it, but she insists that she will win out." He gets angry when one of his slaves is wrongfully arrested and whipped for theft; Pontalba vindicates the slave's innocence, but he is upset because "the poor fellow had nevertheless had his twenty-five lashes."[58]

Pontalba seems most readily moved by the slave children. When he sells one of them to a friend who needs a coachman, he is concerned enough about the child to muse, "I think he will be well off there." A father buying his son's freedom makes the final payment to Pontalba for his little boy. "You have never seen him as happy as when he was being given a copy of the deed, which he kissed fervently," Pontalba wrote.[59] The thought of his own son then prompted Pontalba to give the money back to the man. He had no such impulse, however, when another black came to buy a child.

> Marianne has just bought Poignon from me, *mon amie*, she paid me 200 pi-
> asters for her freedom. . . . You always showed kindness to that family, and I
> felt that I was pleasing you in doing them this favor, as I could probably have
> got 250 piasters just by waiting a little. That child was always ill, and I am led to
> believe that she will not live long; her scurf keeps spreading, and some accu-
> mulations have even appeared lately that seem rather dangerous.[60]

He did give away another slave child, not to the boy's parents but to a friend who harnessed the little Negro and had his own child ride around on him, a game that apparently had amused Tin-Tin when the Pontalbas owned the boy. As Pontalba dispatched more and more slaves he was eventually left with only children to sell, indicating perhaps that he had already sold the parents and separated the families; this was a practice the more compassion-ate owners tried to avoid. The Spanish Crown's rule, observed by Madame Almonester, for one, was that children under ten were kept with their moth-ers. Pontalba described more than one occasion when black parents, former slaves, came to purchase their children's freedom. Moreover, he had no com-punction about placing one of his best Negroes with Tremoulet, a hotel-keeper whose reputation for cruelty Pontalba knew well.[61] Pontalba was sur-prised and a little hurt that his slaves left him so readily.

> I can assure you that all our servants are going . . . without showing regret. I
> had rewarded them all before they left for having so well served us, but they
> showed no gratitude for it. Only Annette seemed at all sorry to leave, insisting
> on waiting on me up to the last moment, after all the others had already left me
> to my own resources, to the extent that without Annette I would have been
> obliged to wait upon myself.

In the end he managed to place all the slaves, even the cook, after first having her teach him how to make gumbo and the rice cakes called *callas*. These preparations he would teach to his wife's servants in Europe.

Pontalba never let his practical affairs or the news and gossip he imparted in his letters crowd his outpourings of longing and frustration. Every letter had its section devoted to the grief, wretchedness, and sense of contingency he was suffering because of his wife's absence. "I am not living," he repeated, describing the emptiness of days without her, "only languishing."

Of Ton-Ton de Pontalba's emotional makeup, her response to his declarations, we have only indirect evidence. She was a poor correspondent—Pontalba often made excuses for her to Miró. Even when Miró complained that Céleste was in tears because she had received no word from Ton-Ton, Madame de Pontalba left it to her husband to send her regards and regrets. Her father, Jean-Baptiste Cézaire LeBreton, had been a Black Musketeer, a member of the French royal bodyguard. In 1771, when Ton-Ton was about sixteen, her father was murdered by a slave at their Carrolton plantation.[62] Ton-Ton was nine years younger than her husband. She was of a cooler temperament than Pontalba and resisted his excessive need for intimacy, if we may hold as evidence certain remarks Pontalba makes in passing. He feels it necessary to apologize profusely for having opened and read, "as if it were for myself " one of Madame de Miró's letters which arrived after his wife had already left for Europe.[63] He offers several excuses for himself and refers to his wife's "habitual restraint" in communicating the contents of her aunt's letters. His craving for tenderness seems to have met with a great deal of habitual restraint. But then, Pontalba's devotion was not without demands, and it is interesting to notice how Madame de Pontalba turned them aside. For example, Pontalba tells her specifically what he wants to find in her letters to him, from "a full account" of her first moments of reunion with Madame de Miró, to "precise information" of her activities. The letters he hoped to receive were to be "so full of details" that he would be able "to follow you each day in the course of your various journeys." He filled three pages outlining "the task I am expecting you to attend to. . . . No matter where you are, write simply of all you do, of all that you speak about, of all that is taking place around you."[64] This was a severe charge to place upon a woman who could hardly spare a line in three months for her adopted mother, but apparently Ton-Ton could shrug off his importunings. He instructed her to have a letter ready to drop in the mail as soon as her ship landed. In a tone full of grievance he remarked that the first news he had of her arrival did not come from her. Nevertheless, he continued fantasizing about the hoped-for letters: "I am going to find in your letters expressions of your tenderness, and a detailed account of all that interests me."

After the first stingy packet of his wife's letters finally arrived, he never quite got over his disappointment. "I expected to receive from you, almost in journal form, an account of all you did, *amie*, where you visited, what you saw; in that way I would have shared in your impressions."[65] Instead, he read through all there was within a few moments. He lectured her for pages on her omissions. "You have given me no details as to your route, and yet you know how interesting it would have been for me. . . . I would have liked to know where you spent the night, where you stopped, the hours of your departures. . . ." Stung by disappointment, he finally concluded: "One has to love as I do, *amie*, to realize how all such details become interesting."

For what she did include in her letters, Pontalba also criticized her. He remonstrated with her about exposing her political views; he disagreed with her choice of an agent to transport her belongings; and he took her to task for having failed to "manage properly" in making currency exchanges. With good reason he was upset when she ignored his incessant requests to have Tin-Tin inoculated.[66] But he was just as insistent about less critical matters. When his wife wrote that her aunt was grieving, he conceived the idea of distracting Madame de Miró with riding excursions. Nothing would do but that Ton-Ton had to buy some horses. "I have never asked you for anything to which I attached any greater importance, and do not refuse to comply. As soon as you receive my letter, charge Monsieur Paul immediately with making such a purchase [horses], because if I were to learn that you had done otherwise, it would cause me great sorrow, and if on my arrival I were to find that my aunt's health had failed," he wrote, with his usual degree of optimism, "I would be led to believe that it was partly your fault. Say that you are buying these to promenade around yourself, to get used to that form of exercise, as you do need it."[67] Such demands did not seem to inconvenience Madame de Pontalba, who apparently did more or less as she pleased without bothering to argue with her husband. Pontalba is worn out with exasperation when he writes that "it is hard for me to understand . . . you let pass whole months without sending letters to your *ami*."[68] When he penned that plaintive admonition, he had been writing several pages every day unfailingly for seven months.

Pontalba's worship of his wife and especially her relatives may have been somewhat rhetorical; he prided himself on his rarefied sensibilities. But his devotion to his little boy was desperate and sincerely neurotic. "Are you not sorry not to have your dear papa put his arms around your neck and squeeze you tighter and tighter?" he writes early in the separation. "Answer your papa my dear lad, just as though he were present." He promises to buy Tin-Tin a little coach; as he fantasizes about it in successive letters, the coach becomes more and more elaborate. He will fill the pockets and the box of the carriage with cakes and candy. It will have a horse with flying hoofs and Baptiste to drive it. "Julien will also be there, riding behind, I promised it to him on the condition that he stop biting his lip." The coach would be painted and gilded, with a little basket inside always filled with cherries, "some small pears, prunes, and a sprinkling of nuts."[69] By the next letter Pontalba has decided that the coach must have a lock so that no one can steal the treats.

He aches for the baby every day, every letter. He is tormented by the thought that his son will forget him and so asks his wife again and again to show Tin-Tin his portrait and see if he can identify his father. He sends further instructions. She is to show the boy a portrait he is familiar with of his father in uniform; then she is to change the picture inside the frame to an unfamiliar one of Pontalba without his uniform. She must leave it in a room without calling attention to it, and observe whether the five-year-old notices it without prompting.[70] Since Pontalba obviously will be heartbroken if the child fails the test, one wonders why he wants to make it so difficult.

"Train your son to repeat to you everything he hears. . . . Be careful that he does not become familiar with the servants," he advises her in one of his frequent preachments. "Take good care to discharge yourself of the commission I entrusted to you, that of buying something for my son each day, and to give it to him as coming from me." She was told to "kiss him twenty times at once and tell him that it is his papa who commissions you to give him all such caresses."[71] He suggests that when his wife sees some child on the street who is poorly dressed in winter, she should "arrange it so that he [Tin-Tin] will ask you to buy a little storm coat for him . . . and when he feels very cold in turn lead him to believe that without him the little unfortunate . . . would have died from the cold." This idea struck in the middle of June, when no one in Spain was likely to die of cold, and people around Pontalba were prone to die of heat. He reminds his son, "When you have something good, keep your habit of saving a little of it for your papa." Tin-Tin in fact writes his father a little note, asking him to send toys and pralines. Madame de

Pontalba is instructed to "buy him some at once." Apparently, the little boy's disposition was not enhanced by such attentions, for he told Honoré Fortier, the mail courier and friend of the Pontalbas, "If you fail to say good day to my papa for me, I will give you a good beating."[72]

Célestin was not to see his father for several more months, for Pontalba left New Orleans a year later than he had hoped. The letters he surely wrote to his wife in 1797 during the last year of their separation must have been lost. We may assume that he was mad to leave as the date approached for his departure, since he had begun imagining their reunion only a few months after his wife left. At that time he confided his daydreams about the life they would have in Europe.

> Sometimes I surprise myself traveling with you, your aunt, and my son; . . . other times I see you and our friend kept busy with deeds of benevolence, helping you myself with them as much as I can, even to the point of outdoing you sometimes. But more often, we content ourselves with mutually recalling . . . the true friend whose demise we will never cease to regret. . . . Sadness will then come to take hold of us, and realizing the emptiness of all our surroundings and occupations, all diversions will become a matter of indifference, and we, from then on, will only find consolation in entertaining each other with our troubles.[73]

It was to this dream of entertainment that Pontalba sailed away in 1797, leaving his rental properties in the hands of a manager.[74]

Pontalba reached France on a Spanish ship with his military clothes in his bags; there his little family joined him. Like Miró before him, he planned to advertise his expertise in colonial military affairs, but to the French, not the Spanish, government. In 1800 he therefore submitted to the French minister of the navy a "Memoir on Louisiana," evaluating the commercial, military, and economic potential of the area. France had begun casting acquisitive eyes on its former colony when the American Revolution broke British hegemony in the region. Periodically the French government gathered information from individuals or its own officials; many "memoirs" on Louisiana had thus been submitted to various French ministers over the years from dozens of people. Pontalba perhaps volunteered his essay to General Victor to "prove his devotion" as he later explained.[75] Pontalba's memoir contained good, conventional wisdom.[76] Much of it had been advocated by Miró in the 1780s and pressed upon the king's ministers when Miró arrived at the Spanish court in 1792. Perhaps Napoleon would have used some of the hundreds of suggestions he received had he kept Louisiana, notwithstanding Robert Livingston's comment that Bonaparte "seldom asks advice, and never hears it unasked."

Pontalba was still in the Spanish service and had been raised to the rank of colonel on February 12, 1800. But soon after submitting the memoir in October, he transferred his fortune to France, renounced his Spanish rank, and voiced his plan "to become French once more." As an immediate reward for writing the memoir, Pontalba asked for admission to the French army with the rank of adjutant general without salary, a position he wanted, he averred, for the honor of serving the French Republic.[77] "He makes the most ardent vows, even at the expense of his own life," he wrote, referring to himself in the third person, "for the precious preservation of the First Consul [Bonaparte]." We can only guess what Miró would have said about Pontalba's political conversion to republicanism; but careerist that he was, Miró probably would have approved of the way Pontalba milked the memoir for a series of compensations he in fact got through the wives of his relatives. As adjutant general Pontalba was to accompany General Victor to Louisiana, apparently to be an advisor to the navy if France fulfilled its plan to repossess the colony. Napoleon of course changed his mind about keeping Louisiana and instead sold the territory to the United States in April, 1803, before Pontalba, or any French advisors, were dispatched.

Meanwhile, Pontalba was traveling between France and Spain, wrapping up Madame de Miró's affairs. In December, 1801, a year before General Victor proposed to go to America, Pontalba purchased the château of Colombes near the Seine. As was usual for large landowners near small towns, he served as mayor of Colombes for 1803 and 1804. Although Pontalba had described himself to Napoleon as "one of the principal landowners of Louisiana," he was actually quite anxious about his financial security, based as it was on rental income from people who might be bankrupted by any change in the slave system.[78] Thus, instead of picnicking in the European countryside or outdoing his wife in charitable works as he had expected, he dabbled in exporting naval stores and lending money at interest. In 1805 he sold the Colombes property and settled into a large, dilapidated estate about fifty miles from Paris. The Château Mont-l'Évêque was just outside the medieval town of Senlis.[79] Here Pontalba was to spend the rest of his life surrounded by his wife, child, and aunt. Napoleon, now emperor, granted Pontalba's request for two more distinctions: first came the title of Knight of the Legion of Honor; then in May, 1810, having established himself in his new domain at Mont-l'Évêque, Pontalba was made a baron, two months after the birth of Napoleon's son, when the emperor was still in a magnanimous mood.[80]

Meanwhile, Pontalba's own son Célestin was enjoying the privileged upbringing of a young nobleman in the capital. His first schooling at Juilly, a grammar school that catered to wealthy foreigners, was apparently his last, for at thirteen he was appointed Page of the Equipage in the newly created court of the newly created emperor.[81] There is a profile portrait of him in his page's costume painted by the same Quesnédy who immortalized his father's Spanish uniform—an overdressed child with a gently blank expression. The pages in Napoleon's service numbered thirty-six to sixty, with six or eight of the group always on duty. They normally were required to attend a page school for one year, to serve at court for four years, and then to enter the army. The major service rendered by pages was to be at hand if anyone at court wanted to send a message. A few pages rode with Napoleon in the state carriage, ran errands, and passed the emperor's guns to him at the hunt. They also served who only stood and waited: when Napoleon was out at night, pages were stationed at the palace gates with torches to light his return. A page received two thousand francs a year. By comparison, the emperor's personal physician was paid fifty thousand.[82] With such preparation, it is no wonder that most of the nobility grew up, as Kenneth Clark once observed, as ignorant as swans.

After five years at court, Célestin entered the army but injured his hand before he could join his regiment.[83] Marshal Ney, whose wife was one of the many French cousins of the Pontalbas, interceded with the minister of war to have Célestin attached to him as aide-de-camp. While waiting for that assignment, Célestin participated in the sieges of Ciudad Rodrigo and Almeida, bitter campaigns intended to dislodge Wellington from his foothold on the Iberian coast. Still not having joined Ney, Célestin was granted six months' leave to go to New Orleans for his wedding. Returning from America, his ship was reportedly stopped by the English who may have detained him and his party until July, 1812. Only after many delays was he finally able to serve as Ney's aide-de-camp and receive, at the marshal's insistence, a promotion to lieutenant.[84] By April 25, 1813, Célestin's military career was over; he tendered his resignation within a year after joining Ney. At twenty-two he was a retired officer with about three years' experience behind him. We do not know whether he resigned for a personal reason, such as homesickness, or because his service in the hard-fought peninsular campaigns made him pessimistic about life in Napoleon's army. His official reason was the injury to his hand. In any case, he got out before the debacle of the Russian campaign, in which, as Ney's asistant, he would have participated.

His father continued to support the Napoleonic cause until the cause departed for St. Helena, although with the discretion of one who intended to survive political vicissitudes. Both father and son resisted Napoleon's desperate call to arms during the Hundred Days. With regard to Marshal Ney, Pontalba's position was ticklish. The marshal had a checkered history in the months before the final collapse of the empire. During Napoleon's exile on Elba, Ney had been received at the court of Louis XVIII. He even promised the king, when news of Napoleon's escape reached Paris, that he would bring Bonaparte to him "in an iron cage." A polite invitation from his former master changed Ney's mind, however. He defected with his troops and assisted Napoleon in losing the Battle of Waterloo. There was then no longer any question of being received at court. On July 11, 1815, Pontalba wrote to Ney, beginning tactfully, "It seems to me that, in the event you would decide to leave France, you would give Louisiana preference over other parts of the United States. . . ." After outlining all the advantages of the region (as if Ney were in a position to reject a sanctuary on account of its barometric pressure), Pontalba gave directions for debarking at New Orleans and included two letters which Ney was to present to Bernard de Marigny and St. Avid.[85] Marigny was requested to supply lodging until Ney could find a house near New Orleans. "Should he perceive that because of his presence there arises . . . some expense because of him, he will leave you to go to an inn; receive him, therefore, with the greatest simplicity," Pontalba advised Marigny, "as if he were not at your house." The letters never reached Louisiana; in fact, they may never have reached Ney, who had fled from Paris in disguise on July 6, five days before Pontalba sat down to write. The letters were seized with Ney's papers and turned up as evidence against him at his court martial. He was shot by a firing squad on December 7, 1815. By this time Pontalba had already been named Knight of St. Louis by Louis XVIII, who took no umbrage at his recent devotion to the Usurper. The Pontalbas experienced no apparent reversals on account of their association with Napoleon's disgraced commander, and the family remained secure in its place among the pampered provincial nobility when the ancien régime was again in control.

The really fateful changes in the lives of the Pontalbas took place several years before France's political crises. In 1810 the elder Pontalba wrote to his cousin Louison in New Orleans proposing the marriage of her Micael to his adored Célestin. That letter, from a man whose missives document so many fatal mistakes, proved to be the worst commitment of his life.

IV

The Widow

IT is easy to find in Micael's personality some traits that she seemed to have
inherited from her father: her energy, her passion for building, her care-
fulness with money, her love of work and business, and her quickness in defending her rights. But, in fact, Micael turned out to be a rather more advanced model of that self-sufficient and restless woman, her mother.

Louise de la Ronde, *Veuve* Almonester, as she signed herself after her husband's death, was bright by anyone's measure. She was literate, interested in
life, full of spirit for all sorts of adventures, and had a head for figures. She
was more than capable of managing Almonester's many projects, at least the
ones she was interested in, the profitable ones. What she had no talent for
was charity, and she let everyone know at once that Almonester's career as a
philanthropist died with him. Three weeks after her husband's burial she
asked the city council to deliver to her all the previous year's surplus in the
treasury as payment for the ongoing construction of the Cabildo. (Almonester's agreement with the council had been that he would build the Cathedral, Presbytere, and Cabildo, and the council would repay him only for the
Cabildo.) She resisted the commissioners' demands that she complete the
building, however, and eventually persuaded them to let her withdraw from
the project. They would finish the building, reimbursing her over time for
the portion of the building that had been completed when Almonester died.
Through her brother, who was now a commissioner, Louison kept abreast
of the council's financial affairs and was punctilious about asking for any surpluses. Within a few years, the council had paid off its debt to her for the Cabildo, a bounty to the estate that certainly would have surprised Almonester.[1]

She could not so easily get out of finishing the Presbytere—that gift was
not as near completion as the Cabildo. In 1799 the bishop of the new Dio-
cese of Louisiana, Luis Peñalver y Cardenas, sued to force her to complete
the rectory according to her husband's promise. She protested in court that
the undertaking would deplete the inheritance of her daughters, who were
two and four years old, depriving them "of the standard of living to which

they have been accustomed and which their social rank in life requires."[2] It was true that her husband had continued to plan costly benefactions even after he had heirs; he had been moved, she said, by "a spiteful feeling he harbored against me because of certain domestic disagreements." The court was unmoved by this interesting confession; however, the king, to whom she was compelled eventually to appeal, took her part and freed her of the building obligation. The Presbytere was not completed until 1813. A temporary roof was put over it, and those rooms that were finished were rented out as stores. It was never used as a rectory.

During the years after her husband's death, Louison had a dozen projects of her own. We find her building rental houses in 1801, and entering into expensive lawsuits with tenants—one proceeding for simple eviction ran to eighty-one pages of testimony and must have cost her more than the defendant's yearly rent. In 1803 and 1804 she rebuilt all the houses on the St. Ann Street side of the plaza, a huge undertaking that she was able to begin only after fighting off a lawsuit by one of the executors of Almonester's will. Miró's old antagonist, Joseph de Orué, also filed a suit against her, with the cooperation of the Marqués de Casa Calvo; meanwhile, she continued petitioning for Almonester's posthumous advancement to the rank of brigadier.[3]

No one could say Louison had not known grief. Four years after Almonester's death, Andrea Antonia, the child named after her father and godfather, died at the age of four. Father Sedella buried his goddaughter on April 9, 1802, in St. Louis Cathedral, "at the side of the bones of her father," as Sedella recorded in his round, expansive hand that even in sadness filled every margin of the page.[4] How the child's death affected Louison or her other daughter, Micael, we can only imagine. The next year, the widow, like everyone else in New Orleans society, attended the gala parties celebrating France's brief repossession of the colony, those lavish events where supper was served at three in the morning. She opened one of the balls by dancing a minuet with Casa Calvo, who nevertheless continued to vote against her in the council whenever he had the chance.[5]

Though she was wealthy, Louison preferred to let people believe her circumstances were modest. The French representative Pierre de Laussat, newly arrived to take over the government of the colony for France, commented that Madame Almonester, for all her property, had meager-looking furniture and personal effects, "not worth 5,000 francs in all." Louison was not living ostentatiously—at least not then. Thomas Ashe, visiting New Orleans in 1806, also had trouble sizing up her true situation. He observed that the "merchant" Don Andrés had erected an impressive plaza "on the condition that he should be made a noble of Spain. He lived to expend two million dollars on these and other public works," Ashe wrote, "but he died before the ambitious honors were lavished on him, and his wife still has the mortification to be called Madame André."[6] Ashe was of course mistaken on all counts. Not only did Almonester get most of his honors, but in 1804 his widow had remarried and was known as Madame Castillon.

Jean Baptiste Castillon was a native of France, described in some lawsuits as a merchant, which is probably correct in view of his frequent recourse to the courts to collect various debts. He was apparently in some financial trouble around 1798 when Almonester died, for his slaves and property were being heavily morgaged in order to buy merchandise for resale. He had been sued by Louison's brother in 1801 for not repaying two loans; had dabbled in local government as a one-year commissioner; and had been named French consul at New Orleans when he married Louison.[7] If Louise de la Ronde had brought "not a penny" to her first marriage, as Bishop Peñalver noted, she made up for it with her second. If her first husband had been old enough to be her father, her second, the townspeople joked, was young enough to be her son. Actually, Castillon was only seven years younger than the forty-six-year-old bride, but even Governor Claiborne referred to her as "an old widow who has lately married a young man."[8] Perhaps Louison seemed old to Claiborne, who was himself a tender twenty-nine at the time. The match was considered sufficiently unsuitable to be ridiculed by an elaborate charivari held in front of Louison's house. For several days a boisterous crowd operating in relays banged on tin pots and sang obscene ballads, keeping up the din until the Castillons agreed, according to Claiborne, "to give a splendid *fête* to the genteel part of Society and one thousand dollars to the poor of the City."

The little that is known about Castillon after the marriage does him no credit. He showed an early taste for wearing Almonester's shoes "in my capacity as spouse and attorney of the widow and daughter."[9] He wrote to the Ursuline nuns in 1805 demanding access to the privileged patron's seat, that is, to Almonester's seat, and to the tabernacle key. Later that year he ran for the House of Representatives from the Louisiana territory. He received two votes, including his own, which was as good a showing as any of the other ten candidates made, except the winner, with his landslide of twenty-three. In 1808

Castillon put a fence around the San Lázaro Lepers' Hospital and tried to in-
corporate it into his own (that is, Almonester's) adjoining plantation. The
mayor compelled him to take down the fence and acknowledge that he had no
claim to the property, which had been donated by Almonester to the city.[10]

Castillon's reputation was further compromised when in 1806 he was
appointed by the Spanish minister to the United States to look after Spain's
interests in New Orleans. Father Sedella procured this dubious honor
for Castillon, who had allegedly endeared himself to the friar by his anti-
republican views. Since the Louisiana territory had passed to the United
States, Castillon's position as a special commissioner made him a sort of legal
espionage agent for Spain. Within one year there were charges that he had
been using his office for personal financial gain. The new Spanish minister to
the United States fired him, although for a year Castillon refused to relinquish his post. Even Castillon's secretary, a man called Angel Benito de Ariza,
was castigated in Spanish diplomatic correspondence as one who was "used
to taking money for himself with impunity or to seeing it so taken, since he
had been secretary to the infamous New Orleans consul Castillon."[11]

Pontalba, who could smell out a n'er-do-well if anyone could, mentioned
Castillon (who was then still unmarried) several times in his letters. Once
Castillon insisted that Pontalba should sell him a slave, but seemed to forget
"that I also told him if he wanted her he would have to pay the price." Castillon formed a partnership with Edouard Dusuau, one of Pontalba's friends in
the import business. Dusuau was constantly worried that Castillon would
disappear when the time came to pay his share of the bills. In one letter to
Dusuau, Castillon wrote four pages about politics, Pontalba reported, but
not one word about his debts. "This made Dusuau pretty mad," Pontalba observed, and caused the importer to conclude that Castillon was too much of a
"youngster" and a "philosopher" to be a reliable partner. But that was not the
end of the affair. A few days later, Dusuau had to miss a party, "having become the victim of dysentery induced by the political arguments of Castillon,
who did not have the good sense to sprinkle these with an outline of . . . how
they were going to pay off their joint debt of twelve-thousand piaster-
gourdes."[12] Castillon's inglorious career was short, however. He died on
August 3, 1809, his chief distinction having been his success in marrying well.
Father Sedella recorded his age as "about 44 years" at the time of his death.

Thanks to Castillon's demise and the careful record keeping of his widow,
we know more about him than his friends probably knew while he was alive.

It was the custom through the nineteenth century to take an exhaustive inventory of a deceased person's possessions, in the presence of a dozen or so witnesses who lumbered through the house of the departed behind a notary, a scribe, and sometimes a special appraiser, counting and evaluating every rag and hairpin. The estate inventories made today are relatively brief assessments of cash, investments, real estate, and cars; a collective figure, usually somewhat arbitrary, is assigned to personal property—the furniture, clothing, etc., of the deceased. But for our nosier and more materialistic forefathers, an estate inventory was long, invasive, and invariably interesting.

Castillon's inventory shows that when he married Louison, he had houses, a large still, twenty-six slaves, land, crops, and livestock, all worth over fifty thousand dollars.[13] But he was deeply in debt and was not making much money from his enterprises. His most profitable risk was his marriage; Louison paid off all his obligations. Castillon's family, a brother and his parents, gained even more from the marriage than he did. Castillon left a will at his death, naming his brother Joseph as heir to all his property and assets. The brother thus inherited half of all the community property held with Louison, in other words, half of everything she acquired during her second marriage. People who had owed money to Almonester paid it to his widow, some of the payments being made after her second marriage. That money came under the purview of community property. The brother got half, that is, the half that would have belonged to Castillon. During her second marriage, Louison paid off contractors for rebuilding her houses on the square; a portion of the value of the houses thus became community property because they were paid for with community funds; the brother again got half of that portion. One extraordinary piece of luck for the dead man's family: Louison had purchased a plantation and a large number of slaves only a few months before Castillon's death—definitely community property. Castillon's brother found himself the happy half-owner of both the plantation and the people. The Tchoupitoulas sugar plantation (the French spelled it Chapitoulas, sensibly) consisted of a number of buildings, including a refinery, a pigeon house, a "hospital," thirty cabins for the sixty-nine slaves who came with the purchase, and a spacious main house ribboned all around with a shaded gallery. Louison must have bought the plantation with the intention of fixing it up, since all the buildings were described in the inventory as being in disrepair.

Castillon's inventory started with about seven witnesses when the succession was opened in August, 1809. By the time the counting was completed in December, the number of witnesses had grown to twenty, more or less, many of whom were glad for the opportunity to purchase items from the estate before these were offered for sale to the public. The first thing the notary, Jean Rodriguez, recorded in the Castillon house on the square was that Madame Castillon had six thousand dollars (or piasters, or pesos—the terms were used interchangeably) in desks and cabinets and 250 dollars in the bank of Louisiana. This was not unusual, for people did not yet bother much with banks. More notably, there were locked desks all over the place containing undetermined amounts of cash—undetermined because the keys had been "lost" and no one present at the inventory could open the drawers. Perhaps the keys lost themselves when Louison realized that Castillon's brother would lay claim to half of whatever cash was found. While Castillon was being ushered out of life with a modest funeral and the promise of twenty masses (at a total of twenty dollars) for the repose of his soul, the brother was suing in court to prove that half of Louison's sugar plantation belonged to Castillon's estate. The brother contended, moreover, that Louison was appropriating assets that belonged to Castillon before his marriage; he therefore hired the notary Pierre, or Pedro, Pedesclaux as his representative, to attend the inventory and protect his interests.

Pedesclaux's abrasive presence must have come as a relief to Louison, giving her something corporeal on which to vent her grievances. As the accountants went through the remnants of Castillon's life, she followed behind them, complaining that whatever they were listing as his separate property was in fact an asset he acquired after their marriage and that what they listed as community property belonged, in truth, only to her. The taffia still had belonged to her husband, she admitted; but the iron buckets and barrels of rice which the counters were toting up had been bought by her.

Louison thought the distinction between Castillon's separate property and the community property was worth making. Everything that Castillon owned before the marriage would have to be turned over to his brother, without exception, whereas Louison was allowed to keep the value of one half of whatever had been purchased during the marriage. While she and Pedesclaux argued, the notary for the inventory was awarding a value of eight dollars to four pieces of wood he found against a wall. Madame Castillon observed that the wood had been bought since her marriage to Castillon and was community property. Pedesclaux insisted she would have to prove when the wood was acquired. And so it went. Occasionally, the brother himself showed up, adding his remarks to the proceedings as he tried to identify the premarital buckets, slaves, or cows, so as to distinguish them from the rest.

Whatever Louison and Castillon had together surely included slaves, so many that the notary once lost track and counted some souls twice. He finally ascertained that there were about 130 Negroes, not counting children under ten who were not to be separated from their mothers (but including one child of ten, valued at $200), and not counting eighty-five others who were Louison's separate property. Some of these latter had been rented out and were not at home at the time of the inventory. Most of the slaves were field hands, and many were rebellious, such as Ambrose, age twenty-four, "good with a pick and ax, but a habitual runaway, being at the moment in a boot and collar as punishment for his vice"; George, afflicted with "crabs on his feet"; Destin, with a gunshot wound, the result of his having run away; and Marguerite, a forty-one-year-old laundress, "pregnant and bad."[14] One Azor was a house slave, and therefore valued high at $800, but was a "bad cook." The notary Rodriguez nevertheless bought him, along with two pairs of oxen and a horse, for $713.

More numerous even than the bodies listed in the inventory were the books, hundreds, on every topic: *Zimmerman on Solitude*, *The Art of Turner*, *Analysis of the Power of Great Britain*, world history in sixty-seven volumes, works of Cervantes, Boileau, Racine, Fielding, Horace, Rousseau, Richardson, Sophocles, and Necker; books about economics, agriculture, medicine, banking, and criminality; maps; dictionaries in French, German, and Italian; titles including everything from *Gnomes* to *The English Constitution*. Almost certainly these were simply items that Castillon bought during his stint as an importer and failed to sell. Madame Castillon stated repeatedly that about half the books had belonged to her before her marriage—the usual protest. But if, indeed, half were hers or Almonester's, and half belonged to Castillon's personal library, then it would appear that she married both her husbands not for their money but for their minds.

The inventory yields other, more certain information about the widow. Her furniture was cheap, but her walls were covered with pictures; she owned two carriages; she subscribed to a newspaper, *La Gazette d'Orléans*; she kept her most important papers, her marriage certificate to Almonester and his *cédulas* from the king of Spain, between two cedar floor planks. She had paid off more than $20,000 of Castillon's debts when she married him, including the $6,000 owed to Dusuau, plus $235 in interest. She had $14,000 in savings before Castillon wooed it from her, and though the house on the square where she lived with him fell partly within the community assets, her Bayou Road plantation and many of her other houses were her own separate properties. Her rentals on the square were so well known that a tenant might give his address as: "Monsieur So-and-So, St. Ann Street, houses of Madame Castillon."[15]

Louison's final accounting of her administration of Castillon's estate, written in a hand as fine and clear as Almonester's, was a little work of architecture. Columns of decimals enumerated the receipts and expenditures, all organized by topic and arranged chronologically according to the date of each transaction. Page after page showed the financial resources of her short, busy, second marriage; where each piaster came from; where each penny went. Unlike present-day successions, in which a tableau of distributions is likely to summarize small amounts or dispense with them altogether, Madame Castillon's account resembled a modern-day tax audit, in which the person making the report unabashedly takes every conceivable deduction. Louison quite properly deducted from the money she paid to Castillon's heirs the two dollars she spent to rent a horse so that Castillon's parents might attend the funeral; the $200 for her widow's clothes for a year of mourning; the $250 she spent on food for the people taking the inventory; the $1.50 she spent to have a slave put in jail, the Negro having been part of Castillon's separate property (if the slave had been community property, she would only have been able to deduct 75 cents); and the three dollars she spent on affidavits against the "so-called brother" of her late husband.[16] She sought expert advice on what she could deduct and deducted the cost of the advice. It appears to have been good advice. For example, she stated in her account that her daughter Micael's patrimony from Almonester was $40,000, which money Castillon had managed for the fifty-five months of their marriage. Castillon had thereby earned, at least theoretically, a management fee of 5 percent a year, totaling $10,834. Since Louison was entitled to half of everything Castillon earned during their marriage, half of that amount was due to her from Castillon's estate. She thus kept another $5,417 out of his brother's hands, along with the $3,192 which she claimed as her own commission for being the estate's executrix. Even after deductions so detailed they included one dollar, twelve and a half cents for a translation of a document, Castillon's estate, swelled by Louison's real estate purchases and payment of debts, was still worth $112,823.81, to the immense gratification of his so-called brother.

Looking over the inventory of Castillon's estate, or of any estate of the time, it becomes apparent that privacy meant something different to Castillon's contemporaries than it means to us. Two centuries ago, one knew that as soon as one departed from life, half the town would be counting the napkins, ball gowns, servants, and almond cakes one left behind. Emotions, however, were private, more than we can now imagine; sex was nearly so; and intimacy of all kinds was shielded from public view. Childbirth was as public as now, illness more so, and death, which was not then considered an indiscreet lapse in an otherwise healthy community, was shared with onlookers. The idea that one might have "private papers" had not yet taken hold; that convention was to develop with the popularity of banks and their promise of semi-confidentiality. In Castillon's time, people who had money often held mortgages for others who needed it, without the intermediary offices of a bank. Such transactions were notarized, as was nearly every transfer of goods, so that the amount and kind of a person's investments as well as his debts was common knowledge. Letters were saved; they were rarely revealing. As for possessions, in a world where nearly everyone either had a servant or was one, these, too, were not personal in the sense that we now use the term. No one thought much about it when the notary went through Castillon's correspondence and listed every sender's name. In fact, one of the last items in Louison's deductions diminished the brother's inheritance by nine dollars: the widow purchased some folders to hold Castillon's "private" letters, after each of the inventory's witnesses had handled and read them, page by page.

Louison had buried her second husband, but she still had to finish her first husband's battle with the city council over Charity Hospital. Almonester died secure in the belief that the king had settled the dispute over his patronage for all time. With the philanthropist out of the way, however, the *cabildo* renewed its pretensions to control of the institution. The governor and the council audited the hospital's accounts a few months after Almonester's death, while Louison was managing the facility through an administrator. According to Louison's old antagonist, Bishop Peñalver, who studied the report, Almonester's widow had expropriated for her own use some six thousand dollars of hospital funds. The council and its magistrate, Casa Calvo, ruled that she would have to pay back the money. Louison retorted that the king's decrees had explicitly exempted Almonester from having to account to anyone for his management; presumably, that exemption applied to his heirs as well. Unintimidated, she threatened to auction off the hospital if the least infringement were attempted upon her exclusive rights. Meanwhile, the hospital was falling apart. The medical historian John Duffy concluded that Louison must have been taking the hospital's funds, since the institution was in deplorable condition. According to a report made in 1804, the wards were dirty, the food bad, medicine was administered without the supervision of a physician, "the dressing of wounds is left to Negroes," and there were no surgical instruments.[17] For eleven years the situation remained thus, with Louison holding off the city council, which had meanwhile passed to United States administration.

Throughout all the debate, no one had bothered to read Almonester's original constitution for the hospital in which he provided for its patronage after his death. When the council did get around to looking at the document in 1809, they joyously discovered that Almonester had pointedly passed over his wife and designated others as future patrons.[18] Almonester had no children when he wrote the constitution; with Micael's birth, the patronage passed automatically to her, over her mother, whom Almonester had excluded, and over the other appointees. Louison had no authority whatever over the hospital, even during Micael's minority.

Before anyone could act on that information, a fire swept the hospital in September, 1809, and reduced the argument to a pile of debris. The mayor moved the patients who survived the blaze to a rented house and asked Madame Castillon to pay the rent. She emphatically refused. Fair enough. But she continued collecting rent from the houses that her husband had donated for the hospital's support, even though she had no intention of rebuilding the facility. She would not even relinquish her patronage of the hospital so that the council could use its meager resources to build another facility. Things were so bad in the temporary shelter that patients were sleeping on the damp earthen floor. Louison donated twenty-four woolen blankets to make their convalescence on the ground more comfortable. The territorial legislature was finally ready to move against Louison to force her to give up the hospital when she suddenly reversed her position. On March 9, 1811, Micael, then fifteen, appeared with her mother before a notary and renounced all rights to the hospital.[19] Louison apparently decided to be finished with the whole business rather than enter into a protracted lawsuit. As soon as she was free of the hospital, she had her house demolished to make way for a lavish new home. The two-and-a-half-story mansion, which was to cost $62,000, contained courtyards, kitchens, a coach house, a wood house, servants' rooms, a dining room almost fifty feet long, and enough space for eight apartments on the ground floor.[20] There was to be a separate apartment for Micael at the other end of the house from her mother's quarters, separated by a courtyard and almost one hundred feet of hallways.

We can only infer what the events of those years meant to the young heiress who was also to live in the grand house on the plaza, in whose name fortunes and honors were negotiated. Micael was two years old when her father died, six when her sister died, eight when her mother's remarriage caused the town to gather in ridicule, thirteen when her stepfather died. She was fifteen when her mother received from Joseph Delfau de Pontalba the proposal that Micael and Célestin should marry. The Pontalbas were now living in France and had not seen Micael since her infancy. Mother and daughter abandoned the unfinished mansion with its young lady's elegant apartment; Micael at sixteen became a French citizen and wife of a provincial aristocrat.

We know nothing of her childhood relationships except that she became close to her mother's half-sister, Victoire de Lino de Chalmet, and especially to Victoire's daughter, her cousin Azélie, who was fourteen years older than Micael. She surely spoke French and not Spanish at home, since her father, the only Spanish speaker in the household, was probably too busy to speak to her and too deaf to hear her by the time she would have begun to talk, a year or so before his death. She learned English at some time. It is likely that she attended the day school of the Ursuline nuns a few steps down from her house, although the Ursulines report no record of her matriculation. Her formal education, whatever it was, lasted only a few years. She must have been an artistic little girl. At thirteen she owned a piano. Her bedroom consisted of "a decorated bed, a table, a little chest of drawers, and five pictures."[21] Her toilet and an armoire were in an adjacent dressing room.

When the letter proposing marriage arrived from France, Micael's mother was delighted. Like Almonester, Louison had always assumed that her cousin Pontalba was a great deal more fond of her family than he was. She did not consider him one of her critics. And she did not hesitate to accept the proposal. "My daughter has shown inclinations to no one, saying that she wants to meet her cousin," Madame Castillon wrote to Pontalba. "She has asked me to beg you to send him as soon as you can."[22] Others had sought the young man's hand, according to a partisan of the Pontalbas who related (some years later) that Célestin "had been desired to the point of . . . embarrassment."[23] In January, 1811, when Célestin had not arrived as early as expected, Louison exclaimed, "What a pity it would be if such a fine match were to fail, as they seem to have been made for one another."[24] Since she had not met Célestin, perhaps she only meant that their inheritances were made for one another. She warned Pontalba to disregard any letters sent in her name by people "prompted by personally selfish motives," who might try to break the betrothal. "My fortune makes people envious, and you may well realize that if your son were a long time coming over, I would have a hard task trying to prevent my daughter from marrying."[25] She assured Pontalba, "I will do whatever you please, and it will be equally indifferent to me whether I stay in Louisiana, or go to live in Paris. . . . You are probably going to say that I seem in a hurry; but that is only because I fear that your son will delay his coming." Louison even invoked the name of their mutual relative, St. Avid, assuring Pontalba that "he will be able to tell you how I have further increased the extent of my fortune." That part was true enough. Negotiations must have broken down in the next few months, true to Louison's foreboding. In April, she went ahead with plans to construct her mansion on the square. But the engagement was on again in June, when Célestin received a leave of absence from his regiment to go to Louisiana.

There is no explanation for Pontalba's choice of Micael as his son's wife except the obvious one. Having had no particular regard for her parents, Pontalba could not have chosen Micael in anticipation of her presumed virtues or superior upbringing. But in an age when marriage was seen as a means of securing wealth as much as affection, a contract made on behalf of two young strangers, each the sole heir to a fortune, was hardly remarkable. Miró had been devoted to his wife in spite of the large dowry she had brought to their union; Pontalba's brother-in-law LeBreton had been so attached to his second wife that he refused to leave her to visit friends; Pontalba, as we have seen, loved his *amie* with lifelong agitation, notwithstanding the legendary affluence of her family, and Pontalba does not appear to have been exceptional. François Guizot, the prime minister of France, once wrote a heartrending letter of sympathy to a widowed friend; though he had many distractions and responsibilities outside his family, he had known "the abyss of grief " at losing a wife. He was to experience it again, with the same overwhelming sense of desolation, when his second wife died.[26] The fact was that arranged matches worked about as well as any other mating system; husbands and wives, matched by their parents, could and did learn to love each other immoderately. As for Micael, her future husband was handsome and dashing, "his youth ripened amidst the dangers of the campaigns of Spain and Portugal," in the later words of his separation attorney. The prospect of living in France may have been attractive, at least to Micael's mother. There were, in fact, very few drawbacks for her in the proposed marriage, all of them serious.

Célestin sailed from Bordeaux accompanied by his mother. Although Pontalba had sworn never again to be parted from his wife, he remained in France while Ton-Ton de Pontalba was charged with concluding the critical nuptial contract. Micael and Célestin had three weeks to become acquainted. They were married on October 23, 1811, in St. Louis Cathedral where Micael's father and sister were buried. Everyone was invited to the wedding, and all noted that the groom was beautiful and the bride rich. The ill-fated Marshal Ney, still alive and respectable in 1811, sponsored Célestin through a proxy, Bernard de Marigny. The young people were accompanied to the altar by an assemblage of Chalmets, de la Rondes, Macartys, St. Avids, and Deverges. The service was in Spanish, which Célestin did not understand, but it was brief.[27] After the ceremony, the wedding party stepped out onto the town square where trees would not grow and stray cows still roamed around the open wells. The couple had to remain a few weeks longer in New Orleans until their ship was ready to leave, giving Micael time to make her farewells to friends and family. Then the bride and groom, towing both mothers, sailed away to France, to live unhappily ever after.

V

Mont-l'Évêque

Iᴛ was not to Paris Micael would go when she arrived in France in July, 1812, but to the Pontalbas' rural estate. The Château Mont-l'Évêque was just outside the provincial town of Senlis which was itself fifty miles from the capital, a carriage journey of eight hours or several days, depending on the state of the ruts that served the scanty traffic.[1]

Senlis today looks like a lovely, medieval tapestry dotted with a few modern buildings; but even to Micael's nineteenth-century eyes, the town must have seemed antique, a sand-colored denseness of massive stucco walls, turrets, winding outside stairs, and many gates, all closed. Senlis had notarial offices, schools, and markets, but above all, the town afforded access to prayer. The narrow streets contained a magnificent cathedral, ten churches, and four convents, as well as abbeys, monasteries, and chapels. It was the sort of town where at midnight one might see the night watchman who called out the hours strolling to the cemetery, as he did in many country places, to tell the time to the dead.

Mont-l'Évêque comprised its own little village. When Micael first saw it, it consisted of two farms of about 130 acres and a few houses which the Pontalbas leased out together with a cornmeal mill, and another great cathedral just next to the estate.[2] The main château was protected from random encounters with the surrounding population by green forests and a moat. Its gardens were much admired in the region, though not perhaps by the young bride. Célestin's lawyer once scoffed that it was "time lost" to try to awaken in Micael "an interest in agriculture and in all other pastimes purely bucolic."[3] It is hard to know how she felt about the country. She had certainly been brought up around cows and crops and barnyards belonging to her mother and stepfather. But sixteen-year-olds often look on compost with indifference. As for the castle that was Micael's new home, it had been used as a fortress until the fifteenth century, and then as a bastion of the bishops of Senlis. Oddly constructed and always in shadow, the château even now has about it an unsettling peculiarity. Here, behind stone parapets moist since the Middle Ages, Micael moved in with three generations of Célestin's relatives: his parents, his aunt, and his aunt's aunt.[4] Her own mother rented a house in a lively part of Paris.

Pontalba did not immediately detest his son's wife, or if he did, he nevertheless treated her well at the outset. He brought her fruit and flowers—a casual enough courtesy in a country infatuated with horticulture—and he apparently tendered some jewelry and furniture. (Pontalba listed these as "investments" in the property inventories he drew up after his relations with his daughter-in-law had soured.) It seems true that in the beginning Micael "found hearts happy at their possessing her," just as Célestin's lawyer later insisted to a tribunal at Senlis.[5]

Even if he had not been a bargainer, the elder Pontalba would have been impatient to see the marriage agreement his wife had concluded in New Orleans. Dowries were a serious matter in any French family. Every marriage was first and foremost a business arrangement turning on the wife's dowry and on her expected inheritance. When the contract was at last brought out after the long delays of the voyage and welcoming formalities, it threw Pontalba (who anguished over any bad deal) into a state of stunned disappointment. He had perhaps expected to get the bulk of the Almonester fortune in the dowry. Instead, the document gave him outright only forty thousand dollars from Almonester's estate.[6] There was more to the dowry, to be sure, but it was to be disbursed by Micael's mother according to specific rules and with unequivocal contingencies.

Possibly because he was in shock, Pontalba continued his solicitations toward Micael for some months. But gradually the full implications of the marriage settlement became clear to him as he ruminated more and more on "the fact that the young wife had arrived despoiled."[7] The dowry then became the only serious matter in the marriage. It was a stain on Micael's existence, spreading and deepening with the passage of time, so that even the old man's death failed to eradicate it. Thirty-five years after the wedding, Célestin was still seeking redress in the courts for a dotal contract by which, he asserted, he had been grievously cheated.

The terms of the contract signed by Célestin's mother and Madame Castillon in 1811, a contract analyzed and attacked in legal proceedings long after Micael was a grandmother, were as follows: Micael brought to the union a cash sum of $40,000, which was said to be her share of her father's estate. (The remaining three-fourths of Almonester's legacy stayed in the possession of Madame Castillon, including the part inherited by Micael's sister which had passed to Madame Castillon when the child died.) Madame

Castillon added to the dowry another $5,000 in jewels. She promised, with strings, an additional $85,000. Part of this generous gift Madame Castillon planned to bestow in a lump sum after she sold some houses; these were listed in the contract together with their locations and appraisals. The remainder of the promised money, amounting to $52,000, would be paid out of the rents expected from her house which was still under construction at the corner of St. Peter's Street and the Place d'Armes. The young couple would get half of the revenues from this mansion, that is, about $6,000 or $7,000 a year, until the $52,000 was amortized.[8]

This, then, was the dowry:

	$40,000	Cash
	$5,000	Jewels
$85,000	$33,000	A lump sum promised after the sale of houses
	$52,000	Rents, to be paid at the rate of $6,000 or $7,000 annually
	$130,000	Dollars total
	(650,000	Francs total)

It is difficult now to judge whether Pontalba had a right to expect more. First, there no longer exists any precise document, such as an inventory, specifying Almonester's cash assets at the time of his death. Moreover, there is now no way to ascertain how much of that cash Micael's mother spent between the time of Almonester's death and Micael's marriage thirteen years later—Castillon spent at least $20,000 of his wife's money before death reduced his expenses. Second, there was no hard and fast rule, either in France or New Orleans, governing the size of dowries, except that the donor offered the smallest amount necessary to confirm the betrothal. Comparisons do not help us much because dowries showed surprising disparities.[9] Considering that 1,200 francs a year was deemed sufficient to support a family of four, and that schoolteachers were paid between 100 and 400 francs a year, Micael's dowry of 650,000 francs should have been an assuaging settlement, even for hands as open as Pontalba's. But there was an attendant stipulation: the last $85,000 (425,000 francs) would be paid only if Pontalba gave the same amount in money or property to his son, a condition to which Ton-Ton de Pontalba had already agreed on behalf of her husband, and which was, in fact, a commonplace provision.[10]

To Pontalba, the contract meant that he and Célestin would get control of a mere fraction of Madame Castillon's fortune, $40,000, plus some jewels that his son could not wear and was forbidden by law to sell. The rest of the dowry would trickle in over the years, canceled out by the disbursements Pontalba would be required to match. The greatest part of the Almonester inheritance remained in the hands of his widow, where, in the interesting words of one of Célestin's attorneys, it "had been exposed to the hazards of a second marriage and might be called on to run the risks of a third hymen." The lawyer expressed Pontalba's disgust with the whole arrangement when he dismissed the dowry as "a few diamonds and cross of the Order of Charles III . . . a piece of land under water. . . ."

As Madame Castillon's only living child, Micael would have eventually received everything left behind by either of her parents, but Pontalba preferred an immediate endowment to a deferred inheritance. It was true Célestin could not sell any part of Micael's dowry or even use it as collateral. "The dowry of a wife is always inviolable," said Célestin's own lawyer in conceding the point; the attorney, however, could not resist adding that "if such a principle had not already been recognized, she [Micael] would have herself invented it." But it was equally true that only the husband could administer the dotal assets. Once surrendered, the dowry was out of Micael's hands, according to law in both France and Louisiana. If the dowry consisted of cash, the husband could invest it as he saw fit; if real estate, he could lease it out; if dividends or rental payments, he could spend them. And if he liked, he could turn all of it over to his father to manage for him. When Célestin protested in one of his petitions that Micael's dowry was his "private property" which helped him defray the expenses of the marriage, he was wrong only in his choice of words; it was not private, but it was his. He was entirely correct in stating that his wife "had no right to claim or interfere in the administration, management, or collection or disposition" of her dowry.[11]

With inherited property, the husband's prerogatives were more confined. In France, he alone had the right to manage his wife's inheritance; he needed her consent only to sell her patrimony. But in Louisiana, an heiress' eager spouse had no legal control over her legacy. Micael's inheritance was exclusively hers to manage.[12] Since the Almonester property was located in Louisiana, Pontalba knew that any dispute concerning it would have to be settled in courts where laws favoring Micael would prevail.

Pontalba unquestionably regarded Micael's dowry as critical to the union. It is therefore difficult to understand why he sent his wife, whom he hardly trusted with traveling money, to negotiate the vital contract. Célestin's own attorney remarked that when the document was signed, Pontalba should have been there "to weigh its terms, think over its clauses." His absence "helped to perpetuate a fatal wrong," the barrister opined, which was "now beyond mending." Certainly, Pontalba must have pressed a hundred instructions on his wife before sending her off to America; and almost as certainly, Ton-Ton de Pontalba put them out of her mind, as was her wont, the moment she boarded the ship.

But for all that, Madame Castillon hardly seems to have carried off any clever stratagem in the marriage contract. Although she was careful not to relinquish her most valuable property to the Pontalbas, she gave them a placating promise of cash with an earnest description of how the funds were to be procured and distributed. Cash money was scarce; her offer of regular payments should have been appealing. Moreover, Madame de Pontalba was not unaided in making the pact, since her cousin St. Avid was at her side in Louisiana and advised her; he apparently thought the settlement fair enough. The only great fault Pontalba could have found in the agreement was the provision, smartingly obvious in the contract, that for Célestin to get the last $85,000 of the dowry from Madame Castillon, Pontalba had to "give the same sum to his son, and in the same proportional payments."

Faced with a contract "blindly signed" in his name and a young woman ratified by everyone as his son's wife, Pontalba "closed his eyes to the deceptions practiced in the dowry," according to Célestin's lawyer, and did what he had to do; he made an obligation to his son for $85,000. Madame Castillon had already given the newlyweds $40,000; Pontalba promised that the same amount would be paid to Célestin with interest whenever he requested it, providing his son gave him six months' notice. The remaining money Pontalba would pay to him in the form of yearly rents from property in New Orleans.

All of the terms of the Almonester-Pontalba contract were thus ostensibly fulfilled. If Pontalba had complied with them in fact and had simply paid off the dowry obligation, it would not now be possible to examine Micael de Pontalba's marriage in thousands of pages of court proceedings, paid for line by line by people who learned even to hate margins. But Pontalba had no intention of giving dowries to anyone. He continued to receive the rents from his (that is, his son's) New Orleans houses as he had always done, sued or evicted his tenants, leased property, and only occasionally pretended that he was acting as Célestin's agent.[13] No money seems to have changed hands between father and son.

As for the $85,000 cash on demand with interest, Célestin simply never demanded it. Soon after she was settled in Mont-l'Évêque, Micael, "while giving some little care to the rearranging of the interior of her husband's study," discovered a paper in his desk; it was Célestin's vow to his father, recklessly committed to writing, that he would never under any circumstances ask for the promised money. This was Micael's first inkling that the Pontalbas had something in mind other than ensuring a nest egg for the marriage. She did not then confront Célestin with the note, probably hesitating to admit that she had rummaged through his desk. But "life became complicated," according to her lawyer, and "clouds began to appear" over Mont-l'Évêque's tranquil gardens.

The next move by the father and son against Madame Castillon was made openly. Micael at seventeen was still sufficiently pliant to sign whatever her husband put before her. On May 7, 1813, soon after Célestin was released from the army, he had her relinquish to him complete control of all her money, property, and possessions. She gave him authority to collect her rents in New Orleans, dispose of her houses as he wished, to represent her in any court, foreign or French, and in a significant provision, to appear in any legal action that concerned her, "particularly in the succession of Monsieur Almonester." This was the first step. The moment Micael lifted the quill from her signature, the elder Pontalba filed a lawsuit in New Orleans against Micael's mother, challenging her right to possess any part of Almonester's legacy.[14] Pontalba apparently hoped that if Almonester's succession could be revoked, the old man's fortune would go directly to Micael who was still a minor. Célestin, now Micael's legal guardian, could thus acquire control over the total inheritance without the inconvenience of waiting for his mother-in-law to die.

It is not clear whether Micael at first understood that the sweeping power of attorney she gave Célestin would be used to attack her mother and the entire succession, rather than to make an adjustment "in Micael's interest," as the Pontalbas assured her. She was either pregnant at the time or had just given birth to a baby who died the following year. Moreover, she was still in the thrall of her father-in-law; his "delicate attentions" filled her with "tender gratitude," she later explained, and made her reluctant to question his actions. The lawsuit was apparently filed by Pontalba, the father, through his intermediary St. Avid, and was withdrawn before it reached trial. Many years after the suit was dropped, Micael's grandson repeated the story that

Micael herself brought the suit, intending to gain access to her inheritance because Madame Castillon was squandering money in Paris. However, nothing of the kind is revealed in the descriptions of the Pontalba versus Castillon affair which turn up in later Pontalba suits.[15]

In fact, far from misspending her daughter's inheritance, Madame Castillon was enhancing it with an aptitude that would have delighted Almonester. Soon after arriving in Paris, she bought a townhouse on the elegant Place Vendôme large enough for several residences for the price of 222,500 francs, or $44,500. She paid off the mortgage within four years and by 1820 had all the apartments leased out for three, six, or nine years at a net revenue of more than $25,000 a year. (Despite the notorious deterioration of Paris buildings, Micael was able to sell Place Vendôme in 1864 for a solid $320,000, to the city of Paris, in order to make way for the reconstruction of the capital.) In 1819 Madame Castillon purchased adjoining houses at 341 and 343 rue St. Honoré from Casimir-Pierre Périer, soon to be prime minister of France. The houses contained forty rooms and cost $60,000. This mortgage was amortized in only two years, during which time the rentals on the first stories of apartments and ground floor shops produced a heartening return of at least $20,000 on her investment.[16] Louison may not have approved of philanthrophy, but in other ways she must have been exactly what Almonester was looking for in a widow.

Pontalba's petition attacked the Almonester succession from many sides. Louise de la Ronde had been poor when she married Almonester, whose preponderant wealth was amassed before the marriage. There was therefore very little property acquired during the community, Pontalba asserted, and Louison had no right to the usual widow's portion, half of the estate.[17] Madame Castillon had refused, he claimed, to render him an accounting of her guardianship, that is, how she spent Micael's money during the years she held it in trust. Pontalba demanded an investigation of her management and a current inventory of the "goods and possessions" of the estate. He pointed out that in the inventory made after Almonester's death, she had left out the money paid to her by the City of New Orleans for the Cabildo. At the death of Micael's sister Andrea in 1801, the widow inherited another quarter of the property. Pontalba alleged that her rights to this deceased daughter's portion ended with her second marriage.[18]

Pontalba's most consequential charge was that Louison had acquired her children's rights to the properties on the Place d'Armes through an improper

procedure in the succession. He therefore demanded that the entire estate—
the cash, houses, slaves, and stores—be reconstituted as it was at Almonester's death and put in Micael's possession, or rather in the possession of her
new guardian, Célestin. To assist the court in figuring out how much
Madame Castillon owed the estate, Pontalba wrote a long memoir on Almonester's resources, listing debts owed to the *regidor* at his death ("6,000
dollars by M. Sigu [Sigur], 17,000 by M. Maxent . . ."), and pointing out
certain economies in Almonester's system which should have added to the
widow's holdings.[19]

Everything Madame Castillon owned was at stake; she defended herself
with appropriate vehemence. If she were to give an account of her management of the inheritance, she replied in her petition, she would deduct the
ponderable cost of raising her daughter for fifteen years before the marriage.
The cottages she acquired on the square were wooden and flimsy; after her
husband's death, she had them replaced with buildings that were brick, fire-
proof, and elevated to protect against flood. Moreover, to the estate she held
in trust for her daughter she had added a mansion that was bringing in rents
of twelve hundred dollars a month. If the Pontalbas wanted the estate as it
was at Almonester's death, she concluded, they would have to pay her for all
the rebuilding.

While the suit against her mother was advanced by the Pontalbas, Micael
still had not perceived "the thought which dominated the family," or so she
later averred. She continued to communicate with her mother, who apparently did not hold her responsible for the lawsuit. In fact, during her first
pregnancy in 1813, Micael spent a good many weeks in Paris near Madame
Castillon. As the time approached for Micael's confinement, Célestin displayed a foresight that was to become characteristic in his later years. He
came to her with a prepared will, short and uncomplicated, stating that if she
died in childbirth, the Pontalbas, not her mother, would inherit her total fortune. Her husband told her that in taking this "precaution," she would
greatly please him and his father. She signed the "Plan for a Will," as the Pontalbas called the document, but the incident troubled her, and she began,
finally, to have misgivings about the marriage.[20]

According to Micael's version of the events that followed, the Pontalbas
then took her away from Paris, abruptly and without explanation, first
to their estate Migneaux, near Versailles, and from there to Mont-l'Évêque
where her son was born. Her mother was not permitted to see her even

during the birth, nor was she allowed near her newborn grandson, Joseph Michel Célestin. The Pontalbas' version was that Madame Castillon "saw her daughter as much as she wanted to." Célestin's lawyer further remarked, "I do not see how she could have been prevented without the actual confinement of Madame de Pontalba, something not very easy under our habits of life, nor likely under those of the husband, and impossible under those of the wife, whom it would have been necessary to hold under a private charter." Of course, it was not necessary to deny Micael permission to travel, even when pregnancy did not impede her. As Célestin showed many times during the marriage, it was only necessary to forbid the coachmen to leave the grounds of Mont-l'Évêque. The France of 1813 was vast; Micael could make no journey to Paris alone.

Confining women for the purpose of extorting money from them or their relatives was an occasional practice among the well-to-do, according to contemporary novels such as Honoré de Balzac's *Eugénie Grandet*. In his memoirs, the baron de Frénilly described with malicious pleasure the nonfictional misfortunes of Madame Lavoisier, widow of the famous scientist. Married at fourteen, she became her husband's translator and valued research partner. That idyllic union ended during the French Revolution when both her husband and her father were executed on the same day in 1792. Her second husband, a chemist named Rumford, found her presence dispensable. Soon after their marriage in 1801, he had the gate to her house hermetically sealed, put her under guard, and finally locked her in the cellar until her relatives offered him a ransom he deemed acceptable. He then released her and left town. Frénilly described how the majority of Parisians laughed at the matter: "This poor woman, with her philosophy, her liberalism, and her mustache, interested no one."[21]

We cannot be certain whether Micael was forcibly isolated from her mother in any such fashion, but within a year Madame Castillon gave in and surrendered much of what the Pontalbas were after. On February 25, 1814, a "compromise" was drawn up between Madame Castillon and Pontalba, the father, duly notarized by Guibourg of Senlis. In exchange for having the succession suit in New Orleans dropped, Madame Castillon added to Micael's dowry all the houses on the left side of the Place d'Armes except for the new mansion. Madame Castillon was to retain control of the right side and continue to enjoy her deceased daughter's portion of the inheritance; she would render no accounting of the rents she collected while guardian of

Micael's estate; and she would be acquitted of the obligation to make the yearly payments promised as part of the original dowry (Madame Castillon's promises of cash had been fulfilled; $52,000 only remained on the annual rents).

Madame Castillon made a few significant conditions: Célestin was not to collect the rents without Micael's express permission, a provision that would be unhesitatingly ignored as soon as the blotter was lifted from the document's last signature, as Micael was still a minor and could not even accept the donation except through her husband.[22] Célestin would surrender the power of attorney his wife had given him. Pontalba would withdraw a second legal action he was pressing in New Orleans. Not content merely to sue her, Pontalba had filed another petition to force Madame Castillon to pay court costs in the succession case he brought against her. The terms in the agreement which affected Célestin were accepted by Pontalba in his son's behalf. Pontalba was likewise freed of the obligation to match a portion of the dowry dollar for dollar. That meant that Pontalba had slipped out of the $85,000 matching obligation of the dowry. He agreed instead to give Célestin some property in Louisiana. But this commitment, too, was to be circumvented. A month after the "compromise," there was another of the Pontalbas' inspired transactions. Célestin transferred the rents from this same Louisiana property back to his father in exchange for the two farms at Mont-l'Évêque.[23] The new document clearly stated, however, that his father would retain all of the farms' revenues.

Thus did Pontalba manage to revoke the hated marriage contract. The gates of Mont-l'Évêque were once again opened to Madame Castillon. She took the precaution during this period of amnesty of buying a small cottage from the Pontalbas on the "highway" leading to the estate, to ensure that she could not be kept away from her daughter in the future. Mother and daughter were probably together in Paris on December 19, 1814, when Micael's first son died there. The baby was buried two days later at Mont-l'Évêque; Micael was already a few weeks into her second pregnancy.[24] Relieved of the Pontalba lawsuit and resigned to the loss of a great part of her Vieux Carré property, Louison turned her attention to real estate in France. She purchased houses in Paris, settling herself at Place Vendôme with several layers of tenants, the wealthiest sharing the lower level with a shop, and the poorest family installed just under the roof, for in Paris the indigent were customarily placed closest to God.[25] The cottage at Mont-l'Évêque served her on such occasions as the birth of her other grandchildren, or the periodic signing of notarial acts which Pontalba continued to sponsor throughout the next years. Sensible woman that she was, Madame Castillon now saw to it that she invested her money in property that would be hard for the Pontalbas to steal after her death.

After such wrangling over the dowry, we might wonder if any hope of compatibility remained for the young Pontalbas. But in fact, after the crisis between her in-laws and her mother, Micael still traveled at her husband's side, had children with him, made over more of her inheritance to him. People in France were accustomed to tolerating intolerable spouses. The law discouraged premature exasperation, and in any case, it appears that Micael did not yet regard her marriage as insupportable, marked though it was by a continual reassignment of assets. Nearly all respectable people married for either money or position, marriages of inclination being considered dé-classé. Moreover, as a critic of French habits observed, "The preliminaries of wedlock are all arranged by third parties. One is spared here the happy wretchedness of falling in love."[26] Those preliminaries included lining up the resources that would support the new family.

Nevertheless, if Pontalba's preoccupation with Micael's dowry did not seem as vulgar to his contemporaries as it seems to us, it was extreme. He exceeded the boundaries of permissible avarice when he wriggled out of the obligations of a marriage contract on the one hand, and on the other, tried to turn all of the property of the bride's family into a dowry. Marrying the wealthiest heiress one could find, getting a fine settlement, insisting on the dowry payments—this was a common enough course of action. Confis-cating the girl's inheritance before both her parents died—that was a suffi-cient attack on the established matrimonial system to make all parents un-easy.

After the 1814 "compromise," the father and son were appeased for a time. Instead of a promise of $52,000, they now had property worth two or three times as much, which supplied yearly revenues of some $17,000. Moreover, Pontalba's own position was not bad. In 1810 he had been awarded the title of baron by Napoleon's government, after applying and lobbying for the reward in the customary fashion. Napoleon created 1,552 new barons along with assorted other nobiliary types, giving the title to mayors of large cities, for example. Pontalba's grant did not include an en-tailed estate—in fact, he had to buy his own *majorat*, Mont-l'Évêque, to qualify for the title—but in any case he could proudly call himself Baron of the Empire, and he began prefixing *de* to his name.[27] Why did Napoleon single out Pontalba? The memoir that Pontalba wrote would not have justified any such reward even if Napoleon had read it and followed Pontalba's eager advice concerning Louisiana. In fact, he did the opposite of what Pontalba suggested. Judging from the letters in Marshal Ney's papers regarding young Célestin, it appears that Ney's wife wrangled the title for her cousin Pontalba, just as she was responsible for getting Célestin his coveted position as Ney's aide-de-camp. The title did not make the Pontalbas part of France's old aristocracy, for upstart Napoleonic nobles were consistently snubbed by the ancient families. Only an old general like Marcel Proust's de Froberville might allow himself the tolerant observation that "this Empire nobility, well, of course it's not like us, but just the same, for what it is, it's very fine of its kind; some of those people fought like real heroes in battle."[28] Xavier de Pontalba was not one of them, but he had his barony anyway.

Like the Napoleonic nobility in general, Pontalba prospered during the Bourbon restoration.[29] He dabbled in credit. It was common for people such as Pontalba to hold a property mortgage together with five or six other creditors; according to the inventory made at his death, Pontalba held part-interest in several such mortgages. This handwritten inventory, which describes sheet by sheet every receipt, debt, contract, and account in Pontalba's personal files, would give us exhaustive information about his financial affairs, if anyone could read it. Even so, we learn from the document's occasional certain word that Pontalba's main income came from rents and leases. In this he was like most of the old and new nobility of France.[30]

In 1806 he bought two rental houses in Paris on rue de Provence and rue St. Honoré, both good deals.[31] In 1823 he was able to exchange the house on rue de Provence for a more valuable château and estate, Migneaux, in Verrières, a property that included farms, mills, woods, and houses. At Xavier de Pontalba's death, the notaries required many pages to list the buildings, facilities, and strips of land at Migneaux which had been leased out year after year.[32] Likewise, he kept 256 St. Honoré constantly rented, mainly to shopkeepers who took six- or nine-year leases. His great-grandson was still renting it in 1879, to a tenant whose lease ran until 1906.[33] Another house the Pontalbas bought soon after they settled in Paris, on rue Argenteuil, continued to attract tenants for long leases when Célestin was an old man. The most impressive moneymaker was a house covering two addresses and several stories at 348–350 St. Honoré, just across the *rue* from Madame

Castillon's rental place. The Pontalbas leased it and leased it, well into the twentieth century, with contracts that would be the envy of any landlord— 3,000 francs a year for twelve years for a boutique; 15,000 francs for an apartment for nine years, with the rent rising to 18,000 francs for the last six; 18,000 francs for a shop for fifteen years (this last arrangement was made in 1886 by Xavier's great-grandson). In 1817, Pontalba bought a *hôtel* on rue du Houssaie and gave it to his son.[34] In short, the father seems to have been doing well enough without Micael's property added to his fortune. But then, his periodic raids on her inheritance were probably motivated as much by revenge as by greed. Her mother had outwitted him, he thought, in the original marriage contract; perhaps he found relief from that humiliation in each of the finely calculated contracts which he subsequently forced on Micael.

Célestin de Pontalba seems to have had the same obsessive and legalistic turn as his father, though he was more elusive, and his impulses regarding Micael were, as might be expected, more complex. He accepted his father's control over his life, just as his father had been receptive to Miró's; but Célestin expected to be the dominating partner in other relationships. At times he was as protective as his father toward people who put themselves in his hands. But he was sly and defensive with equals. As long as Micael consented to any scheme he presented during the early years of their life together, he apparently gave her nothing to complain about in writing. But as she reached adulthood and began putting forward plans of her own, Célestin's reaction was to withdraw rather dramatically. A prefigurative incident occurred soon after their second child, Célestin II, was born. Célestin brought Micael and the baby to the Pontalbas' château at Migneaux for a summer holiday. There Micael awoke one morning to find that Célestin had disappeared with their son. According to the note he left for her, he did not intend to inform her of his whereabouts. The elder Pontalba, who alone knew the location of Célestin's retreat, would act as intermediary for any correspondence between them. Célestin declared that he was leaving in order to free himself from her "control" and did not want to see her until he had "mastered his weakness" from afar.[35]

Micael, at this time about twenty, sent a docile apology through her father-in-law, writing that she had not intended to exert any untoward influence in their marriage. Célestin was mollified by her contrition, motivated though it must have been by anxiety for her son. He sent, if not a love letter, at least a conciliatory reply: "It will be all the more fortunate for us both that I will not be giving you back a weak and blind husband who, by submitting to all your caprices and only lending ear to your will, made himself a weakling unworthy of your esteem." He continued the dialogue in a few more letters, explaining that he ran away because he could not bear to see old haunts and be reminded of his former happiness and courage. In the future, he promised her ominously, he would assume complete control over their life. Sounds as if they had had a heated argument during which she accused him of being weak.

But what exactly were these emasculating caprices? Looking past the rhetoric of the lawyers who quoted, paraphrased, and thus preserved Célestin's communications, it seems he was distraught because Micael wanted him to set up their own household separate from his parents.[36] In the United States, married children might establish independent residences as a matter of course. But in France, it was normal for a man to bring his wife to the family home. A few young women of the upper bourgeoisie insisted on their own homes, and gradually their demand spread to women of all ranks. But as an acquaintance of Micael's, the comtesse d'Armaille, observed in her memoirs, in the 1820s and 1830s the practice of moving away from parents "was only beginning, and only in certain circles."[37] Since Frenchmen were inclined to stay as close to their parents as accommodations would allow, the usual thing was to see "great phalansteries of families" ensconced in the enormous houses of the faubourgs. Célestin thought he was providing well enough for his wife when he offered her the third-best cell in the disintegrating château (Madame de Miró occupied the most habitable apartment) and the attentions of his parents' watchful servants.

Living with his parents was the main issue, but there had also been some unpleasantness over the matter of Micael's playhouse. It seems Célestin had allowed Micael to turn a large room at Mont-l'Évêque into a theater, a project that she approached with understandable enthusiasm; Mont-l'Évêque was probably a quiet place before she moved in, the sort of country estate described in the memoirs of the marquis de Belleval, where carving the dinner meat counted as a diversion.[38] Micael's plays were staged using local people and artists from Paris in the leading roles. Costumes were ordered for the productions. Enough of Micael's friends attended to provide an audience dryly described by Célestin's attorney as "the sort to be found in most salons of good taste: polished, indulgent, resigned." According to the same lawyer, Micael could bear life in the country only "on the days of Comedy, and could not feel happy in the fields except when tinsel and drama were also to be present." These were the problems that caused the first separation.

Célestin, finally confident that he could stand up to his wife, let her know he was in Geneva and sent for her (through his father) to join him. When the couple returned to Mont-l'Évêque, the tinsel and comedy were banished on Célestin's orders. But the Pontalba parents remained. However, Célestin soon gave in to his wife's insistence on a separate home, a capitulation which indicates that Micael did indeed have suasive powers over him. They moved into his father's house at Number 2 rue du Houssaie, a property worth about $60,000. Célestin then purchased two adjoining houses for $20,000 with money he received from his father through one of their complicated property exchanges intended to keep Célestin's acquisitions from becoming community property. Thus, in 1818 he had a rental income and a home, for lack of a better description, of his own.[39]

The house on rue du Houssaie held many charms for Micael. There were two children now, for Alfred was born in 1817. Her mother was nearby, busily turning her second fortune. Throughout the 1820s and beyond, friends and relatives from America passed through Paris and paid their respects.[40] Life at Mont-l'Évêque had been either silently hateful or explosively hateful, in dark, underfurnished rooms with barren cupboards. The painstaking inventory of the possessions in the château at the time of old Pontalba's death revealed sixteen rooms devoid of the material conveniences, not to say luxuries, found in normal wealthy homes. Micael had left cold hearts, to be sure, and also cold, shabby bedchambers. But the greatest comfort of Paris was that for the first time she could order her own life. Here the breakfast rolls from the bakery, the furniture she paid for herself, even the potted plants— though they may have looked like those in any townhouse on the boulevards—were of her own choosing. She could engage her child's wetnurse, instruct the servants, or select for her ablutions any day on which a water porter could be sighted on the street.[41] At Mont-l'Évêque, her very presence at the table had reminded the Pontalbas of disappointment and lost chances. Here there was no one to be reminded of anything. Except her husband, and often he was absent.

Until Madame Castillon's death in 1827, Célestin and Micael thus lived conventionally, if intermittently, in Paris as husband and heiress. In March, 1819, a daughter was born, Michaelle Célestine Mathilde, who was called Mathilde by the family. Having a little daughter at last must have given Micael a flicker of joy, but it was only a flicker. Mathilde died at Mont-l'Évêque in May, 1821, at the age of twenty-six months, leaving no record of the heartbreak with which she was buried. Though children died in droves, their parents generally suffered as piteously as if childhood death had not been a commonplace of the times. Micael was probably no more inured than anyone else to losing her little ones. Once again, she was a few weeks pregnant as she saw another of her infants sealed in the family tomb; a fourth son, Gaston, was born in 1821.[42]

By this time, Madame Castillon was too disillusioned with her son-in-law and his family to maintain even the appearance of amity. In 1821 she made a will awarding her daughter everything the law permitted her to assign, half of her worldly effects, but with the stipulation—ironically wistful considering that Micael was only days away from childbed and that she would bear five children in ten years—that all possessions were "to be enjoyed by her as if she were a wife separated from bed and board, without needing any authorization to administer these goods. . . ."[43] Thus, in the first sentence of the will, in the strongest language testamentary custom would allow, Madame Castillon excluded Célestin from the control of her property.

Louison used careful wording, expensive paper, elaborate authentication, and shrewd foresight in making the will. She instructed that her property in France be considered the disposable portion of her estate, the half that she was allowed to convey with conditions. Micael would inherit the New Orleans property as well; but her mother could not herself assign all of the estate or encumber it with provisions to protect it from the Pontalbas. Madame Castillon apparently thought she could rely on Louisiana courts to do that, to confirm that the right side of the Place d'Armes was Micael's separate property, outside of the marital community. She therefore reserved the protections of the will for the more vulnerable property in France, to ensure that it would be kept beyond the Pontalbas' ardent grasp.

Four years after sealing the will, Madame Castillon at the age of sixty-seven died at her home on the Place Vendôme. Micael later contended that she died of heartache over her daughter's marriage. Madame Castillon died during the night of December 15, 1825. She had been Micael's last protector. At one o'clock the following afternoon, Célestin appeared with Micael at the Palace of Justice in Paris to witness the opening of the will. The event "caused the greatest excitement among the family," Micael's lawyer observed.[44] During the reading, Célestin, giving in to what the barrister called "a tendency toward fantastic emotions," burst out angrily to Micael: "We will break that testament, Madame," he shouted. "Yes, Madame, we will break it."

But Célestin did not need to attack the will. A week after her mother's death, Micael signed a document carefully obviating all of Madame Castillon's protections, a document which, when it was finally examined by a magistrate, threw the jurist "into deep astonishment." According to what Célestin termed "a private contract" between them, Micael turned over her total fortune in New Orleans to her husband to administer as "his portion" of the Almonester-Castillon succession.[45] Célestin, "with a view to being agreeable" to his wife, "acquiesced" in allowing her to take control of her mother's property in France. An inventory found that Madame Castillon had about $7,000 in cash and valuables, and $53,000 in a bank at her death; her property on the Place Vendôme was assigned a value of $70,000 (350,000 francs); the house at 343 rue St. Honoré was valued at $173,000 (865,000 francs); the right side of the Place d'Armes was assigned a value of $96,000 (480,000 francs). Several adjustments were made to present the appearance of dividing the total estate evenly so that the property given over to Célestin in New Orleans equaled to the last cent the portion Micael would retain in France. After many pages of calculations, it was concluded that Célestin would receive $156,000 worth of property, all the future revenues from "his" portion, and a free hand in managing it.[46] Included in his share was $60,000 cash, a particular source of bitterness because Célestin took this money out of Madame Castillon's house when he was notified of her demise. Micael was allotted the rents from the other so-called half of her mother's estate, the property located in France. The left side of the Place d'Armes was of course not included in the calculations, having already been surrendered to Célestin in 1814 as an amended dowry. Célestin was thus in possession of all the property on the square. That was shocking enough, but Célestin's limitless arrogance becomes even more apparent when we examine the true value of the property Micael was allowed to keep. According to the "private contract," Madame Castillon's house on rue St. Honoré produced revenues of $86,000 in two years, in yearly "rents and equity," whatever that meant. The house on Place Vendôme was supposed to have produced $70,000 in four years, according to Célestin's odd addition. In reality, Micael's income from these properties was by then not nearly so much, according to her leases— perhaps $35,000. Whereas half of the Place d'Armes, Célestin's "share," was worth a good deal more than $96,000, a sum that a Louisiana Supreme Court judge eventually found to be a blatant underappraisal. Célestin seized far more than half of Micael's inheritance.

As to why Micael committed this notarized act of masochism, we cannot be certain. A possibility which may not be ruled out is that she was still unsure of her rights. Perhaps she believed the Pontalbas' claim, aggressively put forward then and always, that Célestin had the privilege as master of their marital community to collect all of her income, wherever her properties were located. In that case, she might have decided to strike a bargain with him that would leave her in control of at least some of her mother's money. True, there were people present at the drafting of the "private contract" who might have disabused her of the notion that Célestin had all rights over the property; but then, Célestin himself seemed unenlightened regarding the limitations of his control. Unfazed by American judges who some years later called the agreement between them "an act of spoliation," "an impossible transaction," and "a violation of all fair principles," when it was finally brought to light in a New Orleans courtroom, Célestin continued to press his claims to the Place d'Armes as relentlessly as if he himself believed in them.

Another explanation for Micael's signing away half her money is that she hoped to keep Célestin from abandoning her by giving him the French Quarter revenues to which he was so unfortunately addicted. This would assume that Micael loved her husband, or at least needed him near her now that her mother was dead. It would also suggest, with less probability, that when Micael was thirty years old and had been married to Célestin for fourteen years, she could still be manipulated into doing anything he wanted. However, the "private contract" does not have the tone of a lovelorn submission. Like a dozen other such documents that Célestin co-authored with his father, echoes of sniping rise from the paper as soon as it is unfolded. With no pretense to solicitude, Célestin "pledges himself to furnish her with necessary funds" for repairs to her half of the property, but she "must pay her husband 5 percent interest" on all loans.[47] Micael allows him to tear down her mother's cottage at Mont-l'Évêque "to use the materials in building a tombstone for Madame Castillon." Both of them will share the expenses of opening the succession. It is a coldhearted document on both sides.

The rationalization which makes the most sense is that Micael forfeited half of her property in return for the privilege of remaining in Paris. French law did not permit divorce. A Frenchman could legally separate from his wife if she were proved adulterous. A wife who wanted a separation was unlikely to admit to adultery for the sake of getting her freedom; the civil code specifically stated that any wife guilty of adultery would receive a compulsory prison sentence of three months to two years. In the courts, a wife's affair was commonly referred to as a "criminal liaison."[48] A husband could informally separate from his wife merely by leaving, so long as he continued to provide for her. But a wife was required to take on her husband's nationality and live with him wherever he chose. If she ran away, like the slaves of New Orleans, or refused to follow him where he ordered her, she could be charged with criminal desertion. He could then take control of all of her assets, *whether communal or not, and preclude her access to their children.*[49] A bed and board separation would have been available to Micael only if Célestin had forced her to live under the same roof with his concubine.[50] The law did not offer the least relief from having to live with his parents. Célestin could certainly compel Micael to return to Mont-l'Évêque. In contrast to many of his "rights," this was a real one, and when the "private contract" between them broke down, he enforced it. Therefore, in order to stay in Paris and maintain at least some contact with her children, she probably bought him off with the Place d'Armes property.

With their respective dominions staked out, what happened next seems predictable. On January 23, 1827, three weeks after Micael signed over control of the Place d'Armes to him, Célestin left the breakfast table at rue du Houssaie for a proposed hunting trip to Mont-l'Évêque. The next day he had one of Micael's women friends deliver a message to her: his living with her was a thing of the past. He would henceforth reside with his parents, either at Mont-l'Évêque or at one of their other homes. A notarized paper followed, of course. Micael was to live at rue du Houssaie. Célestin granted her the authority to rent parts of the house and use the income however she liked. In addition, he would give her three thousand francs a month (six hundred dollars) which, had it been paid, would have been less than a fourth of the amount he was collecting monthly from her houses in New Orleans.[51] The timing of his departure was, it seems, a surprise. He carried out the separation so as to embarrass her publicly—making it official through his notary, and so forth—which indicates that he was angry and perhaps ambivalent. Célestin apparently wanted Micael to move back to Mont-l'Évêque with him, although not with the intensity that he wanted her to give him the houses on the Place d'Armes. When she refused to leave Paris, he took pains to let everyone know he was rejecting her. But as he was somewhat pacified by the "private contract," he carried his spite no further than the notary's office and did not force her to return to his family's home—yet.

Was that really all there was to the separation—Célestin's greed coupled with Micael's refusal to live with his parents? If only we might find somewhere a single, fusty packet of letters which could tell us that Micael had a whole other life passionately devoted to velocipedes, or Englishmen, or a short, jolly gentleman with pink cheeks. Unless there are such documents, then for our purposes there was no passion, either, no other issue in the separation. Nothing Micael lived through is real to us now except those experiences that were recorded in some way and saved. Without some dated paper to certify its existence, a devastating love affair or even a quiet, happy decade of marriage can slip invisibly through the finest net of research. The same is true of Célestin. Did he have hobbies, mistresses, sufferings, or redeeming features, other than his face, that might explain him? Whatever there was of Célestin that cannot be traced to greed or filial guilt is lost now—it is at best hearsay or rumor. A few words spoken before a notary, on the other hand, a thoughtless note on a scrap of foolscap, a tooth surgeon's bill—these are the admissible evidences of life. With time they become more real, more biographic, than a lifetime of unremarked patience, wordless tenderness, or robust teeth. The documents of Micael's and Célestin's marriage are clumsy guides to a complicated relationship. An outline of sorts appears as we progress through the months and years of letters, notarial records, and court proceedings; but like the numbered dots in a child's workbook, the finished sketch leaves much to be imagined and presumed. Considering the inherent vagaries of marriage and fidelity, and considering that we are often hard put to explain the separations and reconciliations of people we talk with every day, it should not surprise us that the only thing we know with certainty about Micael and Célestin is that they found wedlock an uncomfortable container for their love.

The ensuing two-year estrangement was one of the happier periods of the marriage. Célestin made a habit of sending his wife produce from the gardens at Mont-l'Évêque, meat from his hunts, flowers, fruit, and even, as Micael's attorney slyly noted later on, "the results of his industry, screens magnificently embroidered." Micael claimed she still had the needlework in her possession ten years afterward, though the court record does not show whether Célestin acknowledged the embroidery as his own. Célestin went to New Orleans and made extensive improvements on his recent acquisitions on the square, all financed by his father. In 1825 he also purchased other property in Louisiana, but managed to keep it out of the purview of community property by a perfunctory assertion that he was acting as his father's agent.[52] Micael's feelings toward him during this period are expressed in a letter to her notary:

> You have misunderstood my letter, Monsieur, in thinking that I wanted to go live at Mont-l'Évêque. I have never had that fantasy. . . . When the time seems right to me, either I will go with my husband or we will get a separation of property; right now I don't want either one or the other. . . . My husband is too devoted to me not to love me always; they can't take away the friendship which is in the depths of his heart for me. I am sure of being well received at Mont-l'Évêque, for he told me himself to come whenever I felt like it; and if he had not told me, I know anyway his kindness and his feelings toward me which nothing will change, no more than I will change in my deep friendship for him, which is worth more than love.[53]

Even when we consider that the letter was edited by Célestin's lawyer before he presented it to the Senlis court, these are significant musings. If it is authentic—and it may not be—the letter suggests that the single issue which kept the couple apart was Micael's refusal to live at Mont-l'Évêque. No matter what recriminations or qualifications one imagines in the omitted portions of the letter, the document shows that Micael looked kindly on Célestin even after he had appropriated half of her property. Moreover, she still had the illusion (or perhaps Célestin's promise?) that a formal separation was an option available to her if she could not bring herself to live at Mont-l'Évêque. She did not entertain the idea, however, that Célestin would ever be persuaded to stay in Paris with her. If one doubted that there really was a nineteenth-century mentality and that it was different from ours, one has only to read the references to the young husband's "kindness" and the young wife's "deep friendship." And one wonders how a twenty-seven-year-old woman in a hostile family arrived at the conclusion that friendship is worth more than love. As for Micael's assessment of Célestin's state of mind, her confidence that he loved her, perhaps she was trying to convince herself that her own warm feelings were reciprocated. Perhaps she was a woman of the Romantic period, in love with sentiment. Or perhaps she knew him.

In any case, the friendly armistice came to an end when Célestin refused to honor one of the terms of their "private contract," his commitment to lend Micael cash at interest for repairing her mother's houses. The mansion on the Place Vendôme was an old building in need of extensive renovation. When Micael asked to borrow $25,000 from him to help pay for the work, Célestin demurred, saying he could not release such a large sum at once.[54] She then planned to borrow the money from a bank, a resource that exacted the same interest as her husband. Since a married woman could not contract debts without her spouse's consent, she sought his permission to make the loan. Célestin, seeing an opportunity to leach a bit more from the Castillon succession, replied (by way of a messenger) that he would consent to the loan if she would exclude from the division of the Castillon estate the $60,000 he had taken out of Louison's deathhouse. He had spent more than that, he stated, making improvements on the property on the Place d'Armes. He did not reiterate what Micael well knew: that he, not she, was the beneficiary of these improvements since the increased rents from the buildings were now his. She should excuse him from having to account for this money and, in effect, halve the estate all over again as if he had not already received $60,000 from it.

At this point, strengthened by two years in an independent household, or perhaps discouraged from trying to bargain further with her husband, Micael decided it was "urgent for her to become enlightened as to her own rights." She consulted a lawyer, Jean-Charles Persil, who wrote out "in an irrevocable manner" the prerogatives of all parties.[55] When she looked at the sheet of lawyers' notepaper on which he had set down the rights of husband and wife, Micael understood, though probably not for the first time, that Célestin had no claim whatever to any of her rentals except those specified in the original marriage contract of 1811. The agreement made by Madame Castillon (in which she added the left half of the Place d'Armes to the dowry in exchange for the withdrawal of Pontalba's suit against her) was without legal standing, a document that Micael's second lawyer described as the act of "a badly frightened mother." Micael's agreement to divide her inheritance with her husband was likewise not binding. The courts in New Orleans, she was informed, would immediately place her again in possession of her fortune, *both* sides of the Place d'Armes. She had, however, to make an appearance in Louisiana in person. It is not clear whether Persil explained to Micael the possible penalty for exercising her rights: that when she came back from America, Célestin might force her to return to Mont-l'Évêque.

Micael's three children were living in boarding schools selected by their grandfather. She had no close family in Paris, and she had not seen her aunt and cousin in New Orleans for almost twenty years. She therefore packed her warm-weather clothes, locked her apartment on rue du Houssaie, and without asking her husband's permission to leave the country, as she was legally required to do, made her escape to New Orleans.

VI

We All Live Here

THE progress and decay of nineteen years had changed New Orleans. In 1811, Micael left a French city where Americans, though numerous, were still regarded as a foreign element by everyone but themselves. In 1830, when she returned, New Orleans was an American metropolis full of new businesses and lately acquired wealth, all reaching out from an old French quarter at the center. The courts still operated tolerantly in two languages. But except in the Old Quarter which was their stronghold, Micael's people were considered a retrograde minority. The population was reaching toward 75,000. Plantations once isolated below the crescent of the river had been subsumed by the city, the land cut up into lots and sold. A pumping system drained streets that Micael may never have seen, since they were under water during most of her youth. There were paving stones and shade trees on a few avenues. Above Carondelet's old canal, cypress swamp had turned into suburbs for wealthy American speculators in sugar and cotton. To this day the division between uptown and downtown remains Canal Street, without the canal.[1]

The Quarter where Micael must have once known every house was now crowded with stores and commercial traffic. The ugly parade ground of the Place d'Armes still resisted all landscaping efforts and probably looked the same as twenty years before; but the St. Louis Cathedral where Micael's father and sister were buried had a clock tower, a genteel promontory with a bell-shaped dome; it was hardly recognizable as Almonester's Spanish church. The Cabildo remained the miserable habitation of criminals as well as the seat of government; since the price of everything had risen, the cost was now twenty-five cents to have a slave whipped at the jail in City Hall. The Presbytere was divided into seven stores with apartments above, all let out at high rents. Like other buildings still unfinished when Micael left, it had grown old while she was gone. Madame Castillon's former mansion, with its airy apartment designated, even on the blueprints, "for Mlle. Micael," was now rented to Célestin's tenants, with the ground floor taken over by shops. For a long time the upper floors were occupied by the infamous

Tremoulets, who kept there one of the few French-speaking hotels in the area, noted for its filth.[2]

On both sides of the square, the most recent and vivid changes were those made by Célestin. With the signing of the "family pact" in 1827, Célestin had been left in possession of all of Micael's Place d'Armes property. He lost no time getting to New Orleans, making improvements to the houses—twice, since after the first renovation the plaza was swept by one of its periodic fires—and raising the rents. By the time Micael arrived in New Orleans in 1830, Almonester's buildings were known to everyone as the property of a Monsieur de Pontalba of France, whose father's agent collected the rents. Possibly the tenants had never heard of Almonester's daughter.[3]

Micael landed on December 4, 1830, with two servants.[4] Though she was set upon by a flock of relatives, she managed to get to Parish Court the very day after her arrival to begin the legal process of reclaiming her property. Célestin was initially represented by a court-appointed attorney who argued first that Micael had never made "amicable demand" for the return of her rents, and second that the houses in question were not her separate property. The lawyer admitted, however, in what he thought was English, that "the property claimed in the plaintiff petition, as her paraphernal property, did belonging to the joint States of her father and mother."[5]

Just as her attorney in France had promised, the judge, James Pitot, dismissed all such protests and put Micael in control of all of her inherited property, both the left side of the square that her mother had yielded to the elder Pontalba in 1814, and the right side that she herself had surrendered to Célestin in 1827—altogether a yearly income of forty thousand dollars. Micael's rights to the Place d'Armes were thus confirmed temporarily. But the quarrel over whether the French Quarter real estate was part of her dowry or her separate property was to continue for nine long years, ending in the Louisiana Supreme Court in 1839. Micael apparently realized even as she filed her first suit that any single court ruling was likely to be only a pause in a long contest. She and Célestin might swap the same winnings—her property—back and forth for years. Either she or her lawyers therefore conceived the idea of threatening her husband with a Louisiana divorce, perhaps hoping to dissuade him from further litigation over the Place d'Armes. A week after the Parish Court's decision, she wrote to him:

> Monsieur,
> Surrounded by many good friends and assisted by able lawyers, I have been seriously reflecting on my situation. . . . Monsieur Desuauneaux, my business

representative, who will hand you this letter and forward me your answer, will let you know of my conditions. As I wish to enjoy some peace of mind, I must inform you that if you refuse to accept without restrictions all of the conditions proposed to you by Monsieur Desuauneaux, *my mind is irrevocably made up. I will ask for and obtain a divorce. . . .*[6]

The demands were: First, Célestin must acquiesce in the judgment of the New Orleans court and cooperate in securing a similar judgment in France giving her control of her property in Paris. Second, he must give up the eternal quest for the $52,000 that he claimed was still owed on her dowry. Third, when Célestin declared in 1829 that a separation existed between them, he had made no mention of their community property, which Micael estimated was worth 950,000 francs or $190,000. She wanted her legal claims to the community satisfied.[7] The only comfort the letter offered was its brevity, for in 1831 the recipient, not the sender, paid by the page for letters mailed to him. It cost Célestin very little to read his wife's demands.

We must not draw too many conclusions from the tone of any of the letters between Micael and Célestin: the letters come to us through their attorneys as part of the record of one or another court proceeding. In this example, the letter was preserved because Célestin's attorney quoted *parts* of it with a view to showing that Micael was mercenary and impulsive. The parts he declined to quote to the court were not preserved in the record.

Mindful of her husband's tendency to evade or delay an issue rather than meet it head on, Micael had added:

> *Above all, no evasions; a consent clear, full, and in totality, or else a positive refusal which will put me perfectly at ease* as to the decision I have reached, one which I will then put into action without the least hesitation or scruple.
> February 21, 1831.   De Pontalba, née Almonester

An American divorce was at best a long shot, as Micael's attorney must have warned her. Married women, like Negroes, had virtually no access to Louisiana courts; to sue their husbands they needed a special authorization from a judge. The legal grounds for divorce seemed broad: infidelity by either party, ill-treatment, condemnation to ignominious punishment, or desertion for at least five years. If a divorce was granted because of adultery, the accused could not marry his or her lover. However, the courts interpreting these grounds were niggardly in granting relief from marriage. A judge who knew well the Pontalba case estimated in 1882 that only three divorces a year had been allowed since the Louisiana Purchase in 1803.[8] Custom even more than civil procedure chained many wives to their protectors. Among the Creoles it was more common to hear of a woman killing her husband than divorcing him, even though divorce was legal and murder, naturally, was not. New Orleans was still the sort of place where one could read in the *Daily Picayune*, alongside the advertisements for runaway slaves, a notice (May 1, 1838):

NEWS OF THE WEEK—
My wife, Mary Curlander, having left my bed and board at No. 146 Chartres Street, and carried with her about $3,000 worth of goods in the fur line, this is to give notice I will not pay any debts contracted by her, and that I will give $299 reward to any person who will arrest her and put her in any jail in the United States.
          David Curlander

N.B. She is the daughter of Judah Litwach, professor of mathematics at Amsterdam, Holland.

Even if Micael had received one of the few divorces granted in Louisiana, it could have had absolutely no effect in France. Only her New Orleans property would be divorced, as it were, from her husband's control. Nevertheless, she did petition the court when her husband, spiting her demand for an unequivocal answer, failed to respond at all to her letter. Célestin wrote instead to the French minister of foreign affairs, a former comrade in the army, pointing out that he was a French national beyond the jurisdiction of a United States divorce court. The minister, Horace Sebastiani, would eventually have reason to consider the advantages of divorce. In 1847, his only daughter, the duchess of Choiseul-Praslin, was stabbed by her husband so repeatedly and viciously that the scene of her death, a bedroom of the Choiseul-Praslin mansion, was reported to resemble a slaughterhouse.[9] Apparently, the husband had been planning to run away with the governess of his nine children. Instead, he went to jail, where he committed suicide before he could be brought to trial. Poor Sebastiani lived only three years after his daughter's ferocious murder, which was one of the famous crimes of the century. But in 1831, Sebastiani was still a man leading a charmed existence; his little girl was quite alive and one of the several pleasures in his life. Perhaps he thought no father should suffer the disgrace of being divorced, for he acceded to Célestin's request with alacrity. He prevailed upon the Louisiana governor to intervene in Micael's case and have her suit dismissed without a trial, on the grounds that her husband was a French citizen.

Micael, meanwhile, waiting for the legal process to take its course, had several months to spend relaxing. Mont-l'Évêque was an ocean away. She decided to take a sightseeing tour of the United States—the western boundary was then Missouri—and for a few months she had the only documented fun she was to enjoy for many years. First, she went up the east coast by steamboat as far as Quebec; she returned to New Orleans by way of Florida, writing letters full of daydreams and nostalgia along the way. Though she found the journey more trying than she had expected and was weary of traveling long before she got back to New Orleans, she set off at once for Cuba, for reasons which we will presently surmise.

America had been a foreign region to Micael even in her childhood, and she was as unprepared as any European for its emptiness. She pronounced the United States a "beautiful country, nearly uninhabited." Along the east coast, she complained of going for miles between steamboat landing and stagecoach depot without seeing a dozen houses. An extraordinary effort was necessary, she observed, to reach a few American cities; then, having made the trip to a population center, one ran out of people. "I arrived here on the 2nd," she wrote from Philadelphia, "and already I know the whole community."[10]

All over the country, people made a fuss over her, though it is hard to figure out exactly why. Everybody made her "feel like a queen," especially in Canada, where she noted that the nobility (including the de la Rondes) retained the same seigneurial rights as before the French Revolution. The governor of Quebec and his wife offered to take her around the countryside; the Ursulines in Montreal gathered at their convent door to receive her. In Washington, President Jackson sent his carriage and his secretary of state to fetch her.[11] Perhaps the hero of 1815 was trying to make amends; it was on the estate of Micael's Aunt Victoire that General Andrew Jackson fought the Battle of New Orleans, devastating both the British and the plantation. In Philadelphia, Micael was visited every day by the French consul and his wife. All along the way, people arranged little soirées in her honor, singling her out with courtesies that awakened her peregrine sense of not belonging to the expansive, new society. "France," she wrote, underlining the words as if to commit herself to them, "is *my country*, for at least there I am with my family." It was July, 1831, and she had been away from her children for six months.

There was something nervous and reckless in the very appearance of Micael's letters during her American tour. Her writing tracked over the thick paper like a locomotive running off the edges, a rapid, unadorned, angular scrawl that left no margin for meditation. The letters crossed the continent without envelopes, usually. The paper was folded, sealed with a dot of red wax, and addressed simply "Mademoiselle Azélie Chalmet à la Nouvelle Orléans." If she addressed a letter to Victoire, she generally enclosed an unsealed note marked "Mademoisel Azélie." Micael's spelling was variable, and her penmanship intense and uncalculated, as if her sentences had been composed by someone intelligent but had then been written down by an eager semiliterate.

Her letters show that at first she was touched by all the attention she received, but when it became cloying, she turned a critical eye on her hosts. It was "really ridiculous" for people to be "as impressed with titles as Americans are." You had to take a voyage in the United States, she observed, "to be aware of your noble status, which elsewhere you don't think much about." Like her countryman Alexis de Tocqueville, she noticed that Americans were quicker than anyone else to make class distinctions. "They make a brave show of democratic pride," she noted, "but then they love important names." A few lines later, she was apologizing for remarking on American pride and confessed that she felt "a little uneasy" about letting her aunt show her letter around. She did not mean to be unkind to Americans, who were always so gracious to her. The relative to whom Micael confided these observations was not an American but a rustic Creole who was herself quite pleased with her niece's position in French society. Victoire de Vaugine de Lino de Chalmet was Micael's aunt, more or less. She was the widow of Ignace Martin de Lino de Chalmet, Madame Castillon's half-brother. Victoire had six children. The youngest, Azélie, was a spinster and Micael's dearest friend. The eldest, also named Victoire, married Antoine Cruzat, who earned frequent mention in Micael's letters as "old Cruzat." Victoire and Antoine had fifteen children, providing Micael with a sorority of second cousins near her own age—Zoe, Malvina, Coralie, Céleste—who circulated her letters among themselves and begged her for details about Paris society. Until the Battle of New Orleans in 1815, the Chalmets lived on their grand plantation on the river, six miles below the city. A few weeks after the battle, Ignace de Lino de Chalmet died in despair over the destruction of his life's work. Victoire lived twenty years longer but was apparently never able to recover financially, since she was reduced to accepting a pension willingly provided by Micael.

Micael's letters to her "dear little aunt," as she called Victoire, were rambling, formless, and flushed with tenderness. Her visit to New Orleans in 1831 was the only time she was to see Victoire in almost thirty years (the aunt died in 1836, before Micael could return again to Louisiana); but her relationship with the old lady remained easy and intimate and never needed renewal. Micael had grown up with her cousins and her aunt's maid, Thérèse. "I always remember the pleasant moments I spent with you," she wrote: "I sometimes think I am back in your little living room. I can see you calling Thérèse, and then lifting your skirt and calling me, 'Goodness me! Not so fast, Madame Champagne!' Dear Aunt, don't become too sophisticated. It's a sin. Don't let them make your bonnets too tall." She chided the old lady for having someone with fancier diction write for her "in a hand I did not recognize and with phrases that were not yours. In the future, I want letters from you," she warned, "or I won't answer them."[12] Thérèse remained with the family through its bad times and outlived most of its members. Micael was still mentioning her in her last letters to Azélie, twenty years after Victoire's death.

Thus, it was with her country aunt, and not with her expensive legal advisers or her notary, that Micael discussed a man who was her companion for over a year and whose name reverberated through her later separation trials. J. N. François Guillemin was a gentleman of fifty-four. He was the French consul in New Orleans, long widowed when he became friendly with Micael, aged thirty-five.[13] When Micael arrived in the city, she had to confer with him as part of the procedure for filing for divorce against a French citizen. Either by chance or design, Guillemin found himself with Micael on the steamboat tour of New York and southeast Canada, although his new consular assignment was in the opposite direction in Havana. Wherever the boat stopped, the two went sightseeing together. Micael was returning to Louisiana when she decided to go out of her way to visit Pensacola with him "so as to know the country better."[14] Judging from estimates of the population of Florida in 1831 (fewer than six people per square mile), country was indeed all there was to know. Once back in New Orleans where she and Guillemin were to part, she revised her plans again, and accompanied him to Cuba for "a tour," despite her repeated complaints about her weariness of traveling and the discomforts of the recent journey. The road to perdition had, it seems, been unpaved whenever they stepped off the boat.

We do not know what Guillemin looked like. Micael's lawyer protested to a court in France some years later that if the judges "had but a portrait of the gentleman, they would see how absurd was the imputation of an improper relationship" between the consul and the heiress.[15] But by then, 1836, Guillemin was dead and Micael, herself disfigured, could hurt no one by disparaging his attractions.

On board the vacation boat, Micael and Guillemin spent their endless leisure time together chatting with fellow passengers, eating, or simply roosting on deck, according to the one letter in which she wrote of him in detail. "Monsieur Guilmin is taking as good care of me as anyone could ask," she assured her aunt, misspelling Guillemin's name as she did everyone's.[16] "Right now he is writing on one side of the table and I on the other. He does not leave me for a single moment." One can picture them swatting each other's mosquitoes in the comfortable old clothes that Flaubert informs us were worn by all French travelers.

Célestin did not have access to Micael's letters. Mailed from points in the United States to New Orleans, they never crossed the Atlantic. He did, however, have bankers whom Micael dealt with during her wanderings, and he was not ashamed to ask them for reports. "Madame de Pontalba was seen only a few days ago," replied a Monsieur de Rhan of New York to one such inquiry, "on her way from here to Niagara, and from this I presume that she will remain in our part of the country until Fall. It seems that she had for the past two months been in New York and taking the waters at Saratoga, and that now she is bound for a tour around Niagara and Canada." Célestin had apparently made some inquiry about a man other than Guillemin, for the banker added, "Monsieur Séherer left for Havre on July 10th last, aboard the American packet-boat *Erie*, in charge of Captain Funk. . . ."[17] Property agents of the Pontalbas wrote to Célestin on January 22, 1832: "Mme. de Pontalba left for Havana the day before last; she was accompanied by Monsieur Guillemin, who has been named consul-general to the Island of Cuba."

From these drops of implication squeezed out of two informants, Célestin's lawyer was able to draw for a French tribunal the lurid outline of an affair which, he said, shocked observers "on two continents" from Canada to Cuba, though it is doubtful that the Cubans were really so scandalized by the gringa's behavior that they found it necessary to secede from North America. No doubt the lawyer could have created a hair-raising story if he had been privy to Micael's letter. For what he did not know or could not prove was unclearly written in Micael's own hand, as she described her travels with Guillemin:

> He stays with me at the inn, where we get on marvelously, and tells me that he will not go away to the consulate until I leave for the country. We dine at the ship's common table. Since my arrival, my room is never empty. He just introduced me to the former Consul. Here are the details, dear little aunt, that I believe will give you pleasure. I tell them to you because I know you love me.[18]

A shipboard romance was necessarily a serious affair for a married Frenchwoman; if found guilty of adultery, she was subject to a mandatory prison term and other unpleasant penalties, regardless of the location of her crime or the ugliness of her partner.[19] But adultery, as everyone knows, is the most difficult of all recreations to document. It is not surprising that despite unsparing research, the Pontalbas never succeeded in proving anything about Guillemin except that Micael took a pre-arranged tour and "kept company" with him for several months. There was no hard evidence offered during the trials that Guillemin had even held her married hand, and there remains none today—Micael's letter, to an objective reader, admits to everything and nothing.

Micael knew that Célestin would pounce on the chance to prosecute her for a "criminal liaison." Therefore, though she might have invited a male friend to accompany her when she visited Célestin's agents who were hostile to her, she was probably too guarded to bring a lover. Nor is it likely that she would effuse about shared lodgings and bedroom visitors to her good Catholic aunt, unless Guillemin was indeed nothing more than a platonic admirer. She did not behave like a woman with a guilty conscience. On the other hand, there is one strong indication that she was having a well-deserved and potent romance: when the time came for Guillemin to depart, Micael left her relatives and her servants "and followed his caravan to Cuba," as Célestin's lawyer energetically pointed out. It is a fact that cannot be dismissed.

Guillemin at any rate was worthy of an intelligent woman's love; he was a refined and reflective man who deliberated over social conditions which the average observer of life merely despised. Alexis de Tocqueville, on a tour of the United States much like the one the two companions had just completed, sought out the consul on New Year's Day, 1832, just before

Guillemin and Micael left for Cuba. Although Tocqueville had only twenty-four hours to spend in New Orleans, he squandered several of them with the consul. Tocqueville described the visit: "We knocked. The Negro who opened the door seemed completely surprised that we should want to visit his master, but of what importance is it what goes on in a Negro's head?"[20] At first Tocqueville was put off by Guillemin's complacent indifference to his guest's ideas. He remarked that Guillemin's courteous manner "concealed an ego which prefers monologue to conversation." Nevertheless, he recognized that "Monsieur Guillemin is certainly an able man and, I think, someone of means. All that is exceptional. For incompetence among French agents abroad seems to be the rule. He has been living in New Orleans some fifteen to seventeen years."

Tocqueville took notes of the long interview. Guillemin began by commenting that people in Louisiana were "more concerned with French affairs than with their own." The Creoles, with their French manners and preoccupation with Europe, "had opened one of the great American doors" to France. He pointed out that almost all the land in Louisiana still belonged to the Creoles, although big business had been seized by the Americans. The French Creoles were no match for the Americans as entrepreneurs, Guillemin observed, because they did not like to take risks and feared bankruptcy as a disgrace, whereas Americans looked on business failure simply as a setback. Moreover, the Americans who descended on New Orleans from the North were "eaten up with longing for wealth," had no reputation to lose, and no scruples about making bad debts.

Tocqueville asked Guillemin the question everyone in 1832 asked about New Orleans, that is, how much bitterness was there between Creoles and Americans. "Each criticizes the other," Guillemin answered. "They do not see each other much; but at bottom there is no real hostility." There was enough prosperity to go around, he said, without the French and Americans having to compete too fiercely. He thought New Orleans was going to become the largest and richest city in the New World. But though Guillemin was a humanitarian, he had no use for democracy in America, and especially in New Orleans. The way business was conducted in Louisiana, he said, was "bedlam." The government was "like Penelope's loom," with a legislature that "ceaselessly makes, alters, and repeals the laws." It was not the spirit of the political party that ran the state, but the spirit of the coterie. New Orleans was neglected and dirty, despite all its revenues, because public money was frittered away. However, he believed that giving everyone the vote was not an answer. The working classes in Louisiana, as in every country, were at the mercy of those who employed them, according to Guillemin. Therefore, the great industrialists could easily manipulate the vote and sway the supposed free choice of the people. Besides, he noted, in Louisiana truly outstanding men did not run for office, so the voters were stuck with mediocrities—"obscure people, lawyers of the third order, village intriguers"—no matter how wisely they voted.

There was nothing particularly original in those sentiments; exasperation with Louisiana politics was already a tradition in 1832. But Tocqueville next turned to the question of race. He remarked that the colored people were reputed to have low morals. "How could you expect it to be otherwise?" Guillemin burst out, since the law "almost forced" women of color into concubinage. Though they might be as cultured as any white girls, "the law still forbids them to marry into the reigning and wealthy race of whites. If they want to contract a legitimate union, they must marry men of their caste and share their humiliations, for men of color do not even enjoy the shameful privileges that are accorded to their women." Even an educated, light-skinned man of color, Guillemin told his guest, was "condemned to continual indignities. There is not a white beggar but has the right to bully the wretch he finds in his way and throw him in the dirt. . . . At the head of any document he executes, the law obliges him to write: 'man of color, free.' He cannot hope for anything." Guillemin observed that the whites in Louisiana were doing what all aristocracies do: isolating themselves. By excluding even the most intelligent men of color from society, they were in effect providing leaders for the people they had made their adversaries, the blacks. The interview then ended. Tocqueville departed from Guillemin fortified by the thought that "France was still represented abroad by people worthy of her."[21]

This was the man—bright, kindly, and perhaps a bit didactic—who did not leave Micael's side for some fifteen months, in New Orleans, New York, and finally, at the beginning of 1832, Havana. Whatever we think about their relationship, it is clear that Micael found Guillemin easy to take, even as far out of the way as Cuba was in those days. No letters from Micael remain from the trip to Havana, so we do not know precisely what she did there. But as it happened, one of her friends, Marshal Ney's third son, Eugène, had made an excursion to the island exactly one year previously. In a long article in the travel section of *Revue des Deux Mondes*, the young diplomat described what the typical tourist might see in Cuba.[22] Micael and Guillemin probably traveled to Havana on a boat with about thirty passengers, possibly with slaves packed in the hold below deck. When they reached the capital, they found a metropolis of about 50,000 Caucasian souls controlling an equal number of slaves and free people of color. Micael probably stayed with Guillemin at the consulate, since Ney found only two "abominable" inns in all of Havana. Cubans had windows without panes and beds without mattresses, according to Ney, because in January the heat was so intense that lying on a mattress was "unbearable." Guillemin's residence was well appointed; Ney commented that all government accommodations in Havana were "palatial," the French consulate particularly.

Cuba was florid, foreign, dirty, many-tongued, and seductive, not without benign surprises for a well brought up French person. Ney described a dinner during which a horse was conducted through the dining room and casually harnessed in the salon, and more routinely, meals during which everyone withdrew to another room so that the table could be reset and redecorated before they returned for dessert. The dinner hour began about two o'clock and continued throughout the rest of the slackened day. Both Ney and Micael were lucky in that they visited during fiesta season. Except for such holidays, Ney complained, there were in Havana no parties, dances, dinners, nothing. Micael, nevertheless, stayed two months after the official parties were over. The idyll, if that is what it was, did not end until March 12, 1832, when she returned to New Orleans, alone for the first time in many months, on a cargo vessel on which she was the sole passenger. Leaving Guillemin must have extinguished some fragile light in her; the captain of the boat judged her age as forty.[23]

When she arrived in New Orleans, Micael was met with one of the surprises that both she and Célestin favored in their dealings with each other. On March 29, 1832, Célestin countersued his wife, demanding that the court return her French Quarter revenues to him. He contended that the Place d'Armes was not her separate real estate but dotal property which fell to him because of $52,000 unpaid on her dowry. All the property in excess of $52,000 he claimed by virtue of the "family pact" between him and Micael made in 1827. If the court rejected these claims, according to his petition, he would then fall back on the argument that the Place d'Armes houses were community property and therefore under his control. If the court found they were not community property, he would claim them anyway as reimbursement for all the repairs to them he had made. Finally, he alleged (wrongly, as it turned out) that Micael had not told Judge Pitot that her husband was in France, outside Louisiana's jurisdiction, and that her supposed misrepresentation to the court disqualified her previous suit.[24] These were not trifling arguments, since even in Louisiana a husband controlled dotal property as if it were his own.

Célestin took further steps. On April 12, 1832, he obtained a judgment in Senlis finding Micael guilty of desertion and ordering her back to Mont-l'Évêque. The judgment warned that if she failed to return to the "conjugal domicile" within two months, Célestin would be authorized "to seize and stop any income of his wife," regardless of its source. In 1832 a French citizen deserted by his wife could have her separate revenues impounded until she returned, just as under our legal system a wife can have her husband's income garnished until he meets his obligations for support, irrespective of whether that income is his separate property.[25] Célestin had declared in notarized documents that a de facto separation of three years existed between him and his wife while she lived at rue du Houssaie. Nevertheless, this "voluntary" separation, as the court termed it, did not excuse Micael from getting her husband's permission before traveling abroad. By failing to procure that permission, she had abandoned their home, recorded as Mont-l'Évêque.

Célestin's next move was to revoke Micael's privilege of collecting rents from apartments on rue du Houssaie. Assisted by the justice of the peace, Célestin seized Micael's furniture and all the contents of her apartment, told the tenants to move, and padlocked the house.[26] With the place closed up, the summons ordering Micael to answer a charge of desertion could not be delivered; the bailiff forwarded the summons to Mont-l'Évêque where it remained, unseen and unanswered by Micael, so that a judgment against her was rendered in default.[27] Therefore, even though she got back to Mont-l'Évêque within the two months the court allowed her, the income from her houses in France was impounded anyway.

The Pontalbas were thus well served by the law, except for one technicality. Mont-l'Évêque belonged to the father, not the son who had legal claim to only one-twentieth of the estate. A man could not call his wife back to a fraction of a house or to a domicile that was not his own. To remedy this, the elder Pontalba executed a property exchange on May 16, 1832. All of the rentals which he had ostensibly given to Célestin to match Micael's dowry were now to be ostensibly returned. In exchange for the imaginary rent benefits, Célestin received the remaining nineteen-twentieths of Mont-l'Évêque, making him the professed owner. However, as in all previous agreements regarding Mont-l'Évêque, the elder Pontalba was to continue receiving all the income from the estate and had the exclusive right of managing the property. The document registering the exchange ("that miserable arrangement," as Micael's lawyer called it) was then backdated so that it appeared to have been made months before Célestin went to court against Micael.[28]

Micael had gone to America on the advice of her first lawyer, Jean-Charles Persil; he became a magistrate while she was gone and was appointed minister of justice after Louis Philippe ascended the throne in 1830. Thus, Micael engaged a new attorney, Antoine-Louis-Marie Hennequin, who was to be her mentor during the next four years, the worst of her life. Like all of Micael's lawyers in both France and Louisiana, Hennequin was well educated, well known, and expensive, part of a generation of French lawyers who were involved in the great judicial and political issues of the day.[29] On paper, he opposed divorce. One of his books was a tepid argument against dissolving any marriage. The little treatise still exists, consigned to the caste of the harmless and untouched in the Bibliothèque Nationale. But on his feet, Hennequin assisted in several scandalous emancipations, including the judicial separations of the baroness Feuchères, the duchess de Berry, and George Sand, who asked Hennequin to let her read Micael's file.[30]

Micael arrived in Paris in the spring of 1832 to find her asylum on rue du Houssaie locked up and deserted; she went to an apartment in her mother's old house on the Place Vendôme. Then she "sought advice," as Hennequin mildly described what must have been a frantic interview between them. When Hennequin read the Senlis court judgment against Micael, he told her that she had no choice but to resume her married life at Mont-l'Évêque.[31] Thus, on June 12, 1832, the last day of freedom permitted to her in the court order, Micael appeared at the château. The Pontalbas knew that Micael had traveled with Guillemin; judging from the cruelty they inflicted on her in the next few years, they must have also believed that she had come but recently from his bed. Old Pontalba did not need proof to believe the worst about Micael, and Célestin's never-sturdy pride was injured by the mere act of her leaving France and filing for divorce. It was easy for him to be persuaded that she deserved the harshest treatment.

Thus, at the door of Mont-l'Évêque, her father-in-law set forth the rules by which she would now live as Célestin's no-longer-estranged wife. She was to be isolated in one small room of the Little Château, the two-story guest-house a few yards behind the castle, since she would now be in the position of "a caller staying too long" in the family circle.[32] She would be permitted at the family table in the main château, but no one would speak to her and her own attempts at conversation would fall on deaf ears. Even visitors to Mont-l'Évêque were soon made to understand, according to Hennequin, that their welcome would end if they showed "any consideration to the mistress of the house."

Long after she had escaped this ignoble penance, the memory of evenings at Mont-l'Évêque haunted Micael like a bizarre dream: "If I am in the salon, no one speaks to me. If strangers come they do not greet me and all in the gathering sit whispering in each other's ears until I am compelled to withdraw to my room."[33] Life at the château, she wrote to her cousins, was only "painful existence." Micael sought the protection of Madame de Miró who had shown her kindness in former years; but Mamma Miró, as Micael called her, was as much under the old man's domination as anyone in the household. "All these people," Hennequin later explained, "had entered into that sad conspiracy of all against one."

As for Célestin, he at least talked to his wife when his father was not about. Though Micael was terrified of the old man, she never expressed any physical fear of Célestin and apparently thought she could manage him if she could get him away from his father. Even during this worst of times, she reported to Hennequin that there were "tender memories" between her and her husband—the lawyer refrained from qualifying them further—and the possibility, she thought, of true reconciliation. Unfortunately, the elder Pontalba also noticed the resilient attraction between his son and his enemy and blocked it, or so Micael insisted. The father would appear at the end of a conversation—"that phantom," Hennequin called him—"and anger and contempt appeared with him," dispelling whatever sympathies might have developed between the couple.

Early on, Hennequin perceived that there was a strategy underlying the peculiar drama at Mont-l'Évêque. Micael, he said, "had been called back in the hope that she would not come, and that in her refusal a way would be opened for seizing her money. If she were so indiscreet as to answer the summons, if she failed to understand, they would make her life unbearable. . . ."

They would drive her to rebellion, since her rebellion was necessary for con-
fiscating her income.[34] The lawyer's task was to keep Micael at Mont-l'Évêque
long enough to collect some proof of what was going on.

From June, 1832, until Micael was shot in 1834, almost everything that
happened between her and the Pontalbas—all letters between them and perhaps most conversations—were calculated acts undertaken for their legal
value. For example, Célestin gave Micael permission to return to Paris for a
few days to supervise the remodeling of the Place Vendôme mansion, but he
would not allow her to stay in the Houssaie house. Then he sent messages to
her at the Houssaie address, so that the letters would be returned to him
with the postman's notation that Madame was not residing there. In that
way, Célestin hoped to document a pretension that Micael had left Mont-
l'Évêque without getting his consent or apprising him of her whereabouts.

Célestin hit upon other strategies as he prepared for a legal fight. The first
time Micael left the château for a trip to Paris which was to last one week,
Célestin wrote to her forbidding her to bring back servants or horses.[35]
Henceforth, she would be allowed only one chambermaid, he wrote, because he could not afford to pay for such luxuries. A maid's usual wage was a
franc a day—five or six dollars a month, if indeed the woman was paid in
money and not in garden produce or milk, as was common in the country.
Keeping a horse probably cost a little more, but even so, Célestin could have
supported an entire village of servants and horses without appreciably diminishing his income. But the letter could be offered in a court as proof that
Micael's extravagances were putting the Pontalba family in debt, an idea that
Célestin's lawyer intended to ingeminate in future court actions. The refrain
of the Pontalbas was that Micael had demanded the finest furniture, silver,
crystal, and so on, while she lived on rue du Houssaie. Her appetite for luxury caused Célestin to borrow heavily. Then she vanished, going to New Orleans with the aim of getting control of more revenues she could devour,
leaving her husband to pay the bills.

Célestin was indeed in debt. Notarial records show that while Micael was
in New Orleans, Célestin made loans totaling at least 115,000 francs from a
number of undistinguished individuals. His parents co-signed these obligations.[36] But whatever Célestin was doing with the money, he was not buying lacquered cabinets and lace tablecloths—Micael bought those with her
own revenues or took them out of her trousseau; when Célestin saw an opportunity to seize her domestic "luxuries," he had to get a court order be-

cause they were Micael's separate assets. Moreover, Micael could not have contracted debts for furniture or anything, not even medical treatment, without her husband's permission, and it is unlikely that he would have acquiesced in any purchases for a home he refused to inhabit. Célestin had never made any loans before 1831, though he had been married to Micael for twenty years, and the household at rue du Houssaie had been established for nine. And he never borrowed money again after the flurry of obligations he incurred while Micael was in America.

If not for furniture, then why did Célestin contract debts in 1831? Possibly for detectives to follow Micael's and Guillemin's steamboat as it breathed its way up and down North America. But after paying out 115,000 francs, could Célestin not find one spy willing to offer himself as a witness to the lascivious behavior the Pontalbas hoped to discover? No such witness was ever deposed; therefore, the money probably was not paid to detectives. Possibly the debts were a ruse, bogus loans from friends or employees, concocted by Célestin, his parents, or his thoughtful lawyer. The loans were all made at the same time, with the same document, from five different individuals, and none of them appears to have been repaid, as far as we can tell from the notarial records. When Micael left France and threatened to get an American divorce, the Pontalbas may have figured that she could be held responsible for the debts of the marital community as well as the assets; therefore, the more debts, the better. In case of a separation of property, she would have to pay out 57,000 francs, half of the total owed by Célestin, which would then find its way back to him. Or Célestin could have pretended to make debts simply to support his claim that Micael wanted to live in Paris so that she could be surrounded by glamour, not because she was being mistreated at Mont-l'Évêque. In fact, this was exactly his argument in court.

Chances are, however, the debts were real. They were contracted only a few months after Micael succeeded in having the courts in New Orleans put her back in possession of the Place d'Armes rents. The Pontalbas had enjoyed half of those revenues since 1814 and the other half since 1827—perhaps a total of 200,000 francs every year. Suddenly in January, 1831, they were forced to manage without the yearly banquet from New Orleans, just at the time when their legal expenses were rising. Thus, they had to borrow money, and at the same time it occurred to them to try to show that Micael was the cause of the family's embarrassment. Their strategy was to complain in writing about her extravagance, to document an ugly portrait of her which they planned to present to a tribunal.

Micael answered Célestin's letter forbidding her to bring back servants, although she knew that she herself would arrive at Mont-l'Évêque before her letter. Her polite and reasonable reply to her husband was something her lawyer could readily read to a tribunal, and Hennequin of course received a copy: "You understand, Monsieur, that if the servants were to become an inconvenience to you, I would not hesitate . . . to pay for them in full. . . . Allow me to assume therefore that money is not the issue here." She assured Célestin that "none of these people has it in his head to show you anything but the proper respect." Nevertheless, she agreed to return with only one maid.

> These pretexts distress me for more than one reason, but I know the power that you hope to use. . . . I am still convinced Monsieur, that my conduct toward you in no way justifies your forgetting obligations toward me while you are so careful to remind me of my own. I placed myself in your hands without hidden motives, and I only wish your conscience would allow you to say the same.[37]

Hennequin believed he had to show a court that Mont-l'Évêque was the father's house, even though the son had ownership of it on paper. To prove that Célestin was not in fact master of the domicile, Hennequin instructed Micael to seat herself at the family dinner table one evening in the center place usually occupied by the mistress of the house—the seat "usurped," as Micael put it, by her father-in-law—and to order the servants to bring the meal. This was a little like telling a foot soldier to walk behind enemy lines to prove that a war is in progress. Mont-l'Évêque was an estate surrounded by unlighted wilderness. Every meter of it belonged to old Pontalba, and every person within screaming and shooting distance was his dependent. Though it must have taken courage in that chamber where even the kitchen maid was trained to ignore her, Micael did what Hennequin advised. "You should have seen father and son exchanging snickers but not daring to say anything so as not to put themselves in the wrong, knowing the law full well," she wrote.[38] When one of the men finally objected to her sitting in Pontalba's place, Micael asserted that her legal position was mistress of the house. "After dinner in the living room, my father-in-law could not leave it there and told me, 'Madame, you are indeed mistress here, but I am master and Madame de Miró mistress also.'" Micael retorted that she recognized only her husband as head of the household. "They found themselves suddenly in the wrong and must have been embarrassed," she wrote to her aunt, perhaps trying to believe that the law, if not the court, was on her side and that she, isolated at Mont-l'Évêque with her one maid, could use it to intimidate Pontalba. Alone with Célestin, she remonstrated about the life she was forced to lead in what was purported to be her own home. "Madame, you are certainly in your own home," he told her. Then, echoing his father, he added, "My father and mother are in their homes and Madame de Miró in hers. We all live here."[39]

Soon Micael was writing her aunt that Célestin was about to be summoned before the Senlis court to answer her demand for "a residence where I can be mistress. He has no right to call me back to his father's," she continued, "to mistreat me as he has, all so he can get money from me that he is not entitled to."[40] Micael savored a fantasy in which the court ruled against him. "He'll have a fit when he has to separate from his family and get a proper house for me, and all that without my giving him any money. Since money is, of course, his primary concern, he will be punished where it really hurts him."

Meanwhile, Micael was making short trips to Paris to which the Pontalbas readily consented. Each time, however, they made it harder for her to return to Mont-l'Évêque. Theoretically, she was allowed to bring a maid with her, but she was restricted to one horse, so that even if the two women wanted to journey to Senlis unaccompanied over that terrain of few highways and many highwaymen, they could not do so on one animal. Micael was obliged to leave her carriage, horses, driver, and any other servants at the village of Mont-l'Évêque. A Madame de Presle kept the horses, causing Célestin to declare publicly that he plannned to snub that neighbor indefinitely. After leaving the carriage, Micael and the maid had to walk to the castle.[41] Next, Micael was informed that the maid would not be allowed to go into Micael's tiny room, though this was still the time when ladies could not get in or out of their underwear without someone to assist with the stays. Hennequin advised Micael to break the rules occasionally, just to see what the Pontalbas would do—to show up with all of her carriage horses, for instance. But Micael was too frightened to test the limits of the hatred that surrounded her. It was not the lawyer, after all, who had to face the sneering men behind the château wall.

Around this time, July, 1832, Micael began having severe attacks of a disorder that was probably epilepsy. At least in this, Micael was lucky to be among Frenchmen, who did not regard the condition with any particular horror. The English reportedly refused to allow epileptics in the public hospitals. Whereas the French were so tolerant of the disease that the French Creoles in New Orleans even permitted their slaves to have seizures. "As you might expect," Micael wrote to her aunt, "all these torments have made my bad nerves come back. Yesterday, they thought I was dying,"—it was while she was in Paris—"I was stiff as a board. . . . The nerves in my neck got big as your thumb and black. Three men could not hold me. Finally Monsieur Hennequin promised me that I will not have to go back until my husband and his parents make a place for me where I can demand to be mistress of the château."[42] From the chimera of freedom in Louisiana, she had come to hope only that the Pontalbas would "make a place" for her in their colony.

To her cousin she commented sadly:

> I do not look particularly interesting in the eyes of strangers. The two Pontalba gentlemen have put me through too much suffering. If I had you near me, my good cousins, one of you would go with me to Mont-l'Évêque and then they would not dare say anything to me. But you feel you can hardly ask strangers to go and make themselves the target of sarcastic comments.

Micael had a close friend who was about to visit New Orleans; he was charged with reporting "everything I am forced to endure."[43]

After what must have seemed like a prison sentence or a decade in purgatory, Célestin's case against Micael for desertion came to trial. There is no extant record of this proceeding. However, in the separation trials of 1835 and 1836, after Micael was shot, her lawyers briefly reviewed for the court all the previous litigation. In this 1832 trial, the tribunal had ruled, as Hennequin recalled the decision, that "the mere presence of her father-in-law was not sufficient reason to justify her staying away from the conjugal domicile. . . ."[44] The judges had confirmed "against every dictate of common sense"—Hennequin made this remark to their faces—that her married life was to be one of permanent coexistence with her in-laws. In vain had the lawyer protested that Micael was afraid of the old man; in vain had he described the ways in which she was being abused. "At that time I could be listened to with a smile of incredulity," he remembered bitterly.

Hennequin appealed the 1832 decision to the Royal Court of Amiens. Here there were no smiles; the magistrates gave the case serious consideration. But after long debates on both sides and intense discussion among the judges themselves, the tribunal on November 16, 1832, upheld the order of the Senlis court.[45] Micael had been living in Paris while awaiting the outcome of the two trials. She was told that she must now return to Mont-l'Évêque. Célestin was authorized "to seize and receive the revenues of her personal property" until she had remained with him and his inevitable parents for six consecutive months, after which period she could again petition the court for the return of her rents. The time she had already spent at the château was not counted.

Micael did not return to Mont-l'Évêque. She lived in Paris on the income she was getting from New Orleans, those revenues that Célestin was trying to take back in his still-pending suits in Louisiana. The Amiens ruling at the end of 1832 was a portent of the terrible years that lay ahead. She had long been engaged in repairing the two mansions in Paris, left to her by her mother, on the Place Vendôme and rue Saint-Honoré. Getting money for these repairs had been her initial reason for going to New Orleans and reclaiming her rentals there. As Célestin was now receiving the rents from the two buildings, Micael stopped paying for their rehabilitation. The unpaid workmen retaliated by placing liens on the property, rent garnishments that took precedence over those of Célestin. Since Micael made no effort to remove the new garnishments, her husband was effectively deprived of the revenues the court had awarded him. Célestin thus re-opened their case before the Senlis tribunal in May, 1833, charging that Micael was deliberately circumventing a court order. This time, the judges transferred to him all of Micael's separate property in France for an unspecified period. Micael appealed the judgment and lost. Since Célestin was already in control of her rents, the transfer would seem to have had little practical effect. However, it enabled him to make Micael a little more wretched by selling her furniture and personal belongings, things she had paid for herself, which he had been keeping under lock at rue du Houssaie.[46]

Célestin's case in New Orleans was by now approaching trial, though Micael's lawyers were purposely delaying a court date, to the point of exasperating the judge. If Micael were going to lose her property, it was better not to lose it right away. The rents from the Place d'Armes were her only income. Without them, she would be forced back to Mont-l'Évêque—"in other words," she wrote her cousin, "forced to die." She envisioned being completely without funds, "reduced to spending my life around the four persons who could, from morning till night, make my life more miserable than you can imagine."[47] Meanwhile, in order to give the appearance of trying to comply with the court orders, she had to provide the Pontalbas with certificates delivered to Mont-l'Évêque by her doctor, attesting to her inability to travel.[48]

She had remained in Paris since August, 1832. When she first returned to the city, even while she was still going back and forth to Mont-l'Évêque, she tried to resume her normal habits. She wrote to her cousins of going to the Gymnase to see *Le Chapéron*; of showing some visiting relatives the Bois de Boulogne and the Jardin des Invalides; or riding on the most fashionable track in Paris, the Champs-Élysées.[49] However, as money became tighter and her problems multiplied, she began letting go of her life in society and thinking more about New Orleans. "Tell Cora not to send me a thing. I received the pistachios; the shipping charges are more than these things are worth. I appreciate her thinking of me, but she can show it by writing."[50]

While her cases were pending, she saw few people outside of a circle of close friends: Marshal Ney's widow, who now shunned the Pontalbas; Madame Vatry, the prominent widow of a prominent Orleanist, who was a noted beauty and would marry Ney's second son in 1833; relatives from Louisiana; and Monsieur de la Croix, Micael's dearest friend. According to Micael, the Creoles who visited France were so indignant at Pontalba's treatment of her that they refused to call at Mont-l'Évêque. Even the LeBretons and St. Avid, people who were Pontalba's relatives and had been close to him, now took her side. "Everybody feels sorry for me, but that does not keep me from being unhappy," she wrote, feeling sorry for herself.[51]

Her cousin Charles stayed near her in Paris for over a year; he was about the same age as young Célestin, eighteen or so, and eased her longing for her own sons. He soon became part of all her letters: Charles was homesick and had wept on reading mail from New Orleans; he was appalled at the ostentations of the nobility in Paris and the misery of the poor; he was looking for a rich wife.[52] Micael observed that the Pontalbas avoided the boy when they visited Paris. She thought it was because her husband wanted to keep him away from Madame de Miró, lest the aunt decide to leave some of her fortune to her younger nephew.

By the end of 1833, Micael was alarmed at her financial state. She had been obliged to rent an apartment to live in after her husband seized her two houses, and she was trying to replace the furniture and items he had sold. Moreover, she was providing pensions to her aunt and to Azélie, and to people such as a Mademoiselle Péguit. "She didn't know where to turn," Micael explained to her relatives. "I had to help her, in spite of my being so pressed for money. But don't tell her."[53] Her income from New Orleans would easily have covered all this, except for the incubus of litigation. "I still do not have a moment of peace," she wrote to Victoire in November, 1833. "Yesterday evening a new summons for me to present myself at Mont-l'Évêque—it is the fourth in two weeks." Each legal summons had to be answered. Documents filed by the Pontalbas had to be countered by rebutting documents. "The fifth of this month, a trial at Senlis," she wrote, "and at the end of the month another at Amiens. Is this living? They have sworn the death of your poor niece." She attempted a wan joke about her cousin's piety: "I think Azélie did not pray for me as she promised."

With Micael's money added to their own, the Pontalbas could afford to keep up the legal pressure indefinitely. There were fees charged by the lawyers' assistants for preparing documents for court, fees for having a case placed on the court calendar, fees paid for papers served, for court attendants, for certified copies of the court's judgment. All such charges were raised by a third when a case was appealed.[54] Moreover, all court costs on appealed cases were paid by the loser. That meant Micael always paid. By the end of 1833, she was worn out with litigation, but too heartsick to think of anything else. Like aching teeth, the lawsuits narrowed her life to one area of suffering. As she continued losing every court fight in France, the case in New Orleans that was about to be tried by Judge Charles Maurian became almost the only important thing in her life. Twice she asked her cousin Zoe, connected to Maurian through his wife, to speak to "Monsieur Maurian" in her behalf, "and have him speak to the other judges. . . ."[55] She wrote of her rising anxiety at the prospect of returning to Mont-l'Évêque: "I will lose my mind if I don't win my suit in Louisiana." She was deeply wounded by the defection of her cousin Charles, who decided after all to seek out Madame de Miró. On Christmas Day, 1833, she was ill and despondent:

I am still in bed, my dear friend, very sick from a hemorrhage which I have every two weeks following an inflammation caused by all the tortures I've been put through here. The Pontalba gentlemen have so little pity for my condition that I've just received yet another summons to appear at Mont-l'Évêque within twenty-four hours. I regret very much, my dear friend, ever leaving you. It is impossible to be more tormented than I am or more miserable. It would frighten you to see me, as I am completely stretched out.

I spend my life in bed, crying endlessly. Since Charles and his sister Justine have gone to Mont-l'Évêque, I see them very seldom. They are all enthusiasm for their aunt Madame de Miró. Meanwhile, I have been kindness itself to them. In life, one finds only ingrates.

Goodbye, my good friend, my dear aunt. Think sometimes of your poor niece who deserves great pity. I embrace all my cousins and wish you a happy new year.

At the prospect of returning to Mont-l'Évêque, she felt a childlike fear and isolation. "I often dream I am with you," she wrote to Azélie, "and find myself so happy that I would not leave you." A technological advance prompted her to write to her cousin: "Do you know that I plan to come see you in a balloon? They announced a few days ago that a balloon was to leave Paris and get to London in six hours." She sometimes seemed to think of herself as an orphan. "If you were near me, I could be consoled," she wrote to her cousins, "but here I have neither parents nor even a friend from childhood." Informed that a Creole acquaintance had somehow lost his fortune, Micael at first expressed sympathy but ended by reserving her most heartfelt condolences for herself. "Good Grief, he is less to be pitied than I am. He has a wife who loves him, parents who cherish him, and peace of mind in his work," she wrote.[56]

She had four lawsuits pending in 1834. "You can imagine my apprehension," she wrote, "as what I am waiting for is to me a judgment of life or death." For months she mentioned wanting to send a nice gift to her aunt and cousins, but she could never find the money. Borrowing was impossible without her husband's signature, "which naturally he would refuse." In August, 1834, she wrote that she was down to three thousand "piasters," as she termed dollars, and had to come up with twenty thousand by the fifth of November. "I hope later on that I can prove to all of you that I am thinking of you."[57] She added, "One cannot keep so many lawsuits going without putting out a great deal."

When the fifth of November came, she was writing to Victoire as if for the last time:

I cannot write long, my dear aunt. I am in bed not even able to sit up. I am having a hemorrhage that has rarely left me for the last month. Since one must always think of death, I am sending my Will to Louisiana in which I have of course not forgotten you, my good aunt. You know that nobody loves you more than I do. I am sending you a warming pan so that you can sleep in a warm bed. I am writing to LeBreton to send you a case of good Bordeaux to warm your stomach when you drink it to the health of your niece who loves you so tenderly. Goodbye, good aunt. May God be with you all your days.

In the war of nerves and money, Célestin seemed to be winning all around. It is only in retrospect that Micael appears the survivor of their embattled marriage, only when we consider that the elder Pontalba destroyed himself in 1834, and that Célestin became deranged in later life.

During the years from 1827 to 1834, the Pontalbas put severe restrictions on Micael's contact with her children, restrictions against which each of her sons rebelled in turn. The three boys hated being away from their mother; the letters of Micael's friends, the Neys, and Hennequin's remarks in various court trials attest to that. It is difficult to know whether separation was as anguishing for her as it obviously was for them. She remarked about the younger boys only rarely in her extant letters, but that may be a measure of her grief at being apart from them; she was equally taciturn regarding her aunt, to whom she was unquestionably devoted, once the old woman had died. In her few comments about Alfred and Gaston, and in her many letters about young Célestin, she wrote as if she doted on them all and ached for them like any mother removed from her children. Gaston made a fetching drawing of his mother at Mont-l'Évêque perhaps just after her return from New Orleans in 1832, at the start of her worst troubles. She looks small and pleasant in the boy's sketch, an agreeable mother. He also saved a creditable drawing of a horse captioned "a sketch by Mother."[58]

However, Micael was able to endure separations from the children that many parents would find unthinkable, even in a cooler familial climate than that of nineteenth-century France. When Célestin left her at rue du Houssaie and returned to Mont-l'Évêque for three years, he had the three boys, or at least controlled them when they were not in the custody of a boarding school. Micael may or may not have acquiesced in this marital estrangement that separated her from her sons—there is no evidence either way; the youngest, Gaston, was only six. When she went alone to America in 1830, she was away from the children for more than a year. They were sixteen, thirteen, and nine when she departed. Despite these lacunae in the relationship between Micael and her children, all the sons, Gaston in particular, were devoted to her when they grew up.

Célestin, the eldest, was eighteen when he openly defied his father. Four months before he was to graduate from the military academy where his grandfather had placed him, he escaped by vaulting over the walls. He insisted on living with Micael in Paris, although he tried to maintain a relationship with his father as well. In response to young Célestin's overtures to his father, his grandfather wrote to him:

> Monsieur de G. has come to tell us that after having defied the paternal authority for three years [by continuing to see his mother] you are asking to be restored to grace, and that were such a favor to be refused you, you threatened to enlist in the army and to have yourself killed before Algiers. He himself was greatly moved by that, but as to ourselves, we were far from frightened. . . .
>
> My father, his two brothers, and six of his nephews did not meet with death in the several campaigns where all won distinction. . . . The brother of your own grandmother was not killed in the glorious campaigns of the Indies. . . . I myself, was not killed in my campaigns in America under Count d'Estaing, who led us tirelessly . . . and for me it was all as so much added glory.
>
> I did not fear to expose my son in the wars of the Emperor because I felt that, if he were to show himself in the world with honor, he had to have a career; he chose that which had been adopted by the men in his family. He was not killed. . . .

Here, Pontalba mentioned each battle his son witnessed, ending with the "brilliant and dangerous retreat of Portugal." The marquis d'Hautpoul, who was with Célestin's brigade during the campaign in Iberia, wrote in detail about the quite inglorious retreat in Portugal, describing Célestin's division and all its activities. He even described General Masséna's mistress, and the mistress' parakeet, both of whom accompanied the troops. But he did not mention Célestin.[59] Pontalba, however, assured his grandson that the elder Célestin "won the esteem of the brave among braves"—a reference to Marshal Ney—"who saw him always first and cool-headed at places always most perilous. . . . After all, were you to be killed, it would at least be more honorable than to meet death in a duel, as might well happen through the sort of life you are leading, and among the sort of people with whom you associate. . . ."[60] When young Célestin failed to comply with Pontalba's conditions for reconciliation, the old man revised his will, depriving his grandson of a yearly income of 80,000 francs ($20,000), which he had settled on him in 1830 when the boy reluctantly agreed to enter the school. Pontalba was to rewrite the will two more times, in July, 1834, and on the day of his death, making each revision more insulting toward all three grandsons.[61]

Alfred and Gaston had likewise been placed in a preparatory school which would groom them for Saint-Cyr, the prestigious military academy near Senlis where old Pontalba planned to enter all of his grandsons. According to a contemporary, such military nurseries were not particularly harsh, having for professors old men who were "ossious, lymphatic, and banal."[62] The main intellectual exercise of the students was trying to circumvent the school rules, and the memorable cruelties were those practiced by the boys on each other. Nevertheless, Alfred and Gaston ran away from their school in 1833, the year after Célestin's defection, when they were sixteen and thirteen. Apparently, they lived in or near Mont-l'Évêque after fleeing their boarding school, probably in another institution but not at their grandfather's château. Micael remarked to Azélie that their father had not seen them a single time in six months, nor had he answered any of their letters though they wrote to him "incessantly."[63] Micael corresponded daily with her children, it seems; mail was delivered in Paris every few hours. However, the Pontalbas allowed her to see the younger boys only once every two weeks when she could have them to dinner. Célestin refused to let them spend their summer vacation with their mother. Micael wrote to Azélie that her one consolation was that her children were "perfect."

Although the younger sons were treated with indifference by both their father and grandfather, young Célestin ultimately became one of old Pontalba's obsessions. During these years Célestin was apparently an exceptionally sweet boy. Every letter one encounters concerning him refers to him as "sensitive," "loyal," "loving," and utterly devoted to his mother.[64] However, as long as young Célestin lived with Micael, he was shunned by all the Pontalbas, who considered him in revolt against his father. The harder the young man tried to approach his family, the more violent his grandfather's rejection became. Having Célestin live with her, Micael wrote, was "certainly a great comfort to me in my sorrow—without him, I would be dead. . . . God knows how all this will end." She repeated again and again how vital his presence was to her. After months of being turned away from his father's door, young Célestin was "broken-hearted" and apparently became somewhat obsessed himself with forcing a meeting. "The poor boy left yesterday to go talk to his father at Mont-l'Évêque," Micael wrote in November, 1833; "probably they won't let him in." The Pontalbas refused to listen to any propositions from Micael regarding Célestin. "I would gladly give him to them for six months of the year," she wrote. "But for always? I don't have the heart."[65] Their attitude succeeded in making Micael suffer. "Read my letter and hide it," were the grave instructions she wrapped around a missive to one of her cousins; "Farewell, my good friends, I have a very heavy heart." The cousin obeyed, and the letter is still hidden.[66]

But Célestin also pulled at his adolescent's leash when he was with his mother. Micael commented uncomplainingly that young men had many expenses. In 1833, Micael's friend Marie, who had just become the duchesse d'Elchingen, wrote to her husband about a visit she received from young Célestin. The boy spent the afternoon with her, "hardly able to speak without crying," because his mother was trying to keep him away from a young lady who had no fortune, one Joséphine Tascher, a relative of Napoleon's Joséphine. Marie sympathized completely with "this poor Célestin." Micael kept sending him back to Mont-l'Évêque "like a pestilence," Marie complained,

> because she's afraid he will be so crazy as to marry a charming, good, pretty, and pleasant girl—that would mean too much happiness! But don't talk to me about fools! The poor unhappy boy told me he didn't know how he would be received by his father and grandfather. That crazy mother did not think of that. She throws her son's devotion to the winds. . . . Célestin is young and loving; he has surely proved his attachment to his mother. Early on she needed him, and he too missed her constantly. . . .

Marie was completely out of patience with Micael, "this goose of a mother who doesn't understand any value outside of money."

However, the Duchess herself was agitated by a preoccupation with wealth. Born Marie-Joséphine Souham in 1801, she married a naval officer who died in 1831, leaving her with a young son and little else. She then wed Michel Ney, duc d'Elchingen (Aloys), in January, 1833. She married for love, both times, as the duc d'Elchingen punctiliously reminded his stepson. "She had no money, nothing, nor did your grandfather. He wanted to give her 10,000 francs as a dowry, but I . . . asked that this money be placed in your name. . . ."[67] Marie could not understand why everyone did not share her indifference to money—it was a favorite theme of her letters to her husband and mother-in-law. When she was not upbraiding her husband by mail for his coldness, she applied herself to showing how happy their marriage was despite their lack of a fortune. "Our lives are filled, not with money and its demands, but with affection and happiness," she wrote early in their war. Fourteen years later, writing to her mother-in-law, she was still not understanding how people could marry with money as their main consideration.[68] The topic of fortune hunting was inexhaustible, not least because it provided Marie with the chaste thrill of ricocheting a little insult through the family. In 1827, Aloys' elder brother, Napoléon Ney, prince de la Moskowa, had stooped to conquer the Laffitte banking heiress, whom Marie and the other relatives genially despised. Money had not been the main consideration in the older brother's choice of a bride; it was the only consideration. Young Célestin's plight gave Marie a chance to pick at one of the family's most cherished little sores.

By the end of 1833, young Célestin was on everyone's mind, for he was being included in the schemes and restrictions by which the Pontalbas hoped to make his mother's life intolerable. A new rule was applied to Micael's entry into Mont-l'Évêque, or rather her hypothetical entry, since Micael was defying court orders to return to the château. She would not be permitted to bring young Célestin with her to the estate, even for an hour. Thus, if she were driven back to her husband out of financial necessity or the courts, she would have to leave her son. "But at eighteen and a half, a man makes his own decisions," she wrote, "and he had firmly decided never to be separated from me. He loves me so much."[69]

Micael, too, described Célestin as "the most sensitive boy you could imagine" and, she might have added, the most persistent, with or without his mother's goading. In August, 1834, Micael wrote to Azélie that her "dear son" had gone to hang around Senlis for a few days, hoping to talk to his father (the quarrel between father and son had now lasted a year and a half), but that when his grandfather caught sight of him, the old man "went into a frightful rage. Can you imagine such a monster?" What Micael did not confide to her relatives was that a new complication had arisen to further poison Célestin's relations with the Pontalbas. Because of an incident in July, 1834, Célestin and two companions were awaiting trial on charges that they had assaulted a hapless stranger on the Champs-Élysées.[70]

Although the Avenue Champs-Élysées in 1834 was little more than a dirt road stippled with litter, every Sunday afternoon it was thronged with carriages and fashionable people out for a bit of fetid air. Micael, young Célestin, and his friends had been riding when the trouble started. According to one Monsieur Laurent, a rug merchant, Célestin hit him on the head with his horsewhip when he failed to move quickly enough out of the path of the young man's carriage. Listeners in the courtroom responded with sympathetic agitation as Laurent recounted how he grabbed the bridle of one of Célestin's horses and was immediately set upon by Célestin's companions: Alfred Mosselman, a scion of manufacturers and the brother-in-law of the Belgian ambassador, and a youth named Klein, the son of a general. Passers-by rescued Laurent from the three miscreants and brought him to the police station. Presenting his blood-soaked shirt as evidence to the court, Laurent added that Célestin's servants stayed behind to buy drinks for some soldiers who had witnessed the fight.

The Pontalbas' attitude toward Célestin could not have been softened by reading in the *Gazette des Tribunaux* that three young men from "the most honorable, elegant, and distinguished families" were seated on the defendants' bench ordinarily reserved for "malefactors, crooks, and vagabonds." However, the incident received only a few inches of print; all the newspapers were far more interested in reporting the trial of Nicoló Paganini, who was accused of having raped a sixteen-year-old girl.

Young Célestin's side of the story was that he had struck the pedestrian initially by accident, and the fracas followed from mutual misunderstanding, before anyone quite knew what had happened. When the judges learned that Micael had been with the men when the incident occurred, they acceded to Hennequin's request to rescind the one-month prison sentence imposed on Célestin and to reduce his fine. Returning rejected time after time from Mont-l'Évêque, Célestin had no opportunity to give his father his lame explanation of the incident. Micael finally decided to go to her husband herself and speak on the boy's behalf. It is not clear why both she and her son considered it critical to reconcile him with the family. The only apparent explanation is that they wanted his pension from his grandfather resumed, but there may have been a great deal more to it than that. Micael wrote to her husband around the middle of October: "I would like to see you as soon as possible to speak to you about your son in order to avoid some great misfortune. . . ."[71]

Before setting out for Senlis early on the eighteenth of October, 1834, Micael scribbled a hasty note to her cousin Victoire Cruzat: "My poor son came back from Mont-l'Évêque yesterday. They would not let him in. The two Pontalbas swore my death."[72] Micael repeats the remark about her death so often in the letters written just before the shooting that one wonders if she had some compelling premonition of the terror that awaited her at the château. If so, she ignored it and set out to see her husband, just a few days before their twenty-third anniversary.

There exist several slightly differing accounts of what happened the next day at Mont-l'Évêque. Micael's account is contained in a letter she had a notary write to her aunt after she had returned to Paris; in it, she took pains to insist that hers was the only "true version" of the shooting and instructed her relatives to disregard rumors that were circulating. There were also letters from Marshal Ney's sons who went to the château as soon as they heard about the shooting and brought out reports of what Célestin and Micael's doctors told them; they were not, however, allowed to talk with Micael. A large and generally reliable compendium of information is the record of Micael's separation suits which came to trial within two years of the shooting. Naturally, the shooting was an important issue in the tribunal's decision as to whether to grant Micael a separation from her husband, and all of the details of the bloody event were described. The lawyers may have deliberately misrepresented what Micael, Célestin, and the family members said and felt toward each other during the crisis, but the court documents do at least quote police and medical reports that would otherwise be lost to us. Newspaper stories are worthwhile mainly for showing what people outside the family were saying about the attack on Micael, or at least what they were saying to journalists. The differences in the various versions of the shooting turn on whether the father-in-law was infuriated by an ugly scene between Micael and Célestin or whether the old man's violence was ignited by just the opposite—a reconciliation and the rekindling of a relationship from which he felt excluded.

According to all accounts, Micael arrived at the village of Mont-l'Évêque on the night of October 18, at about seven-thirty, and went as usual to Madame de Presle's where she left her carriage; she was still not permitted to have horses or more than one servant on the estate.[73] She and her maid and the coachman went on foot to the château. At the gates the male escort was obliged to leave—he went to seek shelter at the gardener's. Micael and the maid proceeded alone. Micael walked directly to her customary exile, the Little Château, where, as it happened, all the family was residing while the main château was being repaired. She asked for her husband and, in order to avoid meeting her father-in-law, went at once to the tiny room she had formerly occupied to wait alone for Célestin.

Her husband joined her between eight and eight-thirty, and they talked until nearly eleven. After the shooting, some newspapers reported that Micael and Célestin had reached a "rapprochement" that "inflamed the elder

Pontalba." Micael's lawyer, on the other hand, pointedly told a court that she and her husband did not make up their differences, and the conference ended without her having "the least hope of reconciliation" for young Célestin.[74] Micael then prepared to spend the night, since at that late hour she did not want to look for her driver and go knocking on Madame de Presle's door.

For once, the account in the newspapers sounds like the right one—that there was some sort of tender interchange between Micael and her husband. Hennequin's statement allows us to infer that Pontalba had been prepared to kill Micael before she even arrived at the château, and that even though Célestin stood his ground and did not acquiesce to his wife's requests (whatever they were), Pontalba went through with his plan anyway. There is much evidence for that interpretation of the events. However, it is hard to believe that Micael and Célestin simply had a long, rational talk—candor and discussion had never characterized their marriage—and it seems unlikely that a calm talk sparked an act of desperation some nine hours later.

More likely, their bitter anger erupted behind the thin, closed door as soon as they were alone. Micael and Célestin had not spoken to each other for many months, and no doubt each had interesting things to say which might have aroused Pontalba's rage. However, if that had been the end of it—two and a half hours of quarreling with no resolution and an exhausted parting—old Pontalba would simply have congratulated his son on having stood up to his curse, and then gone to bed an excited but satisfied man. Something else occurred while Micael and Célestin were together which caused the elder Pontalba to seethe all night and go through with any plan he might have conceived for killing her. What happened was—or might have been—that the couple quarreled in an initial spasm of fury but then extinguished whatever fires had blazed. They did not reconcile the marriage that night, it seems clear. But they parted, at whatever hour, emptied of the evening's tension, and perhaps with enough live affection evident between them that old Pontalba felt devastated and defeated.

Célestin told Micael, when they finally gave up on each other, that she was not to stay in her usual room. He explained that his father was also sleeping in the Little Château, and the old man would not have her in any chamber so near his own. Célestin walked her to the newly assigned room and allowed her to have her maid inside. According to the court records, the maid was the only person who shared Micael's room that night, sleeping on a mattress on the floor.

There could hardly have been a better location for a murder than Micael's new exclave upstairs. It was at the end of an L-shaped corridor which, though not long, was awkwardly positioned so that the bedroom was hard to get to. Not only was there a door to the room itself, but there was a door separating the entire wing from the central part of the house. The hall door closed her off from the main corridor—and also from the stairs that could have been her escape.

The provincial newspapers embellished the grim happenings of the following day. The *Journal de l'Oise* reported that Pontalba, before "going up to execute his daughter-in-law," took a stroll in his garden and commented on the fine weather. But given his tendency to insomnia and single-minded concentration, Pontalba no doubt remained awake in his room all night, drugging himself with hatred until the moment he started out with his guns. Another report noted that Micael was having breakfast in bed when the two pistols were leveled at her.[75] In fact, at nine in the morning of October 19, she was dressed and about to leave Mont-l'Évêque on an empty stomach.[76] Her maid was sent to Madame de Miró to ask whether Micael might come and embrace her before her departure. As soon as Micael was alone, Pontalba, who had apparently been watching for an opportunity, went up to the secluded room with two dueling guns. He found Micael standing near the door with the maid's pallet at her feet. Her own bed was a little distance behind her.

"Do not so much as breathe or you are dead," he told her.

"What do you want of me?" she asked. Though she had often declared that she was afraid of the unpredictable old man, Micael thought the pistols were merely "theater," as she later explained to her lawyer, props intended to scare her into signing some new expropriation of her money.

"Sit down there," he ordered her, indicating the maid's pallet on the floor.

"Me?" she exclaimed.

"Sit down, I tell you, or you will cease to exist this very minute." Sitting and folding her arms, she said, "Very well, now. What do you want?"

"On your knees! You are going to die. I will give you a moment to say your prayers."

To her relatives in New Orleans, Micael later bragged that she then dared him to shoot. But the attentive judges of the tribunal which convened at Senlis the following year heard only that the agitated old man began firing as soon as he had uttered the last words. Two balls shattered her breast, severing an artery. Blood began pouring out of her left side; nevertheless, she got up and ran back toward the alcove where her bed stood. As Pontalba came after her she began screaming, "Don't! I'll give you everything."

"No," he answered, "You are going to die!"

Another ball tore her chest, this time crushing the hand that she had raised instinctively to cover the muzzle of the gun. She pushed him away with her other hand and began trying to get out of the room; but as luck would have it, she ran toward another alcove which again offered no escape. He shot at her again at very close range, but as he, too, was locked in a violent drama, with guns prone to be inaccurate, he missed his target. She pushed past him again, her wounds still jaculating blood, and this time managed to get out of the room. She threw herself into the closed-off corridor where he shot at her again. The gun misfired, perhaps momentarily justifying Micael's retrospective certainty that she had been "protected by God" during the ordeal. The corridor was empty because the old man had taken the precaution of locking the door to the main hall. Frantically twisting the key, she at first succeeded only in giving the lock a second turn; but she corrected herself just as Pontalba reached her. She turned the key twice in the opposite direction and unlocked the door to the stairs.

One story, put out by Micael's doctor who said he got it directly from Micael, was that she managed to get down the steep stairs alone and made it as far as the dining room where the household was gathered. She fell at Célestin's feet, according to this version, spurting blood everywhere, and told her speechless husband, "I am dying. Your father killed me. Forgive me for whatever I've done to you and I forgive you."[77] But Micael wrote to her aunt that once outside the second door, she fell into the arms of her maid who had come running at the sound of the first shot and had heard everything at the door at the top of the stairs without being able to get in. The two women went down the stairs together, the maid half-dragging her mistress as far as the drawing room below. There Micael fell, crying, "Help me!" Pontalba followed them, still holding the guns. He crossed the drawing room, stood over his victim and saw that she was still breathing, although she was unconscious and blood was gushing from her left side. However, instead of shooting her again, he turned away and directed his steps to the main château where he locked himself in his study. Reflective as always, he remained there all day. Sometime near evening he pointed the dueling guns at himself.[78] Only after two shots did he succeed in ending the combat that had obsessed him for twenty-three years. He was nearly eighty when he died.

Micael was more dead than alive. She had four wounds above the heart, two of them shallow and two deep. The doctors from Senlis who were called to the scene believed that some of the material from the projectiles was lodged in her lung, but evidently had not caused the organ to collapse.[79] Her usual doctor, Marjolin, was brought from Paris, along with several eminent others. They collaborated on a diagnosis, necessarily crude, since it was based on what they could see, feel, and hear by probing into the wound with their hands. Without opening her body, which they did not want to do because of the possibility of causing further infection and the certainty of causing hideous pain, they surmised that she had three balls in her chest. One finger of her left hand was "horribly mangled"; the first finger was shot away entirely.[80] If she did not die from loss of blood or the destruction of some vital internal organ, the doctors explained, she would surely succumb to infection within a few days. Firearms of the 1830s discharged their missiles at a slower velocity than modern weapons; pieces of clothing or other debris were often dragged into the wound along with the ball. If that were not enough to contaminate the victim, the material might then be extracted with fingers or forceps fresh from an autopsy. Hence, though they were mystified as to its cause, doctors could accurately predict infection; it was almost inevitable. In the wake of the doctors, the official investigator from Senlis appeared, one Monsieur Faucher. He was later relieved of his duties as *procureur de roi* after delivering himself of the opinion that Dr. Marjolin's medical judgments were worthless.[81]

We do not know how the bleeding was finally stopped—perhaps by packing the wounds with cotton lint. Micael's torment was excruciating the first night and she had a high fever. However, she was always conscious in the days following the incident and nearly always awake, since her torture did not permit her to sleep.[82] Though everyone now believed she was "on the margin of the grave," in her lawyer's words, neither Micael's mother-in-law nor Madame de Miró saw her or inquired about her. In fact, only one person nursed her. He stayed at her bedside the entire first two nights of her ordeal, and thereafter slept two or three hours at a time on a mattress in an adjoining room, within earshot, for she would have no one else touch her. It was he, according to his lawyer, who lifted her in his arms and held her above the bed each time the blood-drenched sheets had to be changed. He promised he would not leave her, and did so only to bury his father.[83]

The maréchale Ney, Micael's best friend, was in Switzerland at Queen Hortense Bonaparte's château when Micael was shot on the nineteenth. The Ney family tried to keep her informed about the shooting as they received information. On October 28, Aloys wrote:

> You have already learned, my dear mother, through the newspapers you re-
> ceive there, of the horrible events at Mont-l'Évêque. . . . I remember so well
> that you told us not long ago that it was really unwise of her to go like that
> all alone out there. . . . She has so much vitality, so much hope and docility
> in following the doctors' injunctions that they think they will be able to
> save her. . . . Célestin arrived from Paris and he and his father do not leave her.

Napoléon Ney, called Léon in the family, remarked, "The two old women, the mother and aunt, live in one corner of the château and do not see Madame de Pontalba, whose husband and son do not leave her for an instant. A surgeon is set up near her."[84]

The Ney sons, quite attached to their mother and protective of her, did not want her to get mixed up in the mess at Mont-l'Évêque, even though Micael was asking to see her friend. Consequently, the sons made trips to the château so as to be able to provide reliable information to their mother and forestall her going there herself. Léon, who was the eldest and most outspoken, wrote on November 8:

> As for this sad affair at Mont-l'Évêque . . . if Madame de Pontalba survives,
> which is uncertain now, you can bet she's going to ask for some sort of advice,
> which you should give her—you can wait to reproach her later. What you need
> to tell her is this: don't consult your business advisers about these things; con-
> sult only your heart when it comes to reconciling with your husband, for it
> alone can guide you.

He went on to suggest that his mother should tactfully warn "this poor woman" that Célestin's tender care of her might have some ulterior motive—as if Micael needed warnings about Célestin's motives. "Especially, don't go yourself to Mont-l'Évêque," Léon cautioned his mother. "I don't want to see you publicly associated with this tragedy, or with that imbecile

Pontalba who was so inept he couldn't even do a decent job of putting a bullet through his head."

Meanwhile, Micael suffered. Her doctors probably had not prescribed the opium palliatives normally given for pain, since it is reported that she had no sleep. She was, however, tended by prominent men of science whose names were well known to Paris' wealthy and infirm. By the fourth day, though the doctors continued to report her condition as "desperate," she had in fact begun to show signs of healing. She had a relapse after five days, a fainting spell brought on by the practice in those times of "starving" wounds and, incidentally, the wounded patient. But as the doctors believed she could not possibly survive such massive injuries in an area of vital organs, they withdrew somewhat from treating her, and she got better. They thought it was a good idea to bleed her every few hours, a little at a time, so as to avert inflammation, though half the furniture and all of the rugs in the Little Château showed that she had been bled pretty radically already.[85] Doctors thought it was a good idea to bleed everybody for everything; Prime Minister Guizot had had bloodlettings to relieve migraine headaches.[86] However, it gradually became clear that despite the doctors' most diligent medical procedures, Micael was going to live. Her fever subsided after a week. As she passed her thirty-ninth birthday on November 5, the torn flesh lost some of its redness and began to form scabs. After three weeks, the doctors delicately reported that her stomach had returned to its normal functions. With two balls still in her chest, she got up and demanded to return to Paris.

It is easier to surmise what Micael was thinking as she left Mont-l'Évêque than it is to hazard presumptions about Célestin. She refused to remain in a house already stained with her suffering. Her husband's demonstration of love, however sincere, was too late and probably too little also, since he did not suggest going with her to Paris, as a man bent on reconciliation might have done. In fact, Marie, the duchesse d'Elchingen, reported on November 9 that all the rumors and noises of reconciliation were wrong, since Célestin "positively told Monsieur Urquhart that nothing had changed in his relations with his wife; that she could count on every care and consideration, but that he had obligations to fulfill toward Madame de Miró and his mother, and he did not want to have his father's memory blighted by the accusation that he had been the only cause of their failed marriage." Hennequin was cynically terse about Célestin's ministrations during Micael's recovery. "I will not seek to interpret his action," he said. "When a man does one honorable thing, we must accept it without discrediting it with a commentary." Regarding Célestin's care of her during her convalescence, Micael remarked only that her husband "behaved toward me as he should."[87]

She held out her hand to him in parting, but "he responded only with angry looks" and would not speak. During those three weeks of healing and endearment, he must have entertained some small hope that she would offer to stay with him and that they could then start over and have a normal, boring marriage. But she was going back to her own home in Paris; and after only a few months, he would be going back to court to expropriate the rest of her money. If he had been willing to forgive her and be forgiven when she seemed to be dying, he changed his mind when she was decidedly alive. A male servant was allowed to carry out her bag. She did not have to walk to the village to fetch her horses. For the first time in years, she left Mont-l'Évêque in a carriage.

Andrés Almonester in 1797, in a painting by Salazar. Micaela's younger sister
was born about the time this portrait was made, a few months before his death
at age seventy.

Courtesy of the Archdiocese of New Orleans

"Portrait of my mother," by Gaston de Pontalba
Courtesy of the Louisiana State Museum

Célestin Delfau de Pontalba. At his wedding to Micaela in 1811, all noted that the
groom was beautiful and the bride rich.
Courtesy of the Louisiana State Museum

Joseph Xavier Delfau de Pontalba, Micaela's father-in-law. His lifelong obsessions
were his son and Micaela's money.
Courtesy of the Louisiana State Museum

Célestin Delfau de Pontalba[?], ca. 1830. He retired from Napoleon's army at the age of twenty-two and devoted himself to hunting, and raiding Micaela's fortune.

Courtesy of the Louisiana State Museum

Micaela Almonester de Pontalba, *ca.* 1825, possibly after Célestin left her to return to his parents. The three-year separation was one of the happiest periods of the marriage.

Courtesy of the Louisiana State Museum

Château Mont-l'Évêque, just outside Senlis, where Micaela lived with her husband and his inevitable parents. Here in 1832 the elder Pontalba instructed the family, servants, and visitors to pretend that Micaela was invisible.

Courtesy of the late Samuel Wilson, Jr.

The commune of Mont-l'Évêque with the gate to the Pontalba château. Micaela was required to leave her coach at the gate and walk to her room in the guesthouse.

Courtesy author

The Little Château where Micaela was confined in 1832 and where old Pontalba tried to kill her in 1834.

Courtesy of the late Samuel Wilson, Jr.

Micaela, *ca.* 1840, when she was about forty-five. The artist (possibly Gaston de Pontalba) has obscured her shattered fingers and has perhaps idealized her, since the portrait shows no evidence of her massive chest injuries.

Courtesy of the Louisiana State Museum

Letter from Micaela to her cousin in 1835, after the shooting and the first trial, when Micaela sent her son Célestin to New Orleans to get him away from the scandal.

Courtesy of Howard-Tilton Memorial Library

Visconti's Hôtel Pontalba as it looked when Micaela lived in it with her sons, before its façade was remodeled by Félix Langlais.

Courtesy of the Louisiana State Museum

The U.S. Embassy residence in Paris, formerly the Hôtel Pontalba, an apt symbol of the two worlds of the Baroness de Pontalba.

Courtesy of the U.S. Department of State

Ange Tissier, "The Architect Visconti Presents his Plans for the New Louvre to the Sovereigns." Napoléon III and Empress Eugénie are seated before Visconti. Behind the emperor, looking away from Visconti, is Léon Ney, Prince de la Moscowa.

Courtesy of Musée Versailles

Micaela's Chinese lacquer panels on a pink and white tile floor, one of the many
lavish accessories she purchased from a royal mansion of the seventeenth century
and installed in the Hôtel Pontalba.

Courtesy of the Louisiana State Museum

The Louis Seize room of the U.S. Embassy residence, used now for small
receptions.

Courtesy of the U.S. Department of State

Micaela's son Célestin [?], b. 1815, in a painting dating from about 1836. Sensitive and loving as a youngster, he was a problem child throughout his life.

Courtesy of the Louisiana State Museum

Self-portrait by Gaston de Pontalba, Micaela's youngest son, b. 1821.

Courtesy of the Louisiana State Museum

Micaela in 1841, when she was forty-six. Two of her children died at a very young age. Three sons grew up to adore and fear their mother.

Courtesy of the Louisiana State Museum

St. Louis Cathedral as Micaela saw it when she returned to New Orleans
in 1849. On the right is her property on St. Ann Street that would be the site
of the Lower Pontalba.

Courtesy of the Historic New Orleans Collection, accession no. 1959.3

Micaela in a photograph taken probably just as she landed in New Orleans from France in 1849, when she was "dead tired," according to Gaston.

Courtesy of the Louisiana State Museum

Gaston's sketch of the Place d'Armes in 1849, before the construction of the Pontalba Buildings and the renovation of St. Louis Cathedral.

Courtesy of the Louisiana State Museum

Gaston's sketch of the Place d'Armes in 1851, after the church was remodeled. German was by this time heard as frequently in parts of New Orleans as French and English.

Courtesy of the Historic New Orleans Collection, accession no. 1940.3

Gaston's sketch of St. Charles Avenue with Gallier's new City Hall. Though many new buildings graced New Orleans in 1850, the city remained the capital of mildew and malaria, with epidemics of cholera and periodic yellow fever.

Courtesy of the Louisiana State Museum

A sketch by Gaston of Jenny Lind in 1851, when she lived in the Pontalba Buildings. After the star's departure, Micaela auctioned off everything she had left behind, including her alleged thimble and her chamber pot.

Courtesy of the Louisiana State Museum

The Upper Pontalba on St. Peter Street, sketched by Gaston. The Pontalbas were monuments to the new vogue for exact duplication which manufacturing made possible.

Courtesy of the Louisiana State Museum

Gaston's watercolor of St. Louis Cathedral, the Presbytere, the Lower Pontalba, and boats on the Mississippi, as seen from his house in the Upper Pontalba, across the Place d'Armes. Trees like the newly planted ones in the picture now block the view between the two Pontalbas.

Courtesy of the Louisiana State Museum

The Pontalba Buildings were mail-order houses, with practically every part sent from somewhere else. They show that Samuel Stewart was a remarkable builder, and Micaela was a lay genius in architecture. The Upper Pontalba encloses Jackson Square on the left side.

Photo: Frank Methe, Jr.

The AP monogram may have been designed by Gaston, whose notebooks show many trial sketches of it.

Photo: Ann M. Ball

The Lower Pontalba encloses Jackson Square on the right. Almonester's St. Louis Cathedral, with the Presbytere and Cabildo on each side, stands between the two blocks of Pontalbas. Micaela's buildings captured what eluded her in life: the predictable, the lyrical, and the lighthearted.

Photo: Frank Methe, Jr.

Beginning in 1852, Micaela reported that her husband was "losing more of his mind by the minute." By the time this portrait was made in the 1860s or 1870s, Célestin had outlived most of life's inclemencies.

Courtesy of the Louisiana State Museum

Despite her hard-won legal separation, Micaela spent the last twenty-three years of her life caring for her sick husband. Marriage was an awkward container for their love. Photograph *ca.* 1860.

Courtesy of the Louisiana State Museum

Célestin *b.* *1813* (died December, 1814)

Célestin II *1815–1885*
+ 1) Blanche Ogden *d.* *1878*

    Edouard *1839–1915*
    + Clotilde Vernois *1841–1924*

        Georges (died at 15)

        Jeanne de Pontalba *1870–1942* (Micaela's godchild)
        + Jacques Kulp

    Michaelle Louise *1844–1906*
    + Georges duMesnil de Maricourt

        Jean de Maricourt (died at 22, Micaela's godchild)

        Michaelle de Maricourt *1865–1947*

    Henri *1846–1880*

+ 2) Marie-Claire de Barneville

    Fernand *b.* *1880*

    son (died in infancy)

Micaela
1795–1874
and
Célestin
1791–1878

Alfred *1817–1877*
+ 1) Cecile de Parseval *1839–1862*

    Michel Delfau, Baron de Pontalba *1860–1942*

+ 2) Louise d'Estrées *1840–1915*

Mathilde *1819–1821*

Gaston *1821–1875*

A Separation of Body and Belongings

MICAEL did not see her husband for several months, and thought that she perhaps might never see him again. She faced that prospect serenely. The shooting was a turning point in her feelings toward Célestin. The ambivalent and intermittent affection she seems to have had for him when she went to Mont-l'Évêque, a comparatively healthy woman, had turned to committed hostility by the time she returned wounded and traumatized to Paris.

The day after she got back, she charged a notary, a Monsieur Dupoux, with composing a letter to her aunt, "the only true narrative" of the shooting that had taken place three weeks before.[1] Sitting near Micael's bed as he wrote, Dupoux explained that Micael had gone to Mont-l'Évêque only for the sake of her son. Her sole motive in seeing Célestin alone was to avoid a scene with the "crazy father-in-law whom she greatly feared." In his blunt, decorous style, Dupoux described the meeting between husband and wife, the preparations for departure the next morning, and finally, shot by shot, the old man's attack on Micael (" 'You would never dare shoot me,' she tells him; for an answer she gets a ball in the chest!"). After assuring Victoire that Micael was expected to live, Dupoux observed that in Paris she was suddenly "the object of interest and attention, even among personages who had stopped seeing her." He noted with resilient optimism that "this event can only work to her advantage."

The Paris newspapers also reported the shooting, generally refraining from elaboration, since nothing was so commonplace in Paris as domestic violence. The conservative *Journal des Débats* speculated that the attack at Mont-l'Évêque was caused by "exalted paternal love which directed the hand" of the attacker. But the paper was less concerned with the "unfortunate old man" than with its continuing report of the Paganini rape case which now had exercised *Journal* readers for four months.[2] The writer Stendhal was offended that left-wing newspapers indulged in waggish remarks about "blue-bloods" and "blood relatives" in reporting the sanguinary incident.[3] Stendhal knew both Micael and Célestin and felt their shame. But it is not surprising that in France, where so many aristocrats were shackled to their in-laws and were alert to the hypocrisies of family life, those who did not know the Pontalbas were wickedly amused by their scandal. People who were acquainted with them were horrified. The Ney sons, who knew all of Micael's querulous little ways, nevertheless felt that neither her husband nor her son were doing enough to help her get over what Edgard called "a bloody nightmare." Léon, the prince de la Moskowa, writing to his mother of "this poor Mme. de Pontalba," commented that he was devastated by the event, even after thinking about it for several days. "It's stupid and cruel, everything you tell me about Mont-l'Évêque. Her husband's behavior is outrageous. As for Célestin [Micael's son], I can hardly believe that he's turning into such a nasty character; he's always been such a self-possessed little gentleman. Poor Mikaël was always exaggerating the slightest irregularities and awarding him a bit too much of the paternal heritage. I don't think he should go to his mother right now for any reason." After indulging in various disparagements of his own in-laws, the bankers, Léon added, "In the Laffitte house, they blame Mikaël for what happened and make her out to be the one in the wrong."[4] Aloys, the duc d'Elchingen, who was thoughtful and open in his letters to his mother, was also depressed by the Pontalba affair.

> For me, the outcome of this horrible mess is that now I understand you; of all of us, you were the one who most loved this poor Mme. de Pontalba. . . . Marie has been terribly affected—also those four good-hearted Urquhart girls, despite what you hear about backbiting between them and Mme. de Pontalba. . . . I don't know anything more appalling than this miserable business. And to think, the evil force behind it was by no means a question of honor. Just money. Filthy money, between two and two hundred thousand francs in fat rents, that got them into something so sordid, disgusting, and tragic. What an awful position for her husband and her poor son—that good, devoted boy—mixed up in all that horror. If she comes out of this, poor woman, she's bound to be scared to death; she was already so frightened and nervous and had so many anxieties. I wonder what all those staunch defenders of the sanctity of marriage would say about this one ending with a murder and a suicide? What violent times we live in![5]

Edgard Ney criticized young Célestin's returning to Paris and his girl-friend before his mother could be moved out of Mont-l'Évêque. "I think Célestin is really behaving badly toward his mother, to abandon her just at the moment when she needs him most." He also had less sympathy than his brother for the "awful position" of the elder Célestin, who, he wrote, "impresses me as a greedy low-life who takes after his father. The poor woman has every reason to complain."[6]

The shooting was not Pontalba's final attack on his daughter-in-law. A last swat was contained in the will that was found with the old man's body, a long document which he had revised while the rest of the household attended to his victim. "The only one of my son's children [young Célestin] to whom I attached special importance and whom I held in great affection," he began, consigning Alfred and Gaston to preterition,

> having made himself unworthy of my regard by his revolt against the best of fathers, by leaving his studies, contrary to advice, in order to devote himself to idleness and dissipation and the worst of companions, under the hypocritical pretext of being useful and necessary to a mother whose example for him will be pernicious, I declare that I revoke all testaments. . . .[7]

Pontalba instructed that his money was to be used for a boarding school for sixty boys to be selected from Louisiana, Senlis, and Mont-l'Évêque. The youngsters, who would matriculate at the age of ten, were to be dressed in uniforms identical to soldiers and were to be subjected to military discipline. During the ten-year program they were never to sleep outside the college, even during vacations, a rule Pontalba stated twice.[8]

If the end of 1833 had been a time of loneliness and hopelessness for Micael, the last months of 1834 seemed to close in on her husband Célestin with more adversity than he had previously known in his shielded life. On November 24, 1834, a fortnight after Micael left Mont-l'Évêque, Judge Charles Maurian of Parish Court in New Orleans rendered a thoughtful decision in the case of Célestin Delfau de Pontalba versus his wife, a decision in which he used the most astringent words in the vocabulary of civil justice to rebuke Célestin on every issue raised in his petition to the court.[9] After refuting each of Célestin's complaints, the judge, who did not yet know of the shooting and suicide, discharged himself of several observations. "I cannot conceive by what process of reasoning M. de Pontalba can call [the lots on the Place d'Armes] his property," he wrote. Maurian enumerated the notarized acts by which the elder Pontalba had conveyed "first this and then that property" to his son in order to avoid matching the cash donation which had been promised in Célestin's marriage contract. One thing was very certain from the transactions between father and son, Maurian wrote: the community between Micael and Célestin "had been deprived of all the profits it could expect" from the dowry Pontalba promised to the couple. "It is really difficult to understand the whole of those continual doings and undoings," Maurian went on, his exasperation gaining heat.

> But when I take the deposition of F. Percy on the record, from which it appears that from the year 1816 to 1827, he as agent of the plaintiff [Célestin] collected nearly two hundred thousand dollars of the income of the property of the defendant, I remain fully convinced that the 52,000 dollars which the plaintiff claims as the balance of the *dot* of his wife have been fully paid to him.

Maurian dismissed the idea that the buildings were in any sense community property or that Madame Castillon's will had given the Pontalbas any pretension to her property, two of Célestin's most insistent points. "It is difficult to understand," the judge wrote, "how, from the contents of that [Castillon] Will . . . the defendant ought to be deprived of the other half of her succession." He conceded to Célestin the right to be reimbursed for his improvements to the property; but he opened the door for Micael to demand a full accounting from her husband of all the rents he had collected during eleven years, a suggestion that must have struck Célestin like the first cold blast of a threatening winter. As if to confirm Maurian's acerb judgment that Micael had been badly treated, six weeks after his ruling the first brief report of Micael's attempted murder reached New Orleans and appeared in *L'Abeille*. Probably no one read it with livelier interest than the judge.[10]

In Paris, Célestin made one attempt to see his wife, or at least to look at her, around the time Maurian was writing his decision. He walked into her Paris apartment and met "a gathering somewhat numerous," since he chose for his visit the first receiving day she held after returning home.[11] He ambled among the guests for a few moments, secured some little information from the visitors who were themselves no doubt avid for privity to the scandal, and disappeared, according to Hennequin, before Micael saw him. Soon afterward Célestin informed Micael that hostilities were to be resumed, presumably meaning that he would appeal Maurian's biting judgment and press his longstanding appeal of the 1831 ruling of Judge Pitot. He continued to garnish her rents in Paris. "It was unbelievable," Hennequin said. Célestin intended to apply "positively the same principles after the 19th of October at nine in the morning as he had applied before that time."

But Célestin's behavior is really not so hard to understand. He had never been noted for having inner reserves of strength or the insight to see through his problems to their center. Yet in the aftermath of the shooting, it was he who had had to look at his father's spattered organs, check the body for any sign of life, find on the desk the will with its fresh ink, and, for all we know, some other guilt that his father may have left for him. The household had frantically looked to Célestin to keep Micael from bleeding to death. He had had the presence of mind to summon doctors; to make his father's burial arrangements; to persuade the local curé to perform the funeral rites even though his father was a suicide, by "proving" that his father had been crazy.[12] In short, Célestin, too, had suffered a profound trauma. He had not collapsed in shock, like his mother and Madame de Miró, although the nightmare was to attack him later on. He had managed to keep going, surviving, like many a more independent thinker in stressful circumstances, by following old patterns of behavior and doing what his father would have done in the same situation.

Célestin could not have repudiated his father in just a few weeks, after what he had been through. After all, he had failed for the previous twenty years to notice that his father was ruining his life. In the miasma of his shock and grief, he could not have apprehended the old man's sins. If his wife would not come back to him when his father was no longer able to stand between them, well, then, that was proof that his father's suspicions of her were correct all along; to abandon his lawsuits would be tantamount to declaring that his father had been in the wrong.

As for Micael, her own pain and debility had come to preoccupy her more than the lawsuits. Three months after the shooting, on January 21, 1835, the *Gazette des Tribunaux* (using who knows what source?) reported that she was "now completely recovered, one finger only has been amputated; two of the three balls . . . have been extracted." This was surprising information to the woman who spent several hours a day with doctors, and who in effect lost two fingers and in fact retained two balls.[13] "You say that I give galas attended by the king and queen," she wrote to her cousins. "But my dears, how can you believe such nonsense?" In the first place, she explained, her condition was always unpredictable, even after nine months.

> I am in bed at six in the evening at least four days a week and I have not appeared in society one single time since my incident. Moreover, kings and queens, you know, never attend any affairs but those given by royalty, and as I do not yet have the crown that I told Malvina I would wear someday, I don't invite the king.[14]

The extent of her socializing since the shooting was having dinner "a few times" at Charles' house and going for a walk afterward with a Creole friend,

Madame Anatole, in the Bois de Boulogne. She had forgiven her cousin for abandoning her in the black winter of 1833, for he was also ill. "The poor devil is suffering terribly," Micael wrote. "He nearly always has a fever." For several years she wrote of traveling to various spas in the hope that "going to the waters" would make the two balls come out of her chest. Charles accompanied her on one such trip to Cottret, not far from Senlis, in the summer of 1835. Then as now in France, the water from certain natural springs was believed to have curative powers if one soaked in it and drank the copious quantities prescribed for a period of a few weeks. Right after the shooting, Edgard Ney had written from his army post that Micael

> should not be disturbed about the balls in her body. Our surgeons, who are accustomed to such wounds, say that nothing is less dangerous, that they will eventually come out by themselves through the skin, by means of a light incision; and they even say—I guess it's a proverb—that the bullet contains the person's soul.[15]

Micael's wounds were layered with scar tissue that raked across her body in three deep lines, according to her doctors; the bullets, with or without soul, were probably firmly sealed within an internal tissue capsule as well. Nevertheless, her physicians never gave up trying to coax out the materials, and blamed the balls for everything from her fainting spells to the alarming convulsions that overtook her if the shooting was so much as mentioned in her presence. Early on, the doctors had begun "numerous and abundant bloodlettings," according to one report, which, it was dryly noted, "weakened the patient considerably and greatly increased her nervous attacks."[16] As late as 1851, many years after the shooting, a doctor was addressing the balls with an application of fifteen leeches around Micael's neck—she wrote a letter to Azélie while waiting for the worms to work their tractive magic.[17]

Micael had been sick even before her father-in-law's attack. There were "bad nerves," abdominal "inflammation," and convulsions of the sort she had described to Victoire after her first experience with ostracism in the Little Château. The doctors thought Micael's seizures were caused by her marital problems. The word *epilepsy* does not appear in either her medical or her legal records. Her convulsive seizures, as they were termed, increased in severity and frequency over the years and were occurring daily in the year after the shooting. She was in unremitting pain from the damaged nerves in her hand. The doctors speculated that one of her injured lungs had not repaired itself, since she was too short of breath to climb any stairs. Micael's letters from 1834 to 1852 attest that although Pontalba did not succeed in killing his daughter-in-law, he caused her to spend much of her middle age in bed.

With the shooting, Hennequin thought he finally had irrefutable evidence of Micael's mistreatment by the Pontalbas. Thus, in February, 1835, as soon as she was well enough to ride to Senlis, he petitioned the court to lift the garnishments on her property—in effect to grant her a separation.[18] The trial that would permit or deny "a separation of body and belongings" was a quite different contest than the divorce actions Americans are familiar with. As in all civil processes, the plaintiff's lawyer filed an initial petition which the defendant answered; the plaintiff responded to that answer and also filed another argument, which was in turn answered by the adversary. Thus, over a period of months, each side submitted its arguments in writing together with documents supporting its position.[19] The entire case was debated, as it were, by correspondence. As arguments and documents were filed by one litigant, the other side filed rejoinders and registered counter claims. Eventually, when the lawyers for both parties believed the file contained enough documentary evidence to support the application of certain points of law, the case was brought before the judges. The Pontalba case went to trial on May 11, 1835.

Neither Micael nor Célestin had great reason to dread the days in court, since no testimony would be taken from them or anyone else. It was the lawyers who lost sleep before a French trial; they alone spoke before the bar, and what they said was critical. First one advocate and then the other addressed the court, their long speeches taking up most of the courtroom proceeding. These pleadings, as the speeches were called, closely resembled the summations to the jury that take place in United States courts at the end of a trial. Like summations, they were usually completed without interruption either from the judges or opposing counsel. Each attorney avoided discussing legal details of the case; he described events in the marriage, from his client's viewpoint, of course, and tried to appeal to judges' emotions. A lawyer might put forth debatable arguments in his pleadings without fear of contradiction until his opponent had his turn (perhaps one or two days later, as in the Pontalba case) to make a presentation or offer a rebuttal. Micael and Célestin were required to attend the trial, but only as spectators whose presence was not acknowledged in the courtroom and who did not participate in the proceedings. Separation trials were not open to the public because of the intensely personal details they might reveal; Micael received a few passes which she sent to her cousin Charles so that he and one or two friends might watch.

After some formalities, Hennequin, being the plaintiff's lawyer and entitled to the first speech, began his discourse. Extemporaneous deliveries were rare; most lawyers read their pleadings, looking up at their listeners as our politicians do when they make speeches. Hennequin, it was said, spoke from memory, reciting "with such naturalness, one wondered if he were improvising."[20] He opened in the usual way by reviewing the history of the marriage, going back even to Madame Almonester's purchase of her children's inheritance in 1798, a task of some hours which, he confided, "condemns all of us to the contemplation of painful memories." As he mentioned each relevant document, he produced it from his folders for the court—an important responsibility, since nineteenth-century jurists liked nothing so much as paper. In the course of his lecture, the table before the three magistrates received a marriage contract; notarized property arrangements; Madame Castillon's will and inventory; documents expressing Célestin's intention to live separately; letters from the spouses, both indiscreet and all too contrived; the court judgments from America; letters to notaries; medical reports; the archive of all the couple's previous court hearings, including the ones that did not result in trials; and decisions written by the same judges who sat across the bar observing the lawyer over the acervate paper.[21]

Hennequin was a courtly ultraroyalist, famed for his rhetorical skill as were all the celebrated lawyers of his day, an orator who, it was said, drew tears from his audiences. Though he had a reputation for "sentimental eloquence," his pleadings on Micael's behalf were fairly restrained.[22] He told the tribunal that the shooting opened an abyss of such depth between Micael and Célestin that continuing the garnishments of her rents amounted to a persecution. Tracing the previous separations, Hennequin said that Micael had turned over her property to the Pontalbas in the hope of buying if not happiness, then at least tranquillity; but that after each donation she had been deserted by a "whimsical" and "capricious" husband. As for her own departure to New Orleans, Célestin knew in his heart, Hennequin said, that he himself had compelled her to make the trip. The lawyer described in all their grotesque detail the rules Micael met when she returned to Mont-l'Évêque, the isolated existence that was "a constant torture." Micael wanted to know, he said, if this was really the life intended for her by her husband, and questioned Célestin "with that persistence full of sweetness which forms the very essence of her character." Only when the marriage seemed hopeless did she resort to seeking legal advice, he said. "She advances no pretensions to possession of a knowledge one does not expect from her sex," he assured the court, but even she could see that "this was not the sort of marriage which society had promised her. . . ." Hennequin then recounted Micael's interview with Célestin regarding their son; the night spent in the isolated room; the shooting; and Micael's convalescence amid "the voices of strangers," since the old man's widow and aunt continued to reject her. Hennequin seems to have read aloud word for word the reports of the committee of doctors charged with describing Micael's physical condition, read their unanimous and strongly stated conclusion that she might not survive another residency at Mont-l'Évêque. The lawyer took pains to make the judges understand that Célestin had never managed to stay long away from Mont-l'Évêque and that any pretense he might make of offering Micael some other home was a ruse: "M. de Pontalba, if he wants to keep his mother with him, no longer has any sort of suitable domicile for his wife." Forcing Micael to face "looks of unabating affliction or hatred" would be heartless both to her and to the old man's widow, he said. He reminded the court of Micael's convulsive seizures. How could they condemn a wife to the fear that in such desperate moments she might fall unconscious into the hands of the widow and son of the "brutal" old man?[23] He ended the speech of many hours by turning again to the husband. Célestin had no right to expect anything except what might come to him of the free will of his wife, he concluded; "no one possessed of the least feeling of generosity or even of sanity, could imagine . . . that coercion was now conceivable." Hennequin addressed, in short, every argument that might have been educed in his client's behalf.

Célestin's lawyer made a similar presentation, reviewing the union from its beginning, this time from the perspective of the Pontalbas, particularly the late father. Léon Duval was Célestin's friend as well as his attorney. He was little known at the time of the Pontalba trial, although by the 1850s he had acquired a reputation of some note. He had visited Mont-l'Évêque during Micael's convalescence, and he implied to the court that he had himself witnessed the husband's ministrations. Duval emphasized the medical progress Micael had made, commenting repeatedly on her remarkable recovery. But he, too, described a marriage in which the only moments of intimacy and happiness seemed to occur when the wife was expected to die.

Finally came the decision, a few terse paragraphs as was customary. Far from agreeing with Hennequin that Micael "should be left to follow her own inclinations," the judges denied her petition for a separation. The garnishments were to remain on her property until she resumed her conjugal life. The tribunal's only concession to her was that Célestin was enjoined from forcing her to live at Mont-l'Évêque; he had to provide some other residence. Since he owned three houses in Paris and the Château Migneaux, that should have been easy enough for him.

How was such a decision possible by men who had heard every detail of the unhappiness, from the silent stares to the maiming, who had received the shrill warning of ten doctors, and who knew every grudge engraved on the marriage from the beginning? Other women, at least a few, were granted separations in France; why not Micael? Who were these blind godlings on the Senlis tribunal?

Of their individual lives, we know only that the three judges were old, contemporaries of the octogenarian Pontalba, and that they were the same men who had for years struck down Micael's efforts to protect her property; Hennequin made that clear as he took the judges to task for their longstanding severity toward his client.[24] Despite their tenure on the court, they may have lacked broad experience. Judges were typically bureaucrats from the bourgeoisie, often men whose fathers and grandfathers had sat on the bench. They neither expected nor received the exalted deference shown to judges in the United States.[25] Hennequin was not unusual in his polite but casual attitude toward the tribunal; both in and out of court, lawyers regarded judges as referees whose decisions had to be followed but who were in no way superior to anyone else in the courtroom. The government salary of a judge was meager compared to the fees commanded by a reputable barrister. However, the magistrates in Senlis were not poor; men appointed to judgeships were generally heirs to comfort and security. All the rulings of a tribunal were rendered as if unanimous, and all dissent was supposed to remain secret. That meant that an individual judge could gain nothing but the enmity of his colleagues by being more forward looking or original than others. Magistrates were some of the most conventional and conservative people in society.

Almost certainly the judges of the Pontalba case were not men of the world. They had no use for theater, opera, balls, dancing, splendid homes, or Paris, if the pleadings of Célestin's lawyer—the winning speech—may be taken to indicate their preferences. Men with any attraction to culture or city sophistication would have been dangerously irritated by Duval's incessant pecking at Parisian life. But the lawyer apparently knew his hearers as well-to-do provincials who shared old Pontalba's prejudices. Duval took no risks when he committed huge portions of his speech to particularizing Micael as a *boulevardière* obsessed with the profligate aristocracy that all the country gentry envied and resented. Micael, who was closer than we to the situation, had no doubt that the tribunal at Senlis was biased. "They tell me I have to be satisfied with the ruling," she wrote, "because all the judges in Senlis are friends of M. de Pontalba."[26]

And yet, the possible limitations of the Senlis magistrates having been noted, we should not assume that they acted only on illiberal or parochial impulses. We may be fairly sure that the higher court at Amiens did not twice uphold their rulings because the appellate judges were neighbors of the Pontalbas, or were awed by the presence in their chamber of a prominent local nobleman. Nor should we suppose that the magistrates were more misogynistic than the rest of French society, any more than we can conclude that our own judges hate the children they remand to abusive parents. There were large issues at stake in the Pontalba affair which no French jurist of the 1830s dared to ignore. All European and American judges of the time re-coiled from interfering with a husband's authority, just as they now hesitate to challenge a natural parent's authority, because the major regulating institution of society was not the police, nobility, church, factory, or company, but the family. The question in the Pontalba case was not, as it might be in a modern court, whether an individual could be forced to follow a law that was harmful to her both physically and psychologically; the individual was at best a secondary consideration. The family, not the citizen, was the basic unit of society, and the husband was responsible for preserving its integrity. All property belonged to the family, not to individual members (a legal nail on which Célestin's lawyer hammered incessantly during the trial). The husband was charged with keeping the property intact. As if to bolster the husband's position as the family's sole representative, women in France were removed by law from public life. Micael's judges were minions of longstanding statutes according to which a woman needed her husband's permission to take a job, be a witness in a criminal trial, obtain a passport, open a bank savings account, enroll her child in school, obtain credit, make a contract, or keep her earnings.[27]

Micael's observation that "Women, poor things, are slaves in this country," was accurate, but the thralldom seemed normal and necessary to most people in Western Europe, including the slaves themselves.[28] Women seldom came into contact with the law and, like Micael in the early years of her marriage, were perhaps only vaguely aware of their legal handicaps. Perhaps they accepted society's compensation—an ideology of domesticity—without realizing that it was a compensation. Only radicals and people with exceptional experiences such as Micael believed that the sanctity of the family, or rather the ideal of sanctity, should be violated by restricting a husband's financial control. Thus, what the judges saw in the Pontalba case, perhaps, was not a "pale, thin, weak" woman having convulsions at the thought of her husband, but a family pressing its legal privileges to have a well-endowed wife remain at home and add her resources to the common pot.[29]

Moreover, by the time Célestin's lawyer finished his presentation, the judges may have had no compelling urge to find a solution, or a dissolution, for the Pontalba marriage. Léon Duval had little of Hennequin's polish, experience, or reputation. Underneath his wig and black robe he was only thirty-one, young in comparison with the forty-nine-year-old Hennequin, and not as schooled in civility as his veteran opponent. The son of a provincial bureaucrat, he had been sent at the age of ten to a boarding school in Paris which he was never allowed to leave, even for vacations, until he received his law degree nine years later. Duval attracted odd clients after the Pontalba case established his reputation. He became something of a specialist in separation cases, but his services were also sought by artists and intellectuals.[30] Even in 1835, before his eccentric career was flourishing, he was quirky and, unfortunately for Micael, amazingly skilled. He treated the court to a brilliant, supple, vicious portrayal of Micael, so thoroughgoing and defacing that if the judges believed half of it, they might have supposed that the intractable woman deserved to be shot.[31]

Duval carefully skirted the fact that the money in question was Micael's inheritance. Instead, he alluded to all the rent revenues as wealth belonging to the family (by which he meant the Pontalbas), wealth that they had liberally allowed Micael to squander. But it was true only as a legal abstraction that Micael's money was part of "the family's wealth," as he called it. She was spending money that she brought to the marriage, not spending those resources accumulated by her husband's family. This was a moral distinction if not a legal one, which the judges might have acknowledged if Duval had not obfuscated the issue. When Duval came to the arrangement by which Célestin divided his wife's inheritance and seized over half of it, the lawyer consistently referred to it as a "family pact." Through this family pact,

Célestin granted his wife "the management and full enjoyment of houses bringing in revenues of 60,000 francs yearly." These were, of course, the houses in France left to Micael in her mother's will. In addition to that "splendid income," Duval said, "the children were allowed to grow up under the eyes of their mother, seemingly heaping on her all the happiness a woman could justly expect from life." It was from such a comfortable situation, he continued, that Micael "suddenly rushed over to America to ask for a divorce . . . acknowledging in writing that she had no other grievance than her *pretension* to a larger portion of *the family fortune* [italics mine], delivering herself, her husband, and her children as so much fodder for all the gazettes of Europe, like some loose woman."[32]

Her suit, Duval said, hid "a nest of corruption."[33] The lawyer would lay bare the sort of marriage it had been for Célestin, "what kinds of deviations he has had to witness, and how watchful he has had to be to protect his honor." The question of money had been raised, "although this was scarcely the place," Duval said. The trial was not about an inheritance but about morality, even though "all the more serious family virtues become in [Madame de Pontalba's] hands a question of money."

Adroitly and without a scrap of evidence, Duval then characterized Micael as a woman whose frantic extravagance and man-chasing had plunged the Pontalbas into debt and subjected Célestin to repeated humiliations. He began with a letter written by Micael's mother to the elder Pontalba in 1811. The letter remarked on the fifteen-year-old girl's many "lovers," or so Duval interpreted Madame Castillon's reference to *amoreux*, by which she surely meant Micael's suitors and sweethearts.[34] Duval perservered in his timeworn contention that the Pontalbas had been cheated out of Micael's dowry through Madame Castillon's "deliberate and deep calculations." Micael wanted a house separate from the Pontalbas so that she could indulge herself in furnishing it. According to the lawyer, Micael could not contain herself, and her husband "satisfied her least desires with an idolatrous weakness. A mansion was bought in a quarter where the rich spread their lands over with gold. . . ." Rue du Houssaie was hardly in a luxurious neighborhood. The house in which Micael and sometimes Célestin lived was the most unprepossessing of all the Pontalba properties. Three years after the trial, the family sold the "mansion" for 21,547 francs—a little over four thousand dollars.[35] Nevertheless, Duval assured the court that Micael's purchase of rugs, hangings, diamonds, and silverware "of a taste and richness rarely surpassed," enabled her to entertain courtiers and famous people who gradually crowded out Célestin's friends. The cost of such magic put the family into debt. But Célestin continued to meet her craving for unbridled luxury. He had, according to Duval, a "prolonged infatuation with his wife," a curious statement that most husbands would be loath to sponsor, unless it were true.[36]

Madame Castillon's bizarre will, as Duval termed it, gave Micael financial independence just at the time when "occasions to stray were getting more frequent, when her husband had to be more watchful than ever because of the many seductions offered by the social world. . . . He had to watch over such things as are known to concern the honor of women." The duties of a married woman were "risked," he continued, in a hectic life full of "capricious dissipations" against which "the needs of her children entered their mute protests." Even in the face of all this, Célestin "consented" to have her enjoy alone the income from the best half of her mother's estate. Célestin's abandonment in 1827 was characterized as a worthy attempt to put a gap between himself and a frivolous existence. " To isolate yourself from your husband is to make a dangerous situation public," Duval lectured the court, as if it had been Micael who left Célestin on rue du Houssaie, and not the other way around. "Elegant vice, fashionable corruption, the idle connivings of roués seem to be ever on the watch for women so separated." By allowing her husband to leave her, Micael had apparently compromised his dignity; Duval referred to Célestin's disappointment when *she* did not return! Finally, having swallowed revenues belonging to her husband, and being refused "outrageous" requests for more, Micael left a mansion where her independent stay had been tolerated for three years and went to New Orleans. She left Célestin in a condition of "despair and stupor."

"Who would ever have believed that the mother of three children would ask for a divorce over a question of money!" Duval exclaimed, in reference to the letter from New Orleans delivered by M. Desuaneaux.

> What civil law itself forbids, what might cause children not to know to whom they belonged, what would offend modesty, what would legalize adultery, what would authorize a wife to leave the arms of one man to fall into those of another, becomes resolved into a mere question of money, one to be settled with a M. Desuaneaux.

The court, he was certain, would find appalling the idea that a woman would expect to collect merely on her own receipts, without permission or control from her husband, the whole of the income from her hereditary properties.

Duval assured the judges that Micael had no hidden grief in her life, that "not the slightest wrinkle" had ever interfered with her night's sleep. As for her treatment at Mont-l'Évêque, Duval called her charges "defamations," "wicked accusations," "rampant calumnies," and "utter nonsense"—her gunshot wounds notwithstanding—from one who had "plunged herself far from her husband into the mad pleasures of the city."[37] The château at Mont-l'Évêque was not a fit place of residence for her, he snickered: "Were not her attempts at conversation forever ignored there? . . . Were her melodies on the piano so much as admired?"

Through his entire presentation, Duval wove insinuations about Micael and Guillemin. He accused Micael of following "that worthy gentleman" over the globe, lying about Guillemin's age to the court so as to misrepresent him as a fatherly escort, and in general exhibiting "reckless" behavior. Guillemin was a decidedly defenseless co-respondent in these accusations, having died earlier in 1835. Guillemin was used as a touchstone to suggest that Micael pressed her uninvited attentions on others. "Has she not brought back from overseas I know not what letters from Monsieur, General Jackson" [Duval should have said "President"], letters which were courteous, the lawyer implied, only because Jackson would not use his leisure "to become severe with ladies who are traveling." But here, Duval said, "we will curb our indignation and throw a veil over these things." At the very least she had paraded her idleness in places strewn with peril for a married woman. The advocate could not bear to uncover so many crudities.

Finally, Duval charged Micael with scheming to lure her son away from school. It was she, said Duval, who led young Célestin into a life of actresses, debts, gambling at the smart clubs, duels, culminating in the incident on the Champs-Élysées.[38] "All this," he concluded, "because an arm was needed for Madame de Pontalba that she might haunt the balls, the opera and the *Bouffes*."[39] The lawyer ended his astonishing performance by congratulating Micael on her "good health," noting that she was "happy today with her excitements, and her joys . . . restored to a life of pleasure." As for her husband, the seizure of the revenues was but an additional burden which he undertook so as "to force Madame de Pontalba to practice economy, to inoculate her with a new sort of domestic virtue."

Hennequin attempted a surrejoinder, but he could hardly begin separating the tangle of half-truths, mistruths, and fabrications that the lawyer had presented so persuasively. Unfortunately, he chose to concentrate on Duval's darkest charge, that Micael wanted a separation in order to do more freely whatever she had done in America with Guillemin. Hennequin might have attacked Duval's silly insinuations about Andrew Jackson, and in that way discredited the lawyer as an oracle of illicit romance; he might easily have refuted the accusation that Micael had put the Pontalbas in debt; he could certainly have exposed the legalism, which Duval treated as practical truth, that in spending her inheritance she was squandering "the family's fortune" to which she had no claim.[40] Instead, he centered his last pleading on the one eighteen-month period in the entire marriage when Micael's actions were open to question. Perhaps Hennequin knew what he was doing. The judges' faces may have told him that the trip to America was the only issue they would listen to. In any case, despite the lawyer's vigorous, perhaps sincere, argument that Micael and Guillemin were platonic and even casual friends, he could not avoid the fact that while her children were on the other side of the Atlantic, she had remained longer than necessary in America, touring the country with a man who was not their father.

Duval's rebutter, the final comments of the trial, left the judges with more thoughts of Micael's sojourn in the United States. Duval pointed out that after she returned in June, 1832, she never remained for long with her husband.[41] Clearly, America (and by implication, Guillemin) had spoiled her for the restrictions of domestic life. In the eyes of the Senlis judges and perhaps many others, leaving France without notice and traveling with Guillemin were serious transgressions, even though her husband had already deserted her and her children were not permitted to live with her. Compounded with the false impressions Duval diffused throughout his pleadings, the case against Micael seemed overwhelming.

And so the garnishments remained.[42] The judges could have had no illusions about the couple's prospects for reunion, much less happiness. But as Micael's next attorney commented, probably intending no irony: "Simple antipathies, angry quarrels, scandalous trials were not sufficient reason to untie the sacred bond of marriage."[43] Micael seemed resigned to the decision, or perhaps was simply too ill to entertain rage. Just before the trial she had marveled at Célestin's hardihood. To think, she remarked to her aunt, "that a man would still have the nerve to attack a woman legally after having tried to kill her." Now she complained to her cousins that while she was unable to leave her bed for anything except an appearance in court, Célestin was telling her friends that she was attending dances. "I am hardly surprised that my husband says I am plump and in fine fettle. He would like people to think that the balls in my chest did me more good than harm."[44] Micael did not give up. Two months after the exhaustive May proceeding, she went back to the judges at Senlis for another hearing aimed at recovering her rents—or perhaps the aim was only to wear down the judges. At that time her petition was dismissed without a trial.

Célestin was understandably delighted with the outcome of these legal encounters, and attempted to prolong his enjoyment of the contest. Young Célestin, wanting to shield his family from publicity, had taken steps to keep the details of the proceedings out of the *Observateur des Tribunaux*, one of the legal journals that reported trials. The younger Pontalba offered the editor of the journal a "quite considerable sum" not to print the lawyers' pleadings.[45] The money was supposedly given to compensate the paper for the stenographic expenses it had already incurred and for its loss of expected sales. Whereupon, Célestin the father compensated the editor with the same amount to have the pleadings re-inserted—not the full pleadings of both lawyers in the case, and not even Duval's complete speech, but only the sections most bruising to Micael. The version of the trial that resulted from this editing so pleased Célestin that he then had it printed and distributed. First, he gave it out among his friends; then, to Micael's friends; and finally, to the entire Chamber of Peers where Micael had relatives—more than five hundred copies in all, each in an esthetic rose binding. Moreover, when he brought the pleadings to Duverger Press, he altered the wording of the tribunal's judgment "so as to give [himself] a crown," according to arguments that Micael's lawyer later presented to the court.

This published brochure attracted as much attention as the trial itself. Micael's acquaintances reacted to the booklet by shunning her. Invitations ceased. Her overtures to many of her usual friends were ignored. Regular visitors stopped coming to see her. And all the unkind remarks anyone had ever heard about Madame de Pontalba were resurrected and exchanged. Micael described the months after the trial as the period when she was "the most pitiable" in her life.[46] " The world is everywhere the same," she commented sadly to her cousin. To endure the trial with its insults and put it behind her "took courage," she explained; "yet it was while I was in this miserable situation that my friends abandoned me." But Célestin's spite was his undoing. When he began handing out his anthology of the legal proceedings, Micael's lawyer thought she had grounds for reopening her case. Another hearing was scheduled, and this time the judges agreed that she was entitled to a new separation trial, a concession worth more to Micael than all the invitations in Paris.

Célestin's publication of his lawyer's pleadings, even the edited version, was in itself no crime. In the absence of any official court record, most lawyers brought their own scriveners to the proceedings to copy their speeches. Later, they themselves might publish four or five such pleadings in a collection, if the cases were of general interest. But by exposing his wife to ridicule, Célestin violated his legal obligation to protect her, or so her lawyer argued.[47] Micael prepared to go through another big trial, to endure hearing again Duval's version of her shortcomings.

In February, 1836, Micael bravely went back to the Senlis tribunal, this time with a new lawyer who was a great favorite of the bourgeoisie. Simon-Philippe Dupin was almost Micael's exact age: forty.[48] Both his father and two quite elder brothers were lawyers and politicians who held various high positions in government; the youngest Dupin lived in their stunting and sheltering shadow with, by 1836, the most prominent legal name in France. Some accounts describe Philippe Dupin as coarse-looking and as having "good, country sense."[49] He was without doubt a direct, plain-speaking man who wore a "righteous and impatient" expression, according to contemporaries, and gave his pleadings in a bellow that must have resonated like a field piece in the small Senlis chamber.[50] For all his serious mien, Dupin was a man who "loved the world"—parties, balls, the theater, and, according to his admiring son, women. His speaking style was sober and eloquent, devoid of the circumlocutions which characterized the pleadings of both Hennequin and the fabulist Duval. The point of his dissertation in February was to show that everything the court had heard about Micael in Duval's pleadings the previous May had been a lie.[51]

Duval's attacks, Dupin said, had been "dusted with a pretense of reticence and wrapped in layers of oratory," enabling the lawyer "to dump on Madame de Pontalba every conceivable insinuation and outrage." Dupin subjected Duval's speech to a critical examination, sentence by sentence, from the attorney's habit of categorizing Micael with loose women to his accusation that she corrupted her children. He attacked all the lawyer's "artistic hypocrisies" and "perfidious rhetoric" that led the judges to conclude that Micael had in some way insulted her marriage vows. He spoke at length of Micael's "innocent relations" with Guillemin. Only then did he turn his angry scrutiny on Célestin's failings as a husband and father. He spoke for several hours.

In a desultory response, Duval renewed his attack on Micael, but in a tone much attenuated. He blamed her upbringing as a slave owner for what he called her "expectations of servitude" in marriage. In contrast, he portrayed Célestin as a kind of ingenuous rustic, "happy like Fielding's baronet with his hunting and his family."[52] Duval avoided mentioning the dozen slaves who had once served Célestin. He quoted St. Jerome, Montesquieu, and Rousseau to support his view that women were necessarily subordinate partners in marriage. But he had been chastened by Dupin's assault, and the fever had gone out of his words. The judges, as worn out as everyone else with the Pontalba fight, this time granted Micael a separation. After April, 1836, Micael's rents in Paris were to be paid to her; her property and income was declared separate from her husband's, and she would suffer no penalties for refusing to live with him.

It had taken a long time. One cannot avoid the realization that there might not have been a shooting and a suicide at Mont-l'Évêque if Micael had been allowed to leave her husband when she wanted to. Similarly, the duc de Choiseau-Praslin, Célestin's acquaintance, might never have butchered his wife and orphaned their children in 1847 if he had been permitted to slink away peaceably with the children's governess, a divorce freeing him to remarry. However, the laws controlling marriage everywhere in Europe grew out of the impetus to protect, not individual rights, but property. Domestic law in every country constrained women far more than men, since in France and elsewhere, men at least could separate at will, if not remarry. The injustice of French law is obvious on that point. What is not obvious is that the desire for legal divorce was widespread among either men or women, that most French people before midcentury saw the dissolution of marriage as an important right. Divorce was not legalized in France until 1885. Though the domestic statutes caused much misery, they were not widely attacked in the 1830s. Women suffered in the courts, though they were not uniformly suppressed or mistreated in society as a whole. Even when we take into account the suffocating influence of the Church in social legislation—an element that can hardly be underestimated—it appears that most people were willing to put up with the strictures against divorce. Ordinary people who had no reason to come into a courtroom may not have been especially aware of the severity of the law concerning separation, child custody, and joint property. Though ignorance was certainly not the major reason for the failure of divorce reform, it was probably a factor, difficult to measure. Only after the public saw an accumulation of scandals such as the Pontalbas' and the Praslins' did reform initiatives gradually gain strength. The separation laws of 1816, put in place during the reactionary period following Napoleon, survived until 1885 possibly because most marriages in that period were working; Micael's life was a cautionary example of what could happen when a marriage failed and there was no practical way of ending the hostilities.

Micael had finally won the right to be let alone. She could not share her joy with Victoire, for the old lady had died in January; but to Azélie, whom she wrote at once, she described her relief as indescribable. "If you knew all I have suffered since I last saw you, without relatives, in a foreign country" [she was now far enough away from America to consider France foreign]. "It is impossible for me to tell you. There are no expressions strong enough. Finally God made a shelter for me and I won my separation. I can now say that I have gone through my purgatory while still on this earth."[53]

The end of the Senlis trial was not, however, the end of Célestin's legal maneuvers. He contested Micael's administration of the Place d'Armes houses for several more years in the appellate courts of Louisiana. Micael's unencumbered rights to the property were not finally and fully confirmed until 1839; in that year she won one of the two suits before the Louisiana Supreme Court, and Célestin dropped the other suit a few weeks before it was to be argued.[54] Thus, the quarrel over Micael's dowry was settled, the quarrel which, in effect, destroyed the family and shattered the happiness of the children, just as Célestin's mother died, and in the same year that Micael and Célestin became grandparents themselves. The court decision was made that ensured peace, at last.[55]

How were they set for money when they parted? The judicial act separating the assets was remarkably fair, considering the court's previous decisions, in that neither husband nor wife profited at the other's expense. Micael staggered away from the marriage with nothing she had not brought to it, except the balls in her chest. After his wife's property was finally extracted from him, Célestin remained in an enviable financial position. In 1836, after the separation, he owned four rental houses in Paris inherited from his parents and worth more than a million francs. These provided him with rentals of about 61,000 francs a year. Madame de Miró's real estate yielded another 165,000 francs yearly, which was his to collect and use. He owned the vast estate of Mont-l'Évêque, which his father had assiduously enlarged since its purchase. Célestin received 46,121 francs in cash from Madame de Miró's estate, and three years after the separation, when his mother joined her aunt in the afterlife, he inherited another 272,121 francs, which had come to the Pontalbas from Madame de Miró. That amounted to more than $63,000 in hand and some $45,200 each year from real estate.

For all that, Célestin lived as thriftily as he loved. The inventory of possessions found at Mont-l'Éveque after his father died exposed a life of cold floors, bare walls, cheap dishes, and stubs of candles to light the emptiness of the château. The cellar contained, in November, enough firewood to keep the bedrooms of the castle comfortable for perhaps forty-five minutes. There were over five hundred bottles of wine in the château, but since not one was valued over one-half franc, all but the most serious alcoholics might have excused themselves from depleting the store. The contents of the coachman's room, counting the cobwebs, were valued at thirty-five francs—seven dollars. In old Pontalba's own study, no picture, mirror, rug, drapery, slippers, books, or bric-a-brac distracted him from his stalwart contemplations. The dining room was the only room in the chateau with enough chairs for the whole family to sit together. The family's most expensive furnishing was a billiard table which together with three balls and a cue was judged by the accountants to be worth thirty dollars.

No wonder Célestin made such a noise at the trials about Micael's extravagant domestic accessories, her unworthy desire to have her own home merely for the pleasure of decorating it. It was not only that he knew how to play a weak hand, though that was certainly part of his show of vituperation. He was also genuinely outraged by the sight of furniture. The Pontalbas were sincere in regarding Micael's wanton preference for tablecloths, silverware, matched dishes, and sofa cushions as frivolous indulgences. One remembers the exuberance with which Célestin sold Micael's cherished belongings when he seized the house on rue du Houssaie in 1831. Micael's chaste fruitwood bed remained a blister between them right through the last legal documents on which they wrote their estranged names. Micael dismissed Célestin's selling of her Bayou Road lots with a wave of her hand and some muttering. But he had to pay her, before she would sign him off, for the insult of selling her private little bed. Furniture had clearly been a sore issue.

Micael began her life as a free woman with $72,450 suctioned from Célestin. This was supposed to represent the return of her dowry, her half-interest in

their property (everything except rue du Houssaie had been fraudulently removed from the community of assets, however), and compensation for her
lots on Bayou Road which he had sold before the separation. He did not
repay her for the rents he had collected on her property. In truth, the money
only compensated Micael for her dowry, of which Célestin had collected just
about $73,000.

The terms of the separation allowed Micael to acquire 41 rue St-Honoré
and to enjoy it as part of her separate property. Micael inherited two properties from her mother. Her mansion at 22 Place Vendôme was a splendid
grandame constantly in need of makeup, but worth every franc Micael put
into it. She leased it for nine years at a time for about 50,000 francs, or
$10,000 a year, before finally selling it to Baron Haussmann and the City of
Paris in 1861 for a lovely profit. Her property at 341–343 rue St.-Honoré consisted of two five-story houses with ground-floor boutiques; the houses
should have produced a minimum yearly revenue of 20,000 francs. Micael's
holdings on the Place d'Armes in New Orleans were worth $520,000. How-
ever, though she was the owner of the third most valuable property in the
Vieux Carré, she did not realize a great profit from it because her tenants
were notoriously delinquent. Her agents may have been able to coerce four
or five thousand dollars a year from the twenty-one dilapidated houses in
1836.

Micael's other property in New Orleans was the Bayou Road tract which
stretched far out from Bayou St. John, acres and acres of land that the Pontalbas had considered so worthless they made only a few half-hearted attempts to expropriate it. Célestin must have been inconsolable when the
value of the property skyrocketed after the separation. Bayou Road turned
out to be Micael's Madame de Miró, the reserve of capital that enabled her to
get on her feet after the separation, and kept her standing while she hemor-
rhaged money to build the Hôtel Pontalba. Mortgage payments from the
Bayou Road sales plopped in steadily throughout the 1840s. In the beginning of the decade Micael was up to her braids in debt; but by the end, she
could see her way clear to financing the enormous Pontalba Buildings, all because of Bayou Road.

In the late 1830s, therefore, Micael assumed a large mortgage burden for
the Hôtel Pontalba, in which she had invested all of her cash, the $72,000
she received from Célestin. She had the responsibility of paying for half of
her sons' necessities, plus whatever else she wanted them to have which their
father would not provide. Against that, she had an income of from $10,000

to $20,000 yearly from her houses in Paris, and dwindling revenues from the Place d'Armes property, maybe $5,000. She was not quilted in security, yet. But she had brains, imagination, a ferocious history, Bayou Road, and at long last, the hard-won right to invest her money as she saw fit.

VIII

Home Alone

DESPITE Célestin's portrayal of his wife as a flirt and compulsive socialite, Micael's life after the separation was as tame as before it. For the first year or two, she soaked in self-pity. "My bad health is really bad now," she informed Azélie in 1836. "I live in bed. I see my doctor every day. Yesterday I had a consultation where they decided that all my ills are related to nerves and that to get well I need time and a lot of peace and quiet. They are sending me to the baths in the Pyrenees again. I have two vesicatories on each arm."[1] A vesicatory was a poultice of some irritant such as mustard, placed at random on the body and allowed to fester until it produced the equivalent of a third-degree burn, which, it was thought, would coax out internal toxins. Burning the skin was used for illnesses ranging from colds to rheumatism. With such treatments added to her usual wheezing and seizures, Micael certainly did not go to balls during those first free years, nor to the opera or theater, for every grand event in Paris meant getting to the top of a grand staircase. Even after she had more or less recovered from the shooting, she continued to be an early sleeper, frequent fainter, and poor breather for at least another decade.

When Micael did go out in society, she had every reason to enjoy herself. She was smart and plainspoken, and she knew a number of lively and thoughtful people who preferred discussions of politics, religion, irreligion, art, and scandal to small talk. Society was variegated. The social upheavals of the French Revolution and the Napoleonic period had not buried the old nobility, but rather, grafted on to the top of society a dense new foliage of military people, Bonapartes by the dozens, and Bonapartists—the so-called Napoleonic nobles. The restoration of the Bourbon king Louis XVIII in 1815 and his successor Charles X did not rid society of those new arrivals; but it did make life in the 1820s noticeably duller, more conservative, and more pretentiously royalist in everything from architecture to manners. Charles X was deposed in July, 1830, the result of a temperate little revolution that brought his cousin, Louis Philippe, to the throne and ushered in the pleasantly named July Monarchy. Also dull, but committed to being a constitutional monarch, King Louis Philippe embodied the bourgeois concerns of the class that was slowly marrying its way up in the world.[2]

"Society," though hard to define during the July Monarchy of the 1830s and 1840s, was easy to factor. Its partitions were the boundaries of three Paris faubourgs, or sections. In the faubourg Saint-Germain, exclusive families left over from the ancien régime lived in haughty seclusion, withdrawn from the court of the bourgeois king. They entertained each other with studied simplicity. Over meager refreshments (the buffet for one ball consisted of rice milk, bouillion, and a milk of almonds), the displaced Bourbon nobles, most of them still marvelously rich, could freely commiserate about the political ascendancy of bankers and industrialists.[3] The Pontalbas, whose star had risen with Napoleon's, were never part of this ultraroyalist élite.

Micael lived in the faubourg Saint-Honoré, the section where the new Napoleonic nobility made common cause with the haute bourgeoise—financiers, the richest manufacturers, shippers, and similar, affluent others. Here the furnishings and entertainment were not yet vulgarly ostentatious. An exception was the wedding of Micael's friend, the prince de la Moskowa, to a banker's daughter who was the granddaughter of a carpenter. Three thousand were invited to the ceremony, three hundred to a feast sufficient for multitudes. Most of the Napoleonic nobility made do with less flamboyance.

The most recently arrived of all the arrivistes in French society were to be found stuffing themselves in the third section, in the new houses of the faubourg Chausée d'Antin. Here lawyers, wealthy bourgeois, and speculators indulged their capacious tolerance for splendor and pampered their guests with every variety of refreshments. In all three faubourgs, dinner was for conversation. Afternoon receptions were for chit-chat and business contacts. Balls were for dancing, cards, and seduction; for these, women marinated themselves in several perfumes and dressed fittingly.

Every sifting of nineteenth-century personal papers brings forth its pile of invitations, reminiscences of parties, diaries crowded with receptions and salon afternoons. For diplomats, many of whom were Micael's friends, and for people of her set who invested fortunes in each other's enterprises, social life was life, not merely a respite from work. Consequently, their attitude toward visits was the reverse of ours in that Micael and her friends did not think they did anyone much of a favor by receiving them at home—the maid, after all, put out the cups and straightened the chair pillows. To pay a social debt one had to pay a call, which took both effort and discrimination since there were always more visits owed than one had time for.

People were far more harried and busy than we might suppose. With the exception of attendants at the royal courts, who lived an artificial and unique existence, well-off men and women were constantly writing and running errands. What is now described as the pace of life was indeed slower when one sat in the weather amidst the unpredictable traffic of carriages and horse-drawn omnibuses, or when one climbed the inevitable splendid staircase to a government office. But a person with business to conduct left earlier, came back later, and, like Micael, complained constantly of being tired. Without telephones or typewriters, every transaction was enormously complicated. We hear incessantly that life is more complex today than a century ago. Technology is more complex; but thanks to it, modern life is comparatively simple.

Micael was probably right when she commented that the people she knew did not think much about their noble status. Except in the faubourg Saint-Germain, society was remarkably exposed. Poor and rich lived in the same buildings and met each other on the doorstep, where they might also bump into each other's visitors or a chambermaid emptying the nocturnal vessels.[4] We may recall that Proust's narrator in *Swann's Way* nursed his infatuation with a wealthy neighbor by standing outside his own door and looking down into her apartment across the courtyard.[5] Senators and servants sat (or more likely stood) side by side on the omnibus when it began crawling through the center of town in the 1830s. Nor was contact between the classes limited to random encounters. Flaubert, that reputable reporter of social idiosyncrasies, described in *A Sentimental Education* a soirée given by an art dealer. The dinner conversation turned to travel, opera, theater, art, and the starvation diet of a bohemian artist who was one of the guests. The host of the evening, a rich bourgeois, customarily paid court to all the stage-coach drivers, Flaubert tells us, and developed contacts among the cooks of the great houses, who gave him recipes for sauces.

Micael, too, mingled with all sorts of people, from diplomats to elderly Creole ladies with twice-turned dresses whose conversation seems not to have bored her in the least. As for her society friends, the ones her cousins wanted to hear about, most of them were typical property owners of the faubourg Saint-Honoré, that is, prospering, liberal families, often with military connections, who had gained prominence during Napoleon's exploits. They generally supported King Louis Philippe after 1830, and rallied to the governments organized by Louis Napoleon following the revolution of 1848—first the republic and then, in 1852, the Second Empire. Micael's main recreation with these friends was riding in the Bois de Boulogne or resting outdoors under the trees, "recovering from Mont-l'Évêque." She had a number of male friends too, apparently platonic despite the promise of Célestin's lawyer that lechers would be lying in wait for a separated woman. "Good old M. Dos had dinner with me a few days ago," she wrote to Azélie. "He says he hopes to live to 117 because he knows somebody who has reached that age."[6] Her most intimate confidant appears to have been a Monsieur de la Croix or Delacroix who was "becoming famous," according to her letters in 1833 and 1834, and who visited her every day. De la Croix advised her regarding her legal problems and gave her moral support during the dark days of the lost trials. When he left for a trip abroad she wrote of being "truly desolate, for I love him so much. He is really a good friend to me, and full of fun."[7] It was common for Parisians to have close friends of the opposite sex. According to her letters, George Sand had almost as many male friends as she had lovers.

Micael knew quite a few celebrities, too, at least casually. Prosper Mérimée, whose name was better known in his lifetime than it is now, mentioned Micael in one of his letters. Honoré de Balzac, who knew everybody, knew and disliked Micael's son Célestin. Micael apparently had some part in matching a Creole friend of hers to a relative of Émile Zolà; she took the bridegroom to task in one of her letters for the way he was treating his new wife.[8] Her doctors were well known. Guillaume Dupuytren was Paris' leading surgeon. François Magendie was a noted physiologist; among his discoveries was a rum punch treatment for victims of cholera.[9] Micael loved opera all her life; although she did not have what we would call a music salon, at some point she seems to have treated her guests to recitals by the *Puritani* quartet, Grisi, Rubini, Tambourini, and Lablache, the four singers who made Bellini's opera the rage of Paris.[10] After the shooting, it was years before she could plan anything so elaborate again, although the dinners and balls of the faubourg Saint-Honoré of course went on without her.

Some of Micael's friends were indefatigable party-goers. The Austrian ambassador to Paris, Rudolphe d'Apponyi, journeyed to eight or nine receptions every night and enjoyed them sufficiently to describe them in his journal the next day. To find so many parties (for Paris contained only about a million people, including the homeless and those in hospitals), d'Apponyi had to mingle with the entire range of the bourgeoisie, the crass as well as the cultivated. But though he might make an appearance at a table burdened with veal and ten varieties of mushrooms, d'Apponyi himself entertained

like true nobility: cakes, ice cream, and weak tea were all that composed one
of his buffets.[11] Invitations to his embassy were highly prized. Micael was on
pleasant terms with him and his wife, neither distant nor close, and was invited to one of his stylish galas. She thought enough of the invitation to
mention it to her young cousins who hungered for details of the gay life of
the capital, but not enough to attend the ball.

It is hardly surprising that Micael de Pontalba knew some of Paris' no-
table figures; in fact it would be odd if she did not have a few illustrious
friends in the gregarious hives of the faubourgs. The population of Paris in
her lifetime was about that of metropolitan New Orleans today, but with a
much smaller clique of wealthy and well-educated people at the top.[12] However, she seldom went out at night, and in comparison with most well-to-do
Parisians, she was a high-ranking homebody, both before and after her separation. One must search diligently through the memoirs of the period to find
so much as a mention of Madame de Pontalba even at the height of her scandal. When she was well, she had receiving days like most of her friends: three
hours—in her case on Monday afternoons—when people who had been
specifically invited or who had a standing invitation came to chat for forty-
five minutes and finally have some light refreshment before moving on to
someone else who was receiving. These gatherings were not as pretentious
or intellectually demanding as the salons of literary history, although the
guests of Madame de Rumford or the duchesse de Dino or Viollet-le-Duc
certainly believed they were part of a salon. Moreover, since Paris had few
offices, no telephones, and much business being conducted by people who
did not consider themselves businessmen, the afternoon receptions were
never entirely frivolous. "The salons are for me a real torture," one government official told his son. "After spending the whole day immersed in public
affairs, I am subjected to an interrogation anywhere I show my face. Each
one in accosting me shakes my hand and after asking about my health, begins without waiting for an answer to talk to me about his railroad, his canal,
his factory."[13] Micael, always manipulating her investments, must have invited many such officials to afternoon tea. She also spent a lot of time with
New Orleans people who turned up in Paris.

> [Mme. Amelung] will tell you how pleasant Paris is; meanwhile she has nei-
> ther horse nor carriage, is living very modestly, and in spite of everything, is
> entertaining society people with four plates of cake and syrup. She gives parties
> in the Creole style that she knows. She didn't invite me to her last. Since I was
> not acquainted with her group of friends, she thought I wouldn't enjoy it.

They play innocent little games there. . . . I'm going to take her for a ride in the Champs-Élysées this evening.[14]

Writing of one Madame Pulcheri, who moved to Paris from Louisiana, Micael complained to her aunt in May, "I see her very little. When she meets me she tells me to come see her. That really makes me laugh. Pretentious airs don't catch on in Paris unless one spends forty thousand dollars. Only then can one say to people, 'Come see me; I don't go out!'"

In July, two months after she lost her first separation trial, she was commenting, "I very seldom see Pulcheri. I don't know what became of her." But in 1836, immediately after she was vindicated by the second trial, she informed Azélie, "Pulcheri and her husband are having dinner here today. She comes to see me often since my return from the waters. She has a feel for things. She came to the conclusion, from reading [Célestin's] booklet, that I would get well from the waters."[15]

She was especially hurt by the reaction of Creoles to the scandal. Friendships she had maintained throughout her marriage cooled dramatically after she lost her first case. The Burthes and the Urquharts shunned her, though they had been her partisans for many years. In April, 1836, Micael discharged her pent-up resentment in a letter to her cousin, one that was particularly ill-timed since Azélie was deep in her own grief over her mother's death in January. "Would you believe it?" Micael wrote,

Charles Lanusse stopped visiting me, the Urquharts, M. and Mme. Burthe, Mme. Péchaud—none came to see me for five months. *Now that I've won*, the Urquhart ladies have written to invite me to their ball. They came to visit, saying that they didn't know why I don't go to see them anymore. Mme. Burthe . . . sent me a notice of her son's marriage. She says that she is my friend and that she doesn't understand how I could have abandoned her in her hour of need. You should know, by the way, that I, as unhappy as she when I returned from the waters in October, nevertheless went to see her, and have not left my bed since. I wrote her in January a very friendly letter inviting her to visit and asking her to excuse me to her sister for not being able to pay a call. I got no response. And today she is my friend, she says, and she holds it against me that I abandoned her! They tell me Mme. Péchaud, whom I haven't seen for five months and to whom I showed many courtesies, will probably come to see me; she mentions it every day; she keeps putting it off probably feeling that she's done wrong.

Micael was going into such detail, she explained, "so that no one can tell you I did something to my friends. It was these women who stopped seeing me."

Everybody believed what M. de Pontalba said and he thought I wouldn't have the strength to rise above so many lies. But God protected me and all the evil that [Célestin] wanted to do to me has fallen back on him. He is completely discredited. His friends no longer see him. How disgusting the world is, my dear Azélie. You can't imagine all the invitations, all the advances which I am receiving. Finally, everything is turned around. I swear that if I can regain my health and if my Célestin returns to me sane [young Célestin was traveling in America], I would put behind me all the unfairness I've been put through, for I am still the same woman that I was. They say that justice is showing me to be right, that it has pronounced in my favor. That is society's excuse. . . . This letter is also for Malvina. My health is so bad that to write exhausts me.

However, Micael was developing a sanguine attitude about her vicissitudes in society. "It is sad, my dear friend. You can't count on anybody. In hard times they abandon you, and in good times they fawn over you."

One companion who remained constant through Micael's unhappiest hours was the widow of Marshal Ney, who had also known the best and worst of times. Princesse de la Moskowa, as she was called, brought Micael into contact with her sons, their wives and relatives, altogether quite a gathering of Napoleonic nobility. They had, it seems, everything but money. When Michel Ney was executed in December, 1815, he left behind four sons: Joseph-Napoléon, known as Léon, prince de la Moskowa; Michel-Louis-Félix, called Aloys, the duc d'Elchingen; Eugène, named after Napoleon's stepson, Eugène de Beauharnais, who was his godfather; and Edgard. All of the Neys were tough, emotional, and acutely aware of their financial indisposition, beginning with the luckless marshal and his wife. Ney, who had been awarded his titles because of his bravery in battle, remained temperamental and courageous in confinement, right up to his final moments.[16] Though his wife and children shattered his jail with their sobs during the half-hour they were allowed to see him before his execution, Ney faced death calmly. He reminded his wife of her strength before all of their previous separations, when he left for campaigns not knowing whether he would return. This was just another such parting, he said, but for a longer time and with the certainty that it would be the last. After his family was forced to leave him, Ney shrugged off the consolations of a priest, marched out to the Jardins des Luxembourg grim but unhesitating, refused a blindfold, and gave the order himself to fire. He had never expected to die in bed. His wife was no weakling either. After leaving the prison, she pulled herself together and went from one official to another, begging for an audience with the king. According to her sister-in-law, who accompanied her, she was still frantically accosting palace functionaries when her husband was shot down in the Carrefour de l'Observatoire.

The eldest son, Léon, was thirteen on that horrible night. He grew up devoted to his mother and the memory of his father, whose name he tried to clear in speeches and writings. He wrote numerous books, mainly histories, and among his many musical compositions was material for ten operas. During the Bourbon Restoration the family lived in exile in Sweden; but after the July Revolution, Louis Philippe rehabilitated the sons and restored their government allowance; in 1831 Léon was named a peer of France, taking his seat in the same body that had tried and sentenced his father. He served in the army in Algeria and in the Crimea, in between government posts that eventually included a seat in the senate of Napoleon III. Like his brothers, Léon wrote to his mother incessantly, sharing secrets in his careless penmanship of his extramarital dalliances.[17] He was sensitive, fun-loving, and esurient, as the readable portions of his letters reveal. After his marriage to Albine Laffitte, that opulent occasion, he expected more or less constant loans and gifts from his wife's father. The old banker used several strategies—procrastination, forgetfulness, and outright refusal—to avoid paying his son-in-law's debts. Léon cheerfully persisted, regarding all loans as insufficient gratuities to which his title entitled him. He had a pensioner's mentality. Not for one moment would he have refused his father-in-law's largesse; nor would he have been particularly grateful if the Laffittes had given him a great deal more. As it was, he had married an allowance of 200,000 francs a year ($40,000), the income on his wife's dowry of four million francs. She had a mansion in Paris which provided him with rents—for he had complete legal control and use of her dotal property—and Albine, as an only child, was to receive more when her parents died.[18] In view of these important qualities, he liked his wife well enough for several years, and usually managed to refrain from reminding the Laffittes that he had transformed their rich, ordinary daughter into a princess. He was better off than Micael, he once remarked lightheartedly, since his wife's family had never met him at the door with pistols. They did, however, try to disengage him from Albine's money after the couple finally separated. In the 1840s Léon lived with Pauline Murat, who became the mother of his natural son in 1849.

Jacques Laffitte may have disdained the man who was attached to his daughter's title, but he was devoted to his grandchildren, to whom he dedicated his memoirs: "My little Napoléon" and "My little Eglé."[19] Léon's legitimate son, Napoléon, died at the age of fifteen. His daughter, Eglé, was the subject of commiseration in Léon's letters because of her skinniness. In 1852 Eglé married Victor Fialin, who would become the duc de Persigny and hold various high positions at the right hand of Napoleon III. Eglé had five children and, proving the adage that a woman can never be too rich or too thin, she also had several lovers. The marriage broke down, finally, because of her open infidelities, while the families on both sides wrung their hands and exchanged concerns. The scandal contributed to Persigny's eventual exclusion from the emperor's inner circle. As for Eglé, she married twice after Persigny's death, but her father did not live to meet all of her husbands. Léon died in 1857 in a campaign in the Crimea. "Prince de la Moskowa was a man without any good qualities whatever," offered Horace de Viel Castel in an obituary entry in his diary, "and his character made him generally detested. Military men say he was a good musician. Musicians ought to rejoin that he was an excellent soldier."[20]

The Ney sons were attached to each other, as well as to their mother. Eugène was a diplomat in the July Monarchy and somewhat out of the public eye. He died in 1845 in Paris, having completed several missions. Edgard Ney, the youngest child, was only three when his father was executed. He, too, served in military campaigns during the July Monarchy, and then rose quickly in the service of Louis Napoleon, becoming a colonel, aide-de-camp to the emperor in 1852, and a general in 1856. He was taken prisoner by the Germans in 1870, but released after the fall of the Second Empire; at that time he was still a bridegroom, having yielded his hand in marriage in 1869 at the age of fifty-seven. The writers of memoirs liked him, and he has enjoyed better publicity than the rest of his family.

Edgard wrote the most literate and urbane letters of all the Ney sons. Shocked by the duc de Choiseul-Praslin's brutal murder of his wife, and his subsequent suicide, he exclaimed to his mother:

That Praslin!!!!! What a wretch! What a butcher! What a tiger! And to think that such animals have faces like anyone else, that you meet them without suspecting anything, that they have no particular mark. This morning I saw all the Sebastiani family, the general, his wife, and one of their granddaughters [the parents of the murdered duchess and one of the orphans]. They stopped for lunch at our hotel; they all looked depressed and with good reason. Well, it's

all over now since he [the duc de Choiseul-Praslin] is dead. I feel relieved for
Léon, who would have had to see him. To think, the worthy ministers and
peers of France—killers.[21]

The duke, like Léon, was a member of the Chamber of Peers and could be
tried only in the Chamber of Peers. If Praslin had not killed himself, Léon
would have had to face him.

A considerable part of the Ney correspondence consists of letters between
the second son, Aloys, the duc d'Elchingen, and his wife Marie, from their
first separation in 1834, through his military campaigns in Algeria and
Turkey, where he died in 1854. Aloys wrote 465 letters to his wife, almost as
many as he wrote to his mother, but in a markedly different tone. Whereas
he was spontaneous and playful with his mother, addressing her as *tu*, decorating his margins with lively little drawings, and generally fussing over her,
his letters to his wife ("My dear Marie") were composed, it would seem,
very, very slowly.[22] He had married Marie de Vatry in 1833 when she was
thirty-two, a widow with a four-year-old son. She was so strikingly attractive
then—during the years when she and Micael were friends—that old men
writing their memoirs fifty years later still thought her face and charm worth
a few lines in a long life.[23] As with many great beauties, people assumed that
she was profound; but she was only profoundly neurotic.

In the first phase of her letters to her husband, eight or nine months
after their marriage, she reproached him constantly for not writing. She
addressed him as *tu* for about two years, waiting for reciprocation, but
switched to *vous* when he refused to take the hint. Despite the constant little
dinner parties which seemed to be part of every Parisian's home life, she was
bored without him, uncomfortably pregnant with their son, and suffering
from migraines: "I really am hoping to have a letter from you tomorrow
morning for my Saint's day, my sad Saint's day. Never have I spent it more
bored and irritated, never have I felt more out of sorts, bad-tempered,
snarling, unpleasant to myself and probably to others."[24] Writing to him
usually at eleven at night, for she was superstitious about the number eleven
having some effect on their relationship, she reeled from depression to overheated devotion:

> Oh, how I love you, how I love you so tenderly and piously—yes, piously—
> with adoration, with respect, you resemble other men so little. My life! You,
> you are my life. I don't just love you, I worship you. I am so sad. I want so pas-
> sionately to see you and press you to me! May God watch over you this night
> as always. May he watch over you for me and our children, our children! I am

going to bed. You are no doubt asleep now. I kiss you with all my heart and soul . . . my only love. Sleep well. I love you. I love you.[25]

She hungered for his tenderness all the rest of his life, for his responses to her outpourings were those of a soldier and a sane man, and thus, hardly ever measured up to her expectations. She rebuked him for being so fatuous as to write her cheerful letters:

> I received your letter. . . . It is quite amusing and interesting, but with all this information, I would still like to have something of you, you, you, always you, that's what I need. The small talk is all right for your brothers and your mother—but I am your wife, your poor wife; I am demanding, pushy, possessive, all very bad, but that's how it is. I am the only way I can be. Save the amusing details for others, if you don't have time to tell me everything, and to me just keep repeating the same thing over and over. Talk to me of love, talk about yourself, long and deeply. You can be amusing for me when you return. Right now, I don't have the heart for it. My love, don't be angry, it's because I love you so much that my life depends on it.[26]

After that, Aloys tried to be more ardent, and received an explosion of encouragement:

> My love, my angel, in a word, my Aloys—for your name says it all for me—I have your letter from Algeria, a letter which shows you, you, you completely! Or rather, everything in the world that is good, adorable, and adored . . . my darling angel, my only love—I would like to write you on my knees, for you are God to me, you make me so happy! happy!—yes. Oh, certainly, these are tears of intense happiness dropping on your letter which I am crushing to my lips and heart. It makes me happy to say to myself that a love like ours will be stronger than death, oh stronger, stronger a thousand times, for I defy death to separate us. You say I tell you quite clearly that I love you. It's that you understand it, that you sense it. . . . It's you, my love, it's you who lets me see your soul, your noble, beautiful soul, so naturally and clearly superior—Oh, thank you, thank you for this letter. Thank you for your love—all mine is yours—all my thoughts, all my actions, all my life is for you, my angel; live for me. Let us die only for one another. . . .[27]

Her letter had begun happily; but she soon worked herself into hysteria and depression, as was her habit. Aloys' life in Algeria could not have been improved by reading her next paragraph:

> Life doesn't go on any longer, sleep has left me, I can't eat any more. When daybreak comes . . . I continue my thoughts by dreaming, but it's horrible—there are things, ideas which I can't stop . . . or else in sleep the fear of these ideas weighs on me. . . . I wake up in terror when I feel I have begun to

dream. . . . My love, I told you I was happy at the beginning of this letter, and now it's already over—it's not my fault— . . . Oh, it's hideous, it's hideous!

She took him to task for having written to his brother that he considered his mission in Algeria worthwhile. "What could I think!" she exclaimed. "You are happy. You are content. I guess that's natural, and I'm not complaining—but my love, don't ever say you love me as much as I love you. . . ."[28] Poor Aloys. No wonder he was satisfied in the army, where men were men and not gods, and he could keep his wife at a breathing distance across the continent. When he was at home, Marie's letters were more lighthearted. She wrote her mother-in-law about the death of an acquaintance: "Her will was full of singular legacies: her mirror to M. Roy, her best white pen to Mme. Roseny, her best bouquet of artificial flowers to Mme. de Taillis, her best brocaded handkerchief to Mme. Baillot, then a thousand-franc yearly income to her parrot with a page of instructions on its health, its character, the sicknesses to which it is vulnerable."[29]

In the 1840s Marie calmed down. She wrote to Aloys of their children, especially their daughter born in 1841. She could spare a word now and then for his brothers: Léon was a "bad man," Edgard an "egoist."[30] The son Marie had with Aloys, Michel Ney, followed in his father's footsteps and became a general. His marriage to Paule Heine produced seven children, whose marriages in turn allied the Ney family with the most illustrious Second Empire nobility. But by then, the empire had fallen.

During the Crimean War, Aloys was sent to Gallipoli. On July 14, 1854, he wrote two letters to his wife. The first was in response to Marie's letter to him, explaining that his mother had died. The princesse de la Moskowa had apparently been a little withdrawn from her adoring sons throughout their lives, as evidenced by their constant pleading with her to answer their letters, and also by the insistent attentions they lavished on her: cherished boys tend to take their mothers for granted.[31] Marie had criticized her mother-in-law for being shallow, and for once perhaps she was right. The widow Ney may have grieved sincerely for her remarkable husband but she had not grieved long. Soon after Ney's execution, she secretly married General Louis d'Y de Resigny. Although Marie called him "the most null and void of beings," Resigny was genuinely loved by the Ney sons, and he seems to have been devoted to their mother. But even he had not prevented Ney's widow from traveling constantly and restlessly moving from one residence to another all over Paris. Aloys described his reaction to her death in a grief-stricken letter to Marie which was, however, characteristically controlled and impersonal.

He thanked her earnestly for having taken care of his mother, and commented on how much his mother had dreaded and feared death. His second letter was written a few hours later:

> My dear Marie,
> I have just felt the first manifestations of cholera. I am not afraid, but I feel sorry for you. Thank you for your care of my mother, thank you for your devotion. I die loving you and blessing you. Goodbye, you and my darling daughter. Remember me to all our friends. Goodbye and have courage.
>   d. E.[32]

If Marie's love for Aloys had been clamorous and cloying, her grief was deep, despairing, and as far as documents reveal, understated. Among the 225 books in her home at her death in 1889 was found her diary of biblical quotations which she had kept over many years. For July 14, 1854, she had placed, between excerpts from her husband's letters, a passage from Lamentations: "Look, Father. How great my anguish! My entrails shudder; my heart turns over inside me. . . ."[33]

When Micael knew the duchesse d'Elchingen, Marie was a bride, and the beloved Aloys' death was still twenty years in the future. It was Micael who was going through soul-scarring anguish, and Marie who, together with her mother-in-law, took her to sit out under the trees and talk away her fears.

Through her friends, Micael thus had ample opportunity to view and appreciate the pretensions of the French aristocracy and the particular self-importance of Parisians. She once related to her aunt a Creole friend's cool observation: "She remarked that Mme. de Pontalba, me, is somebody in her own country, but that I'm supposed to be a nobody here."[34] But she must have observed that neither the Parisians nor the Neys nor anyone else lived on rank alone. "I see that in this country a lot of money is necessary," she wrote, quoting her Creole friend. "Without that, Paris is not so pleasant."

But Micael did have a lot of money. The Senlis court that granted her a division of property granted her a fortune, her fortune, to manage for the first time. She knew exactly what she wanted to do with it: build. Within a year or two she had put the separation behind her and was so preoccupied with her projects that she had little time to nurture grudges and hurt feelings. Micael loved building. She had inherited a passion for contracts, pricing, drawings, and all the reckoning associated with construction. Building and real estate were in her blood. Her friends might flock to invest their capital in railroads, glass manufacturing, dyes, fabrics, industrial iron, or any of the other temptations of the expanding French economy. But Micael, like her father, kept her money in property; and like her mother, she used whatever revenue she acquired to build the best and biggest houses she could afford.

Micael was in her forties before she won control over her inheritance; consequently, she had had years to think about her building projects. When she finally did break ground in 1839, she was like one of those late-talking children whose first words are compound sentences. Her first attempt at construction was an impressive four-level mansion which spread over three addresses.[35] Though the exterior began to look ponderous in comparison with the architectural fantasies that filled the capital in the next decades, the Hôtel Pontalba remained a Paris landmark throughout Micael's life, and as a born-again restoration, it is a visitor's attraction now. Americans live in the house today, and Americans by the dozens troop up and down the grand staircase, when they have passed the guards stationed at the gatehouse portals. The outside façade and roof line of the mansion was redesigned after Micael's death, and there were some further alterations before it became the United States ambassadorial residence in 1977. But despite the changed façade, one has only to step inside to recognize it as one of Micael's airy, elegant, private places.

The Hôtel Pontalba that Micael built was a rectangular affair bisected by stone stairs. The building's strong horizontal rhythm, the rigorous symmetry and heavy masonry of its façade, all looked back to the sober tastes of the 1820s rather than to the exuberant decorations of the next decades. However, the more unfashionable the house became in the years after it was built, the more it gained in dignity, like a stately dowager amid the Second Empire décolletage. Tourist guidebooks throughout the 1860s pointed out that, with its fourteen awe-inspiring reception rooms on the first floor, the "magnificent" Hôtel Pontalba was the largest residence in Paris, second in size only to the Élysée Palace a block away.[36] The boast was probably never true. One does not have to look far in Paris to find houses dating from the 1840s and 1850s that seem larger by far than Micael's. But the advertisement shows that the Hôtel Pontalba was considered an important building even when the capital sparkled with big, new construction.

Micael kept her original façade for the house as long as she lived. In 1876, two years after her death, the banker Edmond de Rothschild bought the mansion from her sons. Rothschild changed the exterior face of the house in both front and back, and added two perpendicular wings to the rectangular floor plan.[37] He turned three of the rooms into a kind of museum—the salons Louis Quatorze, Louis Quinze, and Louis Seize, respectively. For the Louis Quinze room he purchased decorative works, especially a collection of exquisite eighteenth-century wood panels that had originally been made for the home of Louis XV's banker, Jacques-Samuel Bernard. The Salon Samuel Bernard is preserved today in the U.S. embassy residence. Rothschild's dedication to reproducing the Louis styles in his mansion was a little erratic: after lovingly installing mansard roofs and a plethora of eighteenth-century embellishments in the Hôtel Rothschild, he placed an art-deco glass marquee over the front door—an eclectic addition that has since been removed.[38]

The building proved to be adaptable and purposive. The Rothschild family fled to Switzerland during the Second World War. When the Nazis invaded Paris, Hermann Göring requisitioned the house as a club for his Luftwaffe; a building in the garden that was planned as part of a theater for the Rothschilds was by then serving as an air-raid shelter. After the liberation of Paris, the mansion was occupied by the British Royal Air Force Club, and then the United States Embassy located its information and cultural services at 41 rue St.-Honoré for eighteen years. Finally in the 1970s, the site having been purchased from the Rothschilds, the entire premises were renovated so that the house could become the official residence of the United States ambassador, which it remains today. Even the walkways on the back lawn were landscaped to facilitate "the occasional informal diplomatic discussion."[39] The embassy offices are a few steps away on the Place de la Concorde where, during the French Revolution, the guillotine in the square cut short both discussion and diplomacy.

All sorts of changes have been made to the building over the years—bathrooms and parking lots never imagined by Micael. But the mansion is once again a place where people live. Just as in Micael's day, the entire basement is given over to kitchens, offices, equipment for servicing the house, wine cellars, and the like. The *rez-de-chausée*, or ground floor, contains capacious dining and reception rooms—blue-paneled planets connected to each other by a filament of smaller salons. The visitor can walk on Micael's glossy dance floor where she gave balls and concerts in her later years, or stand in her sitting room which, like most of the main rooms of the house, opens out onto the lovely garden. A long time ago one even received a pamphlet explaining that the house was built by "an enterprising American lady whose father was a governor of Louisiana."

The splendid marble staircase that leads to the second-floor family quarters is the same one Micael used, a spacious, exhilarating passageway. The visitor ascends it "like a minnow inside the rippling esophagus of a whale," as Robert Hughes aptly described the experience of scaling one of the gigantic staircases of the nineteenth century.[40] Micael, too, kept the second story for her private apartments as distinct from her first-floor receiving rooms. Living quarters even in humbler buildings were similarly located up and back from the street, so that occupants could open windows without being subjected to the noise, odor, wind-borne offal, and flies of the roadway; and everybody in Paris treasured a window on what was invariably called the *jardin*, even when the garden was a bare backyard. Above Micael's apartments was the third floor, or what was then called the attic story, with its servants' rooms, storage, more kitchen space, and more windows. Micael loved glass and was a great believer in working attics equipped, of course, with servants' bells.[41]

It is hard to know how much the neighborhood has changed. In Micael's time, high yard walls were the only security against intruders, although assassination by bombing was even then much in vogue; the house was flanked by the Japanese and British embassies, and was only a few doors from the Russian embassy and the Élysée Palace. The British embassy had formerly been the house of Napoleon's sister. The street was accustomed to important traffic when Micael lived there, although it was on the edge of the open and wooded Champs-Élysées. Probably St.-Honoré never had the stilted ambience that characterizes the embassy row of other capitals. Today, though hundreds of diplomats are chauffered in and out of the Cercle Interallié next door to the Hôtel Pontalba, Micael's street looks merely busy and unofficial, an expensive piece of real estate surrounded by furriers and the sort of haute couture retailers who are careful to put incense in the fitting rooms.

Micael wanted the house as much as she ever wanted anything tangible. She tried to model it after a townhouse she had fallen in love with on rue de Lille, the Hôtel d'Havré. She bought that old mansion for 560,000 francs and dismembered it, selling the façade and various portions to neighbors.[42] Other accoutrements she carefully salvaged for her new house—elaborate doors; intricately carved and decorated boiseries, or panels; wainscotting; shutters; mantelpieces; balustrades; even an entire ceiling—to use in her new dream house. First, she destroyed the building that was on the St.-Honoré site, an eighteenth-century home called the Boisgelin mansion that was actually two adjoining houses. The doomed buildings and the lot cost her nearly 600,000 francs. Next, she purchased the lot next door at 45 rue St.-Honoré for 65,000 francs. Then she hired a promising and well-connected architect, Louis-Tullius-Joachim Visconti, to draw all the plans, both the general design and the working drawings, and to supervise construction of the house she could already see in her mind.

There is an arresting picture credited to the collection of the Versailles Museum which shows Visconti at the height of his career in the early 1850s, unveiling his plans for the New Louvre to his royal sponsors.[43] Napoleon III is as always imperturbable and attentive; Empress Eugénie wears her habitual and unearned expression of fatigue. The standing attendants, including the fey and distracted Léon, prince de la Moskowa, look past the architect to stare dully out of the picture. A dandyesque Visconti, groomed more meticulously than any lady-in-waiting, gestures before a man-sized drawing as he warmly explains his enormous project to connect the Louvre and Tuilleries palaces despite their different elevations.

Visconti was a few years older than Micael; born in 1791, he was the son of the eminent and wealthy curator of ancient sculpture at the Louvre. He started out with a historic name, a fortune, and membership in the comradely circle of Napoleonic nobility. Micael once explained that she hired Visconti because he was so highly recommended and had impeccable professional references; in 1838, when she engaged him, Visconti was known mainly for being his father's son and something of a specialist in fountain design.[44] The Hôtel Pontalba was the first of his large private homes. It helped establish his reputation just as he was about to undertake a series of important public and private commissions. For example, in his position as director of public festivals, he was placed in charge of the decorations for the celebration that took place in 1840 when the first Napoleon's ashes were returned to Paris from St. Helena. This was no small commission. According to Visconti's elaborate plan, the funerary urn was carried through the capital on a jeweled and sculpted float, held aloft by twelve marble pallbearers in classical poses.[45] The ashes led an army through streets festooned as if for a victory. In honor of the glorious return, welcoming parties were held all over Paris after the ceremonies; it is not known whether the ashes were invited. Visconti's next appointment was as architect of the emperor's tomb in the Invalides Hospital, where the ashes were to repose amid the beds of Napoleon's maimed soldiers and the crypts of his marshals.[46] Visconti, in fact, was sought after to design several of the officers' sepulchers.

It is perhaps unfair to Visconti to look now at the high seriousness of his floats, mansions, statues, and fountains through eyes that remember the ebullience of the late Beaux-Arts or the lucidity of the International Style. Visconti had never seen any of it. He was steeped in the images of Ingres and Gérard, and in the turgid nostalgia for antiquity displayed everywhere in the Napoleonic court. The buildings everyone gushed over were those that symbolized the imperial ego, and the public ornaments that people were willing to pay for were those that resurrected, with archeological dedication, the muscular esthetic of Greece and Rome. Visconti's work was wonderfully expressive of the Napoleonic mentality and the neoclassical style so admired by France's neo-nobility, the marshals and peers who were Visconti's clients and patrons.

Visconti's greatest and costliest work was to be his additions to the Louvre, a project that employed three thousand workers, not counting the priests who came to bless the foundations, and consumed seven million francs in the two years Visconti worked on it.[47] The New Louvre incorporating the Tuilleries was to be the center of the court of the Second Empire. The grand project would have gained Visconti a larger place in architectural history if he had lived to complete it. However, he died suddenly in 1853 of what was diagnosed as apoplexy, before the immense façade was in place. The exterior decorations of the buildings were redesigned by a successor, Martin Hector Lefeul, who gave the structures their famous and much debated ornamentation.

Visconti had a few detractors in his lifetime. However, since he was by all accounts suave, charming, and political, his critics may have been merely jealous of his success. At the time Micael engaged him, Visconti's career was still largely ahead of him, whereas the tragic events of her life were but recently behind her. He was probably eager, overworked, sporadically careless and brilliant—and arrogant. She was intense, suspicious, bursting with ideas and demands, a wounded creature with an obsession. She bore all the secret psychological marks of having swum with barracudas; and it was not long into their association before Visconti was able to see those marks as clearly as he could see her dangling, useless, hurting fingers.

In reviewing their conflict, we must bear in mind that architects of the nineteenth century were also interior designers as well. They were expected to design cartouches, mantels, elaborate cornices, medallions, and every sort of interior and exterior decoration along with their structures. Visconti's papers show walls and doors that he designed to fit around panels and columns Micael brought to the construction. It was not only the structure of the mansion for which Visconti was responsible, but the entire image of elegance that the house presented.

Micael's problems with her house began with the foundation, which was laid while Visconti was away on a three-week trip. The architect had paid a supervisor to take over the construction, promising that the overseer would be present at the site at least six hours a day. At Visconti's suggestion, Micael augmented the man's salary with a monthly bonus of her own. However, when the construction began running over budget, Micael withdrew the bonus, and the supervisor withdrew the supervision. He would not go near rue St.-Honoré except for the most perfunctory inspections; moreover, according to Micael, he "didn't know anything about stone," the primary material of the house.[48] When Visconti came back from his trip, Micael showed him that the workers had used soft stone of inferior quality for the foundation, and that they were about to place the sewer in ground that was appallingly shallow. The foundation had to come up, and the project began again.

Micael was under the illusion that Visconti intended to use the doors, ceiling, and other features from the d'Havré house, which she had reverently entrusted to him "without his having to take one step to call for them." However, as the walls and openings were framed, she realized "to her great astonishment," her lawyers wrote, that the first-floor elevation would not accommodate the doors and other accessories she wanted to use.[49] Visconti's remedy was simply to raise the floor, a solution which satisfied Micael until she realized that he had altered none of the exterior architecture to match the revised interior elevation. The outside handrail was now the wrong height for the stairs. Moreover, the plans did not include balconies under the bottom windows, although the ground floor was no longer at ground level. Anyone who stepped through the floor-to-ceiling windows now fell out of the building.

While the first floor was being reconstructed, Micael ordered work on the second floor to stop. She wanted to prevent the same mistakes being repeated, until such time as she could get up on the scaffolding to see for herself what was going on. She reminded Visconti "incessantly," according to her own account, that she wanted to use the doors from the d'Havré house.

It is interesting, to say the least, to look at Visconti's plans for the entresol, or mezzanine, which he presented to Micael on April 1, 1839. Micael penciled over every door and window and changed the measurements so that the openings were raised by several inches.[50] Another plan for the first floor shows elaborate doctoring—pencil markovers and refiguring of measurements. Even the signatures of Micael, Visconti, and the contractors, showing that the plans were agreed upon and formed a contract, were scratched out. When Visconti assured Micael that the measurements had been corrected for the second floor, construction was allowed to proceed. By this time, June, tensions were rising along with window frames. "Twenty *pouces* [inches]" Micael wrote in her most furious scrawl over the windows she added to Visconti's plan. The architect must have been exasperated with her changes, but they both signed the alterations and hoped the windows would turn out right. Nevertheless, as the second floor was completed and the walls all but finished, she found that there, too, the door openings did not fit the doors she had lovingly tendered to the workmen. She ordered the door openings raised. That required another new wall to be ripped apart.[51]

As the house neared completion, Micael's expenses enlarged along with her problems. In her own bedroom, she had wanted a door "in the middle of the wall," providing a clear view of the garden below. Ignoring the plans, the contractors Laroque and Poizot instead put the door in a side wall, providing a clear view of the alley of the Japanese embassy next door. Micael instructed the workers to close up that opening and cut a new one according to the plans. But the back wall overlooking the garden contained an enormous support beam where the new door was to be placed. To get the door in the middle of the wall, the house had to be shored up from top to bottom.

Sometimes the contractors made their own messes by neglecting to follow the contract, or to explain to Micael why they were not following it. But often it was the architect's plans that got everybody in trouble, at least according to Micael's survey of the problems. For example, she claimed that Visconti's drawings placed three amazing fireplaces in the sloping walls of the attic, where lighting a hearth would have meant setting the roof on fire, but that there were no fireplaces at all in the frigid basement rooms. Micael claimed that he forgot to include chimneys for some of the fireplaces, a mistake that was tortuously corrected by conducting the smoke through false floors out to the walls. In the entresol, it was not warmth that was lacking but light. Micael averred that Visconti had designed the mezzanine so that it was surrounded by walls, without access to sun or air, and dark as a crypt.

Micael solved the problem by placing a terrace on that floor, sacrificing one of the intended rooms; indeed, Visconti's penciled-over plans seem to show that she made exactly those changes. There were other errors, each requiring some degree of complicated reconstruction. Micael herself discovered most of the mistakes and halted work until the miscalculations were rectified. As she later explained when she and Visconti came to court, she realized early in the construction that if she did not supervise, no one would.

Was Visconti really so cavalier in supervising the Hôtel Pontalba? Of the frictions between him and Micael, we have only one account: hers. The trial records that might have provided us with the architect's side of the dispute are lost; we do not even know who won the lawsuit that eventually developed from their quarrels, or whether it was settled out of court before a decision was rendered.

In French courts, technical questions were not argued by expert witnesses from each side, as in the American system. Instead, the court appointed a committee of experts which was supposed to render an impartial opinion even if some of the members knew the litigants personally. The experts were charged with reading briefs addressed to them by both sides; making their own inspections; and finally, advising the court of their expert conclusions. The twelve-page brief that Micael's lawyers filed, "Mme. de Pontalba's Explanation to the Experts," in which she aired all of her grievances against Visconti, is the only extant document of a situation that must have been mutually frustrating. We must read its criticisms of the architect with a certain degree of fair-minded reservation.

According to the "Explanation," Visconti advised Micael in August, 1839, to issue the contractors Laroque and Poizot an advance of 20,000 francs against the 40,000 that he estimated would be needed to finish the house. But in September, Laroque and Poizot went bankrupt; Visconti now revised his estimate and told Micael that 100,000 francs was the amount required to complete the project. Probably the miscalculation was not Visconti's fault; he had no doubt relied on information from the unreliable contractors. After much negotiation, a Monsieur Salles, a stonemason, was engaged to finish the house for 76,000 francs. However, once a new contract was signed and work was under way again, Salles found that he had not included certain necessary charges; he submitted a supplemental contract involving, of course, more money.

If Micael had doubts about Visconti's expertise in his field, she had none about Salles'. She was certain the mason knew absolutely nothing about stone. According to Micael, Salles left porous building materials out in the rain and used soft stone in the construction when he should have used hard.[52] She detested the masonry decorations he put in—they made the buildings look top-heavy, she said—and she had him tear them out, which is of course what she should have done if their presence was going to irritate her for the rest of her life. Salles in turn was emphatic on the point that Micael was an interfering nuisance. Visconti was well acquainted with Salles, having hired him for other projects, including his own house. In the disputes between Salles and Micael, the architect sided with the mason, whom Micael nevertheless fired. Of the lawsuit that ensued between Salles and Micael, we have one fragment, the judgment of the commercial court where the case was given an initial hearing.[53] The tribunal found that although Salles was overcharging Micael on his fee, the mason was entitled to some compensation. Micael was ordered to may him 4,500 francs. Meanwhile, she had yet to finish the house.

Micael was still on speaking terms with Visconti in 1840; however, she felt that he had caused her to squander a fortune on a house that was not turning out at all like the d'Havré mansion, and she was heartsick. She thought that even the outbuildings which she commissioned from Visconti near the end of the project looked nothing like the d'Havré façades she so admired. Perhaps at the court's suggestion, she decided to break with Visconti soon after the dispute with Salles, and to hire a new architect to design the remaining outbuildings. She wrote to Visconti asking for the rest of his bill.[54] With the help of a court-appointed architect, she had already settled the accounts of the carpenters, locksmiths, and other workers. Since she had paid these men directly, she expected Visconti to deduct their charges from the unpaid portion of his fee. However, instead of the 16,000 francs she thought were still owed to the architect, she received a bill for 31,000 francs, a sum she at once refused to pay. Visconti, it seems, then sued Micael. His bill was fair, he claimed, because Micael still had his plans for the outbuildings; unless he exacted some payment for them, she might use them later without compensating him. Micael's defense was that she could not use the plans, and that was the very reason she had to break with Visconti and hire someone else to finish the project. In fairness to Visconti, it is entirely likely that Micael intended to have another architect modify Visconti's designs, rather than pay someone to start afresh.

Meanwhile, the house and the outbuildings were being finished up by workmen whom Micael apparently knew from having made repairs to her rental properties.[55] There was no insuperable difficulty, as far as we can tell, in completing the project, except that two contractors failed to construct roofs over the outdoor terraces to Micael's satisfaction, and she refused to pay part of their fee.[56] One of the contractors sued her (and the other contractor) and lost, then appealed the case and won, partly because he demonstrated to the court's expert that Micael had ordered changes in the construction which delayed the work and raised the estimated costs.[57]

But whereas Micael's quarrels with the contractors were a matter of money, pride was at issue when Micael and Visconti came into court. Micael could have returned Visconti's plans and deflated his argument, or she could have paid him the extra money. Tight-fisted and scrappy though she was, Micael should have seen that an additional 15,000 francs in a building costing hundreds of thousands was not worth an expensive trial. But Micael's society was feverishly litigious; in general, people were not inclined to drop their petitions merely because legal redress was costly. For his part, Visconti had already received a great deal of money for the house. He was stung at having his designs rejected. If he could not make Micael like his drawings of the outbuildings, he could make her pay for the privilege of refusing them.

Their tantrums proved unpleasant. Judging from the response of Micael's lawyers to Visconti's petition which, it must be repeated, is the only available record of the case, the architect's suit was filled with slurs on Micael's emotional stability. In French courts, and in public life in general, men were allowed to ridicule women in a manner that would have been unthinkable in the salon. The architect could avoid addressing the flaws in the Hôtel Pontalba so long as he could keep the court's attention fixed on the flaws of its owner. Micael in any case made herself an easy target. She was high-strung, probably every bit as unstable as Visconti could have implied, and she was all too willing to settle her business disputes in court, where women were unwelcome and vulnerable.

However, it is not at all clear that Visconti succeeded in portraying Micael as a neurotic, though he seems to have been permitted to try. Micael's lawyers refused to respond to what they claimed were personal insults in Visconti's petition. Declaring that their client wished "to have as much calm around her as within her," they pointedly refrained from disparaging the architect and confined their fault-finding to the building. That strategy must have been scarring enough to a man of Visconti's prestige. The "Explanation to the Experts" was a persuasive explanation indeed. The experts on the investigating committee were all friends of Visconti, but that did not necessarily keep them from considering Micael's complaints seriously. Whether or not they were convinced that the defendant was overwrought, they had to go look for themselves to see if her complaints about the design were true. What they decided remains a mystery. Visconti's reputation is safe, and apparently was safe even when the results of the trial were known.

The architect could have been damaged by the trial—even a cherished *artiste* could lose business by having each of his mistakes in a building exposed in detail. But Visconti seems not to have been scratched. The very people to whom Micael sold part of the d'Havré façade, the Callots and the Lauristons, engaged Visconti to design their hôtels after seeing the results of his work on the Hôtel Pontalba. He went on to do extensive work for the princesse Bagration, Micael's neighbor on rue St.-Honoré, as well as for the ill-starred Praslins and Sebastianis, the Ségurs, Livaudais, and many, many others whom he patiently billed, month after month, throughout the 1840s. As far as we can tell from judicial records, he was not often in court again.

But for Micael, the effects of the conflict were long-lived. Her experience in building the Hôtel Pontalba soured her attitude toward all architects and contractors. She went into her first project with at least a little trusting enthusiasm; she initially thought the house would cost less than the architect's estimate, a sure sign of her inexperience. Her excitement was destroyed by the time the mansion was finished and all the court costs paid. Ten years later in New Orleans, she was to be unreasonably defensive in dealing with both Henry Howard, an architect she consulted about the Pontalba Buildings, and Samuel Stewart, the contractor. Stewart in particular was a different type altogether from the spoiled professionals Micael had wrestled with in France. He was less educated, more practical and earnest than Visconti or Salles, unsupercilious, and eager to please Micael. But by the time she met Stewart, she had become indelibly suspicious of all his tribe. Thus, her next collaboration with a builder was likewise destined to end in court.

How much did Micael pay for her house on St.-Honoré? It is hard to know exactly since the court records indicate that she spent much more than the amounts specified in contracts, probably more than she was willing to admit. The house Micael bought for demolition in 1836 cost over 100,000 francs. We can guess that her total expenditure for the Hôtel Pontalba was well over a million francs, that is, over $200,000, a safe guess in view of the insurance Micael maintained on the property: in 1863 the Hôtel Pontalba, all 9,330 square meters of it, was insured against fire for exactly one million francs, a sum that of course did not cover the cost of the land.[58] Visconti's fee probably ran from 5 to 20 percent of the building costs.[59] We could not guess with any pretense of accuracy what such a sum might represent today, even if economic indexes were trustworthy and inflation could be evenly measured for all goods and services. We know that houses like Micael's cost a great deal more than they needed to, that is, more than an estimate of materials and labor would indicate, for splendid homes were wildly overpriced. Architects and builders were the defense contractors of the 1840s and the Second Empire—they and their government sponsors accepted astonishing overexpenditures as normal; consequently, private clients, too, became blithely tolerant of waste. Micael's house might cost two or three times its original price if it were constructed today; on the other hand, with strict budget supervision, it might not.

Luxury in general was relatively expensive in nineteenth-century France. When Célestin, Micael's husband, visited the waters at Vichy in the 1840s, he probably spent about a thousand francs a month for his hotel there. Vichy was a chic spa even then; in the next decade it was the resort chosen by both Napoleon III and the khedive of Egypt for their therapeutic retreats. A high-fashion dress cost 1,200 francs, though frumps like Micael might go about in plain but presentable day dresses which they could order four at a time, all just alike, for fifteen francs each. A consultation with a doctor cost on average twenty francs; doctors provided no magazines, as these were dear—three francs for a copy of *Revue des Deux Mondes*.[60] Servants remained a bargain in Paris. A month's wages for a chambermaid were about the same as a bottle of ordinary table wine, such as the one the Goncourt brothers once ordered for twenty-five francs. At the top of society a really stylish wedding could cost 800,000 francs; however, a first-rate funeral complete with invitations cost only 20,000.[61]

Neither salaried people nor most professionals could afford such memorable ceremonies. A Parisian doctor could expect to earn 30,000 francs a year; a notary, 60,000; and an ambassador to a foreign country, something in between. Senators in the open-handed government of Napoleon III earned only 30,000 francs a year.[62] The emperor's own cabinet ministers earned from 10,000 to 20,000 annually in the 1860s, a salary that was considered enviable by some people.

But how much money did one need to be really rich? Countess de Ségur, one of Micael's acquaintances, wrote twenty novels minutely concerned with contemporary costs and incomes. She estimated that to build a mansion in the capital and furnish it appropriately would require one and a half million francs.[63] According to the countess, who knew the price of everything from candle wax to prostitutes, it cost only 100,000 francs a year to live like a princess, once a residence was established. With effort, one could squander 200,000 annually. Three hundred thousand would be enough, the countess judged, to maintain a townhouse worth over a million and a country château as well. Micael's income is difficult to pinpoint since it came from dozens of real estate conveyances, rents from two apartment houses in Paris, and a number of rentals on the Place d'Armes in New Orleans, but it was probably well over one hundred thousand francs a year when she moved into her hôtel in the 1840s. So she was well fixed.

Even so, why did she want a house that was three times the size of a normal mansion? To impress her friends? To spite those who had turned their backs on her because of her separation? That explanation may seem obvious to us, for in America ownership of a fine house is the most reliable indication of wealth, and wealth, along with race and education, is the basis of class distinction. It was not so in France when Micael's house was built in 1840.[64] Although everyone was aware that the owner of a mansion like hers was not poor, a house might be an undependable measure of the wealth of its owner. The great majority of Parisian nobles lived in apartments, often consisting of a first-floor reception room and a modest living area above. The value of their country châteaux, if they had them, was measured by whether or not these were attached to revenue-producing farms and buildings. In Paris some aristocrats were housed below their means, a thing unheard of now in America. Perhaps among the bourgeoisie Micael's mansion would have stirred jealous comparisons; but people in her circle were more interested in living in a correct neighborhood than in building a house that signaled wealth.

Micael's friends knew she had money, with or without a house, just as they knew who among them worked for a living, who made a fortune in stocks and how recently, who lived off an inheritance, and whether the inheritance represented old money or new. The members of her set were all interconnected by marriage, and they knew the same things about their relatives that we know about ours. Moreover, it is important to realize that for most of Micael's lifetime, wealth was not yet a crucial matter in deciding whom to spurn. This was particularly true during the years of Louis Philippe's reign from 1830 to 1848. The basis of class divisions was not money but family. Money enabled people of humble origins to marry into good families, which they did increasingly throughout the nineteenth century, but it was their new family affiliations, not money alone, that gained them acceptance in the roosts of the faubourgs. Micael's friends, acquaintances, and enemies knew the precise degree of deference to accord to the estranged wife of Marshal Ney's assistant, the cousin-by-marriage to the duc de Noailles. Whether her house had had four stories or fourteen would not have affected the temperature of their relations with her.

Even with all the social climbing and slipping, the increasingly relaxed moral standards, the economic mobility that characterized France during these years, Micael's society was both stratified and highly nuanced, as ours is not. The subtleties of respect or contempt that surrounded Micael are not easily apparent to us through documents, though we may notice a few indicative phrasings. Micael's lawyers chronicled the building mistakes of *Monsieur* Visconti and *Contractor* Salles, never those of *Monsieur* Salles who, being a stonemason, was not a gentleman, no matter how genteel his manners.[65] More subtle turns of speech, the dainty slights of a perfunctory glance or an unacknowledged calling card are harder to weigh, even when they are recorded. Those of us whose "you" is the same equipollent pronoun whether addressed to a servant or senator are particularly handicapped in perceiving the fastidiousness of French snobbery in the nineteenth century; we only vaguely understand it with a Proust or Goncourt as a guide. But Micael perceived quite well that a mere house, no matter how striking, would neither penetrate nor affect the pellicle of indifference she might encounter in society as long as she was a separated wife and a survivor of scandal. She did not build the house for spite.

Chances are that Micael was not thinking of other people when she built the Hôtel Pontalba. She commissioned the house because she liked building, just as she would have ordered paintings had she liked fine art, since she and everyone she knew thought that satisfying one's whims was an excellent way to spend money. One has only to look around Paris to realize that its nineteenth-century inhabitants considered extravagant building to be estimable and patriotic. Architecture, even private homes, needed no more justification than music or poetry, precisely because buildings indicated the esthetic, and not the economic, position of their sponsors. In fact, it pained Micael to spend money on anything except houses. She wore little jewelry; her clothes made a suitable gift for her chambermaid after her death. According to family legend, she bravely resisted her son Célestin's incessant requests for money, although at one point he stopped speaking to her. But she spared nothing in making 41 rue St.-Honoré a remarkable residence.

Seen in one way, it was a house that might appeal only to the rarified sensibilities of an architect, conceived at a time when no one thought about comfort in designing any home grand enough to require a design, nor about whether a dwelling was cleanable or intimate. Until its renovation by Rothschild, the exterior resembled a well-endowed secretarial school. But then, many such mansions looked like institutions. Europeans tended to blur the distinction between public and private architecture except in determining how it was paid for. Not only kings and ambassadors lived in public buildings; the curator of the Louvre under Napoleon III lived in the Louvre when he was not cohabiting with his mistress, Princesse Mathilde; he had a seventeen-room apartment in the museum that was much coveted by his subordinates. The countryside was full of castles—bastions—such as Mont-l'Évêque, which had none of the appurtenances we consider homey; yet children were fed in them and clothes mended, as in any other domicile. If the original Hôtel Pontalba seen in a photograph looks as heavy as a continent, it was surely no more clumsy than many other townhouses of its time.

Moreover, the house is a flowing brightness inside, its walls stippled with gardens that seem to spill indoors through the great panels of glass. We must give Visconti his due. Nothing that was later done to the mansion, not the interior panels transposed from the Samuel Bernard house, not even the addition of perpendicular wings on each side of the rectangle, changed Visconti's basic plan of a building that was cloistered from the street while every main room was pervious to a rear lawn of flowers, trees, and seclusion. The two-acre garden and the openings to it give the entire building the ambience of an arcadian retreat, just a few yards from the worst traffic in Paris. Micael had insisted on the garden windows, took pains over them, and probably was the first of the mansion's decorators to place mirrors on the walls opposite them, so that some of the rooms seem to be veritable bowers, rather than places where indoor life goes on with all its prosaic stress. But it was Visconti who turned her idea into livable reality, whose working out of the engineering details raised a poem of glass and cream-colored stone on what had been a rubble pile. It was probably Visconti, and not Micael, who placed the snug salons so as to break up the electric expanses of the larger rooms, and it was his rounded ceilings and clusters of ornamentation that gave the immense transparent rooms their buoyance.

One of the remarkable details of the house, which in those days was considered an architectural feature, was Micael's Chinese Lacquer Room containing dark-colored Chinese lacquer wall panels and silk-covered furniture. Much in vogue during the reign of Louis XV, Chinese lacquer was painstakingly removed from imported screens and set in rococo borders of carved wood. Micael's Chinese panels had originally been made in 1723 for the duchesse du Maine, the wife of Louis XIV's natural son, and came into the possession of the duc d'Havré. They were among the various elements of the Havré mansion purchased by Micael. There were other precious wood panels in the mansion, too, including at least one boiserie by Jean-Baptiste Oudry. With Micael's taste and Visconti's élan, one can only imagine the house they might have built had they liked each other. Micael, too, must have finally been pleased by the mansion. Except for extended trips abroad, she lived in it without recorded complaint for the rest of her life.

Micael's sons lived with her on rue St.-Honoré, with the exception of Célestin, who was to remain her problem child until he was middle-aged. Immediately after the first trial, when young Célestin was twenty, Micael dispatched him on a tour of America, probably thinking it would do him good to leave his family's scandal behind him for a year or two. Still nursing her wounds from the lost trial, she was going through a lonely time. "Now you no longer need news from me," she wrote to her relatives in New Orleans. "You are going to have my son who will put you in touch with everything. I had promised Malvina an example of a true roué (from a respectable background, of course). I could not have picked a better one. I beseech you dear cousins to take good care of my son. I felt such a terrible emptiness in separating from him, but I think a young man needs to travel. I entrust him to you. Don't let him lose his way. Tell Cora to give him good advice. He speaks English like the English."

After her success in the second trial in 1836, she wrote again to Azélie. Her mind was still on Célestin.[66] "Tell me, what is my son doing? Is he in love? Does he speak of me? Or his father? He has not written a word to his father since he read the lies in the booklet, but his letters to me are full of good things. I thought you'd tell me a little more about what he's doing. He must be in love to stay so long with you."

Thus, it came as no surprise to Micael that two years later, while still in New Orleans, Célestin married Blanche Mérieult Ogden, a descendant of the Mérieults whom Almonester knew well. Blanche was introverted and petty; Célestin was an extrovert, especially regarding money. When they returned to France, Célestin made peace with his father. The couple then resided at Mont-l'Évêque and at Versailles, where Célestin could follow his passion for racing. They had three children.

There is a gap in Micael's letters from 1836 to 1842, which probably indicates only that the letters were lost. We know that during these years she was completely absorbed in constructing her hôtel, collecting the mortgage payments on property she sold in New Orleans, and managing her rental houses on the Place Vendôme and 350 rue St.-Honoré. Even a visit from her cousin Malvina did not distract her from her work; she saved time by dictating letters to her "secretary," Gaston. For a decade Micael busily shifted her assets, selling off some parcels of her New Orleans land, speculating with others. Except for special occasions, her life was mundane, as one's own existence always is. She rose early, like the great majority of Parisians—for stores opened at six and even lawyers went to their offices by eight—and she took time off only to be sick. To the end of her life she would devote loving attention to *mes affaires,* as she referred to the letters, legal forms, and business-related visits that devoured her abundant energy.

It is enormous fun to sort through this waste paper of Micael's life, even when the papers are an incoherent batch of shipping bills, land surveys, theater tickets, rental advertisements, and always, leases. They show us first of all that there was little consistency in the formalities of bourgeois life. Business was much less businesslike than now, and government less official, or so it seems. Property boundaries were sometimes imprecise, even on expensive tracts of land. Or a building might be vaguely described on a notarial inventory as being worth 100,000 francs "in value and rentals." Moreover, in a time when nearly everything was written by hand, all letters looked like personal letters. The phrasing even on bank statements and legal forms might be homey and labored. Public documents were full of mistakes and makeshift grammar. Street names, such as Micael's rue de la Houssaie, might be spelled differently each time one encountered them. Routine matters were seldom expedited with routine or uniform idioms. There was in the nineteenth century an untidy absence of forms, of the standardization we take for granted in every aspect of life, reflecting, of course, a society not yet completely penetrated by manufacturing, by the expectation of exact duplication.

As for personal letters, people delayed writing them as much as they do now, judging from the profuse apologies one reads. However, letters were often dashed off without a heading, sometimes with no greeting of any kind, and little attempt at cleverness or originality. Not only Micael's correspondence was unpunctuated, rambling, and trite; many letters showed a casualness, unself-consciousness, and openness common nowadays only on the telephone. There is other latent information in the letters of Micael and her contemporaries. Their epistles, regardless of the decade, appear at first glance to have been written by old people. Reading closely, one realizes that the writers were preoccupied with symptoms and therapies which in our time are of interest only to the aged. But sickness was part of everyone's news then. The letters of the most lively people in the prime of life—a Thiers, a Mérimée—include descriptions of treatments and convalescences that make them seem like missives from a nursing home.

Micael prized her letters from Azélie during the 1840s and always took her cousin to task for not writing. "I received four words from you," she complained in 1842. "It's been some time since you've written me a real letter. These *séances* in church and your prayers take up all your time. During your prayers say a few for me once in a while; I need them."[67] Her next surviving letter to Azélie finds her, four years later in 1846, happy and incessantly busy, but not oblivious to the opportunities Paris offered to aging, eligible ladies.[68]

> I can't let Cruzat leave, my dear Azélie, without giving you my news. He will tell you how often your name has come up in our conversation and how we would have liked to have you with us on our excursions. Come see me: I will get you married. You are alone and sad, that's what makes you vulnerable to every sickness imaginable. Here, you would receive love letters every day, declarations from everywhere. You need some distraction and not these meetings in church all day long. If you come, I will be godmother to your firstborn, on the condition that you have a son. [As Micael was fifty-one when she penned this letter, and Azélie sixty-five, one can judge her lighthearted mood.] Moreover, I want him to be as good as Cruzat, this cousin whom I love with all my heart. Since his arrival a month ago we are never apart. I started by trying to show him what Paris offered of the beautiful and odd. He ended up by completely changing my habits, for you know I always have so much work that I never go out. Evenings, we walk to the Jardin and I usually go to bed by nine. As soon as he leaves I am going to resume my habitual life.
>
> Cruzat prefers that I don't promise [to visit you] in writing. He will tell you how much I miss you all and would like to see you. It is not impossible that you will see me soon. I will be so happy to be with you again. Goodbye to all, dear friends. Love me as I love you. Kiss all the family for me.

Indeed, she left Paris in 1848; but the idea of returning to America had been in her mind before she even secured her separation. On February 15, 1836, *L'Abeille* in New Orleans reported that she had requested her agent to dispose of her land on Bayou Road "in order to concentrate on improvement of her property around the Public Square. It is the intention of Mme. de Pontalba," the article added, "to erect blocks of buildings that will bear comparison with any in this country and challenge rivalry from abroad."

Throughout the 1840s, Paris was an uneasy place for aristocrats; like everyone else, Micael worried about the political unrest. "Our poor country is in a pitiful state," she wrote in 1842; "it is really frightful, for those who live in it and for those who have money invested in it."[69] The constitutional monarchy of Louis Philippe was coming to a troubled close and was about to be abrogated by another revolution. There were food riots in Paris. Houses on rue St.-Honoré were sacked—we do not know if Micael's was one of them. The home of Dupin the Eldest was saved from attackers by the intervention of the police, according to the police.[70] However, by the time the turbulence began in the streets, Micael was ready to launch her dream project in New Orleans. Her grandson Edouard de Pontalba, Célestin's son, was a child at the time of her trip and described her departure.[71] "My grandmother, seized with foolish terror on February 24, 1848, the day on which the Revolution broke out, had fled Paris. She had gone to seek refuge in London, expecting to remain there until tranquillity should be restored in France. Tired of waiting she decided at the end of that year, 1848, or perhaps as late as 1849, to sail for New Orleans in order to superintend the building of her houses. On that occasion I made for the first time my acquaintance with the sea, my father having taken me with him to bid her goodbye."

Micael was to remain in America for three years, accompanied by both Alfred and Gaston. While Paris shivered with rumors and riots, Micael was happily involved with yet another enormous construction.

IX

New Orleans in 1850

THE Place d'Armes that Micael saw when she landed in New Orleans was set in a slum of squalid houses that were despised even by their tenants. Legal records still exist, though barely, to show that Micael's agents routinely had to sue to collect rents, albeit litigation was as slow, expensive, and unpredictable as now. A typical Place d'Armes tenant was Felice David, a free woman of color, who never paid Micael the fifty-dollar monthly rent for a house on St. Peter Street.[1] She lived there for four months with, apparently, a large family. When the court ordered her furniture seized, the sheriff confiscated six beds, seven mattresses (but only two pillows), eighteen chairs, "4 empty demi-johns," "flour pots," "1 bathing tub," and "2 toilets." This miscellany sold at the sheriff's store on Dumaine Street for $121.96. As the sheriff failed to turn over these proceeds from poor Felice's belongings, he, too, was summoned to court. He explained that he deducted $119.10 for his "costs and charges" but was prepared to remit $2.86 to Micael's attorney. It is easy to see why Micael decided to tear the houses down and rebuild on the expensive land.

To imagine the Vieux Carré as the grand Pontalbas were going up, we must think away the conventions of residential and commercial neighborhoods. There was no restrictive zoning anywhere in the city, except for "lewd women" who might face deportation to the suburbs if they became too conspicuous. The owner of each piece of property decided what sort of commerce would be permitted on it. Owners paid for part of the walkways in front of their stores, though of course the few sidewalks that had been laid were public, to be used by all pedestrians and a few horses, if the streets were inconveniently full or flooded. Panhandling was as common in the French Quarter then as now, but only the licensed "crippled poor" could beg in Jackson Square, once it was refurbished.[2] A number of splendid buildings were being constructed uptown; however, even in the "good" neighborhoods, there was no effort to protect the residents from odors, random squalor, or the sight of indigence. This was as true of Philadelphia or Paris as it was of New Orleans. In one of her letters from Paris, Micael described how she was harassed and handled by a group of paupers as she got into her carriage in faubourg St.-Honoré. In the Old Quarter, well-heeled gentlefolk shared the walkway with rag and moss sellers, shabby Indians, and soldiers going to or from the Mexican War. Walt Whitman recalled that the city was full of uniforms and barrooms in 1849.[3] Moreover, the seamen and soldiers were served by a large number of professional ladies who were not ladylike. The girls might have had hearts of gold, but their mouths were loud and dirty, according to people who had to live near them. A letter writer to the *Daily Delta* complained that the miser John McDonogh "preferred letting his houses to disorderly people, prostitutes, etc., as it depreciated the property adjoining, and he could buy it lower as few people would buy or improve in such a neighborhood."[4]

One of the resilient myths surrounding Micael was that John McDonogh once asked for her hand in marriage. That would have been quite a match, but there is no evidence that the two met during her nubile years. When Micael returned to the city in 1849, she might well have encountered McDonogh; they were both large property owners in the same section of town and, in fact, they were on opposite sides in a multiparty lawsuit over a land title. Assuming that they met, Micael no doubt found that her old flame, if that is what McDonogh was, had turned into her elderly flame in the intervening years, and gave off a great deal of sanctimonious and hypocritical heat to people around him.

New Orleans was one of the five largest cities in the United States in 1850, with a population of 116,000; yet water remained its first and worst problem, just as in colonial times. The "industrious poor" petitioned the First Municipality to put up a public well, since the price of water soared in dry weather. However, in winter the "overflows" of the streets flooded the carpets of the rich, both idle and industrious. Gutters along the sidewalks were installed but never cleaned. The city surveyor noted that after only a few months, one new walkway had ten inches of "green filth" in its gutters, "just like the sidewalks all over the city."[5] In summer, every ditch had its scab of hardened excrement.

In fact, filth of every kind characterized New Orleans. If the citizens of 150 years ago had been told that one day people would travel to their city merely for the pleasure of looking at it and strolling on its lovely streets, they would have laughed. After a walk anywhere in the New Orleans of those days, the hem of a dress was drenched and foul. Traffic and carriages meant horses in the street, feculence that might or might not be picked up by the scavenger

carts—these circled only through the main avenues of the Old Quarter to the
river, where the refuse was taken out a short distance and dumped. Though
soiling of the streets was certain and regular, cleaning them was not. In 1851
the city surveyor wrote to the council of the First Municipality: "I have the
honor to inform you that the Boat used to convey into the river the Offals
from the clearring of the streets is entirely rotten and had sunk last night. I
am in hope to raise it again but [it] being in such bad condition as not to
allow repairing, it is urgent that your Hon. Body should order the construction of a new boat as soon as possible."[6] The letter was read, along with a petition from the postmaster proposing a "regular system of numbering the
houses and putting up the names of the streets on corners."

Sanitation was no better uptown. Turkeys were commonplace pedestrians in the neighborhoods, marched up from the boat landings past the
homes of American socialites, on the way to one of the markets. Hungry
dogs roamed in packs over the business district, despite various measures to
get rid of them. Stray dogs plagued other cities, too. In New York, gangs
were hired to club them to death, until the city hit upon the expedient of
drowning the animals in vats of boiling water.[7] The dogs had few defend-
ers, apparently; people fretted no more about whether they were disposed
of humanely than we think today about whether catching fish hurts them.
In New Orleans, bounties were offered for dead dogs until it was found
that policemen were capturing dogs for a reward instead of chasing unre-
munerative criminals. Eventually, the city settled on an annual distribution
of poisoned sausages which took place in May; by June, the shopkeepers
had stopped complaining of dangerous dogs but were airing their grievances about the decomposing carcasses in the streets.[8] Then, instead of
bringing the carcasses out to the middle of the river where they would be
carried away from the city, the scavengers fell into the habit of standing on
the edge of the water and throwing them in. The rotting bodies either
washed back up on the shore or remained where they landed, in water
where poor people swam and dipped their drinking buckets. Like much else
that was dumped in the river, some of the animals might have been sucked
into the intake valves of the city's water supply to contaminate the "safe"
water that people paid for.[9]

The public, obsessed with the fear of rabies during these years, or hydrophobia, as it was called, wanted the stray dogs killed. It so happened
there was no rabies in New Orleans. From all accounts, hydrophobia was the
leprosy of the nineteenth century, the dreaded New Orleans disease that no

one ever saw. The curse that did strike people every year throughout the century was cholera, caused by contaminated drinking water. The mortality records of 1850 are fairly typical of a year in which there was no yellow fever epidemic. From them we see that there were many deaths in New Orleans from consumption, jaundice, scarlet fever, and typhoid, the predictable culprits; a few deaths from childbirth, lockjaw, and diarrhea; and a variety of fatalities caused by such oddities as hives, teething, and worms.[10] But the perennial leading killer was cholera. Even the Americans, who could cure deficits and were loath to spend public money on an animal pound, died like dogs from it every year.

The strange thing was that despite pervasive sickness, many people lived to a ripe age. There were early deaths in Micael's family; but on the other hand, her godfather Père Antoine died at eighty, her aunt Victoire at ninety, her father-in-law was still a force to be reckoned with when he killed himself at eighty, her husband Célestin died at eighty-seven, and Micael herself, with all of her damaged organs, lasted to an estimable seventy-nine. It is certainly untrue that in Micael's day a person in his forties was considered aged, except by his children. Such an idea would have been amusing to Hector Lefeul; he was criticized for being too young for his post when he was appointed to succeed Visconti as architect for the New Louvre at the tender age of forty-four. Micael's son fathered children in his middle sixties, just as her father had done. Infant mortality was high and may distort some statistics for nineteenth-century longevity. Without a doubt, people died prematurely from epidemic diseases; however, if folks managed to avoid smallpox, influenza, cholera, childbed fever, yellow fever, or a dozen other prevalent infections, then, like Hausman's Mithridates, they died old.

No one pretended to have a cure for hydrophobia or cholera; but the world of 1850 had "scientific" cures for almost all other conceivable sicknesses. The merchandise advertised on every front page and throughout every paper published was not saddles or boots, things that everyone had to buy, but rather, quack medicines. Dalley's Magical Pain Extractor promised the French relief from swelling, hemorrhoids, constipation, sore nipples, broken bones, and erysipelas, a streptococcal skin disease, while the Americans might purchase a one-minute cure for toothache or venereal disease. These miracle drugs were nothing compared to Townsend's Sasparilla, advertised in both French and English, which claimed, in the contemporary idiom of unabashed physicality, to cure scrofula, sterility, and menstrual cramps, relieve the pain of childbirth, delay menopause "for several years," end sores, fevers, rheumatism, the spitting of blood, consumption, despondency, fatigue, and especially, "fits, fits, fits."[11]

Though Micael was as skittish as anyone about the city's infections, she loved New Orleans, partly because it was her home and partly because its land was profitable for her. The money for the Pontalba Buildings came essentially from Micael's suburban New Orleans property, her large tract on Bayou Road. It is difficult to assess the precise value of the Bayou Road land for any particular year; but from the prices paid at various times for one or another part of the property, we can see that the holding was spectacularly valuable. The land was located in what are now called faubourgs Marigny and Tremé, and in the section known as Mid-City. In 1836 we find Micael's agents auctioning off a slice of it for about $210,000. In 1848 another 78 lots sold for $33,000. Still another section consisted of 151 blocks or squares, comprising streets such as Jackson, Napoleon, Bienville, and Carrollton.[12] During the years when Célestin was managing Micael's assets, the Bayou Road gold mine was still under water and produced only timber and mosquitoes. But at the very time Micael began her separation suit, the city started draining these outlying areas. Within a few months, Bayou Road was being converted into new subdivisions for immigrants who were pouring into the city. Célestin began at once gnawing at the property, selling off what he could; but Micael stopped him by winning the separation.

The Bayou Road land was eventually worth over a half-million dollars in profits to Micael. Not that she could ever go to an act of sale and come home with $500,000. But she could sell lots and parcels over a period of ten or fifteen years, accepting down payments and promissory notes, reclaiming and reselling some of the land when the first buyers defaulted, gradually accumulating a fortune. Repossessing, or buying back one's property at public auction after a purchaser defaulted, was a complicated mess because there was so much land speculation and marginal buying in New Orleans. One purchaser might sell pieces of his newly bought land to perhaps a dozen other people; then he would default on his debt to Micael, though it meant forfeiting his down payment and any mortgage payments he had already made. Micael's foreclosure would necessarily involve multiple defendants and usually protracted lawsuits. Even so, she made money.[13]

There was one bothersome problem. Micael had to establish her rights to the land before she could sell it. Almonester was granted title to the Bayou Road tract in 1796, with the usual stipulation that the land had not already been awarded to someone else. Louisiana was a vast, vacant territory then; land was dispensed freely to all takers who would put it to some use. Neither Almonester nor the royal government checked to find out for certain whether a previous grant had been made of the marshland. But when in June, 1836, Micael instructed her agents to auction some of her Bayou Road acreage, she was ambushed with lawsuits which lasted to the 1850s. Dozens of "owners," thinking they had a legitimate claim to some part of the tract, had passed certain sections on to their heirs, who in turn sold their portions to a great many purchasers.[14]

In order to confirm her ownership, it was necessary for Micael to prove that she or Almonester had actually used the disputed land. In fact, at one trial she was able to produce witnesses who remembered her father's brick-yard, his cutting timber, and his slaves working on the property. The witnesses were old and required the court's forbearance. Lawyers phrased and rephrased each question so as to clarify the rambling responses. The attestants spoke in French or Spanish, and the court reporter translated the testimony into English as he took it down. Except in the case of J. B. Ximenes: Almonester's old comrade and fellow Spaniard was so talkative, the recorder could not keep up, and lapsed into his own native French.[15]

Four of the many title disputes brought against Micael reached the Louisiana Supreme Court, where they make up a prodigious repository of documents. Large portions of Micael's separation suit turn up in one case file, as does the entire record of one of Almonester's lawsuits copied verbatim in Spanish. There is a kitchen sink of notarial documents, since fragments of the property had been sold, bequeathed, or donated again and again, each time before a notary, without the titles ever being cured. The lawyers on all sides complained feelingly about the quantity of records they had to review. Micael herself finally resolved the most complicated suits with an out-of-court compromise. She divided the disputed land into four parcels of equal value and put the numbers 1, 2, 3, and 4 into a hat. She drew two pieces of paper and received parcels 2 and 4. Her adversaries drew for the other parcels.[16]

Sounds simple. But in fact, hundreds of documents were generated on the three occasions when Micael used the hat method of partitioning her property, not counting the court records themselves. There were surveys and inventories made for Micael and her adversaries, ancillary claims by people who believed they had purchased a sliver of ground from one side or the other, claims by people who wanted land as payment for their services, transfers and renunciations, documents by which wives proved that they were authorized to act independently of their husbands, and documents by which husbands were empowered to act on behalf of their wives. Not least of the problems was that the land in dispute had been granted and sold at a time when the whole tract was under water and boundaries were vague. What now had to be divided was a bewildering collection of eccentric and overlapping sections, a mapmaker's nightmare. One case against Micael required fourteen years to settle completely—the appeal alone included five hundred documents; thirty-three witnesses testified for Micael's side.[17]

Not all Louisiana Supreme Court cases were so bloated, and most, in fact, were more trivial than anything we might find on the docket today. Micael's lawyer correctly observed that on the basis of money, one of Micael's suits was "by itself equal in importance to at least 100 average suits presented to this court."[18] For every Baroness de Pontalba, there were several Delphine Solets, a free woman of color who won a district court judgment of five dollars against her father for slander. Her father had called her a "thief, the most base and infamous person that ever lived." The father appealed to the Supreme Court, which reversed the ruling, taking into account that the daughter was leaving her father to live in concubinage when the slander occurred.[19]

Besides the title disputes, Micael had to settle one other suit before she was ready to finance the Pontalba Buildings, this one against the City of New Orleans. What was at issue was the land Almonester had donated to the city for the lepers' hospital. The land had been unused since 1810, and Micael had sued in 1836 to have it returned. Meanwhile, she proceeded to auction parts of the contested property, with the understanding that she would hold the proceeds in escrow until the case was resolved. After fourteen years, Pontalba v. the Mayor, Aldermen, et al. was finally heard, together with the city's countersuit, in a trial which itself threatened to absorb another decade.[20] The court considered nothing too extraneous for airing. Witnesses described Almonester's lepers' hospital and the swampy conditions of the land around it. Étienne LeBlanc recollected "perfectly well" seeing "the Leppers and house about forty years ago." F. Lafargue and John McDonogh testified that the hospital was a two-story wooden building which was "yet a pretty good house" in 1800. There had been a fence and a separate house for Negroes. The court heard exhaustive testimony on whether leprosy was or ever had been prevalent in New Orleans, whether it was contagious, and whether it was the same as "Elephantiasis of the Greeks." Micael's birth certificate, marriage certificate, and baptismal records were introduced as evidence, documents remarkable only for their quantity and irrelevance, all copied by an indefatigable hand using quill and ink. Eventually, Micael was condemned to pay the city ten thousand dollars, a judgment that she at first appealed to the State Supreme Court and later decided to accept.

It might nurse our fantasies of covetable wealth if we could believe that Micael's agents managed these tedious affairs without her effort or complete understanding. But in fact, her agents were neither her mentors nor directors; they were assistants and their assignments were at all times specific. She did not hesitate to rebuke Eugène Rochereau, a cousin and close friend, when he proposed selling land to someone Micael archly referred to as "the Countess of Canal," at a price less than the property's appraised value. "There will be no signature and no contract," she crisply informed him, "but I formally authorize you to conclude a contract if she wants to increase her offer by $15,000, which would make it $35,000. . . . I no longer accept the previous terms. The $35,000 must be paid this way: 1/4 down, 1/4 in one year, 1/4 in two years, 1/4 in three years; interest at 5 percent is to be paid each year on all the balance due. I hope that you can make these conditions acceptable to the countess, since she is getting a good deal in buying my land and will enjoy a great profit from it."[21]

She had another bone to pick with Rochereau over his misplaced initiative. "I was astonished that you would tell me about a fee for Mr. Moore, since I don't suppose you pay people to sell my property. According to what you tell me, he came upon the name of the countess. . . . She should therefore pay him and not me. You alone are my agent and you should receive remuneration. . . . However, if it absolutely has to be done, I authorize you to give him a half percent, but no more."

Let people think Madame de Pontalba's property was under the control of her lawyers and cousins to do with as they liked. The agents knew better. Real estate was a game, one of the few games available to her, and a complicated one because most transactions were completed without the services of any bank. Credit was readily available to everyone, but buyers were expected to pay off large mortgages within four or five years; hence, they often defaulted. Today, banks absorb much of the risk of selling on time to shaky investors; but bank-financed mortgages to individuals were not so common in 1850.

Certain other institutions that we now take for granted were also tentative in the American experience at midcentury. Municipal government was still in its formative stages, as evidenced by an odd arrangement that had been in place several years when Micael finally saw it firsthand: the division of the city into three parts. In 1836 New Orleans was legally partitioned into three politically distinct municipalities corresponding to the geographical location of the Creole, American, and immigrant communities. Americans had by then long been settled in the faubourg St. Mary above Canal Street, where they covered the land with their banks, retail firms, wharves, hotels, English-language theater, cotton presses, Protestant churches, brokerages, columned mansions, and commercial devotions. The Creoles, the traditional governing class of New Orleans, continued to own the city's most valuable real estate; from their stronghold in the Vieux Carré, they resisted the steady pressure of Americans trying to seize political power. Until 1836 Creoles succeeded in dominating the city council and controlling the expenditure of public funds. Below the Old Quarter, in the opening suburbs that stretched downriver, the newest immigrants lived, or tried to live, in slouching cabins behind sewer ditches as wide as bayous. Immigrants who had resided in the town at least six months could vote, when roused. However, the Irish, German, Spanish, and Italian dockworkers and hirelings of the new section were either politically apathetic, or they tended to cast their ballots with the Creoles with whom they felt a sense of European kinship. This was also true of the Irish who were freckled across a long, uptown neighborhood known as the Irish Channel. The Creoles in New Orleans, though a numerical minority, thus controlled votes, patronage, and finances, and the Americans were consistently outnumbered and outraged.

Creole and American businessmen differed over whether New Orleans should expand its trade by developing railroads, financed perhaps through increased property taxes. Railroads would mean that the midwestern grain and the cotton of the Tennessee Valley, which already came to New Orleans down the Mississippi River, could be re-exported over rails that would stitch their way east across Mississippi and Alabama and west to Texas. Along with the major exports would go dozens of local and regional products, and goods that could be imported for resale. The Americans, those ideologists of wholesaling, envisioned New Orleans as an entrepot of both north-south and east-west exchange. If the city was to remain the unchallenged port of the Gulf of Mexico, they said, it also had to become a railroad center. They were, of course, right. Creole bankers had attempted some ill-fated railroad investments in the 1830s, and thus preferred putting money into sugar and cotton plantations, insurance, real estate, and proven endeavors connected with the staples of river trade. They were afraid to make major commitments to railroad ventures which were often poorly organized and ended in financial disaster. They too were right.

The most bitter conflicts were over the day-to-day administration of the city. In the city council, the Americans were infuriated by the Creoles' conservatism, inertia, and self-serving leadership. Docks and levees up and down the river were in deplorable condition. The city badly needed a belt railroad to serve the wharves on which the economy of all New Orleans depended. Street improvements, such as they were, were concentrated in the Old Quarter, and were rarely authorized for the impassable ruts of the American suburb. Every idea for improvement met with the Creoles' obdurate resistance. American merchants were even willing to fund a project of uptown wharf repair at no cost to the rest of the city. The city council overruled the proposal in 1836, and the Americans, uttering a chorus of grievances, decided to secede from the city.[22] The state legislature approved a new charter by which New Orleans voluntarily split into three corporations or municipalities. The First Municipality belonged to the Creoles; its boundaries were approximately those of the Old Quarter. The Americans owned the Second Municipality uptown from Canal Street. Below the Old Quarter, the Third Municipality enclosed many of the city's immigrants, free Negroes, and working-class others. Thus, Micael planned the Pontalba Buildings for the First Municipality, went to the Second Municipality for architects, contractors, and building supplies, and paid for it all out of profits gained from her Bayou Road property in the Third Municipality. Each municipality had its own council, or board of aldermen, and its own recorder, or police court judge, who took over the functions of a mayor. There remained a mayor and a general city council for all of New Orleans, scheduled to meet only once a year. They were restricted to legislating on a few common issues and had no power to make appropriations. The municipalities continued to share heat waves and epidemics, but like Micael and Célestin, they could no longer spend each other's money.

The arrangement lasted sixteen years, a surprising longevity for a crazy experiment. But we must remember that breaking up a city seemed neither radical nor unorthodox to the eager urban planners of 1836, whose world did not yet cherish ideals of political wholeness or administrative unity. Parochialism was an acceptable mentality. After all, the Germans in the Third Municipality had come not from any country called Germany, but from independent states such as Hanover or Saxony. Germany was years away from national unification; the same was true of Italy. The large empires of Europe all contained fractious groups struggling to break off into their separate nations. The Irish in New Orleans could have had no philosophical objection to dividing up the city; they had emigrated from a land fervently pursuing its own dream of mitosis. As for the United States, it was of course not yet the placable entity which the mind's modern eye maps out: the big steak dominating the continental platter. The U.S. western border was Arkansas. Florida, Iowa, Michigan, Wisconsin, Texas, and all the West were foreign territory. Each year throughout the 1840s and 1850s saw the southern states within the union scratching more excitedly to get out. The idea of partitioning New Orleans therefore alarmed no one. It was one of those political vogues which had so many echoes in contemporary life and swept people along so readily that for a while it seemed indistinguishable from progress.

In the beginning, the Creoles of the First Municipality and the Americans in the Second competed with each other to run their sections efficiently; each made plans to erect public facilities, hotels, and banks. The 1830s were boom years in New Orleans and in the country at large, and every section of the city prospered. European manufacturers, through their agents residing in New Orleans, sold a variety of items in the city which were re-exported to Mexico. Slaves continued to pour into the city on steamboats from the upper South, to be auctioned off to planters throughout cotton and sugar country. According to one historian, there were twenty-five or more slave depots within a half-mile of the Second Municipality, with carefully dressed slaves lined up behind the fences, sizing up the visitors who came to size them up before the formal auctions.[23] Quantities of lead and tobacco were still coming down the river in the 1830s and 1840s. Tobacco from Virginia and Kentucky was inspected and packaged in New Orleans for reshipment to Europe, especially to Bremen, where it might be turned into "Havana" cigars and brought back to Louisiana on ships carrying immigrant German dockworkers. The Kaintocks who had terrified Creoles and embarrassed dignified Americans of Almonester's day were increasingly rare on the river. A few flatboats still arrived with loads of hay or coal; the rafts were broken up and used as building material, while the pilots disappeared into the waterfront taverns before catching a steamboat back home. Practically all of the sugar that left New Orleans was raised in Louisiana and brought in by coastal steamers and packet boats. The second greatest export, sugar was shipped upstream to the Midwest or to eastern seaboard ports—not to Europe. Handling it provided work for legions of checkers, commission merchants, brokers, clerks, and agents of various sorts.

The single most important commodity that crossed the levee was cotton, for New Orleans was the leading cotton port of the nation. Much of it was sent to New York and Boston for re-export abroad, but cotton from New Orleans also went directly to Liverpool, Havre, Antwerp, Bremen, Genoa, and Trieste.[24] For a few glorious years in the 1840s, New Orleans equaled New York in the quantity of its exports, thanks to cotton; but it was never able to build up its import trade. Ships that left the city freighted with cotton returned with no merchandise, according to their cargo lists, although they carried hundreds of bewildered, overheated immigrants. Micael and her sons arrived in New York on just such a steamer, before making their way to New Orleans. It had left Liverpool six weeks before with a boatload of Cork potato farmers, Londonderry spinners, and Micael, whose occupation was recorded as "Lady."[25] Much of the cotton that went out from New Orleans—perhaps 60 percent—was raised in Louisiana and Mississippi, with smaller quantities coming in on coastal ships from other southern states. Cotton not only kept the labeling clerks and stevedores busy on the wharves; it gave work to bale pressers, classifiers, weighers, sorters, brokers, and warehousers far from the levees, who labored, by and large, in the labyrinths of elderly buildings redolent of burlap and something undefinable like compost.

The growing demand for cotton on the world market seduced both the bankers of New Orleans in the 1830s and the cotton factors, the commission merchants who tried to sell the cotton at the best price. Bankers and brokers extended enormous credit to planters who mortgaged their plantations to expand cultivation of cotton. The banks sold some of these mortgages to European investors and kept others. As the demand for credit grew, established banks expanded and new banks were founded, many of them lending on the basis of the expected value of future cotton crops. The banks' capital was guaranteed by the state, which meant the state treasury was being used to speculate in a kind of cotton futures' market. Meanwhile, in order to finance public projects, Louisiana followed the example of other states and sold state bonds on the European market, in effect, borrowing from European investors. The financial activity and anticipated activity led to an inflation of land prices all over the city, especially in areas where railroads were planned (but never built). Hence, Micael had an easy time selling her Bayou Road properties.

During the inflation, banks in New Orleans as elsewhere began sending forth a flurry of bank notes. These were simply the banks' IOUs, which were theoretically redeemable for specie on demand. But bank notes were only as good as the banks issuing them. Moreover, all paper money was somewhat risky in these years, judging from a popular annual publication called *Bank Note Detector*, which explained in detail how to discern fraudulent bank notes. A weekly periodical, *Bank Note Reporter*, gave the current discount rates of all bank notes and reported bank failures. Banking, we must remember, was in its infancy in America; bankers were amateurs who learned their profession as they went along. Besides the good and bad bank notes, each municipality in New Orleans created an infestation of its own paper money to pay its employees or satisfy ordinary debts. At first the municipal paper notes were accepted by everybody except, significantly, the banks; but as their value fell, discount brokers were the only people eager to handle them.

What was happening in Louisiana was a reflection of inflationary conditions nationwide. The inevitable crash occurred in New Orleans on May 13, 1837, part of a crisis which gripped the whole country and was followed by one of the most severe depressions in the American experience up to that time. European investors, especially in Britain, had begun to withdraw their capital and cut back on their demand for cotton just as the supply from Louisiana surged. The credit system which tied the state's economy to the planters collapsed with the cotton market. Fourteen banks in New Orleans suspended payments so that holders of bank notes could not redeem them. Banks all around the country were doing the same thing. Land values plummeted in many cities. In New Orleans, Micael found herself holding dozens of promissory notes on her Bayou Road sales from purchasers who had no hope of finishing their payments. She had to foreclose on one lot after another. All three parts of the city were swept by bankruptcies and fell into a deep recession.

The three municipalities recovered, though gradually, from the Panic of 1837. By 1845 many people believed that things were looking better, and the banks in the state did become quite reliable.[26] But in truth, the finances and credit of the First and Third Municipalities actually worsened each year, despite the rising fortunes of the state as a whole. In the Third Municipality, there were no good hotels, large retailers, or insurance companies, for the area had not developed economically even before the crash. There was no high school, and even the primary school teachers went unpaid for months.

The municipal council members might have taken steps to meliorate the section's financial problems, if they had noticed them; but council meetings were scheduled months apart, and most of the aldermen skipped them even then. Policemen, under the umbrella of political patronage, were abusive and lazy, as they were in all three municipalities. When a committee was appointed in the Third Municipality to investigate charges against them, half of the investigators did not show up for the first meeting.[27] In 1840 Micael was assessed property tax for her Place d'Armes lots in the First Municipality; but she and John McDonogh and perhaps dozens of landowners apparently paid no taxes at all on ample holdings in the Third Municipality.[28]

The First Municipality was also in trouble. The schools, operating on a bilingual system with French and English teachers and textbooks, showed large deficits in their accounts in either language. Sailors and waterfront riffraff washed over the otherwise unwashed streets every night, ignored by police. By day the area was patrolled by regiments of hogs and dogs moving back and forth across the Vieux Carré. Although the Place d'Armes was the governmental center of the Old Quarter, which was by now referred to as the French Quarter, it was a spiritless place throughout the 1840s, surrounded by run-down wharves and Micael's tenements. The council of the First Municipality now and then considered plans to make the plaza "a neat and agreeable resort for the public," but despite years of talking and piecemeal attempts at beautification, the town's most important square remained a vacant lot where chickens pecked at mounds of rubble and a goat worried the few patches of what the council referred to as "smut grass."[29] City employees were owed back wages recurrently, even in the 1840s, years after the financial crash. There were not enough funds to cover even basic operating expenses.

The Second Municipality was meanwhile thriving, in comparison with the other two. The public debt was high, but the Americans were at least able to obtain credit throughout the period of municipal division. Public schools in the district had a good reputation. Although other public services were wanting, especially during periods of flood and disease, there existed among the Americans a cult of promptitude where money was concerned, a progressive zeal that made the Second Municipality seem more resourceful, perhaps, than it was. Some of the conspicuous ardor for sound management was no more than self-promotion which did not necessarily correspond to the reality of gains and losses, as when the *Daily Crescent*, the newspaper of the Second Municipality, chirped proudly about "Our Workhouse and

House of Refuge, where moral discipline is combined with humane punishments, and the labor of the delinquents made to compensate the public for the expense incurred by their confinement."[30]

Yet, propaganda aside, there is little doubt that the American sector was prospering while the other two were not. Even the French newspapers admitted that the Second Municipality had better roads and streets and well-managed wharves.[31] Its public market stalls brought in rents of $70,000 a year—half the interest on the nearly $8 million debt of the entire city. By 1850 the American section had a massive municipal hall, beautiful by the utilitarian standards of most American buildings. It was designed by James Gallier, Jr., in the solemn Greek temple style favored by pagan worshipers and reverential Christian capitalists.

Small wonder that by the time Micael arrived in the city in 1849, the Creoles had had enough of the tripartite experiment and were ready to rejoin the three municipalities. The Americans at first would have nothing to do with any plan to put them again in the minority in a consolidated city council. The Creoles and immigrants were drowning in deficits in their sections; they would not be allowed to plunder the hard-won wealth of the Second Municipality to liquidate their debts. However, a plan for consolidation was finally proposed that all sides agreed to, though not without wrangling and not until 1852, a year after Micael had returned to France. The American community of Lafayette, which was situated just above the river from the Second Municipality, was joined to the other three districts so that Americans were equally balanced against Creoles and immigrants in the city council.[32] Americans were no longer in a minority, and now had every hope of electing their own candidates to positions of power over the whole city.

Reunification was the beginning of the end of Creole domination in New Orleans politics. For the remaining years until the Civil War, Americans gradually gained control of the police department and through it, supervised local voting stations. The Creoles had for years fraudulently influenced elections, it was charged, by trotting their immigrant friends from one polling station to the next to cast multiple ballots.[33] Since the voting stations were assigned to coffeehouses, a euphemism for saloons, the voters must have found it easy to perform their civic duty as many times as requested. Now the Americans were accused of rigging elections by having voters assaulted at the polls while police looked the other way, or by blocking off the roads leading from the immigrants' neighborhoods to the polls. By fair means or foul, Americans increasingly won mayoral and council elections throughout the 1850s.

Since those antebellum years of political fissure, abundant claptrap has been written concerning cultural hostility between Creoles and Americans, the differences in language, religion, and style which are supposed to have created bruising enmity and kept the city divided into three municipalities. Who has not heard the myth that Creoles refused to cross the "neutral ground," or median, on Canal Street which separated the French Quarter from the American section? Who has not been entertained by the fictitious picture of the Vieux Carré in the 1840s as a quaint museum set in progressive America, its French-speaking curators strolling under wrought-iron balconies, greeting each fellow Creole with a low bow and a praline?

New Orleans, however, was like all big American cities: every section, not only the Old Quarter, was a babble of foreign tongues. More than half the white population of the city was neither American nor Creole in 1850, but foreign born. Overseas immigrants made up 46 percent of the residents of New York in the same period, and there were similar proportions in St. Louis and Chicago. There was nothing remarkable about having a section of a city where a large population was living and breeding in a foreign language. Moreover, to examine the lists of steamship passengers arriving in the Crescent City in the 1840s is to realize that German was heard in the coffee-houses and feed stores as often as French. The Germans had their own thriving newspaper after 1848; the Irish had no paper, but they too had their purchase on the life of the city. Both the Americans and the Creoles looked upon these new people as brawling, drunken, oafish, and superstitious; they were more estranged from them, and from the population they courteously referred to as "colored people," than they were from each other. Throughout the 1850s in New Orleans there were bloody riots and murders, not between Creoles and Americans, but between the immigrant groups who, it was felt, were metastasizing over the city and American chauvinists who had gravitated to the Know-Nothing Party. The one armed standoff that did occur between Creoles and Americans in 1858 was essentially a contest over which politicians would control the immigrant vote.

It is true that Creoles held most of the land in the First Municipality and Americans in the Second; but Americans certainly made real estate investments in the French Quarter, and many Creoles, such as Micael's friends the Urquharts, owned property of equal value in both sections.[34] It is a fact that the treasury of the First Municipality, the reserve of public funds, was empty. But the individual Creole was typically rich and shrewd; he simply had no notion of public policy or the public weal. French and Americans intermarried, according to the marriage records of the period 1840–1860. A man such as John Slidell might walk and talk and invest like an American, but he had as many Creole in-laws as any planter's son raised on *grillades* and rosaries. There was mutual contempt between Creoles and Americans; that is evident from the guarded correctness of their written comments about each other. But it was their struggle for economic control and political power, not cultural friction, that caused the breakup of the city into municipalities; and what reunited the city finally was financial exigency and a redress of the political imbalance, not any melding of the cultures.

Neither should anyone attempt to deny that Creoles and Americans lived in different psychological landscapes, even while they shopped in each other's stores or traded slaves and small talk. *L'Orléanais*, one of the French newspapers read in the Old Quarter, and the *Daily Crescent*, the oracle of the Second Municipality, were published within walking distance of each other. Micael, cantering around town in her sensible shoes, would go from the offices of one to the other with ads for her buildings. And yet they were a mental continent apart. *L'Orléanais* or the *Daily Orleanian*, as its English pages were titled, contained news dispatches from Europe, editorials about foreign affairs, announcements of interest to Catholics, and a reader's digest for francophiles; in 1849 the abridged novels of the elder Alexandre Dumas were being serialized. Local news on October 18, 1850, included a report that a few citizens had been arrested for participating in a charivari. "Several loafers and loaferesses were furnished with quarters in the workhouse," the paper remarked, in the affectedly sardonic tone that substituted in those journalistic days for comic strips. The mayor's court was to have met, the paper reported with an implied shrug, but the aldermen failed to appear.

To unfold the *Daily Crescent*, in contrast, was to enter a world of self-conscious deportment, civic energy, and eager, unpracticed capitalism: "Does Any Body Wish to buy Dry Goods that are almost given away? If so they should call at Andrews', corner of St. Charles and Julia sts. . . ."[35] American readers were assured that this or that house advertised for rent was "suitable for a genteel family." There was comparatively little foreign news, but the paper made up for it with shipping and banking information. Here and there one caught a glancing reflection of a Puritan America beyond the range of the marsh gnat, as in the paper's praise for a minister who recruited numerous people to take a temperance oath—an article unimaginable in the pages of *L'Orléanais*.[36]

As for the durable newspaper of the Germans in New Orleans, *Tägliche Deutsche Zeitung*, it, too, seemed to emerge from some foreign underground place, though it was published on the corner of Poydras Street and Tchoupitoulas. *Deutsche Zeitung* offered the most comprehensive source of international news, a two-page gazette with a paragraph summarizing the most important events in fifteen or twenty countries around the world; this was far more attention to world affairs than one could expect even from the French *L'Orléanais* or *L'Abeille*. A second section was given over to classified advertising, two or three tightly printed pages of ads offering services to German speakers. There were apparently many German doctors in the city as well as German bookshops and a German-English school, not to mention pharmacies stocked with the ubiquitous pain extractors so that customers could be gypped in fluent German. The last page of the paper was devoted to information about arriving and departing vessels—a large number of Germans were employed in shipping and dockwork. Reading *Deutsche Zeitung*, one could be convinced that New Orleans was a German city with an unnoticed minority of French and American inhabitants.

The same contrast was evident in the council meetings of the three municipalities. The third-world Third Municipality kept some accounts of municipal funds; its records show that no matter when we examine the corporation's revenue, it was never taking in enough money to support the public services the area needed. The recorder for the municipality, that is, the mayor, had to seek permission to buy coal to heat a public building so that he could host a warm reception for John C. Calhoun, who was scheduled to visit.[37] Meetings of the seven members went slowly while the council filtered much business through committees. The aldermen did have enough sense to call in a consultant to help them operate more efficiently—a council member from the Second Municipality named George Eustis. His qualifications were first examined by a three-man committee for two months; then he was assigned to seven committees to help dispatch the piled-up work and make recommendations. Eustis may have been taken aback to find that the Third Municipality council meetings were in French, as all the regular council members were Creoles. There was often no quorum for the monthly meetings, which then had to be postponed.

All this was dramatically different from Eustis' experience in the Second Municipality, where weekly council meetings were intense and precise, like

the proceedings at an auction or stock exchange. The American aldermen
had as their first priority in every meeting the presentation and inspection of
their many accounts. Each meeting included reports on monies collected for
wharfage and drayage, rents from public buildings, municipal notes re-
deemed, interest earned or owed, or taxes figured to the half-cent by gentlemen responsive to the thrill of a penny saved or gained. Each chart offered
columns straight as church pews and emphatic decimals planted with the
fussiness of people who loved numbers. The collection-plate passers who ran
the Second Municipality knew the satisfaction of correct addition, and respected both the linear clarity of credits and debits and the dignified, strin-
gent etiquette of showing how money was spent.

In a typical week in 1846, the Second Municipality dispersed about as
much on the workhouse as on lighting for the area (over $500); the munici-
pality spent the same amount for new sidewalks as for police pay (around
$300). The largest expense was for night watchmen, some $2,500, indicating
that the position and the paycheck was a political favor liberally bestowed:
the municipality was spending $100 more for night vigilance than for all the
salaries, books, and building maintenance of the public schools. After sub-
tracting a big scoop of public money for their own salaries (the third highest
expenditure), the seven happy administrators were able to show a balance
for the municipality of $2,470 for the week.[38]

The council of the First Municipality, on the other hand, seems to have
been a kind of private club whose purpose was to spread out the work at
hand and keep each of its sixteen members occupied as long as possible. Accounts were rarely offered for examination or for placing in the record. The
funds for the First Municipality were kept in an iron chest, not in the bank.[39]
Each expenditure, even for pressing issues such as cumulating garbage, required goodly time and many papers. Every scrap of business undertaken by
the council was referred to one of its ten committees. The jailkeeper requested authority to sell slaves who had served their sentences and remained
unclaimed. The matter was referred to a judiciary committee. A police officer
protested that ten dollars had been deducted from his pay on account of
sickness. That was handled by the police committee. One man petitioned the
council not to authorize the emancipation of one of his slaves; he had had a
hardening of heart since his last petition. The matter went to the judiciary
committee.[40] Several committees dealt in turn with Dennis Cronan, who
was employed by the council to replace the curbstones on Chartres Street

and the sidewalk flagging around the Place d'Armes. He started at the same time the Pontalba Buildings were begun, in October, 1849; but long after the buildings were rented, he was still causing "a great inconvenience" to pedestrians. In 1851 the shop owners whose entrances had been blocked for two years declared themselves ruined and threatened to sue the council for damages. But the council had its revenge on Cronan; it took as long to pay him as he had taken to pave.[41]

Micaël's ideas for the Pontalba Buildings became more elaborate as the project developed. She realized early on that the rest of the square would look humble between her two palaces. Thus, on August 28, 1846, her agent Le-Breton addressed the city council in her behalf: "Mme. de Pontalba, although not making it a positive request, respectfully calls your attention to the useful improvements that might be made to the Place d'Armes. I have the honor, Gentlemen, to submit for your consideration a plan for this purpose. . . ."

The council of the First Municipality was as unimpressed with Madame de Pontalba's building enterprise as its predecessor, the *cabildo*, had been with her father's. The council was engaged in the lawsuit against her for possession of the "Leper's Land"; in 1849 it was to receive her reluctant payment of ten thousand dollars; and it considered her no friend. However, the city had everything to gain from new buildings on the square, and the council welcomed the improvements if not the improver. Micaël was apparently willing to finance the refurbishing herself. Recognizing that the square harbored "loafers and vagabonds who are seen lying drunk under the trees," the council resolved to allow Micaël to turn the plaza into "a garden smiling with verdure during the entire year."[42] Micaël herself contracted with Samuel Stewart to renovate the Place d'Armes.

The project excited a certain measure of derision among Creoles who opposed any change, on principle, and especially any change fostered by an outsider. One wag addressed a longish piece of doggerel to the council of the First Municipality, in which Micaël's father's name was invoked with mock reverence:

> Almonester! Death did not end your generosity;
> Your daughter extends it with luminosity.
> In the midst of her celebrations
> She has noticed our vexations

And abandons her security
To battle our impurity.
She comes, that appariton,
To better our condition,
Our squalor to abate
And a philanthropist to reincarnate.[43]

In return for her contribution to the city, Micael wanted to be relieved of paying taxes on the property for a period of twenty years. Such tax credits to encourage new enterprise in a particular area are common government practice now, and were used by administrators then. At first the council agreed. Micael submitted plans for buildings with arcades that would extend over the street, like those surrounding the Place des Vosges in Paris. Micael then decided against the overhanging arcades—even without them, Jackson Square and the Pontalba Buildings still seem strikingly like the Paris park. The council of the First Municipality, with its singular talent for doing the wrong thing, used the change in the design as an excuse to renege on its promise of tax relief, even though Micael notified the council of the changes in advance and asked it specifically to let her know if her tax obligations would be affected.[44] Micael had no choice but to go forward with the Pontalba Buildings; however, it seems that at that time she abandoned her project to improve the plaza between her houses.

Nonetheless, the square got its face-lift. While St. Louis Cathedral was undergoing one of its periodic restorations in January, 1850, the central bell-shaped tower collapsed, carrying with it part of the roof and walls. Major restructuring was unavoidable; and so, after some months the church received an entirely new façade designed by J. N. B. de Pouilly. When Gaston de Pontalba sketched the new St. Louis Cathedral in 1850, the spires were open through graceful webs of iron—a reflection of the nearby balconies of the Pontalbas.[45] Eventually, the Place d'Armes itself was cleaned up in earnest, repaved, and replanted. In 1851 the plaza was renamed Jackson Square in honor of the hero of the Creoles who, like them, avoided banks. Jackson had personally laid the cornerstone of his monument in 1840 when he visited New Orleans; but as with all civic matters, the First Municipality council had not been hasty in erecting the statue. Sixteen years later, a statue of the old warrior by Clark Mills was finally unveiled; Micael sent fifteen hundred dollars from France to help pay for it. In 1851 there was as yet no Jackson in Jackson Square; but there were two blocks of sparkling red buildings on each side, ornate iron benches in the public strolling area, a new fence, and even a guard to indispose the vagrants who liked their old haunt better than ever.

While working on the Pontalbas, Micael was managing her property in France, which did not rent itself. Most of the people acquainted with her knew nothing of her business affairs, though her private life was an open book with a rose binding. In the years after the shooting, they assumed, as did a reporter for the *Daily Picayune*, that she "recovered from the wound and resumed her duties as a mother and a lady."[46] A healthy woman would have wilted under her workload. She was never healthy; but she labored over the management of her property twelve hours a day. She had something better than intellect: inclination, ambition, drive. Like her father, she counted minutes as if they were money. A writer on the *Daily Delta* was particularly impressed with her as she visited the newspaper's offices. Though the weather was bad, she was there at seven in the morning,

> a fine-looking middle-aged lady, with a bright eye, intelligent expression, viva-cious manners, and energetic movements. From her frank and unostentatious style, one would no doubt have taken her for one of those energetic ladies who, thrown upon their own resources and compelled to lay aside much of their feminine reserve and shrinking delicacy, devote themselves so industri-ously and energetically to the support of their dependent families.

The writer commented upon her

> prompt, business-like style, her quick sagacity, her shrewd observations upon passing events—taking in her range political, municipal, and commercial mat-ters—now belaboring the red republicans of Paris, then, with an emphatic gesture toward her forehead, asserting the superior strength of head of the Americans, and deploring the want of energy of the Creoles, denouncing the municipal division of the city as a source of "jalousie" and ill-feeling, and de-claring her determination to devote the rest of her life to the improvement and advancement of her native city.[47]

The reporter liked her. Micael's agents liked her too, even though she told them off whenever she felt like it. They remained with her for decades, which they would not have done if she had truly abused them, since she cer-tainly did not overpay them. Probably Samuel Stewart liked her when she first met him in New Orleans. She approached him with an exciting idea, a plan to erect not a house, but two magnificent blocks of houses. Micael had a clear, fluent command of English, and they both spoke the language of

builders. Stewart was an immigrant Irish tradesman, for all his homespun
courtliness. But like Micael, he was vigorous and independent, with more
mother wit than erudition. As in any close communion, the two working
partners were to discover each other's limitations. Micael could be niggardly
and stubborn over small expenditures, inconveniencing everyone for the
sake of a few dollars. Stewart was not the engineer/architect/straw-boss that
Micael's project demanded, and he was soon exasperated with his finicky and
frugal patron. But during the months they cooperated, they added something to each other's lives. Each was for the other a unique acquaintance,
and together they created something unique for the city. Jackson Square and
the Pontalba Buildings were *their* work, lasting and harmonious. Even after
Micael and Stewart had become sour adversaries, the transformation they
brought about in the dingy Place d'Armes must have given them each more
abiding satisfaction than friendship ever could.

X

Building

THE Pontalba Buildings seemed to materialize overnight. In April, 1849, Micael was still pressing the city council to approve her final plans for the buildings so that work could begin in October. By September, 1850, less than a year later, she had moved into Number 5 Pontalba Row with her sons and was receiving "persons who may desire to rent any of her houses."[1] By the following February, the Place d'Armes had been transformed into a paraphrase of Paris' Place des Vosges.

So far, no one knows who designed the Pontalba Buildings. Both the architecture of the buildings and the idea of the twin blocks were worked out either in Europe or in New York; Micael had the plans with her when she arrived in New Orleans.[2] At some point after she landed in the city, she consulted James Gallier, Jr. His name appeared on the plans as "supervising architect," that is, the one who would see to it that the contractor followed the blueprint, but not necessarily the architect who designed the building. His name was crossed out, however, and replaced by Micael's signature. The Pontalbas mildly resemble some of Gallier's buildings; but Gallier never visited the construction site or supervised any of the workers, according to the construction foreman, nor did Gallier claim the Pontalbas as his work. Some preliminary sketches were made in Gallier's office for the floor plans; it is not certain whether they were developed and used. Apparently, he had nothing to do with authoring the exterior design. Not even Henry Howard, the architect who became involved in the construction problems, knew who designed the buildings. He recalled in court that he and others speculated a great deal as to who the architect might have been and whether he was from New York. In was in New York that Samuel Stewart first saw the architect's plan for the Pontalbas in September, 1849, when he went there to contract for the iron columns.[3]

The genius whose unverified ghost seems to flutter through the design is Henri Labrouste, a French architect who lived in Paris the same time as Micael.[4] Among his works were the Bibliothèque Sainte-Geneviève, and the Bibliothèque Nationale, where he replaced Visconti as architect. The

Pontalba Buildings are not listed in Labrouste's archives (housed, of all places, in the Bureau des Architectes in the Place des Vosges).[5] And yet, looking at Labrouste's day labor, one has the sense that he might have dreamed the Pontalba Buildings at night. His spirit haunts the New Orleans buildings, not only in details but also in his conception of the way iron and curved space can be used to create a feeling both of airiness and solidity. Nevertheless, there is no evidence that Labrouste was responsible for the elegant Pontalba design.

The Pontalba Buildings must have looked quite foreign at first. Row housing was a European tradition that had made its way to the northeastern United States but was still unusual in New Orleans at midcentury. Even in the North, identical rows often did not look identical because the owner of each house might paint or ornament his vertical strip differently from the others in the row. It was only where a line of houses had one owner, as in the case of the Pontalbas, that the buildings could exert the effect of a single, exhilarating expanse. Moreover, the only monumental architecture in New Orleans before the Pontalbas were public buildings. The Pontalbas were the biggest residential buildings most people in New Orleans had ever seen. They were also the most eccentric. To what category or style did they belong? The balconies with their dancing cast-iron were French; cast-iron lace became characteristic of New Orleans only after the Pontalba galleries set the taste. But stripped of their iron jewelry, the buildings had plain Georgian faces, that is, they were the English version, popular in 1850, of a classical Greek temple whose pediment, or triangular part, was supported by columns. The Pontalba columns are slender and graceful, rather than massive like Greek columns, and there are three pediments, not one. Instead of the traditional marble, the buildings are constructed of red brick and iron. Nevertheless, the Greek ancestry of the design remains distinct and distinctive. The Pontalbas were a conjugation of styles on the outside: Greek, English, and French; and they were different from anything else in the Vieux Carré. It was only inside the houses, behind the exotic look of the façade, that one returned to a completely Creole world.

Part of the charm of the Pontalbas is that, even today, they seem transposed from somewhere else. And yet, not having had the plans made locally was Micael's first mistake in constructing them. Bringing the drawings from afar meant that a sophisticated four-level design was worked out by an architect or company of architects without consideration of any of the peculiarities of

New Orleans soil. Micael thought it would be a simple matter for a New Orleans architect to adapt her drawings to the two sites on the Place d'Armes. When she arrived in the city, therefore, she brought her plans to Henry Howard, who would later design many noteworthy buildings.[6] Howard wanted five hundred dollars to make detailed plans and specifications. Her response, as later described in the abbreviated mode of court reporting, was that she "did not wish to go to that expense, said that Howard had no studying of what he had to do, that she had done all that herself—all the figurings of dimensions appertaining to the Plans were made by herself & he only did the labor. . . ."[7]

A little foresight or the wisdom of middle age should have nudged Micael into giving Howard his five hundred dollars, along with the clear responsibility of providing practicable drawings. Instead, she gave him a fourth of the price he asked and he gave her a superficial working plan with no specifications. She then went on her way, momentarily satisfied with the bargain. If we may believe Howard's later court testimony (it is worthwhile to bear in mind that court documents contain as many lies as any other human record), Micael was needlessly blunt with him, remarking that she was a good architect herself, that Howard could learn a great deal from her, and he ought not to charge her anything for the plans. Micael had no university degree, but then, neither did Howard. Architects learned their skills through apprenticeship and practical experience; hence, contractors and builders called themselves architects. Howard had studied with his father in Ireland.[8]

Though at the time of their encounter he was only thirty-one and still something of a journeyman builder, he had at least one thing to teach Micael. The land in New Orleans was highest near the levees and sloped down as one moved back from the river, as every builder in the city knew. The Pontalba Buildings were to be perpendicular to the river, with one end at Levee Street and the other end at Chartres, a block away from the river, on an incline of thirteen inches. Instead of going to the site himself or getting ground levels from the city surveyor, Howard "merely made the plan for her at her suggestion"; he observed disingenuously to the court that his plan could not have been used on the lot for which it was intended without destroying the harmony of the design she had in mind.[9] Yet he had taken her money and let her go off with it, knowing it was unusable. Normally, he explained, he would have computed the height of the roof by taking a measurement at the proposed center of the building and averaging the height at the ends. He did not do so because Madame de Pontalba "did not employ him and pay him for that." Micael had some specifications at her house made by someone else, according to Howard. "He thinks certain specifications were read to him before the contract was figured," noted the court reporter, "but he did not pay much attention to them." When they were presented to him in court, he admitted disinterestedly that the roof described in the specifications could not possibly fit onto the plan he gave Micael.[10] The specifications and plans were also inconsistent in the matter of drainage. He said he offered advice about where to place the drains, but Micael overruled it. Howard concluded his testimony by pleasantly noting that it was usual for the person who made the plans to furnish the working drawings.

It fell to poor Samuel Stewart, the contractor for the Pontalba Buildings, to turn two sets of incompatible directions into plumb columns and snug roofs, to erect thirty-two houses "in conformity with the plans and specifications accepted and signed. . . ."[11] The contract between Stewart and Micael was detailed, down to requirements for "two-inch axle pullies" on the window sashes and cypress flooring "secret nailed, the heads tongued. . . ."[12] According to the contract for the Upper Pontalba (so called because it is closer to Canal Street, the division between uptown and downtown), Stewart was to demolish all of Micael's old buildings on St. Peter Street and have that side ready within a year. His price, including materials which he provided, was $156,000 for the first building, payable in eight installments over the period of construction. A second agreement was concluded for the Lower Pontalba on St. Ann Street, for which the price was $146,000.[13]

Stewart's own draftsmen provided the working plans for the construction and drew numerous details of the design. Micael inspected all the drawings as they were in progress, made many suggestions, and irritated the people in Stewart's office by taking her time over various decisions. She made changes in the iron columns and in the walls originally planned to separate the back yards, which she wanted two stories high for privacy. She added outside privies along with the indoor water closets she had already specified, and decided that the floor joists ought to be reinforced with cross bridging.[14] She was careful to see to it that the contract's requirements for fire walls were fulfilled. She knew enough about building, apparently, to be a significant nuisance to Stewart, a nuisance he avoided by being out of town most of the time, arranging for the purchase of materials. "I am to leave here for Boston this day at five o'clock," he wrote to his foreman in his clear, graceful hand, "and intend to close there for the Granit and Return here in four days and the following week I Expect to leave for Philadelphia & Baltimore and close

for the Baltimore press bricks and perhaps for the Marbel & Iron & Bannis-
ters & Mahogony. . . . I have ordered working plans of Iron Columns and
Gallery Railing and varanda althou I am very perplexed to know the Sise and
Stile and manner that was intended or that would please the Madam, provided the cost was not extravagant."[15]

Stewart probably brought back pattern books from which Micael selected
ornaments such as interior moldings or decorative fittings for the chandeliers. What imagination and fearless optimism she must have had to order
expensive accessories for thirty-two houses from these catalogs! They contained only simple black-and-white drawings, unshaded diagrams, and some
assurance on each page that "the design presented is original and appropriate
to parlors of the first class. It may be varied in size to accommodate many
situations."[16]

At the beginning of the construction and throughout the winter of
1849–1850, Micael and her sons lived in rented houses. Gaston's favorite
seemed to be a large, comfortable house on Burgundy Street, from which
Micael could walk over to the square every day and irk the workers, while
Gaston sat in the window of his upstairs bedroom and sketched the neighborhood.[17] Stewart's men vented their exasperation by remarking about Micael's being "an obstinate lady," or taking "a long time about making up her
mind."[18] But it seems that her deliberations did not seriously delay progress.
Her alterations in the plans after construction was under way did cause
problems. But, though numerous, her changes were not unusual for buildings costing $300,000.

She did, however, place Stewart in an impossible predicament when, for
some unaccountable reason, she refused to provide him with a copy of the
plans she had brought from New York. As she began making changes in the
working drawings, those made by Stewart's own draftsmen, it became necessary to consult the original plan made by the mystery architect. At first Micael insisted that this plan had to remain in a notary's office where, she suggested, Stewart's draftsmen could go to make tracings. Then as the yellow
fever season set in, she and her sons moved away from the infection to East
Pascagoula on the Mississippi Gulf Coast, and she took the plans with her.
Stewart sent to Pascagoula, about one hundred miles from New Orleans,
to get them, but she refused to let them out of her possession.[19] Possibly
she feared that if she released the plans, someone would copy the design
of the unique Pontalbas or take undeserved credit as the originator of the
buildings. Maybe she wanted to keep the builders from going ahead with the

construction, closing up walls and the like, before she had a chance to inspect the work. For whatever reason, she seemed perversely determined not
to allow Stewart access to plans that he had every right to assume would be
given to him. Stewart's subcontractors—the bricklayer, welder, and others—
sometimes had to work without plans and wait for Micael's random visits to
the construction before they could get directions as to how various jobs
were to be finished. The documents still resonate with the sounds of pacing
and Irish imprecations.

Stewart next appealed to Howard. He hoped that if Howard did not have
a copy of the plan, the architect could at least look again at the original in
Pascagoula and resolve some of the problems Stewart's men were having
with the working drawings. Howard refused to be bothered with what was
sure to be an unrewarded labor. Stewart, aware that the days allotted to him
in the contract were ticking away, must have been fairly desperate by the
time his foreman Jewell "ran across" another architect who agreed to try to
patch together a feasible plan out of the confusion of trial drawings and tracings that had already been made.[20]

The patchwork sufficed until Stewart got to the point in the construction
where he had to fit the roof specifications to Howard's plan. Stewart was reduced to sending for Micael, who of course could not figure out how to put
together two sets of ill-matched directions. Micael sent for Howard, but he
refused to come, according to his later testimony, "because she would not
pay him for it."[21] Using Gaston as a messenger, Micael asked him several
times how the roof was to be put on, and he explained it to Gaston several
times, he said. Finally, she sent Gaston to fetch him yet again, "because she
could not well understand" the directions. Gaston returned without Howard. The architect steadfastly refused to leave his office "except as he was paid
for it." Nevertheless, Gaston, a man of remarkable forbearance, was dispatched again to Howard. His mother "requested to get a small sketch . . .
in order to know how to make the roof."[22] Howard threw off a few lines so
as "to get rid of the young gentleman" (Gaston was three years younger than
Howard, but decades behind him in self-importance) and sent him back to
Stewart and Micael. Stewart did what he could with such a blueprint. When
he and Micael faced each other in court in 1851, the roof had been leaking for
over a year.

Many of Micael's alterations to the plans were reasonable and worthwhile
improvements to the design. But she also gave Stewart plenty of reason to
lose his manners. For example, when she inspected the first backyard wall

which was to divide two houses, she decided that it ought to be carried up to a second story, roofed, and plastered, so that it could hold a privy. She got an injunction against Stewart to stop construction of the other walls until the plans were amended to reflect the new height.[23] The change was made and the yard wall completed with its roof and privy when she next instructed that an archway be opened in the new wall, through the fresh concrete, for the convenience of any tenant who might rent the two adjoining houses.

Surprisingly, relations between Micael and Stewart did not completely break down until the construction of the Upper Pontalba was almost completed. She appeared happy with the quality of the work, and Stewart seemed to make every effort to please her as they muddled through a proliferation of working drawings and trial plans. However, there can be little doubt that in dealing with Stewart and his men, Micael showed a tactlessness permitted only to the very old. R. P. Rice, a foreman for Stewart, testified that he had made several working plans before Micael finally approved one. He asked her to sign the chosen plans. Perhaps he was being snide, but more likely it was a customary and harmless request, in view of the possibility of confusing those plans with the others. Micael replied that her word was as good as her signature, and refused.[24]

Stewart asked her, while they were inspecting the completed building, if she had succeeded in renting any of the houses. This was not a harmless question; Stewart was trying to find out whether Micael had any grounds for charging him for lost rents, since the building was not completed on schedule. Micael told him without hesitation that it was none of his business. According to the workmen, whose patience was even more frayed than Stewart's, she frequently made the unendearing revelation that she was herself a knowledgeable builder.

It is hard now to judge whether Micael's manner and intentions were as obnoxious as her soundbites. With her ugly, mangled hand, her seizures, and the rancid story of her "incident" following her, she knew that she was something of a curiosity to be whispered about. She seemed resolved not to be put off by other people, whatever their reactions to her. Informed, for example, that a cousin hesitated to visit her in Pascagoula, apparently on account of her "nervous attacks," Micael replied, "I don't think she will be more bothered by being around me than I'll be bothered by her. We both say our prayers the same way. So she should not be afraid of me."[25] Her adversities had deprived her of female vanity; she avoided fashionable clothes, jewelry, and her noble title. She was, if not prim and ladylike, conversable, down-to-earth, and good-humored—and perhaps merely brusque rather than intentionally hurtful. Even so, she should have been nicer to Stewart.

As the Upper Pontalba neared completion in the fall of 1850, the problems Stewart had been grappling with began to show up in the houses. Micael had changed the plan for the gutters, against advice; possibly as a result, the yards and entire lower story were flooded after every rain.[26] The building was not uniform in height from end to end, nor as tall as Micael specified, because Stewart had had to alter measurements to compensate for the uneven ground. Stewart used ordinary bricks in the kitchen fireplaces instead of fire bricks, as the contract called for; he left out two fireplaces entirely; and he neglected to place a single bell in any house. Apparently, he had been dealing with so many revised plans, he got confused.

The ground-floor stores were virtually finished when Micael realized for the first time that none of the plans had called for doors separating the rear of each ground-floor shop from the living quarters upstairs, which might be leased to a separate tenant. Circular brickwork had just been installed in eight stores to make arched, open entranceways at the back of each shop, leading to the stair. Inserting doors required cutting into that circular brickwork. The work was already behind schedule, and Stewart was looking ahead to the possibility of having to pay Micael a penalty if the building was not finished on time. When Micael spoke to Joseph Jewell, the foreman, about changing the circular archways to rectangular door frames, he protested that it would be "a pretty large item" and that Stewart would certainly charge her extra. Micael's response, said Jewell, was that "Mr. Stewart had better do it; that he might be a good Builder but that he knew nothing about the law; that Mr. Stewart had better take care; she had carried on a lawsuit in France about something for nearly twenty years, that it was not ended yet."

The October deadline came; Micael withheld the last installment of Stewart's fee and refused to accept the houses until he corrected everything that was wrong with them. Moreover, she threatened to hold him accountable for her lost rents, even though she was abundantly to blame for his delays. Stewart knew enough about the law to file a petition against Micael. He had apparently been undecided about what to charge her for the additional work she had ordered.[27] However, after their concussion over the last payment of his fee, he made an itemized bill of over $4,000 "for the Extra Work," which he now presented to the court, along with his demand for the $26,000 still owed to him on the contract.[28]

It was an unchivalrous list. Stewart not only charged extra for the doors Micael requested; he charged extra for the hinges. He charged her for the braces that she insisted he put up when she discovered the balcony railing wobbled; for the marble hearths he had to replace because the first ones he installed were cracked; for the American locks she demanded when she saw that he had disregarded the contract and used French ones. The bill was an inventory of Stewart's frustrations throughout the whole vexatious year: "Item 27: 152 Iron bars to front window Shutters by orders of Mrs. Pontalba refusing to receive said building allthou the above shutters had the yousale [usual] fastening: one dollar each. . . ." Stewart charged for everything not specified in his contract, even though some of the extras were obviously essentials. Micael was at a disadvantage for, like anyone making a building contract, she had not foreseen the need for "vaulting piers of wood between the joists to prevent them from springing," one of the particulars for which she was charged extra.[29]

Who could blame Micael for not accepting a flooded building with cracked marble and a leaky roof? On the other hand, how was Stewart to defend himself against a person who thought nothing of asking him to rip into fresh concrete and bricks? Having been ill used for a year, he was fighting back with the only means he had of making up his losses. Work on the Lower Pontalba meanwhile proceeded more or less on schedule. It seems that the two warriors settled out of court, with Stewart withdrawing his demand for the $4,000 for "extras" and Micael yielding the final payment on his contract. A notarial act filed by Stewart on November 30, 1852, twenty months after Micael left New Orleans, granted her "a full release of the privilege in his favor" for $156,000 (the price of the Upper Pontalba), "the total price having been paid."[30] The compromise reached by Stewart and Micael reconciled them sufficiently that the Lower Pontalba could be finished.

Two things are clear from the Stewart v. Pontalba court record which, once deciphered, is more concise than most such files. For all her badgering and self-serving garrulity, Micael did know a great deal about building and was something of a lay genius in architectural design. It was she who found the versatile interior shutters which, when open, disappear into the embrasure of the window and become part of the frame. She "found" the columns, that is, she borrowed the style of a column she had seen somewhere and coerced the subcontractors into adapting it to her buildings. She conceived the idea of having the grates of the fireplaces and the iron fittings on the mantels reflect the iron motifs on the exterior of the buildings. She, not the architects or contractor, wanted flagstones in the yard, crane eyes in the chimneys, roofs on the second-story galleries, and archways over the interior entrances to replicate the design of the façade.[31] It was she who decided the flooring joists needed to be reinforced, and that the front of each building had to be anchored in the center to prevent its springing in or out. She saw to every detail, from the brickwork on the privy sinks to the hardware on the workroom doors (knobs, not latches).[32] She was, if not the supervising architect, then certainly the supervising person, whose changes added as much to the solidity and beauty of the buildings as they took away from the building schedule.

The other thing that becomes apparent in reviewing the lawsuit is that Samuel Stewart was an energetic manager and a building wizard (aside from being the prodigious father of thirteen children). His subcontractors testified that they were rarely delayed for want of supplies, even though the whole immense construction was a mail-order building: the granite, marble, stone flagging, thousands of bricks, and iron were all shipped to New Orleans from out of state.[33] None of Stewart's subcontractors or employees troubled themselves much about discrepancies in the plans or sufficiency of materials. When tangles appeared, it was Stewart who worked them out while the workers took off for the day. Yet the buildings were almost ready within a year. The problems Micael saw in them were the kinds of flaws any enormous construction might reveal on the first inspection. And the fact that the buildings have remained livable and sound for more than 150 years attests to Stewart's workmanship.

Little is said on either side of the Stewart/Pontalba lawsuit about the cast-iron galleries, the first feature of the building a viewer notices. W. A. Tallen, Stewart's draftsman, wrote that Madame de Pontalba "was much pleased with my Strictly following her french Ornamental Scroll Work in all the Casting."[34] The iron lace patterns Tallen was copying set the taste for the ironwork balconies for which New Orleans is famous; they were the prototype for dozens of balconies that then began appearing all over the city. The Old Quarter had had decorative iron galleries before the Pontalbas, but they were wrought iron and relatively simple.[35] The Pontalbas were the first balconies in New Orleans to use cast iron in highly elaborate designs on an imposing scale.[36] The C curves that slide rhythmically around a monogram on each porch reflect Micael's coming of age in Paris; iron curls in the galleries of Louis Philippe's capital were like snatches of street music, popular everywhere.

The famous *AP* monogram which echoes through the long railings is a masterpiece of design in a building full of adroit details. The letters are perfectly clear and perfectly unobtrusive; they give a focal point to the pattern without detracting in the least from the diffused loveliness of the iron tracery. The monograms vanish into the delicate weaving of the galleries as soon as one stops thinking about them, letting the balconies again become a flowing panorama. The monogram was surely Micael's own idea and possibly her design, although it appears from Gaston's notebooks that he and not his mother designed the *AP*.[37] The notebooks show several trial drawings and variations on the monogram as it was finally cast. In fact, it is entirely likely that he designed all of the scrollwork that Tallen so assiduously copied.

Gaston probably made other contributions to the buildings, for he was a perceptive draftsman with an eye for tranquil compositions. He loved the buildings in the old city; he made painstaking pencil drawings of St. Louis Cathedral before and after its renovation, of the new Pontalbas before the sycamores in the Place d'Armes were cut down to clear the view across the square, and of the house on Burgundy Street where he and his brother and mother lived when they first arrived in New Orleans.[38] He walked across Canal Street to the Second Municipality and sketched St. Charles Avenue looking up to Gallier Hall, which was then the new city hall and probably still unfinished.[39] Included in Gaston's picture is the shop of Madame Blair, a modiste of American ladies, and a large, corner gift shop featuring combs, perfumes, "fancy articles," and "gents' furnishing goods." Even though Gaston drew only one mudhole and not a single turkey, hog, or dog, his St. Charles Avenue looks neither new nor stylish.[40] In a humorous mood he sketched a bedroom with agitated occupants barricaded against mosquitoes.[41] People had not yet made the connection between the mosquito and the hideous epidemics of yellow fever that were striking New Orleans each year with increasing severity, so the "beasts," as Gaston called them, were still a fit subject for jokes. No one could have imagined that one day it would be possible to live in New Orleans without thinking much about mosquitoes, and not at all about yellow fever.

The most modern thinking at midcentury held that yellow fever was an alien affliction brought to the city through the port.[42] True, every kind of germ in the world visited the Crescent City, and many contagions were carried in on international ships.[43] But New Orleans promoted its own pathogens, too; even luxury hotels were known to dump their capacious privies into busy streets.[44] Consequently, as in every decade since the city's founding, people still came down with "the fever," meaning any sort of internal misery that might or might not be fatal. No sickness, however, terrorized the community as did yellow fever, not even cholera, although it was just as devastating because it recurred year after year, whereas yellow fever might skip a year or more. Reverend Theodore Clapp, who witnessed many black vomit epidemics in New Orleans, described the horrors and desolations he saw in 1853, when cholera and yellow fever epidemics struck simultaneously. "Words can convey no adequate idea," he wrote. "In some cases, all the clerks and agents belonging to mercantile establishments were swept away, and the stores closed by civil authorities. Several entire families were carried off—parents, children, servants, all. Others lost a quarter, or a third, or three-fourths of their members, and their business, hopes, and happiness were blasted for life."[45]

The symptoms of yellow fever included intestinal hemorrhages and vomiting, the so-called black vomit being the regurgitation of partially digested blood. "Often I have met and shook hands with some blooming, handsome young man today," wrote Parson Clapp, "and in a few hours afterward, I have been called to see him in the Black Vomit, with profuse hemorrhages from the mouth, nose, ears, eyes, and even the toes; the eyes prominent, glistening, yellow and staring; the face discolored with orange color and dusky red."[46]

The classic victim was a newcomer to the city; therefore, Micael took her sons to Pascagoula in the summers of 1849 and 1850. Azélie, an old maid to her neurasthenic fingertips, declined to give up her habitual life in order to accompany them, although Micael hated moving to Mississippi away from her cousin, hated "the awkwardness of a new setup," as Gaston expressed it.[47] Once ensconced in their rented clapboard house on the shore of the Gulf Coast, Gaston swam, sketched, and wrote letters which provide us with mundane details of Micael's life. The attentive son informed Azélie that his mother occasionally had "nervous attacks."[48] She went back and forth to the city fairly often when she had to supervise work on her buildings, taking a packet-boat from Pascagoula like the ones that carried mail. The boats left three mornings a week and served breakfast. At the outskirts of New Orleans she transferred to a train that brought her into town; then finally, she took a carriage which Rochereau generally had waiting for her at the station.[49] If his mother got on his nerves in the isolated country house, Gaston never revealed it on paper. But then, he was a polite man, circumspect and probably manipulative; he would not have allowed himself the relief of candid complaint. He seemed only too happy to write letters for Micael and involve himself in household affairs. "Perhaps I told you in my last letter that we got rid of our two white servants," he wrote to Azélie.

> My cousin Malvina was kind enough to try to find some people for us, but perhaps that is a difficult task at this time of year. My mother is thinking of re-hiring the mulatress Cecile who was with her all last year. She does not know her address, but this girl was the niece of Don André Babet. My mother is hoping, dear cousin, that you can send Thérèse to the Babets to get the address, which you can then send to M. Rochereau. She would be much obliged to you. . . .[50]

This was the same Thérèse, a free woman, who had been the maid of Micael's Aunt Victoire and was now Azélie's servant, as neither Victoire, Azélie, nor Micael owned slaves during the years of Micael's correspondence.[51] She was sent on other errands for Micael. "Send Thérèse to get news of our washerwoman's child whom she left very sick."[52] It is clear from Gaston's letters that all the servants had legs. "My mother asks you, my dear cousin, to get back from Madame Deverges a wool dress which Létis brought to my cousin to have her take apart."[53] Since fabric never wore out, even people such as Micael who could afford new dresses remade their clothes again and again from the same material. Gaston continued, "If this dress is not already unstitched, she asks you to have it taken out and then dyed a *bronze green, very deep*. As she is expecting our cousins Rousseau the 1st of September, she thinks they could perhaps bring that dress to her."

Micael received the dress, somehow, but not the Rousseaux. A week later Gaston was writing, "As the boat is about to take off, I hasten to ask you to have my mother's dress dyed the same color, but darker; if it turns completely black it's all right with her."[54] (No one can wear wool in September in the Deep South. Why was she in such a hurry?) Gaston went on to say that his mother was morose from all the talk of yellow fever. "I'm waiting impatiently for the moment when my cousin Madame Rousseau can come see her. Her example, her contagious cheerfulness, will I am sure be enough to reassure my mother, who will then stop thinking about sickness. . . . Try to send us M. and Madame Rousseau."

Gaston was quite close to his brother Alfred all his life, and he seemed to have had no documented discord with his eldest brother Célestin until after the New Orleans trip. His relations with his father were strained. During the years while Micael was building the Hôtel Pontalba and traveling to America, the elder Célestin remained alive and unwell at Mont-l'Évêque. After leaving France in 1846, Gaston did not write to him for three years, all the while sending letters to his brother's wife, Blanche, in the same household. However, it was the inoffensive Gaston, and not Alfred or Micael herself, who wrote to Célestin in 1849 when Micael needed a favor.[55]

> My dear father,
> Since the letter which I wrote in Liverpool the day I sailed, I have often thought of writing to you and would certainly have done so had I not been afraid that my letters would bore you. When Blanche has allowed me to write her, in each of my letters I have not forgotten you, as I think she would not neglect to tell you. It could not have been otherwise; and in whatever country I find myself, I would never forget the kindness you have shown me and the welcome you always gave me at Mont-l'Évêque. I entreat you my dear father to preserve for me, whether far or near, a little of the good will you have so often shown me, the memory of which is so precious.
>
> I hope that today's letter will be welcome, as I have to speak to you of a very important matter pertaining to my mother's interests, which are also ours. Perhaps you know that at this time one of the sides of the Place d'Armes is being torn down. My mother, ascertaining the amount which must be given to new construction and realizing that more extensive repairs to the old buildings would not be profitable because the ancient buildings are not suitable for commercial use, has decided after due consideration to strike a bargain. . . .

Gaston then explained that Micael wanted to borrow some money in France, using her securities as collateral.[56] Banks in New Orleans, he wrote, were charging 9 percent interest, whereas in France, banks only charged five. However, for any such banking transaction in France, Micael needed Célestin's permission, which Gaston hoped would be granted. After discharging his chore, Gaston could hardly wait to conclude the communication; but he managed a convincing filial tone:

> I do not wish to prolong this letter, particularly if you will permit me to write you again sometime before my return to France. If I receive word from you that you are well and that you sometimes think of me, I shall be very happy. I hope, my dear father, that the Vichy waters have had the beneficial result that you anticipated. I send you all good wishes from my heart and I beg you to believe me always your loving and devoted son.

In his letters to New Orleans, Gaston invariably described how much his mother missed Azélie. She longed for cool weather, so she could return to the city and stop in to see her cousin every day while she went about her affairs. However, Micael had developed a certain resilience to the grief of others, if we may judge by one of Gaston's letters regarding a death. "As for your servant's child," he wrote Azélie, "my mother only regrets the pain that you have gone through because of this loss. She knows your good heart and the suffering that an event of this kind brings on your house. But," he continued without apparent embarrassment, "she points out that now there is one more angel in heaven who, if he had lived among men, might have become a real devil. She also says that this bond being broken, the mother will perhaps return to a better frame of mind and it will be easier for you to convert her to virtue and keep her near you."[57] Evidently, Micael did not regard the death of a youth as the tragedy it was worked up to be. However, while she was obviously becoming hard-shelled to outsiders, her relationship with her own family was more intense than ever.

Alfred seemed as devoted to his mother as Gaston. He accompanied her to the city and slept on the floor of Azélie's living room; Micael used the same small room she had occupied eighteen years before.[58] He traveled with her to visit relatives in Mobile, and eagerly entertained a steady transit of cousins who took the boat trip to the coast; visiting, it seems, was the recreation of anyone who could afford to leave home, especially visiting on the Gulf Coast, which was almost as much of a resort area then as it is now. In one of his gracious letters to Azélie, Alfred apologized for missing her the previous day, but he entreated her to join some other cousins who were "risking a bad dinner" by visiting him in the country. "Come as an act of charity, for if I go too long without seeing you, not even Yellow Fever will keep me from coming to find you."[59]

Alfred and Gaston spent some of their time in Pascagoula attending to the sick people in their midst. In that era of stark, sudden malady, when no one thought much about going to a hospital, whoever was well nursed whomever was ill. Men tended women, when necessary; employers cared for their clerks; masters served their slaves. If the automobile has been the leveler of the twentieth century, making all classes and races compeers on the highway, the equalizer of the nineteenth century was the sickbed, for everyone was ailing and dependent sooner or later. The nurse suffered along with his invalid, if he followed a physician's directions, since most treatments were aimed at inducing diarrhea and vomiting in bedridden patients and subjecting them to pain.

The common sickroom practices are appalling to us now, as ours will be to another generation. Richard Beebe, a wealthy New Orleans merchant, had been afflicted with a "fever" for five days before the doctor allowed him to eat a bit of gruel. "He begins to acquire a strong appetite and a desire to sit up, which are both good symptoms," his nephew wrote, "but of course, neither can be gratified as yet."[60] As Beebe fell ill in August, he suffered very much from prickly heat and fatigue from lying so long. "The skin on the sharp corners of his bones is worn off and the flesh sore and that makes him uneasy," the nephew observed. "He has not yet been permitted to change his clothes."

Gaston and Alfred took turns at the bedside of a Monsieur Hepp, their friend and agent who fell ill in Pascagoula just at the time Micael was called to New Orleans on business. "I had to get up five or six times to get him a drink," Gaston reported, "but the rest of us were just as bad, as we've never had such a hot night." As soon as the doctor visited him, Hepp began vomiting and continued throughout the next night, perhaps as a result of the healer's medicaments. The doctor's remedy for this new development was blistering. Micael herself had submitted to blistering, along with the other standard treatments, bleeding, purging, and leeches, to relieve her seizures. Monsieur Hepp was tortured by the blister. Gaston closed his letter by noting that "Jules, his Negro, came to ask me for the linseed oil."[61]

Although four-fifths of all newcomers died of yellow fever during their first summer in New Orleans, neither Alfred nor Gaston contracted it, thanks to their mother's prudence in keeping them away from the city. Micael's dread of the disease was appropriate. She managed to elude both of the worst epidemics in New Orleans history, in 1832 and 1853, by leaving Louisiana a year or so prior to their outbreak. But even when there was no epidemic, black vomit was pervasive enough in the hot months in New Orleans to scare anyone susceptible to it. "My mother is feeling well," Gaston wrote to Azélie in September, 1850, "but always sick with fear. If you say the word 'fever' around her, it almost suffices to land her in bed. . . . We're anxious to know whether Madame Bahier is better. . . ."

Once yellow fever struck, doctors were helpless against it, despite their energetic treatments. The old calomel was still being prescribed, together with castor oil and quinine, and administered "until salivation."[62] Calomel given in such toxic doses was a violent laxative; it caused the breath to become fetid, the gums and tongue to be ulcerated, and the teeth to fall out. A regimen similar to the yellow fever treatment—bleeding, evacuating the intestines, administering calomel in lethal doses, and if the patient lived long enough, blistering the chest—was also the up-to-date relief for pneumonia in the 1850s.[63] Thus Micael had every reason to be terrified of the local fevers and the local doctors, too.

Staying in Pascagoula was hard on Alfred and Gaston. Despite the diversions of caring for the sick and writing to their spinster cousin, they began to long for some activity. In 1849 Alfred even made plans to return to Europe. He wrote a lovely farewell to Azélie, got as far as Mobile, and changed his mind.[64] Gaston, writing to Eugène Rochereau in his most crabbed, conspiratorial hand, asked his cousin to send him ten-foot oars but not to tell his mother, who for some reason disapproved of his exercising on the water.[65] As obliquitous as his mother was direct, he planned to go out rowing after she went to bed or before she got up at sunrise, though the mosquitoes on the water were sure to be wide awake. He did not explain to Rochereau how he would receive a package of oars without arousing her suspicions.

By October, 1850, cool weather had blown yellow fever out of the city, and Stewart thought he had one side of the Pontalbas ready for occupancy. Micael at once sent for confirmation from Azélie that the summer fevers had abated.[66] She was impatient to get back to New Orleans, possibly because her only bathing facility at Pascagoula was the Gulf of Mexico near her house, and the water, according to Gaston, was the first thing in the area to cool off. She and her sons moved back to the city for the last time. They settled into the new Pontalba Building, in a house now divided into several addresses. The other houses began renting; Micael charged $95 and $150 monthly for most of them, and $325 for corner locations, which newspaper editorials described as moderate rents for the most modern and luxurious residences in the city.[67] The French Market down the street still stank, of course; but then, so did many streets in town.[68]

In January, 1851, Micael had a light stroke of luck in her fairly unlucky life. Jenny Lind, touring America under the sponsorship of P. T. Barnum, came to New Orleans for thirty performances at the St. Charles Theater. During her month-long stay in the city, she resided in the Upper Pontalba (in what was even then being called an apartment), providing public exposure for the new buildings. Jenny Lind's welcome in New Orleans was typical of her reception all over the United States.[69] According to one report, her advance manager, LeGrand Smith, arranged a lighthearted competition among the *cuisinières* of the city to determine which one would be hired as her regular cook. A committee of tasters was appointed, one of whom later wrote, "We first interviewed the great Madame Pontalba in person. . . . Her desire was that New Orleans should be seen as a mirage of Paris reflected from the intervening ocean."[70] A competitive cooking examination was held, which the chef Boudro won. He received a crown of parsley with a gold medal and a title, in French, "because all the cooking was to be done in that language." He also received a contract to cook for Jenny Lind.

On the day of the singer's scheduled arrival, a crowd of about two thousand waited the entire day at the river to meet her boat.[71] The crowd was so pressing and ardent that Barnum despaired of getting Jenny Lind's carriage the few hundred feet to the Pontalba Buildings. Barnum first sent out Jenny Lind's chambermaid, heavily veiled, in a carriage that drew off a number of followers. A second false Jenny was sent forth—this time Mrs. Barnum was martyred—and a little more of the dense gathering was scattered. "Nearly every person on the wharf was by this time pulled into the narrow street [St. Peter] in front of the house to be occupied by Miss Lind," wrote one observer.[72] "She was repeatedly called for, as was Mr. Barnum." This was the pattern of Jenny Lind's arrivals: a scene at the dock, followed by a throng at her residence, begging for a glimpse of the singer.

"An immense cheer went up when old Madame Pontalba good-naturedly presented herself on the balcony when Jenny Lind was called out, and [she] smiled and bowed her thanks to the laughing multitude."[73] While "old Madame Pontalba" was entertaining the crowd—at fifty-five she was decidedly older than the twenty-nine-year-old goddess they were looking for—a small, dirty-looking hack inconspicuously inched toward the middle of the block, and Jenny Lind slipped from the carriage through the door inscribed with her name in silver plate. Micael went to meet her and escort her upstairs to her rooms. The crowd, according to a reporter, "bore the appearance of being all engaged in carrying out an excellent joke. The greatest good humor prevailed. . . . Each man was astonished to see his neighbor there, and one half the crowd appeared to wonder what the other half came to see and do."[74]

Although the Pontalba houses were generally rented unfurnished, Jenny Lind's residence had been provided with every convenience, including a piano.[75] As she did in most of the grand apartments prepared for her, from New York to New Orleans, the singer exclaimed over the elegance of the accommodations and walked through all of her twelve rooms. Then she stepped out on the second-floor balcony with Micael, shook her handkerchief at the crowd for a brief moment, and withdrew, ending her last unremunerated public appearance until she left the following month.[76] The parades and holiday atmosphere around the square continued for some hours. The local fire companies braved the crowd and circled the block three times with all their carriages while a shop on Magazine Street burned to the ground.[77]

It is not surprising that New Orleans adored Jenny Lind. Although America in general was starved for music in 1850—New York had the only resident symphony orchestra in the country—New Orleans people were experienced opera lovers. The city was a national center for opera, just as New York is today, where the most famous singers and productions were offered every season. The Americans in the Second Municipality went often to the St. Charles Theater; the Creoles went on foot to the smaller Orleans Theater on Royal Street, which seated 1,344.[78] But everybody went. The Creoles loved any opera, so long as it was French, whereas the Americans welcomed exposure to Italian and German composers. Society people attended the opera on Tuesday or Saturday; humbler ears and slaves appeared on Sunday.[79] Pickpockets went every night. Like television today, opera was the one recreation shared by all races and classes, from the wealthiest to the poorest of the city. Both blacks and whites, for more than half the people in New Orleans were black, filled the city's opera houses a remarkable three nights a week for a five-month season—this from a population of about 116,000. The directors of today's New Orleans opera company, drawing their audience from a population nine times greater, would weep with joy to see so many bodies in their velvet seats. Since going to the opera was an everyday outing, no one bothered to put on his newest clothes or best manners; brawls sometimes broke out, just as they do nowadays at sports events.

Jenny Lind's thirty performances were sold out; many of the most expensive tickets were distributed as complimentary gifts to special guests.[80] First gallery tickets cost eighteen dollars; front row seats, twelve dollars; and single upper balcony tickets, one dollar fifty cents. Free people of color got in for one dollar, and slaves for fifty cents.[81] The theater expected to take in $75,000 a week during Jenny Lind's stay. "There may be a great deal of humbug about this," the *Daily Crescent* observed on February 21, 1851, regarding the Jenny craze, "but it is very evident that the people have a great taste for it." The singer's front-page publicity took precedence over the paper's political headline for the day, "The Imbecility of our Diplomacy," which warned readers of Daniel Webster's activities in Central America. The reviews were as breathless as the advance gushings. "Not to have heard Jenny Lind is to have heard nothing," pronounced the *Daily Picayune* to readers who had, in fact, heard everything.[82] Even the sophisticated New Orleans audiences melted at the rendition of "Home, Sweet Home" which the singer included on her program.

Jenny Lind must have become quite friendly with her next-door neighbors, the Pontalbas. Gaston sketched her—one of his deft, expressive portraits probably done around the same time that he drew his own amiable likeness. His drawing found its way to the *Daily Delta*; it covered half the front page.[83] Gaston and Jenny Lind were about the same age, and perhaps they both enjoyed some time together away from their managers. When she left the city in February, 1851, Jenny Lind stated publicly that the two persons whom she would always remember "with the warmest gratitude and the most pleasant associations" were Madame de Pontalba and Boudro, the cook.[84]

Long after the Swedish idol had left New Orleans, people were still making money from her visit, auctioning off things she might have used or touched, or breathed upon, or looked at, and giving their shops and merchandise her name. Mrs. Rink, who together with her husband, a portrait painter, had been one of the earliest tenants in Pontalba Row, was lucky enough to have her notions shop situated one or two doors down from Jenny Lind's residence. The very day the singer debarked for the next city on her tour, Mrs. Rink began pointing out in her advertisements that "one of the most admired of Jenny Lind's toilettes has been purchased at Mrs. Rink's."[85] Micael's agents sold the furniture from Jenny Lind's apartment within a few days after the singer left, and Micael herself, who was never sentimental about her famous friends, went aboard a boat docked at the river to auction off the personal items. All of the furniture brought $3,061. The singer's chamber pot sold for three dollars, fifty cents; her alleged thimble for fifty cents.[86]

Following the publicity that Jenny Lind generated for the Pontalbas, Micael began systematically advertising the buildings. Leases for stores were available for three and a half years; for the houses, eight months. Since many people moved out of the city during the fever season, year-long leases were not practical.[87] As the 1851 yellow fever season approached, most of the houses were leased. Micael's business in New Orleans was more or less complete, while in Paris she had projects waiting for her. Moreover, she seemed at last to realize that Louisiana, with its heat and epidemics, was a good place to call home, but she did not want to live there.

The buildings that she left behind decayed along with the Vieux Carré and seemed prematurely time-worn within fifteen years. No one could have foreseen their fading. In 1836, when Micael planned the Pontalbas, her houses on the Place d'Armes were shabby little rentals occupying prime land. She made the best financial decision possible in replacing them with chic residences that would have been enormously profitable had it not been for the disaster of the Civil War. New Orleans was economically ravaged by the war and its aftermath. By the late 1860s the Pontalba buildings were half-empty. They gradually refilled with ever-poorer tenants—immigrant families who in the 1880s and 1890s hung their laundry from the iron lace balconies and raised chickens in the courtyards. Jackson Square became their parlor and concert hall, warm with the life of river and market but squalid with poverty. By 1915 the corner of the Lower Pontalba had become a shelter for the homeless. Men could sleep for whatever donation they could afford, while in the rest of the buildings, animals roamed in and out for free.[88]

But even in their humblest years, the Pontalbas stood out with their imperishable grace from the ponderous architecture of the nineteenth century. Their pervasive triangles are the syllables of a composition that echoes through the square. Our view is pricked first by the triangular cathedral tower that outreaches the Pontalbas by just one story; then the image widens to the trinity of church, Cabildo, and Presbytere. Finally, our eyes sweep over the vivid spatter of triangles, the flying peaks that form the Pontalbas' rooflines on both sides of the square.

Seen from the levee walk or the shade of Jackson Square, the front walls of the Pontalbas look straight and sharp, without any recesses or variations in the façade. But if we look again, we see that the center pediment, or triangle, and the two pavilions on either end are each projected forward just one subtle foot. The magic of those jutting pediments leads the eye down a dilating channel from one end of the building to the other. The three pediments reach out to us without our being aware of them, and provide a satisfying sense of beginning, middle, and end. A pediment, then a recessed wing, then a pediment, and so on, covering an enormous space, give the Pontalbas the dynamism of skyscrapers, twin skyscrapers, set on their sides and dressed in iron lace.

Everything in the design is calculated to hold our interest. Just as the gentle projections in the surface of the houses give the pediments a volumetric independence from the rest of the building, the porches, too, are varied to avoid predictability. One is covered, in accordance with Creole convention, and one is open, an inflection devised by their meticulous owner. Without their iron lace, the massive Pontalbas might have blocked in Jackson

Square with gabled fortresses. But the ironwork, set against the vivid red brick of the original façades, made the structures light and pretty, gay rather than oppressive. Because of their iron webs, the façades are as open and as private as the faces of people protecting an interior life. The exquisite rhythm of the buildings, the predictable repetition of certain forms may be what has kept them exempt from architectural fashion. They delighted the generation which first saw them in 1850, when tastes favored opulence and density, and they charmed the twentieth century, despite its preoccupation with the functional and abstract.

Inside, the Pontalba houses were much like raised Creole cottages. Each front door was for a ground-floor shop. To get to the residences, one entered through a passageway at the back of the house where the stairs were located. These led over the shop to a second-story parlor and dining room. The third floor was reserved for bedrooms. The rear of each house was given over to the stairway and to a working courtyard with kitchen and laundries.

The Pontalbas contained all the modern novelties of the day—gas lighting, interior water closets, Micael's versatile, easy shutters. The buildings were monuments to manufacturing, to the new notion that things could be ordered from one place and assembled in another. With their matching iron galleries and repeating details, they reflected the fashionable preference for exact duplication, a vogue made possible by manufacturing. Andrés Almonester, who had to train his own slaves to be the architects and bricklayers of the first buildings on the site, would have liked everything about his daughter's houses—except their name.

Micael never saw them again after 1851, and expressed no regrets about leaving them to go back to France. She started out on a return journey that promised to be "the nicest trip in the world," making friends with American ladies on the steamboat *Belle Key*, which took her and her sons from New Orleans to Louisville.[89] There was no ice on the vessel; passengers drank the Mississippi, hauling it up in buckets on the tourist side of the boat while the steward was emptying refuse on the pantry side. Gaston found the boat so comfortable, he averred that it was more like being in an excellent hotel for seven days than being on the Mississippi. From Louisville they made their way to New York. Micael wanted to show Niagara Falls to her sons before leaving the country. Then they boarded a steamer for the Atlantic crossing.

As the monotony of the sea set in, grief descended on Micael. She was heartsick over leaving Azélie; perhaps she had a premonition that she would never again talk with her cousin. Micael had once complained that Europeans did not understand intimacy. In many letters she expressed her frustration at not being able to talk to Azélie face to face, so that she could confide secrets too private for the mails. Azélie with her church-going and provinciality was the very opposite of her businesslike and worldly cousin. But Micael, who saw her for only a few months in a space of forty years, loved her with all her heart. Even after Micael was halfway home, several weeks after their actual leave-taking, Gaston wrote that she still wept piteously for Azélie. The vocabulary of unhappiness did not make much use of "depression" in those days; Micael, according to her son, shed tears "too natural to yield to any consolation."[90]

Gaston, at least, was having fun on the trip home. Once out of New York harbor, he made a rocky sketch of passengers in their staterooms, retching miserably into bedside containers.[91] "You remember, I'm sure, how my mother hates steamers," he wrote to Azélie. "She dreads them so much that as soon as she boarded, she went to bed not intending to get up until it was time to get off. The sea was very bad for the first two days, and nearly everybody was sick—except my mother, who was only afraid of getting sick. As soon as she got up she was really surprised that the boat moved so little and that she had not been ill for an instant."[92] Since she had no problems with seasickness, Gaston continued, she would not hesitate to sail again if her business in New Orleans required it or if she were overcome with longing for her family. Gaston, who was ready to please and to be pleased, thought the steamship was "truly a floating palace" where they were treated to feasts. An American friend who had left New Orleans with them was down with a relapse of "the fever." But the trip had been like a tonic to his mother who, despite her sadness at parting, was plump and rested. Even as Micael was separating from her cousins, she and her sons were planning another building project which they had apparently discussed in detail with Azélie. Gaston assured Azélie that despite the project in France, she would see his mother again rather soon.

Perhaps Micael did intend to revisit New Orleans after the completion of another project in Paris, but the next two years changed whatever plans she had made. There were to be no more buildings in Paris after the Hôtel Pontalba and no more trips to Louisiana. In 1852 Azélie died at the home of her sister Malvina. At seventy-one she was not young, but her death shocked Micael and pierced her with grief too deep for tears. Then in 1853 New Orleans suffered the worst epidemic of the century. One person out of twelve died, so many that there were no means to bury them. Mule carts passed through the Old Quarter like so many garbage wagons, calling to the residents to put out their dead. Once at the cemeteries, the bodies swelled and burst their coffins because even the gravediggers had died or abandoned the city. No one with common sense visited New Orleans for a pleasure trip in 1853, surely not Micael, if there was to be no Azélie waiting for her.

She never returned to the United States, in fact. There were business affairs to take care of in Paris, more than in New Orleans, and grandchildren in Europe to replace the cousins she had left in America, though no one replaced Azélie. The moment she returned to France, she was greeted by those who wanted and needed her. Among them, of all people, was her husband Célestin.

XI

The War Is Over

WHATEVER Célestin's grievances against his wife during their forty years together and apart, he had known all along that he could trust her, that underneath their recriminations, he had nothing to fear from her. He had squandered thousands of francs trying to convince the world that Micael was a spendthrift and a tramp who deserved his father's violence. And yet, when she returned from America, it was as if none of it had ever happened. Célestin let everyone see that his accusations had been lies, all lies. For it was his wife he turned to when he was sick and desolate; it was Micael he wanted. As soon as she landed in March, 1851, he was waiting for her, a lost soul unable to cope with his son and desperate for her help in saving what remained of his property. He took steps no court had ever been able to coerce from him. He left Mont-l'Évêque, moved permanently to Paris, and offered himself to her—with his problems. Micael, who had had to fight with her life for the right to manage her own money, was soon managing all of his. She had left her children rather than live with him; but now she sat with him every day in a house she chose for him in Paris, saw to his meals, and hired his servants. Where once their marriage had been no more than a legal connection, now their separation became a formality.

"I'm taking advantage of a free moment to come chat with you, my dear Azélie," Micael wrote a month after her return, in a letter that has been partly destroyed.

> You can't imagine all the things I've had to take care of since I got back. You have found out from Gaston how much good it did me to be back in the climate of France, but also how much I miss you. You know my heart, and I know you understand me when I tell you that I have no friends here who can make me forget my Azélie, whom I would rather have near me than anyone else.
>
> You have probably learned that my husband left Mont-l'Évêque where he was living with my son, and then sent for me, both to straighten out his affairs and to help him support Célestin, who had driven him to the end of his rope.
>
> This poor man is so disheartened, we have had quite a time distracting him. I leave Alfred or Gaston with him at all times. Célestin sees neither his father

nor me; he is afraid of my reproaches. Unfortunately, he will soon need me to come to his aid. He has already spent part of his inheritance since I left France, and before long he would have fin— of my husband if I had not come to his rescue.[1]

She did not seem surprised at the turn in her relationship with Célestin, but the reconciliation flooded her with emotions: "Why am I not in your little room, dear friend, where I could have the satisfaction of really talking with you. The things I would tell you which are impossible to say by mail! My heart is full as I write to you; you don't know how much I love you."

Micael was never able to give Azélie her private account of what happened during her first meeting with her husband. We can only guess now at the resentment and hunger of their coming back together, for 150 years is a long distance from which to read the fine script of a marriage. But given Célestin's tendency to avoid confronting any issue head on, and considering his awe-inspiring capacity for self-righteousness, there may have been nothing dramatic to report about the reunion. It is doubtful whether he asked his wife's forgiveness during those first awkward hours, or ever. Only fifteen years had passed since he had handed out his lurid account of her marital crimes—the rose brochure—while she was hobbling about with an oozing chest and a freshly mangled hand. He had believed then that Micael had cruelly wronged him, and time may not have weakened his conviction that he was the one to whom apologies were owed. Moreover, it was still her money he was after, in a way. Had she been penniless, he might not have reached out to her for help. Even if Célestin regretted everything and wanted to redeem his marriage, the evidence of his life suggests that he had no knack for remorse, for holding the poor, limp fingers or tracing the sash of scars across her breast as the two of them contemplated the wasted years. Célestin was ill and pathetic by the time he called Micael back, and so depressed that she was afraid to leave him alone. Self-pity, not conciliation, was what occupied him.

How can we break out of our psychological conventions to comprehend their fatigued, half-married, indestructible tendency toward each other? To us, all love worth talking about is young love or an imitation of it, a monomorphic obsession. Their attachment was something quite else, both more calm and more disturbed, and in their time, probably more commonplace. It was as secure as a filial tie because, despite absence or rejection, they both knew that no other marriage was possible. Being chained to each other freed them to acknowledge broader emotions they would not have permitted themselves if they could have renounced each other and started a new life with someone compatible. "I *know* my husband loves me," Micael wrote more than once; and it seems he did. What besides love could have made him behave with such blind spite in the months after the shooting toward a woman who only wanted to be left alone? And Micael must have loved him, too, during those fierce years, even at times in some romantic and erotic way. Why else would she have driven eight hours to the dark château in 1834, where she was sure to encounter her foaming father-in-law, all to talk alone with Célestin?

There was a palpable, quixotic element in their relationship, a sense of something withheld on both sides, which is perhaps why they never got tired of each other. Célestin did not own Micael completely except during their first years together. By the time her mother died, fourteen years into the marriage, he had long been manipulating her, and she had long been aware and wary of it. During their mature years, it seems certain, he never received her open, defenseless, committed love. Nor did she possess him in the decades when he was worth having. Célestin was anxious and ambivalent even when they were young, before he found out that she had traveled with Guillemin. His affection was rationed by his father until the shooting; and after it, his love was mixed with guilt and frustration over not being able to control her. He was a difficult, intense man, too elusive to provide the security that love craves. And yet, in 1851, when Micael was fifty-five and Célestin was sixty, she crossed an ocean and arrived at a new phase of their marriage. The resistant knots of forty years yielded. If it was not precisely love that made her take him back into her life, it was a sense of duty and connection at least as compelling. They continued to live in separate houses—Micael kept the protective integument of legal separation—but they were never far apart again until death parted them.

There was cruel irony in the reconciliation; whatever attraction they still felt toward each other was futile within a matter of months, for although Célestin regained his physical health under Micael's care, he steadily lost his mind. Micael and Gaston began writing of it as early as 1852. By the 1860s Célestin was completely incompetent. Micael or a *mandatoire*—a representative—signed all of his papers. When Célestin himself put pen to paper, the effort of writing his name produced laborious, eloquent evidence of his helplessness. At first his "illness" was attributed to the strain of trying to outwit his grasping son while the younger Célestin lived with him at

Mont-l'Évêque. A year after Micael began caring for her husband, Gaston gave Azélie one of his fastidious reports of Micael's activities. Gingerly, eventually, he discussed his father:

April 21, 1852

It was a year last week my dear cousin since we left New Orleans and were separated from our family and from all the affection which was showered on my mother and on us. The climate there was pernicious to her health, but in order to leave, she had to pull against the longing in her heart. In wrenching herself away she not only parted from the treasury of her childhood joys and memories, but also from the genuine and precious devotion which all our relatives demonstrated, especially you, my dear cousin. . . .

Since our return to France, my mother has been completely preoccupied with business details, those she was dealing with in New Orleans and the ones created by an absence of more than three years. There have been other, sadder, concerns which have had their part in absorbing all her time. My father's health and affairs being in complete disorder, she had no qualms about taking charge of both, and her efforts have been rewarded with abundant success, praise God. My father, forced to move to Paris by his troubles, is getting well little by little. My mother sees him nearly every day, just as Alfred and I do, and we stay constantly busy coming up with new subjects to distract him, striving to make him forget the torments he endured during our absence. But, my dear cousin, we are getting into details on which I don't wish to dwell a moment longer so as not to lose the reticence which delicacy requires. The one thing I want you to know is that my mother has had great anguish, many worries which often kept her from having either time or heart to take up her pen when she might have wanted to write to the people whom she loves most. All the problems to which I refer, and perhaps even the change in climate, left her in constant pain this winter, but now she is doing better.[2]

Micael added a postscript:

April 30

I am sure you are convinced that I've even forgotten your name, my dear Azélie. Since my return I've been crushed by burdens here of all sorts. I asked M. Rochereau to see you and explain what my life has been like here. I was suffering terribly all winter and had to stay in bed. Exhaustion almost kept me from taking care of my husband who is losing more of his mind by the minute. He has given me so much trouble. He is doing well now, thank God, and I am busy renting him a charming house near me on the Champs Élysées where he'll be fine. I have hired a sitter for him, a woman who used to be a friend of his and who does not leave him for a moment. This way my children and I have more freedom. I have taken charge of his affairs and business interests.[3]

What exactly were these torments? What was driving Célestin to despair? When Micael sailed to America with Alfred and Gaston, Célestin, the eldest son, stayed behind with his wife and three children, as if to get revenge for the tortured adolescence his father had put him through. Célestin's friends were racehorse owners like himself, and all free spenders. He bet and lost lavishly and was constantly falling into debt. His wife Blanche liked clothes, gossip, church, and her children. She did not presume to interfere with Célestin's mismanagement of their finances. By the 1840s Micael had begun refusing money to her son; he then went to live with his father, who paid off some of his gambling debts by selling off pieces of Mont-l'Évêque and other property.

In 1845 the younger Célestin (who at thirty was no longer forgivably young) was facing some serious obligations. He needed money, and the obvious source was to sell more and more of his inheritance—Migneaux and Mont-l'Évêque—or to use them as collateral for loans. While his mother was out of the way in New Orleans, he collected a ponderable 251,680 francs by parceling off Migneaux.[4] He had his magnetic fingers in his father's Paris property as well, appropriating the profitable building at 350 rue St.-Honoré for himself, to the exclusion of his brothers, and renouncing his interest in two less valuable rentals.[5] Alfred and Gaston, who were still in America, of course knew nothing of this rearrangement of their inheritance. By the time Micael returned, her husband had seen part of Mont-l'Évêque slip away from him. Much of the land of Migneaux was in the hands of seventeen separate purchasers. He no longer received income from 350 rue St.-Honoré, nor indeed from any of his houses, since his son had appropriated the right to collect all of his father's rents and dispose of his property. Some of the New Orleans stores were gone. And despite all that, his namesake remained in an abyss of debt. That was when Célestin wrote to Micael asking her to come to him and take charge of her son.

First, Micael settled her husband in a house with a garden about two blocks from her, near enough that she could trot over every day even with her unreliable lung. Alfred and Gaston helped out with their father. For if Micael was never completely appreciated by her husband, she was adored by Alfred, Gaston, and, intermittently, Célestin. She shared her life with her two younger sons. Her home was their home, her friends also theirs, and her travels their travels. But remarkably, even during the anguished years when they were growing up, she never made them accessories to her bitterness toward their father. Gaston's letters reveal emotional distance between him-

self and his father, but no rancor or even indifference. Both he and Alfred
gave up their time each day apparently without question to care for him.
From the tone of Gaston's letters, they were never even tempted to remind
the disordered old man that when they were young and dependent and he
was the regulator of visits, he had allowed them to see their mother all of
twice a month. But they were not so forgiving toward their brother and, in
fact, remained angry with him for the rest of their lives.

Micael was more sanguine about her prodigal son, or perhaps just more
resigned. She took the news about his manipulations as if it were not news
at all, and began finagling at once to free all the property. In September,
1851, she drew up documents to supercede those which her son Célestin had
concocted during her absence. In one of these, Célestin *père* gave all three of
his properties in Paris to Alfred and Gaston, who immediately turned over
the management of the houses to Micael. Célestin *fils* remained in possession of Mont-l'Évêque; he lived there with his family and collected its
revenues. Micael next had her husband sell another part of Migneaux to
liquidate more of their son's debts. Then on Christmas Day, 1851, she mortgaged the Hôtel Pontalba to pay off the rest of Célestin's obligations. It
would take her fourteen long years to become free of that mortgage; it took
the younger Célestin only a few months to wade back into debt.[6] Micael
next sold her mother's rental at 343 St.-Honoré, that indefatigable little
money machine. "My mother just sold one of her hôtels in Paris," Gaston
wrote in his long missive to Azélie, "to pay her debts . . . and spare herself
anxiety and responsibilities so that she can get some rest which she badly
needs and has surely earned." But though she was sharply depleting her
capital, the expenses continued to rise. So did her responsibilities because,
fundamentally, Micael enjoyed overwork and never missed an opportunity
to burden herself.

Micael's ambition was the normal parental impulse to protect young
Célestin from his own folly and to leave Alfred and Gaston a decent fortune
despite their brother's machinations. A normal parent would have let her
two reliable sons manage the tide of paper that washed over her desk each
day, since both were capable of handling bigger tasks than catching up on
letters to relatives: Alfred was thirty-five in 1852, and Gaston thirty-two. Yet
the minutiae of her business remained for the most part in her own restless
hands. Minor lawsuits, such as one over hunting rights on her husband's
land, dragged on for years, pullulating paper, going through appeals, until

long after Célestin himself had given up hunting anything more fugitive than his eyeglasses.[7] Often it was Micael who prolonged litigation.

There may have been recondite satisfactions for Micael in caring for her husband. They were to be together, more or less, another twenty-three years, the same span of time they had been more or less together when the shooting occurred. But though she was never a widow, she must have known a widow's emptiness more often than satisfaction during these years, going to bed night after night without the snug comfort of a husband's back folded against her, its ridges and cushions more familiar than the bed quilt, waking at dawn with no proprietary leg sleeping across her own. For decades she woke up alone, but to the burdens and compromises of marriage. In an obituary for Micael in 1874, *L'Abeille* described Célestin as having been *"infirme et idiot"* during his later years, a diagnosis the paper would not have dared to repeat unless the information was provided by the family. Judging from letters and documentary scraps of information, Célestin was not present at weddings and those events he surely would have attended if he had been dependably lucid.

There is, however, a striking painting of him made in the late 1850s or 1860s, so lifelike that it might almost be a photograph. In it, he is splendidly bearded, benign, and presentable, a portrait of a lovely old gentleman.[8] It is a curious document, considering that both painting and photography in those days required the subject to remain sane or at least calm for several minutes. Perhaps Célestin was often more normal than not; or perhaps his pleasant appearance was due to his being well adjusted rather than rational. It does not seem likely that there was a marriage of true minds between him and Micael even intermittently after about 1858. But there were, one hopes, moments when they looked at each other clear-eyed and felt the surprising stab of affection that scatters even cogent and long-embedded enmity, moments when they recognized each other as comrades—the only remaining veterans of a war that both sides lost.

Much more than Célestin, Micael's relatives in New Orleans seemed important to her as she subsided into old age. Her home was Paris. She did not want to live in a tropical American place with infected ditches, even if she was born there. But nearly all the people she loved other than her children and grandchildren were in Louisiana. Her suffering in parting from Azélie and her warm nest of Creole cousins was as devastating as grief. Indeed, she almost mixed up the dead with the living when she tried to name everyone whose absence pained her. "This letter is for you and my kind Malvina," she wrote to Azélie on August 16, 1851.

> Thank you, dear Malvina, for writing to me. Your letter made me happy. You can't doubt my deep affection. . . . Do remember me to Odile, please, and to my good Zia. She touched my heart when she cried over my leaving. I will never forget that sign from her of her fondness, which I feel just as much for her. Will you hug Eulalie Villeré for me, my old cousin and good friend? My little Eugène wrote an adorable letter to Gaston; it made me cry. He reminds us of our stay in Madison [Madisonville] and the pleasure it gave me to be around this dear little one who was so affectionate. I am really attached to him and would like to know he's in good health. Don't forget to remember me to Nisida. She showed me so much kindness that I could never stop loving her. You know my old bond with your mother. That will only die when I do. Give Cora my love. I would like to know that she's happy. She knows how much I care about her.
>
> Goodbye, my good friends. Remember you have all the love of a cousin who will never forget you.
>
> Micael

In a postscript, Micael remembered the maid: "Tell Letís I always think of her and Baby."

Gaston was particularly close to Eugène Rochereau, notwithstanding his mother's crisp letter to the agent regarding the "Countess of Canal." "Speak to our wonderful friend Eugène," Gaston wrote to Azélie, referring to the cousin whom Micael always addressed as "Monsieur Rochereau."[9] "Tell him again that we love him. . . . And you, my dear cousin," Gaston continued in his grandfatherly fashion,

> you will not tell us yourself how your health is, and when you do, you report how things are going in the family and what has transpired since we last had news. You know how my mother loves you and you won't deprive us of the pleasure you can give us by a few strokes of the pen. . . . Permit me, my dear cousin, to embrace you not only as I did the day we arrived three years ago, but like a relative whom you know, enjoy and love. Alfred joins me in sending his love.

Micael encouraged Louisiana friends to visit her when they came to Paris. "Odile Marigny came to see me. I received her in my best fashion and invited her to dinner." Remarking on one Aristide Berger, she noted that he had made some friends among the people he met at her house, both men and women. "It is surprising to see the shyness of the Creoles when they get to this big city. When we are alone he [Berger] is always so uncomfortable, but I cannot go on with this because I'm afraid my letter will be misinterpreted, even though I have only good intentions toward him for he is an excellent fellow. . . ."[10] Despite an army of Parisian companions, Micael kept her Creole friends, speech, and habits like trinkets of a long-vanished home. She changed gradually, as people do. By 1852, the date of her last letter to Azélie, she could compose a grammatical paragraph. Her pen still raced madly across the page, and in the characteristic style of penny-pinchers, spared no margins.

Azélie's death in 1853 was an amputation that nothing—neither grandchildren nor friends nor business involvements—could replace. But she had a few exasperations to distract her. The same year, Alfred got married. He was thirty-six, with all the dents of a man whose adult life had been spent with a domineering mother. His wife, Cécile Marie de Parseval, was fourteen, but her name at least was old. Presumably theirs had not been a protracted courtship; but it was a real marriage, so far as we can perceive from documents that are garrulous only in money matters. Cécile was from Senlis. It is doubtful whether Alfred married her for her wealth; according to their marriage contract, he gave his wife forty thousand francs which was to be used for the purchase of 135 shares in the railroad company, Chemin de Fer d'Orléans.[11] To this investment the bride gave her fourteen-year-old consent. She brought a dowry consisting of lace and other railroad stock, both of which might have been valuable or worthless in the France of the Second Empire, it is difficult to know. In sealing the betrothal, Alfred's writing, which was usually as deliberate as cuneiform, danced floridly over the document, the signature of a man in love. The little bride produced a grown-up autograph, quite self-possessed and sure. Alfred had to get his parents' permission to marry. At first the couple lived with her father in Senlis; they had a son, Michel. In 1861 they moved in with the elder Célestin. But no sooner had the bride grown up than she died, in 1862, at the age of twenty-three. Her father became the child's guardian.

The unlucky widower tried again the following year. He was by this time forty-five and still young at heart; his new bride was twenty-three like his former wife, and young all over. Louise de Loynes d'Estrées was expected to inherit land when her parents died. Meanwhile, they gave her a *dot* of ten thousand francs and an annual allowance of fifteen hundred.[12] Alfred was again required by law to get his parents' written permission before marrying, which meant assembling the notary, witnesses, and both parents on one of his father's good days. How tense those signing sessions must have been, as Célestin's pen tremulously vanquished his title and initials, only to fall down the strained staircase of his last name! It should not surprise us that in the 1860s, the signature of the elder, crazier Célestin began to look as if it were forged by Micael—only their notaries knew for sure.

As for the younger, craftier Célestin, Micael's headaches with him were far from over. He continued to be a problem child deep into middle age. Célestin was the only one of the three sons who attempted to lead an independent life or to find an income apart from his mother's bursary. His efforts were foredoomed by his own profligacy—he seemed never to be free of debt—but also by the constrictions of aristocracy, by the way wealth circulated in society and flowed down in families. We must remember that dependence on parents, not independence, was valued in young men; Alfred and Gaston had always been models of dependence.

In his youth, Célestin had been among the well-to-do young men striking poses in the cafés, conspicuously wasting their parents' money. He ran around with the duc de Morny, Hortense Bonaparte's illegitimate son, and frequented the Jockey Club, that Parisian symbol of everything aristocratic, anglophile, and meretricious. And yet, one had only to scratch the brittle surface to see the other Célestin, the semi-hysterical youth risking his inheritance rather than leave his mother; or a few years later, while still hardly more than a boy, presenting himself at newspaper offices, cash in hand, to try to shield his mother from humiliation. He was emotional, for all his suave exterior.

Like his mother and father, Célestin came to adulthood with no resources other than his inheritance. As we have seen, by 1851 he had lost his grandmother's legacy and borrowed to the hilt against that part of his inheritance which his family still controlled.[13] Since both of his parents were alive, that meant he had nothing other than the pensions they allowed him while he waited for them to die. He tried for years to find some way out of his confining nest in the family's financial tree, but he lived in a time when a man's most important asset in making his way was not a good education, as it is in our time—hardly anyone had that—but a good name, that is, a wealthy family or powerful connections. Success was not simply a matter of finding a promising job or entering a profession. High public offices paid only modest salaries, hardly enough to keep a man like Célestin in a carriage and calling cards. Then as now, people wanted government positions for the power they might convey or for the opportunities they brought: chances to buy lucrative stocks and bonds, to buy real estate, to use one's influence with other officials and earn fat commissions legally. So, while Célestin milked his parents for their grudging donations, he also sought positions wherever he could, serving on government or company boards for a small honorarium, and then finding buyers for stocks issued by the friends he made in those situations.

Célestin was not unusual in his eagerness to make a killing. Nearly everyone in France in the 1850s was enthralled with credit, speculation, and financial gambles, starting at the top of society. Napoleon III consolidated his political power in 1852 and proclaimed a Second Empire; then he began a program in which the state directed an aggressive, expanding capitalistic economy by supporting enormous private enterprises. French entrepreneurs rebuilt towns, opened mines, penetrated foreign markets, and funded an ambitious imperial foreign policy. The emperor fostered programs for the poor and laboring class, and initiatives for public parks, public safety, and public comforts. All the activity was propelled by the government's systematic policy of providing easy credit. Money was suddenly available to businessmen of every sort who could promise increased employment, services, or markets. The government issued bonds directly, especially for large construction programs; and it guaranteed security to private investors willing to put their money in certain companies, such as the Crédit Foncier, a loan fund for private building and massive urban renewal. The imperial court opened its prestigious doors to the upper bourgeoisie—industrialists, financiers, stock promoters—who were at the heart of the new projects. Access to credit was a potent encouragement both to the economy and to individuals like Célestin who could not resist a lucrative gamble. Mineral production soared, the volume of French goods multiplied, and railroads scored the countryside during the Second Empire; French harbors became centers of world shipping, sending out modern iron steamboats in place of wooden sailing vessels; the Suez Canal, largely a French enterprise, was completed; steel production boomed. Most lasting in its effects was the building surge that hit Paris like a tidal wave, washing away the winding lanes of the medieval city and leaving instead a dazzling new capital. For the first time in history, the major cities of the country were properly supplied with water, light, drainage, parks, and broad, airy streets.

Men, too, were transformed in the atmosphere of energy and mobility, where getting rich quickly was a patriotic contribution to the common weal.

Jules Mirès, an uneducated watchmaker's son who was a small-time broker in 1848, had become a multimillionaire by 1860, installed in a lordly home, his daughter a princess by marriage. Great financial power was suddenly in the hands of people like Mirès who knew everything about money, but nothing about wealth. The government's easy credit policies propelled business; but easy credit also meant that gigantic and shaky deals were given the backing of municipal finances, while the accounts for these projects were hardly glanced at. Conditions were ideal for marginal enterprises and irregular trading, for stockjobbers and financial manipulators who blithely accepted and embezzled the life savings of small investors. For if bourgeois capitalism was a new phenomenon on such a large scale, government regulation of it was an entirely novel idea. Nobody really expected diligent supervision of the moneymakers.

Mirès had only begun his extraordinary rise to power when the younger Célestin became involved with him. In 1849 Mirès, together with a partner, Polydore Millaud, began purchasing newspapers. Some of these periodicals he turned into financial papers addressed to provincial investors. Others were Bonapartist papers that he enlarged and dedicated to aggrandizing the government.[14] In 1851 the two publishers set up an investment company which was a great success, earning lively profits for subscribers and directors. The company was reorganized in 1853 as the Caisse Générale des Chemins de Fer. Under the control of Mirès and another partner, Félix Solar, it became a powerful financial institution, a rival to the Péreire family's Crédit Mobilier. Mirès organized several other companies dealing in varied securities, similar to today's junk bond funds. Like many shrewd bankers and directors of organizations in the Second Empire, he used his newspapers to promote his enterprises. People who read the exciting publicity surrounding this or that project were but dimly aware or completely unaware, when they decided to invest their savings in a new venture, that the owner of the newspaper was the agile director of the venture. The government was a solicitous partner in Mirès' railway building, sometimes selling the shares of his projects directly and always providing state credit. Railway bond interest was guaranteed by the government, which meant that while all profits were privately owned, the losses were part of the public deficit.

Célestin's involvement with Mirès dated from about 1850, when Célestin and Mirès' partner, Solar, began a short-lived political journal, and then founded a bank with a third partner. When this third man withdrew, Mirès took his place as co-director. Célestin installed himself on the bank's supervising council. The other council members, to no one's surprise, were Mirès and Solar, who apparently agreed to supervise themselves. From 1854 until 1860, according to Mirès, Célestin remained the watchpup of the bank. He never made any complaint about its management, and he never hesitated to borrow money from it.

Solar was the one acquainted with Célestin; Mirès claimed not to know much about him except "that everybody knew him, that Madame de Pontalba his mother lived in a magnificent house in the faubourg Saint-Honoré, for which, they said, she had turned down an offer of 6 millions from Count Demidoff."[15] Demidoff was the inconvenient legal husband of the emperor's cousin, Princess Mathilde. "I also knew," Mirès continued, "that she [Micael] owned other property on rue Saint-Honoré, on Place Vendôme, etc., etc., property of considerable value, that she had large property interests in the United States, and finally that M. de Pontalba owned the magnificent estate of Mont-l'Évêque, estimated to be worth around 2 million. All this seemed like such a large fortune, I failed to realize M. de Pontalba's true situation. When I finally found it out, it was too late, since he was already into the bank for a considerable sum. Being a conscientious guardian of the investors' interests, I asked for some collateral to cover his overdrafts. . . ."

The result was that by 1858, Mirès' bank, the Caisse Générale des Chemins de Fer, held a mortgage on Mont-l'Évêque for 1,075,000 francs, the amount of loans which had been granted to Célestin "thanks to his friendship with M. Solar and the reputation of his mother's wealth." Célestin also owed money to Mirès' rivals, which his mother eventually paid.[16] Still, Célestin remained fast friends with Solar, who invited him to participate in setting up an immense project, La Société Générale des Ports de Marseilles, a parent company organized by Mirès to bring gas lighting, blast furnaces, and foundries to Marseilles. Célestin was described by Mirès as one of the "administrators" of the Société, which was to be financed through bonds issued by Mirès' new credit fund and sold to the public.

According to Célestin, Solar and Mirès promised him a commission of some half-million francs out of the five million which the Société directors expected to reap. The bankers knew that Célestin had rich friends naïve enough to take his financial advice. Along with the duc de Morny, the emperor's half-brother, Célestin had kept up his friendship with Alfred Mosselman, an accessory to the youthful incident on the Champs Élysées. Mosselman had become a banker; his daughter, Countess Charles LeHon, was Morny's most long-lasting and generous mistress. She had once maintained a correspondence with Queen Hortense, the mother of both Morny and the emperor. For his own mistress, Mosselman had the taste to choose Apollonie Sabatier, the friend of Flaubert, Gauthier, Berlioz, and Baudelaire. "I had many acquaintances," Célestin wrote. "I got busy getting subscriptions. Two million shares were sold through my efforts, and from that time on, the directors considered me like a partner in their operation."[17]

Célestin was of course only a well-connected nursling in Mirès' shark tank, but he must have been somewhat useful to the entrepreneur since Mirès kept him around for several years during the project. Like any large and complicated undertaking, the municipal improvements in Marseilles ran into bureaucratic problems. The prefect was at one point so put out with Mirès that he made the extraordinary threat of holding the company to the letter of its contract with the city. Mirès' concession was about to be revoked when he dispatched Célestin, who talked with the city officials for eight days successively and won back their cooperation.[18] For the next two years Célestin continued serving as liaison between Mirès, based in Paris, and the Marseilles project. According to Célestin, he averted the unraveling of the project on other occasions. The mayor and prefect of Marseilles were incensed, for example, that the announcements for the bond sales implied that the securities were municipal bonds. Célestin mollified the officials by collaborating with them on a correction and bringing it himself to each newspaper. According to Mirès, that was Célestin's only contribution to the project. Célestin did very little, Mirès insisted, was promised nothing, and expected the moon—an outrageous payment of 500,000 francs for his piddling efforts. Eventually, Célestin moved his wife and children to Marseilles, an indication that he was sincere in believing he had some important business there.

Throughout this time Micael was steadily borrowing money on her own houses to keep Célestin's property from being attached. Mirès was paying Célestin's living expenses, but the huge commission on his stock sales, whether promised or merely hoped for, had still not been paid when the banker asked Célestin to undertake another assignment. This time Célestin moved to Rome with his family, transporting, in his words, "horses, carriages, servants—my whole household." He was charged with pushing through a railroad in the central Italian peninsula, a project expected to cost thirty-three million francs, which was opposed by various Italian authorities. Though Célestin claimed great credit for eventually getting the railroad accepted, his real contribution seems to have been that he convinced the emperor's council of ministers to allow the public sale of stock in France for foreign enterprises; thus the new railroad could be financed by French stockholders. Probably Célestin was an effective front man for Mirès' operations. He was charming, by all accounts, and if a picture of him in mid-life is to be believed, he was three or four times as handsome as an opportunist should be.[19]

Mirès' version of this assignment was that he indeed promised Célestin a generous honorarium and the nullification of the mortgage on Mont-l'Évêque if Célestin could get the Roman government's approval of the project; but he considered Célestin's mission to have been a failure. Célestin and Solar obtained approval for an entirely new railroad concession which was to be awarded to themselves and a third party, not Mirès. Since public subscriptions had already been sold for the first railroad project, that project could not legally be subsumed by another company—or so Mirès argued. Célestin was therefore owed nothing, in his view, although Mirès deigned to give him 259,000 francs for his expenses in Rome for twenty months, which was a better living than he enjoyed on his mother's allowance. To Célestin's mind, his enterprise had been a success. He had, after all, procured a concession for Mirès' partner, and the Italian government no longer objected to the whole railroad project. He had been assured that his exertions would be rewarded. Even his mother in Paris was congratulated on his work; yet he did not receive either money or mortgage cancellation. His attempts to negotiate with Mirès dragged on for several months in 1859 and 1860. At one point Célestin offered to settle for 200,000 francs; later, after the affair had heated up, for 1,700,000.

Célestin alone among his parents' children seems to have inherited both his mother's and his father's combativeness, along with his grandfather's disposition to obsession. With his genetic appetite for vengeance aroused, Célestin decided in November, 1860, to bring to the public prosecutor some noisome disclosures about Mirès' financial operations. Mirès and Solar determined then that the affair had to be stopped and began in earnest to seek a settlement. Mirès sent for one of Micael's notaries, who was also one of his, Constant Amédée Moquard, and through him brought Micael's influence to bear on her son. Célestin agreed to withdraw his accusations about Mirès' business dealings; Mirès agreed to lift the mortgage on Mont-l'Évêque and to pay Célestin 200,000 francs.[20] A contract was drawn up and submitted to Micael so that she could inspect every syllable. But by then, the whole business had gone too far. The foreign press had picked up the news that charges had been filed against Mirès. Mirès had just a few days previously arranged a loan of 154 million francs to the Ottoman emperor. Napoleon III desperately wanted that money to be delivered into Turkish hands, but he did not want the French government to be publicly associated with the loan. Mirès' offer to provide the money—money which would be gathered from French subscribers—had rescued the government from a ticklish position. Now everyone across the continent heard the news that Mirès was going to use investors' money in a loan to Turkey simultaneously with the news that Mirès had been accused of corruption and mismanagement by one of his associates.

The imperial prosecutor acted on Célestin's complaint. Mirès, charged with fraud in February, 1861, was thrown into Mazas Prison where, like many other defendants charged with felonies, he was held in strict confinement, unable, he complained, even to talk with his lawyer. Solar had sold his library at auction and left the country at the beginning of December; he was indicted in absentia. This was an earthquake to the business community of France, like the shock American investors would have taken had Andrew Carnegie and Henry Frick been incarcerated. Mirès was found guilty in July, 1861, together with Solar, and sentenced to a minor fine and a major prison term of five years. He appealed the verdict and lost.

That Mirès had embezzled mountains of cash through his Caisse Générale seems never to have been in doubt. Specifically, the prosecutor proved to the jury's satisfaction that over a period of time Mirès sold a large number of securities attached to his Italian railroad enterprise at a premium price, but kept the sales secret from his depositors. Then in May, 1859, when Italy was on the verge of war, he claimed to have sold the securities very cheaply. He gave his investors the proceeds of the lower price from this fictitious sale and kept for himself and his associates the difference of several million francs.[21] Célestin was not alone in wanting to bring Mirès down, and his complaint to the imperial prosecutor was the occasion for general rejoicing among Mirès' adversaries. The banker's best enemies were Pierre Magne, Napoleon III's minister of finance, and the duc de Persigny, that unlucky husband of Marshal Ney's granddaughter, Eglé. Persigny was the emperor's minister of the interior and intimate advisor. But Mirès was hardly isolated. With the prince de Polignac as his son-in-law, he could count on considerable support from legitimists, those Bourbon supporters who had little love for Napoleon III or his government. Morny, though he had been Célestin's companion, supported Mirès since, according to rumor, he was to receive a commission of millions of francs if the Turkish loan went through, and the loan would probably not be granted if Mirès remained in prison. Mirès was well aware of his secret power over his free-spending royal friends. At his trial he cannily stated that he had not appropriated five million francs for his own use; he had given it away in presents and could name the recipients. The court discreetly refrained from pressing him to expose the gift-takers.[22]

Moreover, Mirès had the prospect of financial panic on his side, the fears of thousands of investors that their savings would be lost if Mirès were replaced as head of one of his companies. There was a nagging intuition on the part of manufacturers, shippers, mine owners, large stockholders, and especially, the government itself, that they could all face bankruptcy if Mirès' empire fell. As months went by, Mirès grouped his partisans around him. His newspapers saturated the public with arguments in his favor, while he relieved his prison solitude by writing a three-hundred-page defense of his case, *À Mes Juges*, in which he was not kind to Célestin. Célestin fired back his own heavy brief.

Even without Mirès' and Célestin's books, the details of the case were widely circulated. People knew that Mirès and all the other financial matadors were swindlers; but the general opinion was that Mirès was no worse than any of the others in that thriving and debased system. Prosper Mérimée, writing to Empress Eugénie's mother with his usual casualness, remarked, "I see that people here are beginning to feel sorry for Mirès. They think he's much less a stinker than Pontalba and Solar. That's not to say that he's a paragon of virtue. To tell the truth, I'm afraid that if they judged most bankers by the rules they are applying in Mirès' case, they would uncover every sort of filth." A friend of Gustave Flaubert commented to him that Pontalba was "the worst scum of that whole lot."[23]

The emperor, who had at first rejected Polignac's pleas that he interfere, decided in the end to save his protégé. He ordered a special tribunal to review the case, that is, to reverse the previous rulings. Mirès and Solar were acquitted of all charges in 1862. The court then used the occasion to formulate a juridical theory of stock trading which, according to Mirès' prosecutor, "made it nearly impossible to win a case against any of the financial criminals."[24] Within a few weeks, Mirès was issuing a prospectus of a new business undertaking, to be capitalized at two hundred million francs.

Not only did Mirès go free. Not only was Célestin deprived of his stock commission. He had the supreme humiliation of having to accept his

mother's intervention to save Mont-l'Évêque. After Mirès was found guilty
by the first tribunal, the banker, hoping to win on appeal, again offered to
cancel the mortgage and thus silence his major critic, Célestin. But the liquidators who were called in to end Mirès' directorship forbade any such arbitrary forgiveness of a legitimate debt. They were prepared to foreclose on
Mont-l'Évêque. As they began sifting through the technical details of that
procedure, however, they found that Mirès' bank could not legally seize the
property contained in the *majorat* of the estate, the buildings and lands of
Mont-l'Évêque which constituted the estate when Pontalba's barony was assigned to it in 1810. They would have to squeeze the cash out of Célestin
some other way. At that point, Micael offered the liquidators half of
Célestin's debt if they would drop all action against her son and his property.[25] By the time various costs were added to the payoff price, Micael had
to forfeit more than 530,000 francs. That took care of the bank but by no
means placated Célestin's other creditors, any of whom might have placed
liens on certain parts of Mont-l'Évêque. Micael could see that Célestin was
likely to lose his brothers' fortune before they could inherit it.

Micael's expensive solution, therefore, to the continuing problem of her
eldest son, was to purchase from him the only property in France that remained in his inheritance, Mont-l'Évêque, for exactly one million francs.[26]
No doubt Célestin fantasized about what he could do with such a princely
amount of money but, in fact, he never got to touch a centime of it. Included in the eighty-five-page sale was a list of Célestin's creditors whom Micael paid off directly with the money she would have paid him for Mont-
l'Évêque. In 1865 Célestin owed nineteen individuals various sums which
had been guaranteed by his father, amounting to 320,050 francs. Micael next
subtracted fees that were owed to the servants and commune of Mont-
l'Évêque; she subtracted from the purchase price of a million francs the half-
million she had paid a few months previously to the liquidators of Mirès' interests. When everything she had paid off was deducted, Célestin wound up
owing his mother 85,000 francs, a sum that he never got around to paying
and that she forgave in her will. Célestin and his wife Blanche no doubt resented Micael for taking Mont-l'Évêque from him; but Micael had more
sense than to leave the estate in his hands so that it might be lost to the next
set of creditors.

Where did Micael get the money? She sold her mother's house on Place
Vendôme to the city of Paris for exactly 1,600,000 francs. Baron Haussmann negotiated the purchase of the house which, after the renovation of

the capital, was now located in one of the most expensive, elegant parts of the city.[27]

In a few little years everything had been turned around. Micael's mother's property was gone, sold to pay off Célestin's debts. Place d'Armes in New Orleans, which old Pontalba had coveted, was filled with Union troops, and Micael's dream houses were more than half empty. But the Pontalba houses in Paris and the Migneaux estate, all in her sons' names, were Micael's to do with whatever she pleased, authorized by notarial acts signed by her husband and children. And Mont-l'Évêque belonged to her as completely as St.-Honoré—even more, since St.-Honoré was now mortgaged, but Mont-l'Évêque was hers free and clear. If her father-in-law Xavier could have foreseen that by the year 1865, everything he had worked for would belong to Micael, that she would inspect the clanking mill at Migneaux and tramp around the fields at Mont-l'Évêque, pacing off strips for tenants and giving orders for new construction, his rage would have been so fatal as to render suicide unnecessary.

The next few years proved something about Micael that her family probably knew all along: the way to make money out of property was to give it to her to manage. In the 1830s Célestin, her husband, had been getting small and inconsistent rent from his Paris property. By 1870 Micael was collecting 88,100 francs a year from the same rentals, according to extant leases, four times Célestin's highest revenue.[28] It is true that rents went up in the intervening period simply because of the inflation of commerce, population, and money in Paris; but as the buildings got older they required more attention and investment to command good rents, and they had to compete with much better looking new residences. Micael constantly improved the property and extended the leases to an average of twelve years. Then there was Migneaux. That property was Célestin's least important source of income when Micael took it over. She at once began leasing out more of the land, selling the milk and produce, renting passage rights to neighboring farmers, and so forth, so that by 1870 Migneaux produced a brisk income.

As for Mont-l'Évêque, Célestin *père* had been buying up small pieces of land around the estate even while he was selling larger pieces to satisfy his son's debts.[29] Micael bought more. She purchased several houses on the road that ran through Mont-l'Évêque from Senlis to Meaux, demolished the cottages, and made the land part of the estate. In some cases she allowed the owners to live in the buildings until their deaths.[30] Then she leased hunting rights and rights of passage to neighbors whose access to pastures, water, and prairies had been closed off by her purchases. She sold milk and lumber, and leased strips of land to tenant farmers and to the town of Senlis, charging her lessees for the right to sublet their strips to others. She leased out the mills, with clever stipulations: the tenants using the mills had to bear the expense of keeping the river flowing. Micael contributed 5,000 francs in a lump sum to put the estate's largest mill in working order; the tenants were then obliged to lease the mill for nine years at 1,700 francs a year and to make whatever further repairs were required. She would not pay more than 5,000 francs toward the repairs even if the tenants expended more. And even if they ended up spending 10,000 francs, the agreement stated, the mill would still belong to Micael.[31] Not the least of her accomplishments was simply maintaining the château, the infamous (to her) Little Château, and all the outbuildings; the castle and some of the structures were hundreds of years old and were continually crumbling and needing repair.

Célestin and Blanche lived both at Mont-l'Évêque and Versailles. Célestin continued to dabble and stumble in financial ventures, though there were no more hair-raising failures like the Mirès mess. During the American Civil War, Célestin, together with his son Edouard, age twenty-five, and some of Blanche's relatives, invested in a copper smelter that they built at Ontonagon in the Upper Peninsula of Michigan on Lake Superior.[32] They had high hopes for the enterprise and believed it would make them all independently rich—independent, that is, of Micael. Edouard was the chief stockholder with $60,000 invested, an endowment he must have somehow coaxed out of his grandmother. Célestin apparently thought he could attract the business of the largest copper mining company in the area, the oddly spelled Minesota Mining Company. However, he was not able to open his smelter until 1864, after the war was well along. By that time Minesota Mining had already invested heavily in another smelter in Detroit, five hundred miles to the south, and had even purchased ships to transport its copper to the new smelter. Minesota's ore steamed right past Célestin's smelter. The next year the war was over and so was the demand for copper; Célestin's smelter shut down in 1866. It had been a typical Célestin venture: an aleatory enterprise far from home in a technical field he knew nothing about but which offered a modest hope for immodest riches.

Even with her profligate son, sick husband, and financial problems, Micael must have been relatively happy in the 1860s. The Civil War brought unsettling news from New Orleans; but Paris was to remain for a few years longer the pleasantest place in the world for a materialist with a privileged niche in society. By day the new boulevards rumbled with carriages on their way to important appointments. Night in the elegant quarters was animated by dinners, masques, and other costly ways to waste time. The capital was full of dynamic scenes, even for dull eyes. Europe's royalty gathered in Paris in 1867 for the Universal Exposition, and marveled at the machinery on display, the shimmering new architecture of the city, and the underground sewers where princesses gladly descended to take boat tours.[33] Even doll clothes might come from the city's leading dressmakers, and little boys brought toy boats that were worth a tanner's weekly pay to parks recently opened to the public.

In the delirium of spending and indulgence, decorative ladies had the best time of anyone. Though Empress Eugénie was pious and strait-laced, several women of the imperial court had unconcealed liaisons. Whereas the English aristocracy contained repressed and unhappy wives, in France, it was said, the wives were merely unhappy. The emperor's cousin, Princess Mathilde, lived openly with two successive lovers. The first one, Comte de Nierwerke, expected to become a member of the royal family as soon as Mathilde's husband and his wife did him the favor of expiring. (Tactlessly, both spouses were to outlive the empire.) Society's tolerant attitude toward all sorts of excess made Parisian life theatrical even for people who were not themselves pushing back the barriers of taste. Comtesse de Brimont appeared at a party with live animals disporting themselves in her gown—butterflies, lizards, beetles, and an excited squirrel in a cage on her head.[34] That was something to see even in a town full of sights. At palace balls, according to diarists, one could observe a great deal of a Madame Rimsky-Korsakov or a Madame Ollivier, wife of Napoleon III's eventual prime minister, as they appeared in portions of a costume. When Micael, long a grandmother, advised Azélie to stop going to church and have some fun, she indicated that the fun she had in mind was the sort that might produce a godchild; even Micael with her terrible marriage had somehow found out about "fun." Not everyone at these affairs was in a good mood, however. There is a photograph somewhere in the papers of one of Micael's correspondents—one of those pebbles every researcher comes across—of Napoleon in a suit and tie, grimly clutching an umbrella; it turns out only to be Prince Napoleon, Napoleon I's worthless nephew, dragging his dumpy wife behind him to one of their many soirées.

As might be expected of a generation infatuated with progress and technological improvement, Parisians tended to ignore distinctions between the real and the fantastic, the futuristic and the merely synthetic. Artificiality often accompanies wealth, like an unavoidable side effect; but in Paris, artificiality was sought after. The Bois de Boulogne was not a nature preserve in those days. It was landscaped and tailored to look as little as possible like "the repulsive realities of our fields and woods," as one wag described it.[35] However, it is easy to misunderstand Parisian clinquant. For all its pervasiveness, flashiness did not necessarily reflect the esthetic taste of its promulgators, no more than it does today in a place like Las Vegas. Gaudiness was not an artistic style during the late empire, but a means of systematic self-advertisement, a way of attracting attention—and investment—to a pulsating capitalistic economy. The flamboyance was not the unexamined intemperance of nouveaux riches who knew no other standards—not yet, although the bourgeoisie copied the garishness they saw and eventually extended it. Most people in society in the 1860s still knew the difference between exuberance and ostentation, and could make fun of vulgarity. It was not until the 1880s and 1890s that Paris began turning into the city of bulemic excess that it was at the end of the century.

Where did someone like Micael fit into the vitality and acquisitive frenzy of the Second Empire? She was too weathered to wear revealing ball gowns and too busy to enjoy the playful diversions she had longed for when she was a young wife locked up in Mont-l'Évêque. Fresh scandals of her own were unlikely at her age—she was seventy in 1865—though her son Cèlestin made sure that the family remained the object of whispering for the rest of her life. She could be counted on in any social gathering to be out of everyone's way after dark. However, though she seems to have had no leisure time, she did have friends and obligations apart from her work of managing the family's money. In August, 1851, when she returned from New Orleans, she wrote to Azélie:

> You can imagine that I have had neither heart nor time for amusements. Nevertheless, I have had to receive sometimes so as to make a polite response to everyone's gestures. On the 18th of this month, the day before yesterday, I gave a magnificent concert; I had 500 people. And on the 27th, I am giving a ball. I'm so frantic right now that I don't even know what I'm saying. Patience, my good friend. I will write soon at greater length. A thousand good wishes to the family. Kisses for Malvina as well as for Mme. Rochereau. Wait for my letter. I love you with all my heart.

These two galas were a way of reclaiming her friendships in Paris after her three-year absence. She did not have such parties every month nor every twelve months. Another reference to a festivity at the Hôtel Pontalba turns up some eight years later in 1859: a sentence in a newspaper about a huge ball she gave that must have resembled a mass rally.[36] She knew society people by the hundreds, to judge from the number who showed up for her parties (although her guests may have only been acquaintances; the beau monde of the Second Empire mobilized for balls as people now do only for sporting contests and revolutions). Some of those people must have sincerely liked her.[37] While she was cracking heads with Stewart in New Orleans, more than one hundred friends in Paris thought enough of her to pass by rue St.-Honoré to leave their calling cards.

It was true of Micael that she did not care to entertain incessantly or to be entertained, but in one way she was absolutely typical of her time: she loved to keep house. One of the longest documents of her life is one she did not sign, which gives exhaustive details about what surrounded her at home. It is an inventory of every marketable object she owned at the time of her death. Two hundred sixty pages of crabbed, bored writing, the inventory described minutely what she bought, touched, valued, saved, or forgot about during her last twenty years on earth.

Since inventories began with the courtyard, moved to the wine cellar, and then upward through the house, we learn first of all that Micael did not share her son's passion for horses. A number of people lived with her in Paris, yet she owned only "one old pony" and two presentable horses to pull her good coupe, which could hold four passengers; she had two other quite modest carriages.[38] She also paid taxes on some dogs, considered a luxury in Paris. Wine was not her weakness either; the best in the cellar was worth only five francs, and that was a gift brought to her from Cyprus by her granddaughter Louise.

She was not penny-pinching when it came to her property. Everything she owned, including Mont-l'Évêque, was heavily insured against fire. She parted with forty francs a year for an electric doorbell, one hundred francs to have the city water filtered, and since she did not like the lanterns that the city provided for her gate, she assumed the cost of mounting her own lights and supplying them with gas. All these little indulgences were later discontinued by Alfred and Gaston, who were untroubled by the possibility of tainted water, dim driveways, or unanswered knocks at the gate.

And what of the blue and white paneled world inside the door? It was unimaginably packed with things. Like most wealthy people in the faubourgs, Micael considered furniture and accessories in the house like flowers in the garden: the more the better. Every space in the hôtel was planted with empire divans, armoires, cabinets, chairs, sofas, and ornaments—gilded bronze bowls held aloft by gilded bronze infants, barometers set on lacquered angels who presented the face of Louis XIV along with the air pressure. There were rococo tables, their surfaces replete with countless, priceless knickknacks which the inventory accountants were obliged to count and price; jewelry boxes; fruit bowls; preciously decorated containers of every sort; and clocks held up by cherubs whose eyes lifted delightedly toward six-thirty. The Hôtel Pontalba was no more congested than an average Paris mansion, for an ambitious class loves proof of its success; but a different generation would have smothered in the plenitude of objects. Even when people moved in those days, they did not have to fear vacant rooms. In a century when moving vans were horse drawn, it was common to sell houses completely furnished—Micael's house was eventually sold this way—so that new owners might look forward to someone else's expensive clutter in addition to some of their own. The emptiest room in Micael's mansion, the ballroom with its shining floor, contained, according to solemn affidavit, over one hundred gilded chairs and seven sofas. The silk brocade on the chairs and curtains was illuminated by a crystal and gilded bronze chandelier with eighty-six lights worth 40,000 francs, that is, worth the wages of Micael's concierge for thirty-three years, three months of service.[39]

In what appeared to be the best guest bedroom, called the yellow room (there was also a green room and a rose room), a visitor was greeted by a dozen Sèvres porcelain pieces and another dozen tables and chests, all decorated in some way with gilded bronze. The house contained more than thirty such rooms. Some, such as the grand salon, were more elaborate; many were modestly appointed bedrooms. Alfred's room was simply and expensively furnished, as was that of Micael's grandson Edouard. But the room designated for Georges, her granddaughter's husband, had its own piano (one of three in the mansion), many, many chairs and divans, paintings, and meters of velour and brocade. Micael's own sanctuary was comparatively ascetic: it contained an armoire, a drying rack for clothes, a table, a rosewood chiffarobe, and a mahogany bed. Her bathroom held a toothbrush, toothpaste, footbath, a washstand with a "toilet"—a seat with a removable chamber pot—a bidet, and no bathtub. Each family member had a private bathroom without a bath. A true citizen of the City of Light, Micael loved sparkling things: chandeliers were the most expensive items in almost every room. She may not have played billiards, but billiard tables were a standard status symbol and she had several; she paid a luxury tax on them, sixty francs, which was about half the tax she paid for her horses and carriages. (Income, remember, was not taxed, only the money people spent.)

Any close look at the material life of the Second Empire reveals that disparity between the classes which takes various forms in various centuries. The owner of the mansion and the people who resided in it merely to serve her lived differently, though they both called the Hôtel Pontalba "home." Micael's "help" could consider themselves well off. They had their own dining room with a large table, fourteen "chairs and stools," and exactly twenty-six earthenware dishes for the six or seven domestics so lucky as to be employed in a great house where the leftovers were tasty and the secondhand sheets embroidered. Their bedrooms were decently supplied with about 55 francs' worth of furniture. But what a contrast to Micael's own dining room, the one she used for parties! It had an inlaid ebony and bronze table with twenty-four matching chairs covered in silk and velour. Several weeks were required to count the dishes, serving pieces, and silver: "about 1,000 crystal candle rings," "18 fruit compots in gilded bronze with embedded crystal coats of arms," and a matched set of dishes, service for no less than 180. Three of Micael's decorative bowls in gilded bronze and borne by the inevitable pudgy cherubs were worth 6,000 francs. The silver in the dining room was appraised by weight: a breadbasket had the same price as 240 of Paris' child prostitutes—240 francs.[40] Altogether, Micael's furniture, dishes, and silver were valued at 328,000 francs, not so much when we consider that the hero in Stendhal's *Lucien Leuven* had 100,000 francs' worth of furniture in his bedroom alone.

Gilded bronze, we see from this and other contemporary inventories, was the plastic of the Second Empire, used in everything from saucers to desk chairs. Cotton cloth was the paper, the indispensible material in a period when everything had to be covered, not only women's ankles, but the arms of chairs and legs of tables, the laps of sofas already covered with something else, the bow-legged knees of bedroom dressers, the shades of lamps, frames of beds, tops and corners of chests—even office chairs, diaries, and Sunday missals—all were wrapped in cotton cloth.

Micael kept a good deal of lace at the bottom of her armoire, little pieces worth thirty or forty francs each, which she had willed to the servants. The talented notary could distinguish the imitation Cluny from the authentic Chantilly, a service the servants no doubt appreciated. Micael had a lorgnette in a box together with a costly fan worth the price of a square of real estate, but no eyeglasses. Aside from the fan and some jewelry, her most expensive personal items were traveling trunks, only two, for she always traveled light.

For a woman who was indifferent to clothes, she kept a certain quantity of jewelry in her notary Berçeon's office, including a lapel pin with a picture of Napoleon's son, probably passed down to Célestin from old Pontalba. She had a brooch, a bracelet containing a lock of hair—whose?—and at home, a pile of junk jewelry of the sort little girls are allowed to play with when they visit their grandmothers. She owned some costly shawls and wraps, a few in cashmere. The rest of her wardrobe was cheap and serviceable, the kinds of dresses worn by a woman whose main concern was comfort. Altogether, her dresses were not worth one of her vases, for Micael's clothes were the oldest things in the house: petticoats limp and numerous, crinolines which the thickest starch could not redeem, an Arapaho embroidered petticoat probably acquired during her 1831 tour of the United States, and chemises dating from the Louisiana Purchase. Since cotton clothes never wore out in those days, the dress from her 1850 New Orleans trip remained in her armoire, "dyed green, almost black," and worth three francs. Like many a grand old lady, Micael apparently wore tattered housecoats while she wrote letters and paid bills in the morning. She owned some presentable frocks, many in black, others in blue or violet, but none of the fabulous ball gowns in Mardi Gras colors favored by society women of her time, even though she had a sewing machine and a woman who came regularly to sew. She owned twenty or twenty-five almost worthless bonnets and hats valued at less than a franc apiece—twenty cents—but, if one is to believe the inventory, no slippers and only one pair of shoes, which stayed on her feet during her journey to the next life. One of her two overcoats was worth five francs, half the price of a glass of water in Paris today. Cold-natured, she owned many warm undershirts and underskirts. Otherwise, she seems to have eschewed all underwear. Only two corsets survived her, both practically new, and no underpants whatever, except for a single pair made of scratchy twill which she could only have worn for penance or warmth. Her nightgowns and twenty cheap, well-worn nightcaps remind us that even mansions were drafty in the nineteenth century. She probably suffered from severe allergies: she had hundreds of handkerchiefs, all used. Her garments, counting every thread in the house, hardly took up two pages of a nearly three-hundred-page inventory.

So far as we can tell, she never immersed herself in either a bathtub or a novel. She cared nothing for literature, philosophy, the life of the mind. She owned not a single book, except for three address books and the account books where she recorded her daily expenses. Her chambermaid, cook, concierge, and maître d'hôtel also had expense books. She did not subscribe to any newspapers, went to sleep without the lenitive of fiction, and possibly had never looked at a poem she remembered. Though her home contained beautifully illustrated panels, there were no paintings, except in one bedroom not her own. She seems not even to have kept drawings made by friends or, for that matter, herself, since she had an artistic flair.

However, she saved everything that had to do with money, in lovingly organized files and accounts. Virtually every important document dealing with her property showed up in her estate inventory: the file on Mont-l'Évêque alone took weeks to examine. All her papers were meticulously arranged: the St.-Honoré file, the Bayou Road file, the separation file, with every paper chronologically ordered in its folder. She was a businesswoman to the tips of her untended fingernails. When her mind was not occupied with managing property, she seems to have been deeply fond of music, coffee, small children, baked fish, soft beds, and blue. She had little use for cosmetics, though her complexion had the hue of stored muslin, nor did she care for locked desks, soap, stays, chocolate, mirrors, or pink.

As the years passed, Micael more and more resembled Almonester, the father she probably did not remember. Working and talking incessantly, sputtering about whatever vexed her at the moment, she could turn stalwart, taciturn, and reliable in the face of true crisis. Like Almonester, she was both sentimental and insensitive. She was, of course, complicated, as is anyone we really get to know; but on the surface, she seemed very much a type in her later years. We have all encountered someone like her: bustling, never quite elderly regardless of her age, blurting whatever comes into her head—the passerby who remarks on our garden with trusting assurance that her evaluation of it is welcome; the stranger on the streetcar who compliments our clothes, and then offers a suggestion for making an even better appearance. Such people would be obnoxious if it were not for their simple-hearted openness. One cannot even say that they are impolite. They are forthright, opinionated, and engaging in a way that bypasses politeness. Micael's statements can be quoted in isolation, as they were in several of her trials, to give the impression that she was imperious and cunning. But that is to miss her style, which was fundamentally humorous. She was the very opposite of cunning. She held people to accounts and made no apologies for doing so; she had every reason to believe that one must watch every penny entrusted to someone else. She was exacting about details and blunt to the point of rudeness. But there was nothing personal or malicious in her agitations. Just the same, her fussiness could get on people's nerves.

In her later years, Micael was preoccupied with her family, which was not unusual for a French matriarch. What is odd is that her family was just as obsessed with her, no one more so than Célestin's wife, Blanche. There is, for example, a curious letter written by Blanche to her son Henri, describing the wedding of his older sister at Mont-l'Évêque.[41] Blanche was about forty-five when this letter was penned. From it we learn a little about the relatives, the hectic activity surrounding the nuptials, and the medieval flavor of a provincial wedding. But the true subject of Blanche's attention is testy Micael, her reaction to the wedding gifts, her opinion of the food, as if the hated mother-in-law were the bride.

> Mont-l'Évêque, May 6, 1864
> Dear child, I have so much to tell you: where to start? They are married and gone—to Versailles! . . . But let's . . . begin at the beginning. Saturday we signed the contract at your grandmother's [Micael], who refused to sign it and who, throughout the reading, was talking away to Georges about the faults of his future wife and in-laws, and the wrong which she saw being done to him, Georges, in the planning of Edouard's marriage.

Célestin and Blanche, we recall, had three children. Edouard was twenty-five at the time of this letter and was to marry Clotilde Vernois in two weeks. Michaelle Louise, called Louise, was the twenty-year-old bride whose wedding was being described. Georges de Maricourt was the groom; hence, his future in-laws whose faults were being detailed were Micael's son Célestin and Blanche herself. Henri, the son to whom the letter was addressed, was to wed another Maricourt in a few years.

> She [Micael] had made it known to Georges that she would not come to the wedding so as not to be faced with Clotilde! Monday morning we received a letter here from her in which she told us she would come if Clotilde were excluded—that on top of a big uproar. Louise, Georges and I declared that Clotilde would be there. Reasonable Edouard arrived unexpectedly and decided that we had to make this last concession, and that the day after the mar-

riage he would take his revenge. . . . Then to tell the poor little thing [Clotilde], who with her angelic sweetness only said that your grandmother must really be spiteful to prevent her from seeing little Louise! She came herself to deliver your sister's wedding gown, and I was taking her back to her house as your grandmother was arriving. . . .

A thousand complaints began. She [Micael] was furious about the celebrations arranged for your sister and the happiness which appeared to surround us—seeing that we would have had to forbid the partying in the village, telling herself that all that only took place because they learned she was coming. But the next day in all the compliments, in all the talk, nothing was said about her! Imagine what fury! . . . Finally, we get to seven o'clock the next day. Dinner was a thunderstorm . . . detestable gumbo, mediocre grillades, all bad, all bad! M. de la Roche was in a rage. He had brought your sister a lovely gift, a complete tea and liqueur service in English metal, English porcelain, and Bohemian glass. Your grandmother thought it looked showy and cheap, just a gewgaw. At last, she went to bed, after having shivered, she said, all evening because of our mania for doors! . . .

Came the morning of the big day, the 4th of May . . . at ten o'clock we were in the salon, receiving the young people and the flower bearers and all the nice congratulations. Then we all left in the carriage for the town hall, where the deputy mayor and the municipal council were waiting for us before the wedding. . . . From there to the church where in a body they presented us with flowers and candles, and Monsieur le Curé, profoundly moved, made a speech full of tact and courage, touching on the most delicate things very adroitly. Your grandmother was foaming at the mouth. Everything had been boring. The church was packed, only the family and the village, as not a single invitation was sent out. The offering brought in 130 to 140 francs for Monsieur le Curé.

After church we came home. New furor. Lunch was not served. She wanted to leave! Finally, we ate in the middle of her carryings-on. Everybody was flabbergasted. Gaston didn't know where to hide. He had been very nice to her. Your grandmother had been ready since eight o'clock. She came down to the salon and found poor M. Romany, whom she proceeded to draw into a conversation about Edouard.

At last, after lunch the mighty blow was about to be struck. After letting his uncle know what was going on, Edouard took his grandmother into the billiard room and told her it was he who had conceded to her latest demand, but that for *certain insults* she had to make prompt reparation and that the banns for his wedding would be published Sunday! She left, saying to herself that everybody would see who was right. But here, at least, everybody thinks Edouard is right, and she had hardly gone before your father went to get Clotilde and the Vernois, whose arrival was welcomed all around [Clotilde was from Senlis, three miles away].

We had dinner, then the newlyweds departed, leaving heavy hearts in spite of their radiant happiness. . . . The family is quite charming . . . furious with their Aunt Michaelle who gives us reason, they say, for remaining close to one another without seeing each other. Uncle Charles is charming and never stops talking about their joy over Georges' marriage, about the happiness which awaits them, and about their affection for Louise. As for the Viscount and Viscountess, he wrote me this morning, they are happy as can be; they will come in a week.

Georges' father, the viscount, was French consul to the Isle of Cyprus; his mother was from Senlis. Georges himself was a lawyer.

I must kiss you goodbye now. I'll have to keep my description of the Arch of Triumph and the gifts for a while, as lunch is about to be served and I am not dressed. . . . As for you, my child, I send my boundless love with a warm embrace from everyone.

M.

It is hard to say who seems less congenial in this account, sixty-nine-year-old Micael, trying to ostracize a defenseless girl, criticizing the hospitality, and wrinkling her nose at the wedding gifts, or Blanche, watching Micael's every move and keeping an account of each offense so as to make allies of the children against their grandmother. If nothing else, the letter shows that relations between in-laws have not worsened since the era of the vaunted extended family. Aside from what it reveals about Blanche and Micael, the letter gives some specific information about the rituals of life in a wealthy family headed by a woman. Louise's and Georges' marriage contract was signed at Micael's house because she, Louise's grandmother, was paying for the wedding. That contract shows that neither of the newlyweds brought much of a dowry.[42] Célestin and Blanche gave Louise shares in the Michigan copper foundry, shares to which they assigned a value of 40,000 francs. As we know, the venture never made money and collapsed within two years, so the 40,000 francs was imaginary. The worthlessness of the dowry may not have been a complete surprise to the Maricourts. They took great pains in the contract to make sure that their son Georges could in no way be held responsible for his father-in-law's obligations to Mirès. On their side, the Maricourts gave the young couple a not overly generous pension of 2,500 francs a year. Georges had few resources other than his noble title, judging from the way Louise continued to depend on her grandmother after her marriage.

At the wedding feast, the family ate gumbo and grillades as if they were sitting down to dinner in the shadow of St. Louis Cathedral; actually, only Micael and Blanche were Creoles, and both had left Louisiana when they were young girls.[43] The mail service in and around Paris during much of the nineteenth century might be the envy of any modern society, as we have had occasion to note. Micael wrote to her son and daughter-in-law on Sunday and the horse-and-rider delivery service dropped the letter at Mont-l'Évêque on Monday morning. The curé of the provincial church, even in an ancient bishopric such as Mont-l'Évêque, could look forward to collecting only 130 or 140 francs, though an unusual number of wealthy visitors were present in the church. Aristocrats were not great givers, even with their hostess watching them and noting what went into the plate. Célestin, Micael's son, apparently kept out of the crossfire between his mother and his wife. Célestin the grandfather was noticeably unmentioned in the letter.

There is no reason to doubt that Micael was as cranky as Blanche described her, although, as with Browning's last duchess, we are left wondering what happened before all smiles stopped together. For Micael, spending any night at Mont-l'Évêque, even thirty years after her "incident" and even after all her tinkering with the property, must have been a cheerless experience. But it is questionable whether the old lady got under everyone's skin as she did Blanche's. Blanche implied that Micael was such a holy terror, even Gaston was embarrassed by her and had to exert special effort to be nice to her. Whatever his private aggravations, Gaston was a classic adult child afraid of his mother; he was never anything but nice.

Edouard almost certainly did not bully his grandmother into concurring with his marriage plans, although he may have charmed her into giving him his way. Micael had faced the hostility of lawyers, judges, architects, contractors, businessmen, and one madman; she would not have been intimidated by a twenty-five-year-old dependent. Besides, Edouard's marriage to Clotilde was a good match, as such things were judged, and as Micael would have judged them. The Vernois dowered Clotilde with 44,000 francs to be spread over a six-year period, and other less easily measured contributions. Both Edouard and his sister were to be parents themselves in less than a year; Louise's daughter Michaelle, whose great-grandmother was also her godmother, was born ten months after the wedding to the day.[44] If Edouard was angry with his grandmother on that wedding day, he got markedly over it, for in his later years he devoted himself to collecting Micael's letters and papers. By the time he himself was sixty-nine, one of his chief occupations was putting together the pieces of her life, assisted by the descendants of Micael's beloved Cruzat cousins. Micael could not have wished for a more devoted grandson.

As for the two ladies, grumpy Micael and giddy Blanche, we may note that the letter was written on May 6, 1864, one year before Blanche and Célestin would sell Mont-l'Évêque to Micael in return for her paying off their mass of debts. Only three months previously, Micael had surrendered half a million francs to the liquidators of Mirès' enterprises, who in fact liquidated nothing except Célestin's obligations to Mirès. Everything that was part of the wedding—the gowns, grillades, flowers, even the carriage with which Célestin went to fetch the Vernois after Micael's indignant departure—were paid for by Micael. The trip to Paris that Blanche referred to was paid for by Micael, along with the dressing gown or whatever Blanche was wearing as she wrote her letter to her son. Also the stationery and the postage on the letter. Perhaps Micael wanted simple acknowledgment of her contribution to the occasion, an effort at curbing the costs, or some attention other than resentment.

Her family's hostilities were not the only civil wars Micael was to experience. In the ten years between Blanche's letter and Micael's death in 1874, her life's work was nearly undone. First came the American Civil War and its aftermath. Then Paris was stained by a savage class war fought on the streets of Micael's own neighborhood.

New Orleans was captured by Union troops early in the Civil War and was thus spared the physical devastation of battle. However, everything that had made the place economically functional was crippled by the end of slavery and the defeat of the South. There had been over a thousand sugar plantations in Louisiana in 1861 whose products poured in and out of New Orleans. In 1865 there were fewer than two hundred, all struggling. Cotton planters were ruined; cotton brokers and exporters left the state or went bankrupt. The clerks, sorters, labelers, and lesser folk who depended on the crop fell on harder times. Without labor, cash to pay for labor, or any sort of financing, the best land was valueless. The once strong banks in New Orleans, having sent most of their gold to the Confederate government, were left with worthless Confederate paper. Merchants who depended on the planters shared their ruin, as did insurance companies, hotels, and everything connected with shipping.

Property values consequently plummeted all over the city, especially for luxury and commercial real estate like the Pontalba Buildings. The Pontalbas had all been leased in 1860; Micael's tenants had included the Bank of America, a planter, several stockbrokers, the secretary of the Ohio Railroad, and over ten attorneys dealing with maritime law, insurance, and commercial contracts.[45] Micael's agents generally did not have to threaten eviction to collect the rents, which together exceeded $6,000 a month. By the end of the war, practically none of these people had money. The buildings were more than half-empty, and the tenants who remained were not able to pay regularly; many simply stopped paying rent altogether while they waited for the eviction process to catch up with them. "The words 'To Let' are posted on nearly every door," a newspaper reporter remarked, concerning the Pontalbas; "They look as though they might be mausoleums."[46] Like so much else, the Pontalbas took a long time to recover from the Civil War. Even in March, 1874, a month before Micael's death and nine years after the end of the war, rents from the Pontalba Buildings totaled only $3,402.[47] When Micael died, her tenants owed her a substantial $4,929 in back payments; she must have carried nearly everyone in the building at one time or another. Moreover, her tenants sent her a petition on May 11, 1874, asking for a 25 percent reduction in their rent. Micael received the audacious demand with uncharacteristic serenity, having died almost a month before it arrived in Paris.

But though the Civil War affected Micael, it was geographically and psychologically a continent away. The shadows that haunted her during the 1860s were the Mirès affair, the expectation of losing Mont-l'Évêque, and the rising possibility of a lower-class revolt. Surrounded by servants and comforts, she and the people in her circle in Paris were deprived of nothing—except a feeling of security. As early as 1852, Micael had mentioned a coming revolution; she hoped the cataclysm could be held off until 1859. Among many people like her there was a chronic sense that the brocaded world of French prosperity might come apart at the seams, that Paris, with its vagrants, unemployed or unemployable workers, paupers, rabble, and rabble-rousers, would soon become a dangerous place for everyone. During the gayest years of the empire and despite welfare programs, the doors of orphanages had revolving boxes attached to them so that mothers could abandon their babies without having to face the attendants who would retrieve them. Underneath the skin of affluence, Paris was angry and cynical. The rebuilding of the city had been desirable for many reasons, not least of which was the employment it provided for the working classes. However, the construction attracted double the usual population of laborers to Paris just as housing for them was being destroyed in the central city. By 1870 the building programs were being curtailed. These newly unemployed people were forced out to the suburbs, where they created a fringe slum of provincials and malcontents surrounding the wealthy business district. Montmartre was one such waste of railway yards, shacks, and half-finished factories.

Then Napoleon III was drawn into war with Prussia in which the unprepared French army was defeated before it struck a single blow. One force was bottled up at Metz; the other was quickly surrounded at Sedan, where eighty thousand men were taken prisoner, including the ill and agonizing emperor. He surrendered on September 2, 1870, and abdicated his throne only a few weeks after his foolhardy declaration of war. However, the city of Paris, or more precisely, the republican deputies in the imperial parliament, refused to accept defeat and voted to establish a republic that would keep fighting. While the Germans methodically closed off the capital from all communication, the new minister of the interior, Léon Gambetta, dramatically escaped in a balloon in order to raise troops in the provinces. But the eventual surrender of Paris to the Prussians was inevitable, cut off as it was from food and fuel supplies during a winter when the temperature fell to eight degrees Fahrenheit.

The Germans surrounding the city waited. Milk gave out by mid-December. The butcher shops soon sold nothing but overpriced horse meat. One by one the exotic animals of the Jardin des Plantes were shot, butchered, and sold, mainly to the wealthy, since the common folk would have nothing to do with such fare and could not afford it anyway. Dead cats and rats were for sale in the markets for a few francs, though it is questionable whether these were bought by anyone other than journalists eager to report a novel experience. Pigeons in the city disappeared. People of means found ways to feed and warm themselves even during the worst days of the siege. Edmond de Goncourt survived on donkey meat located by his maid, and larks; he did not record what the maid ate. Everyone else settled down to "the regular siege ritual," as described by one historian: "eating horses and dying of typhus," at the rate of five thousand deaths a week.[48] Goncourt reported a commonplace incident—being followed by a young girl who begged him to come to her room in exchange for a piece of bread. The Germans bombarded the city for a few days. The shells were apparently more spectacular than lethal; hundreds of people gathered each night in the Place de la Concorde, a block or so from Micael's house, to see the fireworks. They were out of doors anyway, foraging for food and escaping black interiors where gas had been cut off and candles were cherished stubs.

The provisional government of Paris finally signed an armistice at the end of January, 1871. Then a newly elected national assembly headed by Adolphe Thiers agreed to what some Parisians regarded as a humiliating peace. Prussian troops, in a symbolic invasion of Paris, marched up the Champs Élysées as far as the Place de la Concorde, where they found all the statues draped in black. Unarmed, they visited the Louvre, as specified in the peace agreement, and left, except for some forces that were to occupy two suburban forts until France paid an indemnity. For a few days tourists flocked to Paris to see what it looked like after the siege, but within a week they too were evacuating the hotels. Thousands of Parisians swelled the exodus, many to join the government at Versailles, not far from Paris. Micael was probably there already with Célestin and Blanche, or at Mont-l'Évêque. She may have concluded early in the war that the reluctant hospitality of her daughter-in-law, who was after all only an unskilled sniper, was preferable to remaining in the sights of the Prussian artillery.

The lower classes had nowhere to go but did not welcome the armistice. They were embittered by the four-month ordeal and reviled the National Assembly at Versailles, the "capitulators," as much as they resented the Germans. Battalions of poor people had died, sixty-five thousand by the time the siege was lifted, not from the German bombardment but from malnutrition, smallpox, influenza, and pneumonia. What completely infuriated the populace was that as soon as the nightmare was over, the government, those "traitors," required the immediate payment of back rents and promissory notes which had been suspended during the war. The National Guard, just discharged and still holding some of their weapons, turned on the government. On March 26, 1871, the insurgents, insisting that they wanted to save the republic from both the Germans and the capitulators, repudiated the National Assembly and elected their own government, calling themselves by an old name popularized during the Revolution of 1789, the Commune of Paris. There was now one government for France, headed by Thiers and operating from Versailles, and one for Paris, headed by a committee of workers, lawyers, and cranks.[49]

The Commune uprising was to end as a real and terrifying revolution; yet, most of the two months of the experiment passed in an atmosphere of circus unreality. The Commune leaders—there was a large central committee and its members kept changing—included shopkeepers, journalists, a janitor, sword-swallower, concert master, and washerwoman. They were in no sense an organized revolutionary party with a doctrine. They were not disciples of Marx, though the Marxists fervently adopted the insurrection in their history. The rebels included the sort of activists that every revolution attracts. One of the Commune's secretaries was described as a crystal-gazer and somnambulist. The man who took command of the elder Célestin's neighborhood had been involved in two assassination plots against Napoleon III; but his reputation rested on his system of telepathy using what he termed "sympathetic snails." Another was said to haunt the cemeteries, holding interviews with the great departed. One of the less conspicuously unbalanced leaders was a doctor and engineer who instructed his men that society had but one duty toward princes, which was to kill them, and but one formality to observe, which was to ascertain their identity. These agitated souls marching up and down St.-Honoré made the homeowners understandably nervous.

While the remnants of the German army watched with pleased indifference from its positions on the outskirts of Paris, the Commune planned social reforms, such as free compulsory schools, and issued proclamations abolishing the regular army (an order the army ignored). The vast majority of Parisians were uncommitted bystanders to the fight, which was basically between the Commune's leaders supported by the rebellious National Guard on one side, against the government of Thiers on the other side, elected by the National Assembly and dependent on the regular army. The insurgents believed, with some reason, that if given the order to fight, the demoralized army troops would not battle their own countrymen and would join the rebellion. The republican leaders in fact feared the same thing. The Communards therefore never made any serious plans for defending Paris, nor did they seem to understand that they were engaged in a war and that they would have to win or die.

As time went on, Parisians wearied of hardships and tension. The holiday atmosphere of the first days gave way to outrage over troops billeted in houses and frequent looting—the Péreire mansion next to Micaël's was ransacked and two moving vans of furniture and wine were carted away.[50] Shootings of suspected government sympathizers increased, and violence grew as the central committee lost control of the hooligan commanders in some sections. In April the Communards mustered a force that may have numbered thirty or forty thousand—the largest it ever gathered—for a march on Versailles.[51] They were stopped at Meudon where the larger Versailles forces were more than a match for the mob army. In Paris a decree went out for the conscription of men under fifty-five for service in the Commune army, along with all saddle horses. Edmond de Goncourt seriously considered hiding out in the zoo to avoid the draft. The Versailles press and the army leaders meanwhile put out atrocity stories and reports of secret chemical weapons. The anti-Communard propaganda shocked bourgeois sensibilities and may have hardened the National Assembly troops which began attacking Paris in April. The army did not need propaganda to insure victory, however.

The government's bombardment of Paris proved far more destructive than that of the Germans. Buildings were set on fire by the artillery; barricades went up everywhere against the invasion of Paris by Frenchmen. The insurgents, among their gestures of desperation, felled what they thought was a symbol of militarism, the column in the Place Vendôme. Gustave Courbet, the realist painter and Communard panther, carried out the project with some fanfare. The Versailles troops found many welcomers inside the city, for as fighting intensified, the Communards torched the public buildings they vacated, along with others that happened to be at hand. Fires were set in order to block advancing troops—an enormous conflagration at the corner of rue Royale and St.-Honoré was apparently one of these. The collapse of burning houses on St.-Honoré gave rise to the fear that the neighborhood was mined and would blow up at any time; the whole quarter was a furnace. Seven people were found suffocated in a house down from the Hôtel Pontalba. Nearby, the entire front of the Ministry of Finances fell forward into the rue de Rivoli, its arcades which were said to have inspired the Pontalba Buildings crumbling with the rest of the masonry. Photographs, some perhaps taken by the Germans who watched with interest from their forts, show whole squares of the city enveloped in fire. On May 21, a desperate frenzy of carnage began. Both sides savagely murdered their hostages and indiscriminately shot citizens on the flimsiest suspicion that they might be partisans of the other side. The Communards retreated to their neighborhoods and fought with insane tenacity. They were by this time leaderless, widely scattered, and overwhelmed. Within days the last of them were cornered in the cemetery of Père Lachaise where they fought on until they were massacred. By the end of May, 1871, the shooting was over and the Thiers government again controlled the capital.

Many sources have documented the barbarities of Bloody Week, as it came to be called, describing the cruelty of both sides. But no one has succeeded in explaining the bloodthirsty horror of those few days. Those who sympathize with the insurgents blame the generals of the National Assembly for the carnage. They unleashed the army without much supervision and turned a blind eye to mass executions. The number of casualties is a forceful indictment of the army's wholesale massacres: 10,000 to 30,000 Parisians died in the fighting, perhaps half of them after having been taken prisoner. The army itself admitted to 8,000 executions, and in fact seems to have killed more people than had ever fought in the Commune, while itself losing between 400 and 800 men. The army took some 30,000 prisoners. Those who sympathize with the government point out that before the uprising was crushed, twenty-five public edifices had been destroyed by fire or blown up, including the Tuileries and the Palais Royale, the Ministries of Finance, War, and Treasury, and the Hôtel de Ville.[52] There is ample evidence that the Communards would have destroyed Paris if they had had time. They had specifically targeted for destruction the Louvre, Luxembourg Palace, the Cluny Museum, Notre Dame, and everything they could get to "in the reactionary quarters." The sight of Paris burning may have convinced the Versailles troops that, just as they had been told, they were dealing with animals who deserved no mercy.

The Commune uprising, with its wanton destruction of Paris by Parisians, fed conservative fears of revolution and justified hatred of the "dangerous classes" who remained, when all was said and done, an ineradicable part of society. On the other side, the ferocious suppression of the uprising, the martyrdom of the Communards, created a powerful image of class war that socialists invoked again and again throughout the remainder of the century. The confused and hideous affair became one of France's great myth-making events. Thirty-five years after the Commune, French socialist propaganda was still suffused with references to Bloody Week, to the government's carnage of workers, to the rage that no one really felt any longer except as a generational echo.

Where was Micael through it all? The notarial records which would have allowed us to follow her trail—proxies to property managers, contracts for guards at her houses—were destroyed when Communards burned the buildings holding public documents. Chances are that Micael left Paris in September, 1870, when the government advised evacuation because of imminent war. She was not one to expose herself and her dependents to need-less danger. Everyone down to her grandchildren and servants looked to her for directions. She probably brought her whole family with her, including, of course, her husband. By then, no one attempted to get his stuttering sig-nature on a document; everything was signed by a representative. Célestin the son was safe during the siege. The republican government tried unsuc-cessfully to deprive him of his commission as captain of the National Guard of Seine-et-Oise for having deserted his command at the outset of the war.[53] We must not make too much of his refusal to fight. When the war was an-nounced, many provincials declined to attend.

The end of 1871 closed what was perhaps the second-worst year of Mi-cael's life, a year when people in her district were shot by snipers, when bod-ies lay shattered amidst the rubble of the Place de la Concorde, when man-sions on fire were the only light on rue St.-Honoré. Middle-aged people can absorb such events and, with time and a sense of history, recover from them. But for a very young person, or a rather old lady such as Micael, terrible crises are indelible. Wherever she was during the siege and civil war, we can be fairly certain that she never got over them. Nevertheless, 1871, a year of want and sickening violence, was followed by one of general prosperity. The Prussians were astonished to see that France soon paid the hated indemnity and was rid of its occupiers. The ravaged palaces were repaired. New streets, houses, theaters were completed as planned, symbols of the official ego re-stored. French firms were again building railroads in Europe and Africa and looking toward Indochina. The bloodbath of the Commune was followed by some forty years of gaiety, interrupted only by another war.

Micael lived three more years "in the reactionary quarters" after life returned to normal. She actually learned to spell rather well before she died. The year after the Commune uprising, 1872, she wrote out a will as sage as it was cor-rect.[54] Her writing had gotten larger, as handwriting tends to do when eyes get weaker, but it was still a vigorous, willful hand that wrote her last wishes. Her primary concern in the will was to maintain the fragile peace between Célestin and the rest of the family, and to keep Alfred's and Gaston's inheri-tance out of the grasp of their reckless brother. "I hope that my children will respect my wishes as well as all of the acts executed by their father and me, especially that of . . . September 14, 1851," that is, the Pacte de Famille by which Célestin gave up his heirship to his father's property in return for having his debts paid. Célestin had agreed to everything in Micael's will in previous arrangements, trading off his inheritance in exchange for various considerations. But just to make sure he did not try to go back on his word, she stipulated that if one of her sons challenged the will in any way, he would forfeit his share of her estate to his brothers and the donations to his children would also be nullified. This was aimed at Célestin, whose children were the only other major beneficiaries. Alfred and Gaston were not to claim from Célestin "what he owes them or what he owes his father, so that the division of my property among them will conform to that which I know best how to make."

Alfred and Gaston alone inherited Mont-l'Évêque, valued at 1,200,000 francs; Célestin's son Edouard was residing there. Micael forgave Célestin the 85,000 francs he owed her from the Mirès affair; but she excluded him from sharing in the Bayou Road property. Alfred and Gaston got the 243 lots, worth altogether about 36,000 francs; Célestin received forgiveness of a somewhat hypothetical debt which he never intended to pay anyway.[55]

Micael left the Pontalba Buildings in New Orleans to all three sons, but she gave Alfred and Gaston together the St. Ann Street side, worth 590,000 francs ($118,000), and Célestin the St. Peter Street side, valued at 460,000 francs ($92,000). That was the extent of Célestin's inheritance from her, except for his share of the marble ornaments and table silver in her house. To forestall any concussion over that, she ordered her executors to place the marble and silver in three roughly equal parcels and have her sons draw lots for them. Célestin was to be free to dispose of his portion of the inheritance as he chose; Alfred and Gaston could do what they wanted with theirs without consulting the eldest brother. Célestin was always on one side, Alfred and Gaston on the other. Micael did not have the legal authority to give away her husband's houses in Paris, but these had already been renounced by Célestin *fils* in exchange for previous donations of money from his father. As for the Hôtel Pontalba, Micael ordered that within five years of her death it was to be sold to any buyer whom two of the three sons approved. She had already been negotiating with prospective purchasers over the price. The money from the sale of the hôtel was to be distributed to her grandchildren, as the will directed. Thus, there was almost no way her sons could avoid selling the mansion, since in her will she had disbursed the proceeds from the transaction.

Micael tried to be impartial toward her sons. She loved her eldest long after the rest of the family had given up on him. But when it came to grandchildren, she let her preferences show. She favored Edouard and Louise, and after them, their children. These were the grandchildren who were to benefit from the sale of St. Honoré. "400,000 francs to Madame (Louise) de Maricourt, my granddaughter," she wrote. "400,000 to my grandson Edouard." And then, making him a rich man as an afterthought, she added, "A like sum to my grandson Henri." She then awarded Louise and Edouard, but not Henri, an additional pension of 1,000 francs a month each. Micael, who knew everything about every family member's finances, knew that Louise and Edouard would need their allowances before the sale of the Hôtel Pontalba; she therefore directed that their pensions were to begin on the day of her death and would be taken out of the revenues from New Orleans until such time as the Paris house was sold. As for Alfred's son Michel, who was twelve at the time Micael made her will, his legacy from his grandmother was a lean 50,000 francs, the least of all the grandchildren.

Micael's will gave the appearance of fairness to her two daughters-in-law, so that neither woman should be humiliated at the reading of the document. She left Blanche her diamond earrings, and Alfred's wife Louise, a diamond brooch. The rest of her diamonds went to Louise de Maricourt and—surprise!—Clotilde, Edouard's wife. However, when we look at the inventory of Micael's jewels, it turns out that Blanche's earrings were worth 10,500 francs, and Clotilde's loot amounted to 9,131. Whereas Alfred's wife received "a large and beautiful breast-pin of antique diamonds with flowers and pendants." The notary, who had an imaginative eye for jewelry, appraised it at a cool 55,000 francs, noting that it "could easily be made into diadems." Berçeon, who read the will, was of course not fooled as to which of the ladies was getting the most valuable gift; Micael had kept the brooch in a safe in his office.

Micael made provisions for paying the incomes and allowances owed to people attached to Mont-l'Évêque who had been named in the wills of the Pontalbas. Their pensions were like taxes on the estate—they had to be paid by whoever owned the land. One of the recipients, Eleonor LeBoeuf, Madame de Miró's chambermaid, had been present at the death of one of Micael's children and signed the village burial register at Mont-l'Évêque. She must have been nearly a hundred when Micael's will was probated. Micael bequeathed 5,000 francs each to her notaries, her two old friends; 3,000 to her former maid and the maid's husband, both of whom lived at the Hôtel Pontalba; 2,000 to her maitre-d'hôtel, René Vincent; 1,000 to her coachman; and 500 each to the three domestics who had been in her service over one year. She left her clothes, except for the desirable pieces, to her new

chambermaid and the housekeeper. Her last testamentary words were to her
son Célestin who, "recognizing that I have tried to benefit his children in the
greatest possible degree, alone should make up for any deficiency" in case
her gifts exceeded her fortune.[56]

The will seems stingy toward the servants, as all such pharaonic disper-
sions do to our egalitarian eyes. But in every other way, there was utter
method in her meanness. She gave Célestin roughly 100,000 dollars' worth
of marble, silver, and Jackson Square. She gave his son Henri 400,000
francs in cash. Henri was still living at home with his parents at Versailles,
and perhaps, like them, was a magician who could make money disappear.
Micael's legacy to Célestin was based on the presumption that he would
never be able to hold on to either money or property, no matter how much
she gave him. On the other hand, she did leave him a permanent income in
the form of rents from New Orleans.

She took care of Célestin's two children whose habits she was sure of. She
believed their father would have nothing to leave them and so she provided
for their future by giving them, in effect, her hôtel on St.-Honoré. The proceeds from its sale were to finance their lifetime allowances, plus 400,000
francs. Alfred and Gaston were thus deprived of any major benefit from the
Hôtel Pontalba and they were stinted in having to share one-half of the Pontalba Buildings, whereas they might have received two-thirds. But they got
all of what was left of Bayou Road, 243 lots worth altogether some 36,000
francs. Moreover, they were to inherit what was unmentioned in Micael's
will, their father's two moneymakers: his apartment houses in Paris which
had already been turned over to them, as well as Migneaux and Mont-
l'Évêque. Their brother would have no part of any of these. And what of
Michel, Alfred's son, whose young life was to be haunted by death and grieving? Why was he treated in such a miserly fashion? There is every reason to
believe that Micael discussed her will thoroughly with all three of her sons
before she presented it to her notary. It was probably decided then that
Michel would eventually become not only his father's heir, but the sole legatee of his bachelor uncle, Gaston, who had always been an inseparable part
of Alfred's household. So he too would be magnificiently fixed, and Micael
knew it.

There were indications throughout the will that Micael was not yet ready
to go gentle into her good night. She referred to constructions at Mont-
l'Évêque which she might make, and bequeathed property on the condition
"that I have not sold it by then." There were still building projects buzzing in

her head, deals to be made, and situations to improve upon. But whether she was ready or not, she did die, on April 20, 1874. No one except her mother had noticed her birth in 1795; her death was much the same. None of her children or grandchildren were in Paris the day she took sick. If she did not rage against the coming darkness, it was because she herself did not know it was coming. She apparently began suffering some undescribed illness on April 19. Someone called a doctor who performed six hundred francs' worth of ministrations and prescribed thirty francs' worth of medicine. She felt well enough to record these expenses in her day book as usual. But by night she must have taken a turn for the worse. A servant remained at her bedside and knew the exact time of her passing; or perhaps she died suddenly and alone, and the concierge who reported her death to the authorities simply guessed at the hour: two forty-five in the morning.[57]

And so her life, her formidable life, as the French might describe it, was over. The two notaries designated to keep Célestin and his brothers apart and to finish her unfinished business found out how much work there was to maintaining the Pontalba family on its exclusive roost in society. Though Micael had paid her monthly debts up to the first of April, 1874, and scrupulously kept her accounts, Moquard and Berçeon still had to deal with the everyday river of payments and papers. There were fees, taxes, and premiums that had to be sent to New Orleans, similar payments due in Paris, and fees for gas, lighting, and sewage. Micael had already paid the yearly expenses for Mont-l'Évêque, but bills remained from the stove setter, blacksmith, stone extractors, carriage repairman, feed supplier, and a few others.

Where the notaries really earned their fee was in handling the younger Célestin, who was always a problem where money was concerned. If there had been any doubt during his mother's life as to whether Célestin was really as rapacious as he seemed, his actions after Micael's death set his record straight: he was. The first proof came from the notary Moquard. Célestin seems to have asked Moquard for a monthly allowance of 2,000 francs, starting ten days after his mother's death. Moquard, though he had watched Micael refuse Célestin's requisitions for years, abashedly handed over the money and recorded it as a funeral expense. Moquard had seen to all the household bills during the four months of taking the estate inventory. He had receipts to show that he had given severance pay to all the servants and paid the funeral expenses down to two plants for the mortuary chapel (60 francs) and a consideration (100 francs) for the Sisters of Hope, who either prepared Micael's body for burial very inexpensively or offered up some costly prayers. Though Moquard attended to all these details, Célestin nevertheless demanded a reimbursement of 500 francs which he said he spent "for the upkeep of the house."[58] Moquard surrendered this money, too, without insisting on receipts for the supposed expenditures.

Everything had thus been dispensed and Berçeon and Moquard were winding up the last threads of the inventory when the notaries disclosed that there had been 31,877.60 francs in the Hôtel Pontalba at the time of Micael's death, which sum they now turned over to Alfred for division among the three sons. The notaries were preparing to gather everyone's signatures and go home; but Célestin was not one to allow loose cash to elude his prehensile touch. He suddenly remembered that he had expended other money during the previous months for which he had not asked compensation. By a remarkable coincidence, his expenses amounted to exactly 31,877.60 francs. Célestin had no receipts, but he did produce his own precise account. It included a sum for funeral flowers; a generous 104.60 francs for tips; "various sums" that he claimed to have given to his imbecile father, amounting to 200 francs; and money expended by his wife, son, and daughter on such things as taxis. Célestin's agent claimed that Célestin had paid the cook 411.15 francs and Micael's chambermaid 421.60, though Moquard had already given these people their wages and dismissed them; that he gave his children their grandmother's pensions for the month of April, though Micael died on the twentieth and had made all the welfare disbursements at the beginning of the month. Célestin declared that his mother had been "in the habit" of giving him and his wife 1,000 francs per month, Edouard and Louise 500 each, and Henri 400; he therefore added another 2,400 francs to what he claimed was owed to him from the succession—this in addition to the pensions Micael provided in her will, which Moquard had commenced paying at the moment of Micael's death. Célestin claimed he bought mourning outfits for the servants to wear to the funeral—the servants who had since departed—at a cost of 1,297.50 francs; candles for the church; an offering for the priest. He even wanted reimbursement for money he claimed he put in the collection plate during his mother's funeral service. Grief had not kept him from remembering the amount: thirty francs. All of these demands were made over a period of two days through an agent, Monsieur Hughes, a man of courage and gall, who faced Alfred, Gaston, and the two notaries in Célestin's place.

Alfred and Gaston made no recorded response to this outrage by their brother. Perhaps they were years past being appalled at anything he did. Moquard, who should have been more jaded concerning Célestin's frauds, fairly sputtered into the margins of the inventory and would have put up furious resistance, but Alfred and Gaston abandoned the money to their brother. Célestin succeeded in seizing the cash in the mortuary house, just as his father had done the night after Micael's mother died. They were both men who knew what they wanted out of death.

By this time, Micael at least was at peace. Her funeral seems to have been small and dignified, neither showy nor stingy. No Masses were offered for the repose of her soul, but her soul probably reposed anyway; in all three floors of her mansion there had been not a rosary, crucifix, picture, or missal to aid her prayers. The day of his mother's death Gaston wrote out his own will, leaving most of his worldly goods to his nephew Michel.[59] The will was already on its way to being registered when Gaston kissed his mother for the last time. He had only a year to grieve, for the next death at 41 rue St.-Honoré was his own, on November 1, 1875, when he was only fifty-four.

Alfred then took on the care of the properties and his father. He moved out of the Hôtel Pontalba and began the process of selling it; but he too was not long for the world. Fourteen months after Gaston's death, Alfred, aged sixty, followed him to the grave, leaving all the real estate in the hands of his wife, Louise d'Estrées, who, judging from abundant leases, managed it well for her young stepson.[60] Michel de Pontalba, fourteen when his grandmother died, is remembered today as "Grandfather," as if he had never been young, much less an orphan. The current Baron de Pontalba recalls that his grandfather Michel spoke of Micael as an intimidating old lady who would fix him with a half-malevolent, half-mischievous glare and pull his ears. Michel died in 1946, the last person to use a horse-drawn buggy at Mont-l'Évêque, the last eyes that looked into *her* eyes. Mont-l'Évêque passed from Michel to his son Alfred, then to its present owner, Baron Henri Delfau de Pontalba; he married the countess next door and manages their two estates, La Victoire and Mont-l'Évêque.[61]

Célestin and Blanche continued to live at Versailles, presumably on the revenues from the Jackson Square houses. Blanche, noting all the attention and appreciation Micael received at her funeral, had perhaps wished she were the corpse; she did not have long to wait, for her own life ended in 1878, four years after Micael's death. Célestin, then sixty-three, remarried within a few months and fathered two more sons. When he died in 1885, his children ranged in age from forty-six (Edouard) to five (Fernand).[62]

Old Célestin was formally alive when Micael died. He was not present at the funeral, since he had long ago reached the stage of his life when he was attended by others but attended nothing himself. When a death certificate was issued for Micael, the sons had to procure a certificate of life for their father in order to prove to the authorities that, though he might be pallid as a fresco, he was indeed still sentient and a legal person.[63] Having outlived most of life's inclemencies, Célestin nearly outlived all his caretakers. He remained on one of the floors of his two-story house, the house Micael had rented for him, supervised by servants until his death at the age of eighty-seven. René Vincent, Micael's faithful helper who had laid her to rest, had moved to 350 St.-Honoré to manage that house. He was with Célestin when death came at four in the morning on August 20, 1878.

Within four years of Micael's death, they were all gone: Gaston, Alfred, Blanche, the elder Célestin. Within eleven years, the younger Célestin was also dead. The fabulous house on rue St.-Honoré was sold to the financier Edmond de Rothschild in 1876. The Pontalba Buildings, though constantly in decline, survived several more generations of Pontalbas. One side was finally purchased by a philanthropist who willed it to the Louisiana State Museum; the other side was bought by a group of businessmen and eventually came into the possession of the city of New Orleans.[64] The renovating that began in the 1930s continues periodically to this day.

Micael is buried in the town of Mont-l'Évêque near *her* estate. She is in a tomb with Célestin, side by side in death as they seldom were in life, near the quiet woods where she walked alone and prayed to be delivered from the place. Her father-in-law, who would not sleep in any room near her, sleeps next to her in the vault.

New Orleans Street Names
Family, Friends, and Intimate Enemies of the Baroness de Pontalba

Alfred — Second son of Micaela and Célestin.

Almonaster — Micael's father, Andrés Almonester.

Andry — In 1811, a large slave uprising began on the plantation of Manuel André (Andry); his son Manuel was murdered.

Antoine — Père Antoine, Father Antonio de Sedella, was Micael's godfather.

Baronne — Carondelet and his Baroness (Baronne) are one block apart.

Benjamin — Judah P. Benjamin (b. 1811) was a member of Jefferson Davis' Confederate cabinet.

Bienville — Ancestor of Pontalba, Jean-Baptiste Le Moyne de Bienville explored the lower Mississippi and founded New Orleans.

Bourbon — France's royal family was deposed during the French Revolution and restored after the fall of Napoleon.

Burthe — New Orleans family mentioned in Micael's letters.

Cabildo — Spanish municipal council of which Micael's father was a member.

Calhoun — John C. Calhoun (1785–1850), U.S. statesman and vice-president (1825–1832), visited New Orleans at the time the Pontalbas were being constructed.

Calvo — Sebastian Marqués de Casa Calvo, one of Almonester's enemies in the *cabildo*, was acting governor of Louisiana from 1799 to 1801.

Canal — The Carondelet Canal was a project to drain New Orleans. In a letter, Micael discussed selling land to someone she archly referred to as "the Countess of Canal."

Cardeñas — Luis Peñalver y Cardeñas, first bishop of Louisiana, brought suit against the Widow Almonester.

Carondelet — Governor of Louisiana and West Florida, 1791–1796.

Casa Calvo — *See* Calvo.

Celeste — Ton-Ton de Pontalba's aunt was Céleste de Macarty.

Celestine — Micael's husband was Célestin.

Chalmette — Victoire and Azélie Chalmet, Micael's aunt and cousin, were her closest family in New Orleans. The Battle of New Orleans was fought on the aunt's plantation.

Chalona
The Widow Chalon entrusted Almonester with handling a dispute involving her land. The Chalon heirs later charged that he misrepresented her claim.

Charbonnet
One of the families that fled from rampaging slaves in the 1811 insurrection.

Claiborne
W. C. C. Claiborne was the first American governor of the territory, later the state of Louisiana (1803–1816). Micael was friendly with the family.

Coralie
Micael's second cousin.

Creole
A person such as Micael, born in the New World though one of her parents was born overseas.

De Armas
Member of the *cabildo,* contemporary of Almonester.

De Bore
Mayor of New Orleans in 1803–1804, Étienne de Boré's plantation was the site of the first large-scale production of granulated sugar. His plantation is the present site of Audubon Park.

Delaronde
The maiden name of Micael's mother.

Derbigny
Pierre Derbigny was a justice of the Louisiana Supreme Court (1813–1820). He assisted in compiling the 1824 Civil Code of Louisiana.

Destrehan
Jean Noël Destréhan married a relative of Micael's and the Pontalbas. His plantation was involved in the 1811 slave revolt.

D'Hemecourt
His survey of New Orleans property was the basis for settling some of Micael's real estate transactions.

Dreux
Guy Dreux, a friend of Pontalba, murdered a slave.

Duffossat
Gui Soniat du Fossat (b. 1726?), a planter, married Françoise Claudine Dreux and had nine children. Micael was friendly with the women in the family.

Dumaine
The duc du Maine was Louis XIV's natural son; the accessories in one of his wife's mansions were eventually bought by Micael for the Hôtel Pontalba.

Fazendville
Pontalba's brother-in-law LeBreton developed a mad infatuation for a Fazende; the affair is described in Pontalba's letters.

Fortier
A family involved in the slave revolt of 1811; Michel Fortier was a colleague of Almonester in the *cabildo.*

Forstall
Nicholas Forstal was a *cabildo* member (1772–1785).

Gallier
James Gallier, Jr., architect of Gallier Hall, was consulted about the Pontalba Buildings and made some sketches for the interiors.

Galvez
As governor of Louisiana (1776–1785), Bernardo de Gálvez secured East and West Florida for Spain.

Gayoso	Manuel Gayoso de Lemos was governor-general of Louisiana and West Florida, 1797–1799.
Iberville	Together with his older brother, Bienville, Pierre Le Moyne d'Iberville explored coastal Louisiana and discovered the entrance to the Mississippi River.
Jackson	Andrew Jackson won the Battle of New Orleans on the plantation of Micael's aunt; he remained Micael's friend.
Jean Lafitte	His band of privateers helped Jackson win the Battle of New Orleans.
Jefferson	Third president of the United States, he authorized the Louisiana Purchase in 1803.
Jewel	Joseph Jewell was Samuel Stewart's foreman on the Pontalba Buildings.
Lafitte	*See* Jean Lafitte.
Lafon	Barthélémy Lafon (b. 1769) was an architect involved in a dispute with Xavier de Pontalba.
Lausat	French commissioner to Louisiana, Pierre Clément de Laussat presided over the brief transfer of Louisiana from Spain to France in 1803.
Lavoisier	French scientist guillotined during the Revolution; his widow, known as Mme. de Rumford, was an acquaintance of Micael's.
Le Moyne	*See* Bienville and Iberville.
Livaudais	Relatives of both Micael and Célestin.
Livingston	Born in 1764, Edward Livingston was a friend of Micael. He was a U.S. senator (1828–1831), secretary of state (1831–1833), and ambassador to France. He was one of the jurists who revised the Louisiana Civil Code of 1824.
Louisa	Micael's mother's name. Louisa Street is near Almonaster Blvd.
Mandeville	Pierre Marigny de Mandeville represented Marshal Ney at the wedding of Célestin and Micael.
Marigny	Bernard Philippe de Marigny (b. 1785), Pierre's son, is mentioned in Pontalba's letters as an obnoxious teenager.
Maxent	Gilbert Antoine de St.-Maxent was a friend of Almonester and father-in-law of Gálvez.
McDonogh	Born in 1779, John McDonogh was a property owner, philanthropist, and famed eccentric. He gave much attention to the education and moral training of his slaves; his profit-sharing scheme enabled some eighty of them to buy their freedom and emigrate en masse to Liberia in 1842. The rumors of a romance between him and Micael are part of New Orleans legend.

Miro | Esteban Rodríguez Miró, interim governor of Louisiana (1782–1785) and governor (1785–1791), was an uncle by marriage of Xavier de Pontalba.

Montegut | A doctor and surgeon in New Orleans, Joseph Montegut treated many Spanish colonial officials, including Almonester and Pontalba.

Moore | Mentioned in Micael's real estate transactions, Thomas Moore (b. 1810) became governor of Louisiana in 1860.

Murat | Married name of Napoleon's sister Pauline.

Napoleon | Micael's husband began his army career as a page to the emperor.

Ney | Micael's husband was aide-de-camp to Marshal Ney.

Onzaga | Governor of Louisiana (1769–1777), Luís Unzaga, like Gálvez, married one of Gilbert Antoine de St.-Maxent's daughters.

O'Reilly | Second governor of Louisiana, Alejandro O'Reilly was related to Pontalba's wife.

Pakenham | Edward Michael Pakenham (b. 1778), commanded the British troops in the Battle of New Orleans, in which he was killed in 1815.

Pakenham Oaks | *See* Pakenham.

Pontalba | Usual designation of the family Delfau de Pontalba.

Poydras | An aborted slave revolt in 1795 began on the plantation of Julien Poydras in Pointe Coupée.

Rampart | Named after the ramparts which marked the city limits in Almonester's day.

Riviere | Madame Rivière's teasing of Micael's mother is described in one of Pontalba's letters.

Robin | Robert Antoine Robin de Logny was a cousin of Pontalba. He married Jeanne Dreux, the daughter of one of Pontalba's friends.

Rothschild | Edmond de Rothschild purchased Micael's mansion in Paris from her sons in 1876.

Rousseau | Micael's cousin and for many years her agent.

St. Avide | Laselve de St. Avid was a cousin to both Madame Almonester and Pontalba. He helped to arrange the dotal contracts that poisoned the marriage between Micael and Célestin.

Salcedo | Manuel de Salcedo (b. 1743?) was about sixty years old when appointed governor of Louisiana in 1799. His wife died in Cuba on route to his post, in which he served from 1801 to 1803.

Segura | The Ségurs were debtors of Almonester; the family was on good terms with Micael later on in Paris.

Sibley — A member of Governor Claiborne's advisory council, John Sibley first visited Louisiana in 1802 and wrote down his impressions.

Slidell — John Slidell was born in New York in 1793. First a U.S. congressman (1843–1845), he was important in state politics in the 1850s, finally becoming a U.S. senator (1853–1861). The city of Slidell, Louisiana, is also named in his honor.

Soniat — *See* Duffossat.

Stewart — Samuel Stewart was the contractor of the Pontalba Buildings.

Ulloa — First ill-fated Spanish governor of Louisiana, appointed in 1765.

Urquhart — Thomas and David Urquhart were businessmen, politicians, and civic leaders. They were agents at various times of both Xavier de Pontalba and Micael, who was friendly with four of the women of the family.

Villere — The Villeré plantation was near the Chalmette place, the scene of the Battle of New Orleans. Micael remained friends with the Villeré ladies.

Notes

Sources frequently cited have been identified by the following abbreviations:

AGI Archivo General de Indias
AGI Catálogo *Catálogo de Documentos del Archivo General de Indias*
AGS Archivo General de Simancas
AN Archives Nationales
Ét. Étude
H-T Howard-Tilton Memorial Library at Tulane University
La. Hist. Ctr. Louisiana Historical Center, New Orleans
LHQ *Louisiana Historical Quarterly*
NONA New Orleans Notarial Archives
NOPL New Orleans Public Library
RE Répertoires d'Études in Archives Nationales, Paris
SD Santo Domingo (the section of AGI dealing with New Orleans)
Spec. Coll.,
Manuscripts Special Collections, Manuscripts Section, Howard-Tilton Library
UNO Earl K. Long Library at the University of New Orleans. Contains Louisiana Supreme Court Records.

INTRODUCTION

1. Spain did not actually take possession of its new colony until May, 1765.
2. For an explanation of Spain's position in Louisiana vis-à-vis France, Britain, the United States, and the Indians, see A. P. Nasatir, *Borderland in Retreat* (Albuquerque, N.M., 1976), 6–50.

I. NEW ORLEANS IN 1795

1. The colony stretched from the Gulf Coast in the south to a desolate and uncertain border along the Missouri River in the north; from the Appalachians in the east to the Rockies in the west. After 1783 the Spanish took over Florida (known as East Florida) and the entire Biloxi-Mobile-Pensacola Gulf Coast (West Florida.) A map clearly illustrating the complicated swapping of territories in the region among the European powers may be found in Charles Gibson's *Spain in America* (New York, 1967), 184; see also p. 96.
2. Letters of Baron Joseph X. Pontalba to His Wife, manuscript letter diary in Pontalba Family Papers, WPA translation, Louisiana Historical Center. Construction of the Carondelet Canal was abandoned after Governor Carondelet left New Orleans.
3. Amos Stoddard, *Sketches Historical and Descriptive of Louisiana* (Philadelphia, 1812), 154. See also C. C. Robin, *Voyage to Louisiana: 1803–1805*, abridged and trans. Stuart O.

Landry, Jr. (New Orleans, 1966); Minter Wood, "Life in New Orleans in the Spanish Period," *Louisiana Historical Quarterly*, XXII (July, 1939), 642–737. The Cabildo and Presbytere had flat tops; mansard roofs and dormer windows were added in 1847. See especially Gilbert C. Din, "The Offices and Functions of the New Orleans Cabildo," *Louisiana History*, XXXVII (Winter, 1996), 5–30. Din quite rightly observes that the building housing the council was the *casa capitular* and was *never* referred to as the Cabildo in the Illustrious Body's records.

4. Letters to His Wife, May 13, 1796. For executions, see Records and Deliberations of the Cabildo, July 20, 1798, Sept. 30, 1803, WPA trans., microfilm, Louisiana Collection, New Orleans Public Library.

5. Records and Deliberations, Sept. 10, 1784; see also Oct. 1, 1779, Nov. 9, 1781. Although the stucco arcades of the French Market were not built until 1813, a roofed strip extended from St. Ann Street to rue de l'Arsenal (Ursuline), under which were stalls of randomly grouped produce.

6. *Ibid.* June 3, 1791, Oct. 21, 1796. Officials constantly inveighed against dumping in the street: "Orders of Miró," *ibid.*, June 1, 1786; Laura Porteous, trans., "A Regulation Concerning the General Police . . . 1795," *LHQ*, VIII (Jan., 1925), 598; "Auto de buen Gobierno de Don Manuel Gayoso de Lemos, 1798," in Special Collections, Manuscripts Section, Howard-Tilton Library at Tulane University. For remarks by contemporaries on the city's filth, see J. A. Robertson, ed., *Louisiana Under the Rule of France, Spain, and the United States (1785–1807)* (Cleveland, 1911), I, 63; [?] Berquin-Duvallon, *Vue de la Colonie Espagnole de Mississipi* (Paris, 1803), 26 ff., 90; Dunbar Rowland, ed., *Official Letter Books of W. C. C. Claiborne, 1801–1816* (Jackson, Miss., 1917), II, 273; Laura Porteous, trans., "Sanitary Conditions in New Orleans Under the Spanish Regime, 1799–1800," *LHQ*, XV (Oct., 1932), 612. Contemporary documents contain many references to deliveries or visits that were prevented because of impassable streets.

7. Laura Porteous, trans., "Index to Spanish Judicial Records of Louisiana, XXXVIII," *LHQ*, XV (Oct., 1932), 686–87.

8. Samuel Wilson, Jr., ed., *Impressions Respecting New Orleans by Benjamin Henry Boneval Latrobe* (1905; rpr. New York, 1951), 41–42.

9. Records and Deliberations, Nov. 11, 1793. See also Oct. 30, 1789; Feb. 14, 19, Apr. 9, 30, 1790; and "Droit de Levée du Baron de Carondelet, 28 juin 1792," French and Spanish Document #209 in La. Hist. Ctr. An arpent was equal to about five-sixths of an acre.

10. Records and Deliberations, June 8, July 13, Oct. 5, 1787; Francisco Gil, *Disertación físico-médica . . . para preservar a los pueblos de veruelas (1784)* (Windsor, Ontario, 1979), 49, Vol. B-2 of *Documenta Novae Hispaniae*; John Duffy, ed., *The Rudolph Matas History of Medicine in Louisiana* (Baton Rouge, 1958), I, 264–65.

11. Berquin-Duvallon, *Vue de la Colonie*, 97.

12. Letters to His Wife, Apr. 20, June 25, July 10, July 17, Sept. 23, Oct. 16, Oct. 22, 1796.

13. Joseph Xavier de Pontalba à Estevan Miró, 6 oct. 1792, manuscript letter diary (in French) in La. Hist. Ctr.

14. *Ibid.*, Sept. 14, 1796. Miró a Pontalba, 26 dic. 1792, Correspondance du Gouverneur Don Estevan Miró à son neveu Joseph Delfau de Pontalba, ms. letter diary (in Spanish, though the title is in French), La. Hist. Ctr.

15. Letters to His Wife, July 24, Sept. 15, Oct. 2, 10, 1796. Pontalba à Miro, 5 sept. 1792, letter diary in La. Hist. Ctr.

16. Duffy, ed., *History of Medicine*, I, 275.

17. Porteous, trans., "Sanitary Conditions in New Orleans," 613.

18. Records and Deliberations, Oct. 27, 1797.

19. Carondelet to las Casas, New Orleans, Feb. 17, July 12, Oct. 26, 1793, Mar. 28, 1794, Despatches of the Spanish Governors of Louisiana, WPA trans. in Spec. Coll., Manuscripts, H-T. See also the long, rambling depositions by informers reporting on people alleged to be French sympathizers in messages of Sept., 1793, and May, 1795. A. P. Nasatir expressed the view that the French in Louisiana were never reconciled to Spanish control, and that during the French Revolution New Orleans was, in Nasatir's words, "filled with jacobins" who were "begging to return to French rule." *Spanish War Vessels on the Mississippi, 1792–1796* (New Haven, 1968), 4–5.

20. Goeau Duffief to Julien Poydras, 1795, "Private and Commercial Correspondence of an Indigo and Cotton Planter, 1794–1800," typescript in La. Hist. Ctr.

21. Poydras to Claude Poydras, Aug. 25, 1796, *ibid.*

22. For the official version of colonial trade, see "Regulations and Royal Tariffs for the Free Commerce of Spain to Louisiana, the Indies, and her other Possessions, 1788," WPA trans., La. Hist. Ctr.

23. Carondelet to las Casas, New Orleans, July 12, 1793, Despatches.

24. Miró to las Casas, Nov. 25, 1790, *ibid.* See also Miró to Don Joseph Espeleta, Aug. 16, 1788; Miró to las Casas, Aug. 12, Oct. 6, Nov. 13, 25, 1790. Even after he left New Orleans, Miró remained preoccupied with the importance of dealing justly with the Indians in Louisiana and securing their loyalty to Spain. See his *Obra*, as he called it, addressed to the Duke de Alcudia in 1793, reprinted in *Publications of Louisiana Historical Society*, IX (1916), 80–85.

25. Miró to las Casas, Aug. 12, 1790, Despatches. See also Vincente Manuel de Zespedes to Domingo Cabello, Dec. 10, 1789; Miró to Espeleta, Nov. 2, 1788; to las Casas, Dec. 12, 1790; to Cabello, May 19, 1790.

26. Miró to las Casas, July 15, Aug. 12, 1791; Sept. 10, 1790.

27. Rowland, ed., *Letter Books of Claiborne*, I, 314.

28. Records and Deliberations, Apr. 30, 1784; "Auto de . . . Gayoso de Lemos, 1798," H-T. Ira Berlin, in *Slaves Without Masters* (New York, 1974), devotes an entire chapter to the argument that free blacks in Spanish Louisiana and on the Gulf Coast were better off than those in the English colonies.

29. Porteous, trans., "A Regulation Concerning the General Police," 598.

30. "Orders of Miró," Records and Deliberations, June 1, 1786. Some scholars have attempted to dispel what they consider is a myth concerning the pampered life of the quadroon concubine. See Eugene D. Genovese, "Free Negroes," in *Neither Slave nor Free*, ed. David W. Cohen and Jack P. Greene (Baltimore, 1972), 258–77.

31. Records and Deliberations, Aug. 27, Oct. 8, 15, 1773; Apr. 30, May 28, June 4, 14, 1784. Although the whites made legal distinctions between free Negroes and slaves, they looked on all people of color as belonging to the same category. The free Negroes of mixed blood, however, looked on themselves as a group apart. Unlike blacks in America today, who often consider themselves black regardless of light skin color or mixed blood, free Negroes in 1795 carefully distinguished themselves, and were often distinguished on official documents, as mulattoes, quadroons, or octoroons. See Alice Dunbar-Nelson, "People of Color in Louisiana," *Journal of Negro History*, I (1916), 361–76.

32. Claiborne to Robert Smith, Jan. 14, 1811, in Rowland, ed., *Letter Books of Claiborne*, V, 100.

33. Records and Deliberations, Apr. 30, 1784.

34. *Ibid.*, Mar. 7, Apr. 18, 1788; Feb. 20, 1789; Sept. 17, 1790. *Cimarron* was first used in reference to domestic animals that escaped into the woods; later the term was applied to fugitive slaves.

35. Records and Deliberations, July 3, 1790. The Spanish revised the French Black Code that was in place when they took over Louisiana and supplemented their regulations with later edicts.

36. "Orders of Miró" in Records and Deliberations, Apr. 30, 1784; "Auto de . . . Gayoso de Lemos, 1798," H-T.

37. Las Casas to Carondelet, June 15, 1795, Carondelet to Godoy, Mar. 30, Apr. 1, 1796, Despatches; Records and Deliberations, June 20, 1795.

38. Poydras to Claude Poydras, "Private and Commercial Correspondence," Aug. 25, 1796. Carondelet to las Casas, Apr. 14, 1792; June 30, July 25, 1795; Carondelet to Council of the Indies, May 1, 1795, Despatches. Carondelet claimed he was pressured by the planters to make examples of the slave rebels. After investigating, the Crown judged that the governor had acted properly in executing all but one of the slaves, and for that too-hasty execution, fined him three hundred pesos. Carondelet gave several reasons to his superiors for the mildness of his punishment of the three whites, which was carried out without a trial. Mainly, he feared that a trial might stir up more controversy and sympathy among the French Creoles, and it was better to get rid of the troublemakers quickly.

39. Records and Deliberations, May 3, 1795; Carondelet to las Casas, May 3, 1795, Despatches. Not everyone in the song was to be punished. The Intendant "has nothing to fear if he remains the same good man." The slaves promised never to forget his kindness.

40. As early as Jan. 16, 1793, Carondelet began begging las Casas for "at least 200 men from Havana, all Spaniards, or else men from the Negro battalion who have their families there and will surely be reliable." Carondelet commented that the houses in Pointe Coupée were scattered on both banks of the river and separated by a distance of one-fourth to one-half league. Carondelet to las Casas, July 30, 1795; las Casas to Carondelet, Havana, June 15, 1795, Despatches.

41. Letters to His Wife, Mar. 27, 28, 29, 30, 1796.

42. *Ibid.*, Feb. 25, 1796.

43. Carlos de la Torre Reyes, *La Revolución de Quito del 10 Agosto de 1809* (Quito, 1961), 153 ff.

44. The interrogation and sentencing of slaves involved in the rebellion is recorded in uncatalogued manuscripts bound in a volume, "1810–1811, Original Acts, Judge Pierre B. St. Martin, St. Charles Parish Records of Commandants, Judges, and Recorders, 1734–1871," located in St. Charles Parish Courthouse, Hahnville, La. I am indebted to Charles Oubre, St. Charles Parish clerk of court, Harold L. Montegut, Jr., clerk of court of St. John the Baptist Parish, and also to my former student Ann. M. Ball, who directed me to the records. For Governor Claiborne's comments on the uprising, see Claiborne to Major St. Amand [St. Amant], Jan. 9, 1811, and Claiborne to John M. Destrehan, Jan. 19, 1811, in Rowland, ed., *Letter Books of Claiborne*, V, 94, 107. The Major André of the documents was also known as Andry. François Trepagnier, one of the two white victims of the revolt, had been questioned by Carondelet in 1795 concerning a charge made by some blacks that Trepagnier was planning to arm the slaves in his area for a revolt. A search of Trepagnier's plantation was made; no arms were found. See Carondelet to las Casas, May 9–11, 1795, Despatches.

45. Nasatir, *Spanish War Vessels on the Mississippi*, 29.

46. For judicial and certain other matters, the captain-general went through the viceroy in Mexico before the communication reached the Crown.

47. Francisco Luis Héctor, Baron de Carondelet, de Noyelles, Seigneur d'Haine St.-Pierre. Thomas Marc Fiehrer's "The Baron de Carondelet as Agent of Bourbon Reform" (Ph.D. dissertation, Tulane University, 1977) is an exhaustive study of Carondelet's administrative career. See also Carl A. Brasseaux, "François-Louis Hector, Baron de Carondelet et Noyelles," in *The Louisiana Governors: From Iberville to Edwards*, ed. Joseph G. Dawson (Baton Rouge, 1990) 64–69.

48. Miró a Pontalba, 17 junio 1792, letter diary in La. Hist. Ctr.

49. For information concerning Miró, Carondelet, Gayoso, and the intendant, Martin Navarro, see Nasatir, *Spanish War Vessels on the Mississippi*. Caroline M. Burson's *The Stewardship of Don Esteban Miró, 1782–92* (New Orleans, 1940) is the major work on his governorship; see also J. D. L. Holmes, *Gayoso* (Baton Rouge, 1965).

50. One of Salcedo's many detractors whose comments have found their way into the standard histories of the period was the French commissioner assigned to oversee the transfer of Louisiana from Spain. See Pierre Clément de Laussat, *Memoirs of My Life*, trans. Agnes-Josephine Pastwa, ed. Robert D. Bush (Baton Rouge, 1978) I, 28. For Casa Calvo's self-important airs, see Rowland, ed., *Letter Books of Claiborne*, II, 266–67.

51. "Plan Showing Location of Fire—March 21st 1788," ms. in La. Hist. Ctr; Miró to Espeleta, New Orleans, Apr. 1, 1788, Despatches.

52. Records and Deliberations, Dec. 19, 1794; Oct. 9, 1795. A fire broke out in 1792, but was controlled before there was much damage.

53. Samuel Wilson, Jr., *The Cabildo* (New Orleans, 1961), 62.

54. Records and Deliberations, July 17, Sept. 4, Dec. 4, 1795.

55. Laura Porteous, "Torture in Spanish Criminal Procedure," *LHQ*, VIII (Jan., 1925), 20.

56. Records and Deliberations, Aug. 22, 1792. Laws set forth by the Council of Castile and the Council of the Indies quoted by Charles Gayarré, *History of Louisiana*, 3rd ed. (New Orleans, 1885), III, 13.

57. Records and Deliberations, Apr. 3, 1798.

58. John Lynch, *Spanish Colonial Administration, 1782–1810* (London, 1958), 204. For a long overdue study of the municipal council, see Gilbert C. Din and John E. Harkins, *The New Orleans Cabildo: Colonial Louisiana's First City Government, 1769–1803* (Baton Rouge, 1996). Neither this book nor Din's insightful article "The Offices and Functions of the New Orleans Cabildo" was published in time to benefit the present work.

59. Records and Deliberations, Apr. 15, 1785.

60. *Ibid.*, Mar. 18, 1785.

61. Bartolomi Bennasser, *The Spanish Character: Attitudes and Mentalities from the Sixteenth to the Nineteenth Century*, trans. Benjamin Keen (Berkeley, 1975), translator's preface.

62. Quoted in Rafael Altamira, *A History of Spain: From the Beginnings to the Present Day*, trans. Muna Lee (Princeton, N. J., 1949), 458.

63. Usually they did not. Describing church services, Dr. John Sibley wrote: "Few Gentlemen except the Officers attend, but the Ladies Generally go Once a day in high dress, in parties, stay about a quarter of an Hour & return. . . ." G. P. Whittington, ed., "The Sibley Papers, Journal and Letters," *LHQ*, X (1927), 478. His observation is

confirmed by Robin, *Voyage to Louisiana*, 58. In daily letters to his wife, Pontalba never mentions hearing Mass.

64. Miró quoted in Edwin A. Davis, *Louisiana: A Narrative History* (Baton Rouge, 1971), 143.

65. Carondelet quoted in Nasatir, *Spanish War Vessels on the Mississippi*, 339.

66. Burson, *Stewardship of Miró*, 282; Robin, *Voyage to Louisiana*, 58.

67. Pontalba à Miró, 6 oct. 1792, letter diary in La. Hist. Ctr.

68. Records and Deliberations, June 17, 1796.

69. Robin, *Voyage to Louisiana*, 37.

70. Letters to His Wife, Oct. 11, 1796.

71. Miró quoted in Burson, *Stewardship of Miró*, 240–41. Miró was not the only governor who complained of not being able to live on his salary. Carondelet in his dispatches dropped periodic, desperate hints that he needed a raise.

72. "Cuenta Corrte. de d. Josef Reynes y d. Pedro Ancil, 7 dic. 1797," and "Debe y dedro Don Pedro Ancil y Compañíacon Don Josef Reynes, 7 dic. 1798," mss. in John Smith Collection, La. Hist. Ctr.; *Le Moniteur*, Nos. 333 and 334, and *Supplément*, 5 mars, 6 mars, 1803. Compare these with the import and export reports of *Le Moniteur*, No. 304, 14 août 1802, and with F. X. Martin's tables in *History of Louisiana* (New Orleans, 1882), 313 ff.

73. Letters to His Wife, Sept. 11, 1796; Poydras to James Freret, Oct. 25, 1800, "Private and Commercial Correspondence"; order for foodstuffs from J. de Castenedo, 18 mayo 1795, in John Smith Coll., La. Hist. Ctr.

74. Prices: "Cuenta Corrte." and "Debe y dedro"; wine imports: *Le Moniteur*, No. 333, 5 mars 1803 and *Supplément*; whiskey imports: Edward Channing, *A History of the United States* (New York, 1917), IV, 311–12; Martin, *History of Louisiana*, 313.

75. Claiborne to James Madison, Jan. 31, 1804, in Rowland, ed., *Letter Books of Claiborne*, I, 355.

76. Records and Deliberations, Nov. 18, 1803.

77. Quoted in Burson, *Stewardship of Miró*, 241.

78. Porteous, trans., "A Regulation Concerning the General Police," 578.

79. Pontalba à Miró, 21 avril 1792, letter diary in La. Hist. Ctr.

80. Letters to His Wife, Mar. 19, Apr. 27, May 9, June 17, Oct. 17, 1796; see also Laussat, *Memoirs*, II, 81.

81. "Orders of Miró," Records and Deliberations, June 1, 1786; "Auto de . . . Gayoso de Lemos, 1798," H-T; imports in Martin, *History of Louisiana*, 313.

82. Miró a Pontalba, 17 junio, 24, 25 sept., 26 dic. 1792, letter diary in La. Hist. Ctr.

83. *Le Moniteur*, No. 333, 5 mars 1803 and *Supplément*; "Occupational Chart of New Orleans," in Burson, *Stewardship of Miró*, 246; Martin, *History of Louisiana*, 313; Robin, *Voyage to Louisiana*, 45. For an interesting description of shoe purchases for a family and slaves for a period of several months, see "An Account of Purchases by Joseph Vidal, Feb. 5, 1789," ms. in John Smith Coll., La. Hist. Ctr.

84. "Inventory of the Estate of Sieur Jean Baptiste Prévost," LHQ, IX (1926), 411–98; Martin, *History of Louisiana*, 313. On the other hand, Carlos d'Aunoy, who owned more than 100 slaves, left no wigs, only 17 vests, and 24 "very old shirts"; "Intestate Succession of Carlos Favre d'Aunoy, Oct. 10, 1780," WPA trans., La. Hist. Ctr.

85. Porteous, trans., "Index to Spanish Judicial Records," 686–87.

86. See "Proceedings related to the estate of Francisco Maria de Reggio, 5 oct. 1787," Spanish Document #1635 in La. Hist. Ctr.

87. Burson, *Stewardship of Miró*, 246.

88. Letters to His Wife, July 17, also Mar. 21, July 13, 1796.

89. Roger P. McCutcheon, "Books and Booksellers in New Orleans, 1730–1830," *LHQ*, XX (July, 1937), 607.

90. *Ibid.*, 614.

91. Berquin-Duvallon, *Vue de la Colonie*, 295.

92. *Ibid.*

93. Pontalba à Miró, 21 avril 1792, letter diary in La. Hist. Ctr.

94. Stoddard, *Sketches Historical and Descriptive*, 308.

95. *Le Moniteur*, No. 304, 14 août 1802; *Supplément* to No. 341–43.

96. John G. Clark, *New Orleans, 1718–1812: An Economic History* (Baton Rouge, 1970).

97. "Summary of a Representation by Gilbert Antoine de St. Maxent Relative to the Commerce of West Florida and Louisiana," in Arthur P. Whitaker, ed., *Documents Relating to the Commercial Policy of Spain in the Floridas, with Incidental Reference to Louisiana* (New York, 1931). The summary, dated Oct. 4, 1781, offers many insights into the contraband trade. See also Miró to Don Joseph de Espeleta, Mar. 1, 1788, Despatches; Michael O'Connor to Nicholas Low and Company, Oct. 31, Nov. 24, 1783, in Robert Smith and Nicholas Low Papers, 1782–1811, Spec. Coll., Manuscripts, H-T. In both its legal and illegal trade, Louisiana always bought more than it sold; the difference was made up with specie from Spain.

98. The terms of the treaty were: Americans were to have free navigation of the Mississippi River, that is, without having to pay export taxes. They were permitted to deposit their goods at New Orleans for three years while waiting for overseas ships to call for them. They could re-export them duty free. The treaty also established the boundary of West Florida. As a result of all these concessions, Americans began taking advantage of Spain's liberal immigration policies; a large amount of Spanish land was given free to settlers up until 1798.

99. Letters to His Wife, July 8, 14, and 21, 1796.

100. Letters to His Wife, Oct. 17, 1796.

101. Claiborne to James Madison, in Rowland, ed., *Letter Books of Claiborne*, I, 358–59.

102. *Courier de la Louisiane*, 30 août 1809.

II. ALMONESTER

1. Records and Deliberations of the Cabildo, Nov. 6, 1795, WPA trans., microfilm, Louisiana Collection, New Orleans Public Library.

2. The village was Mayrena del Alcor; see Eric Beerman, "Colonial Andrés Almonester," New Orleans *Genesis*, XVIII (Sept., 1978), 389–94. Almonester's birth year would be 1725 if we deduced it from his age on his tombstone and from Funeral Records of St. Louis Cathedral, April 26, 1798, Archives of the Archdiocese of N.O. The tombstone and funeral record were not necessarily accurate; Madame Almonester probably provided information for them at the time of her husband's death. Beerman used Almonester's baptismal certificate as his source; moreover, in military records, which were generally precise, Almonester's age reflects a birth date of 1728. See Archivo General de Simancas, (hereafter cited as AGS), Hojas de Servícios Militares de America, 1785–1815, dic. 1796 and dic. 1797, ms. in Latin American Library in Howard-Tilton Library at Tulane University.

3. Rafael Altamira, *A History of Spain: From the Beginnings to the Present Day*, trans. Muna Lee (Princeton, N. J., 1949), 470.

4. "Mercurio Historico y Politico," Madrid, May, 1761, quoted in W. N. Hargreaves-Mawdsley, *Spain Under the Bourbons, 1700–1833: A Collection of Documents* (Columbia, S. C., 1973), 125.

5. Records and Deliberations, Jan. 22, Feb. 1, 12, Mar. 11, 1796; Edouard de Pontalba à J. W. Cruzat, 20 oct. 1902, Correspondance de Baron Edouard de Pontalba, 1904–1914, in Cruzat Family Papers, Special Collections, Manuscripts Section, Howard-Tilton Library at Tulane University.

6. Will of Andrés Almonester, Spanish Document #3166, Aug. 20, 1794, WPA trans. in Louisiana Historical Center.

7. Records of Andrés Almonester, Mar. 20, 1770, New Orleans Notarial Archives, hereafter cited as NONA; Records and Deliberations, Mar. 16, 1770; the king's edict naming Almonester Public Secretary for War and the Royal Treasury was dated Aug 11, 1765, although royal confirmation of the post was not issued until 1773, according to *cabildo* records of May 13, 1774. This sort of delay between appointment and confirmation was customary and gave the recipient time to send to Spain the purchase price of the office, plus tax and proof of the "purity" of his blood. Notary Public of War was one of the positions usually appointed by the governor, though not in this case. Berquin-Duvallon wrote that Almonester landed in New Orleans "poor as Job but less scrupulous," *Vue de la Colonie Espagnol du Mississipi* (Paris, 1803), 200. That view of Almonester as a penniless adventurer was then copied by subsequent writers.

8. Laura Porteous, "Torture in Spanish Criminal Procedure," *Louisiana Historical Quarterly*, VIII (Jan., 1925), 5–27. For the rewards of the office and methods of payment, see J. H. Parry, *The Sale of Public Office in the Spanish Indies Under the Hapsburgs* (Berkeley, 1953), 6.

9. Records of Almonester, Mar. 20, 1770—May 28, 1782, NONA; José de la Peña y Camara, *et al.*, eds., *Catálogo de Documentos del Archivo General de Indias (Sección V. Gobierno-Audiencia de Santo Domingo) sobre la época española de Luisiana* (New Orleans, 1968), I, Santo Domingo #2547, No. 1392, Nueva Orleans, 27 mayo 1779, hereafter cited as *AGI Catálogo*.

10. Records of J. B. Garic, Jan. 23, 1771, NONA. The two sides had been the site of decayed barracks that were demolished in 1759 and had not been rebuilt. The lots were actually offered for perpetual lease, the yearly rent (132 pesos) being a kind of city tax. It was the leases that were transferred to Almonester, beginning in 1774. He finally did get ownership title just before he died; Records and Deliberations, Apr. 3, 1798.

11. He leased a house on Levée and St. Peter: Records of J. B. Garic, Nov. 4, 1808, NONA; bought and sold acreage on Bayou St. John and bought a plantation near Bayou Road: Spanish Doc. #1846, 18 ago. 1788, La. Hist. Ctr; and bought a tract of land in Metairie from the Capuchin monks: Act of Sale, Almonester to Mauricio Conway, 1791, Spec. Coll., Manuscripts, H-T.

12. Quoted by Edouard de Pontalba to Cruzat, 20 oct. 1902, Spec. Coll., Manuscripts, H-T.

13. A Marie Almonester, a free quadroon whose brother had the surname Barbe, died in 1821, leaving an estate inventoried by Michel de Armas. Margarita Tecla Carmelita Almonester was born June 10, 1793. Her godmother, one Maria Alom, was incidentally allowed a divorce in 1796, according to records of Carlos Ximenes, NONA. Maria Antonia

Almonester was abandoned on Sept. 18, 1798, and was raised by someone named Levia, a worker at Charity Hospital; Earl C. Woods, *Sacramental Records of the Roman Catholic Church of the Archdiocese of New Orleans* (New Orleans, 1987), V, 4.

14. Albert Robichaux, Jr., ed., *Louisiana Census and Militia Lists, 1770–1789* (New Orleans, 1973), 50.

15. *AGI Catálogo,* Santo Domingo #2555, No. 2771, Miró a Valdez, Nueva Orleans, 31 jul. 1789. This document deals with St. Maxent's reimbursements to Almonester. For settlement of the case and freeing of St. Maxent's funds, see *AGI Catálogo,* 10 Oct. 1787, SD #2611, Navarro a Valdez, Nueva Orleans. When he retired as colonel of the militia, St. Maxent proposed Almonester as his successor.

16. "Picaro adulador," Miró a Pontalba, 17 jun. 1792, Correspondance du Gouverneur Don Estevan Miró à son neveu Joseph Delfau de Pontalba, ms. letter diary, La. Hist. Ctr. Guillemard was the nephew of both St. Maxent and Sedella. With such kinsmen, it is no wonder Miró disparaged him.

17. Miró-Sedella letters, No. 249, Box 3, Folder 8, Cruzat Family Papers, Spec. Coll., Manuscripts, H-T; F. L. Gassler, "Père Antoine, supreme officer of the holy inquisition . . . in Louisiana," *Catholic Historical Review,* II (1922), 59–63.

18. Caroline M. Burson, *The Stewardship of Don Esteban Miró, 1782–92* (New Orleans, 1940), 240; Almonester's lending: Spanish Doc. #910, 31 enero 1784; #1846, 1788; #1045, 10 ago. 1788; #1029, 16 feb. 1789; #2320, 20 nov. 1789; #2699, 7 feb. 1791, La. Hist. Ctr.

19. Records and Deliberations, Sept. 18, 1778; Apr. 30, June 10, 1785. An excellent account of the struggle between the governors and the *cabildo* for control of the hospital is Stella O'Connor, "The Charity Hospital of Louisiana," *LHQ,* XXXI (Jan., 1948), 12–28. John Duffy also gives a good account of the dispute in the volume he edited: *The Rudolph Matas History of Medicine in Louisiana* (Baton Rouge, 1958), I, 250 ff. An interesting early document concerning the hospital during the French period is "Condemnation of Villeneuve, workman, for killing dogs and selling them as edible meat to the hospital," Spanish Doc. PC-A23–3, Sept. 13, 1723, La. Hist. Ctr. John Salvaggio, in *New Orleans' Charity Hospital: A Story of Physicians, Politics, and Poverty* (Baton Rouge, 1992), brings the history of the hospital up to modern times.

20. Records and Deliberations, Dec. 13, 1782, Mar. 20, 1783; Almonester's petition in *AGI Catálogo,* SD #2531, No. 34.

21. "Constitution for the New Charity Hospital New Orleans, 1793," WPA trans., La. Hist. Ctr. It is not certain whether the orphanage was ever constructed as a building, or whether Almonester contented himself with providing for the maintenance of the children in the homes of the "housekeepers" employed by the hospital, as he suggested (p. 26).

22. "Constitution for Charity Hospital," 28, 30, 32, 33 ff. For the rules governing colonial hospitals, see *Constituciones y ordenazas para el régimen y gobierno del Hospital Real y General de los Indios de esta Nueva España (1778),* Vol. B-1 of *Documenta Novae Hispaniae* (Windsor, Ontario, 1980).

23. "Inventory and delivery of the effects and utensils of the Charity Hospital, April 17, 1801," ms. in H-T. For inventory of 1794, see Duffy, ed., *History of Medicine,* I, 254–55.

24. Records and Deliberations, Nov. 26, 1786. Almonester made three proposals to which the *cabildo* made various contrived objections. For example, the cattle ranch he offered was deemed an unreliable source of income "due to a plague that from time to

time spreads among black cattle in this vicinity." Almonester's fourth offer, which was accepted, was to donate the rental from six stores on the bottom floor of his own residence on the plaza, amounting to 1,500 pesos a year. He donated several slaves and agreed to repair five houses given to the hospital in previous years so that these could produce revenue.

25. Miró quoted in Lauro A. de Rojas, "The Great Fire of 1788 in New Orleans," *LHQ*, XX (July, 1937), 584; Miró to Porlier, Aug. 10, 1790, Despatches of the Spanish Governors of Louisiana, WPA trans. in Spec. Coll., Manuscripts, H-T.

26. Records and Deliberations, Apr. 27, 1785; Dr. Paul Aliot to Jefferson, April, 1804, in J. A. Robertson, ed., *Louisiana Under the Rule of France, Spain, and the United States (1785–1807)* (Cleveland, 1911), I, 97.

27. Quoted in Lawrence Kinnaird, ed., *Spain in the Mississippi Valley, 1765–1794* (Washington, D.C., 1946–49), II, 373. In Robertson, ed., *Louisiana Under the Rule*, I, 97, Aliot refers to there having been some "two score lepers" at one point. The facility was badly neglected after Almonester's death, as there were no more lepers to use the hospital after about 1808. It then became the run-down refuge of Indians who allegedly burned it down. Micaela inherited the remainder of the property.

28. Roger Baudier, *The Catholic Church in Louisiana* (New Orleans, 1931), 217; J. Edgar Bruns, *Archbishop Antoine Blanc Memorial* (New Orleans, 1981), 33, 36; Records and Deliberations, Aug. 14, 1794. On surveys of the 1780s, the Ursulines' old chapel was designated "Ancient Church." The new chapel, 114 by 45 feet, faced Ursuline Street on the site later occupied by St. Mary's Italian School, now demolished.

29. Records and Deliberations, Aug. 19, 1788, Oct. 12, 1789.

30. Records of L. Mazange, May 3, 1783, NONA.

31. Robichaux, in *Census and Militia Lists*, 30, reproduces part of the Campderos census.

32. The plantation of Louison's half-brother, Ignace de Lino de Chalmet, has been restored nearby; it is the site of the 1815 Battle of New Orleans.

33. Records and Deliberations, Oct. 18, 1789.

34. Spanish Doc. #1113, La. Hist. Ctr., refers to the number of slaves. In Spanish Doc. #1071, May 21, 1785, Almonester charges one of the boyfriends with theft. It was characteristic of Spanish American cities that eminent citizens should have their residences on the central plaza next to public offices. Social classes, in fact, distributed themselves outward from the plaza. Medical treatment reported in J. D. Holmes, "Dramatis Personae in Spanish Louisiana," *Louisiana Studies*, VI (Summer, 1967), 183.

35. Henry Dart, "Courts and Law in Colonial Louisiana," *LHQ*, VIII (Jan., 1925), 275.

36. Carondelet to las Casas, Aug. 20, 1792, Despatches.

37. "Proceedings instituted by Bishop Luis Peñalver y Cardenas vs. Widow Almonester, 1799–1801," WPA trans. of ms. in La. Coll., NOPL, 55. Almonester begins petitioning for "some grace": *AGI Catálogo*, SD #2549, No. 252, 28 abr. 1787.

38. Ordinances of O'Reilly, quoted by Dart, "Courts and Law," 277.

39. Spanish Doc. #2304, 24 oct. 1789; #2033, 24 abr. 1793; fight: #2205, 27 jun. 1789, La. Hist. Ctr. The records, now barely legible because of age and with parts missing, do not show how Almonester resolved the last case.

40. Records and Deliberations, Mar. 1, 1793; Mar. 20, 1795.

41. *Ibid.*, Jan. 28, Apr. 20, 1792; Oct. 29, 1791.

42. *Ibid.*, Feb. 1, 1793; Jan. 22, Feb. 12, Mar. 11, 1796; Dec. 22, 1797.

43. *Ibid.*, May 2, 29, June 20, 1795; Jan. 22, 1796; July 3, 1797; Jan. 19, 1787; Sept. 12, Oct. 3, 1788. The hangman insisted on a raise after he was required to perform four executions in a year; Records of the New Orleans City Council, Sept. 4, 1804, NOPL.

44. Records and Deliberations, Oct. 21, Nov. 11, Dec. 2, 1791.

45. Carondelet to las Casas, Aug. 20, 1792, Despatches.

46. Records and Deliberations, Jan. 17, 1796.

47. *Ibid.*, Apr. 25, 1795; Carondelet to las Casas, Apr. 29, 1795, Despatches.

48. Records and Deliberations, Oct. 7, 1797. Six members were eventually added, so that there were twelve by the end of the Spanish period.

49. *Ibid.*, May 29, 1795.

50. Edict recorded in Records and Deliberations, Aug. 14, 1794.

51. Miró a Pontalba, 3 dic. 1794, letter diary, La. Hist. Ctr.; Records and Deliberations, Aug. 14, 1794 .

52. The petitions sent by Almonester to the Crown (through the usual channel of the captain-general of Cuba) are impersonal business letters similar to communications we might send today to the Social Security Administration. We can see from the microfilms presently in the Historic New Orleans Collection that some of the original manuscripts (in the Archivo General de Indias in Seville) are illegible and disintegrating, while others are clear and sound. Several published catalogues guide us to those documents in the archive that deal with Louisiana; the catalogues briefly summarize the contents of each letter or petition.

53. *AGI Catálogo*, 28 abr. 1787, SD #2549, No. 252; 1 jun. 1787, SD #1891; Miró a Porlier, 12 feb. 1789, SD #2553, No. 2312; 3 abr. 1790, SD #2553, No. 2330; Records and Deliberations, Mar. 18, 1791; Mar. 18, 1796.

54. Gálvez to Diego Joseph Navarro, Aug. 20, 1779, Despatches.

55. Almonester's appointment: *AGI Catálogo*, Miró a Valdez (includes memorandum from St. Maxent), 31 jul. 1789, SD #2553, No. 2215; Miró a Valdez, 16 mar. 1790, SD #2555, No. 2771. Duties: Carondelet to las Casas, Aug. 12, 1790, and Philipe Trevino to Carondelet, June 14, 1792, Despatches.

56. Pontalba à Miró, 20 mai 1794, letter diary in Pontalba Family Papers, WPA trans., La. Hist. Ctr.; Archivo General de Simancas, Hojas del Batalion de Milícias Disciplinades de Nueva Orleans, dic. 1797, ms. in Latin Amer. Lib., H-T.

57. Miró to Porlier, Aug. 10, 1790, Despatches; Records and Deliberations, Apr. 14, 1788; Dec. 12, 1789.

58. *AGI Catálogo*, Miró a Porlier, 25 nov. 1789, SD #2554, No. 2322; for amounts paid by Almonester for lineage research and other costs, see Records and Deliberations, July 21, 1797.

59. Miró to Porlier, Aug. 10, 1790, Despatches; *AGI Catálogo*, 28 abr. 1787, SD #2549, No. 252; Miró a J. de Gálvez, 1 jun. 1787, SD #2553, No. 1891; Miró a Porlier, 12 nov. 1788, SD #2553, No. 2310; 12 feb. 1789, SD #2553, No. 2313; 3 abr. 1790, SD #2330; 20 ago. 1790, SD #2554, Nos. 2335 and 2336.

60. Carondelet to las Casas, Aug. 20, 1792, Despatches.

61. The Heirs of Joseph Chalon vs. M. L. A. de Pontalba, Nov. 28, 1837, First District Court, No. 14.832; The Heirs of Joseph Chalon and Marie Elizabeth Desruisseaux vs. M. L. A. de Pontalba, Jan. 15, 1838, First District, No. 15.126, mss. in NOPL; "Transaction Heriteurs Chalon avec Mme. de Pontalba," Nov. 8, 1839, Records of Felix Grima, NONA.

62. Miró to Ezpeleta, Dec. 3, 1789, Despatches.

63. AGS, Hojas de Servícios, jun. 1792, leg. 7291, C. 3, Latin Amer. Lib., H-T; Carondelet to las Casas, Aug. 20, 1792, Despatches.

64. Carondelet to las Casas, Sept. 17, 1794; Aug. 20, 1792; Apr. 30, 1796, Despatches; Carondelet to Bouligny, Nov. 20, 1793, in Spec. Coll., Manuscripts, H-T; AGS, Hojas de Servícios, dic. 1796, leg. 7292, C. 6, Latin Amer. Lib., H-T.

65. Carondelet to las Casas, Sept. 17, 1794, Despatches; Pontalba à Miró, 5 sept. 1792, letter diary, La. Hist. Ctr.

66. Carondelet to las Casas, Jan. 10, 23, 1793; las Casas to Carondelet, Mar. 6, 1793, Despatches.

67. Baudier, *Catholic Church in Louisiana*, 226.

68. Records and Deliberations, May 2, 1795; Oct. 13, 1793; Pontalba à Miró, 26 avril 1792, letter diary, La. Hist. Ctr.

69. Records and Deliberations, Nov. 6, 1795, Jan. 8. 1795. The controversy is well laid out in "Legal Action to Take Possession of the Charity Hospital of St. Charles by . . . Almonester . . . 1794," WPA trans. in Spec. Coll., Manuscripts, H-T. In trying to complete the priest's house, Almonester was similarly hampered by lawsuits.

70. The architectural transformations of the three buildings are described in several short books by Leonard V. Huber and Samuel Wilson, Jr., particularly in *The Basilica on Jackson Square* (New Orleans, 1966), 29–40.

71. Letters of Baron Joseph X. Pontalba to His Wife, Sept. 8, 1796, ms. letter diary in Pontalba Family Papers, WPA trans., La. Hist. Ctr.; for Almonester's certified genealogy, see Records and Deliberations, July 21, 1797.

72. *AGI Catálogo*, las Casas a Azanza, 13 dic. 1796, SD #2566. Louison did not give up the quest for the title after his death and filed posthumous petitions on his behalf: 11 abr. 1804, SD #2531, No. 34. Almonester first applied for the title in 1789.

73. Records and Deliberations, Jan. 16, 1795; July 21, Sept 30, 1797.

74. *Ibid.*, Oct. 20, 1797 (three days after the birth of his second child).

75. *Ibid.*, Nov. 3, 1797.

76. *Ibid.*, July 21, 1797. The painting, owned by the Archdiocese of New Orleans, is usually exhibited in the Louisiana State Museum, New Orleans.

77. ". . . by reason of the disablement of the hand which my present illness causes, I shall not be able to sign. . . ." Will of Andrés Almonester, WPA trans., La. Coll., NOPL, one of several slightly different versions.

78. Funeral Records of St. Louis Cathedral, 26 abr. 1798, ms. in Archives of the Archdiocese of New Orleans. Though the Charity Hospital was moved, the cemetery still remains at the corner of Toulouse and Rampart Streets. Almonester's remains were then installed within St. Louis Cathedral, a customary burial place for high officials. Almonester and, later on, his younger daughter were at first entombed in front of the Altar of the Virgin; both were then moved to another location in the church, before finding a final resting place in the outdoor cemetery behind the cathedral.

79. Records and Deliberations, Apr. 4, 1798. Duffy, ed., *History of Medicine*, I, 262. The doctor who made the inspection, Louis Giovellina, was Almonester's appointee for the chief physician of Charity Hospital. Two years after his report of the hospital, the *cabildo* blamed Giovellina for the spread of smallpox in the colony and recommended to the governor that the doctor be imprisoned. Records of the New Orleans City Council, Mar. 5, 1802.

80. Records and Deliberations, July 11, 1800.
81. Edouard de Pontalba à J. W. Cruzat, 18 juin 1904, Spec. Coll., Manuscripts, H-T.

III. PONTALBA

1. Letters of Baron Joseph X. Pontalba to His Wife, Feb. 24–Nov. 10, 1796, ms. letter diary in Pontalba Family Papers, Louisiana Historical Center, WPA translations except where noted. The translator renders *amie* as "Sweetheart."
2. Report by Jean Baptiste le Moyne, Sieur de Bienville, June 15, 1740, *ibid.*
3. His parents were Jean Joseph Delfau de Pontalba and Marguerite Madeleine Broutin. Delfau was the original family name; Pontalba was one of the provincial estates owned by the family in the Department of Lot, France, and was attached to the family name by Xavier's father. See Edouard de Pontalba à J. W. Cruzat, 6 oct. 1902, 19 sept. 1904, Correspondance de Baron Edouard de Pontalba, 1904–1914, and Joseph Emile Ducros, "Genealogical Papers Series, 1946," both in Cruzat Family Papers; "Index aux Documents" in Pontalba Family Papers; all in Special Collections, Manuscripts Section, Howard-Tilton Library at Tulane University.
4. Pontalba served in France as a lieutenant in Montauban from 1771 to 1775. He next accepted a demotion to sub-lieutenant in Guadeloupe, giving as his reason his family's reverses in Louisiana. The Pontalbas had invested in colonial treasury notes that were discredited by the mother country. Pontalba fought in the Siege of Savannah in 1779: Pontalba Family Papers, La. Hist. Ctr.; Archivo General de Simancas (hereafter cited as AGS), Hojas de Servícios Militares de America, 1785–1815, dic. 1787, ms.in Latin American Library, H-T; Pontalba to Minister of the Navy, July 8, 1776, and letters of Baron de Stedingk, Feb. 27, 1781; Adm. Count d'Estaing, Mar. 3, 1781; Marshal de Noailles, Mar. 14, 1781; Marquis de Castries, undated; Minister of the Navy, Sept. 3, 1784, in Pontalba Family Papers; Edouard de Pontalba à J. W. Cruzat, 19 sept. 1907, in Cruzat Family Papers; all in Spec. Coll., Manuscripts, H-T. See also "Proceedings Instituted by Jos. X. Pontalba . . . pertaining to the succession of his father . . . ," Nov. 4, 1787, Spanish Judicial Records, No. 2768, La. Hist. Ctr.
5. Miró a Pontalba, 1 mar., 26 dic. 1792, Correspondance du Gouverneur Don Estevan Miró à son neveu Joseph Delfau de Pontalba, ms. letter diary, La. Hist. Ctr.; Miró to Ezpeleta, Mar. 10, May 2, 1789; Miró to Cabello, Oct. 30, 1789, Aug. 10, 1790; las Casas to Miró, Oct. 1, 1791, Despatches of the Spanish Governors of Louisiana, WPA trans. in Spec. Coll., Manuscripts, H-T; Pontalba à Miró, 21 avril 1792, ms. letter diary in Pontalba Family Papers, La. Hist. Ctr.; Peña y Camara, *et al.*, eds., *Catálogo de Documentos del Archivo General de Indias (Sección V. Gobierno-Audiencia de Santo Domingo) sobre la época española de Luisiana* (New Orleans, 1968), I, Santo Domingo #2550, No. 1742, hereafter cited as *AGI Catálogo*. Miró a J. de Gálvez, Nueva Orleans, 15 nov. 1785.
6. Miró to las Casas, Mar. 26, Oct. 24, 1791, Nov. 8, 1790, Despatches. The "coast" was actually not a coast but both banks of a river.
7. Jos. X. Pontalba as agent of Mauricio Conway v. Pedro Villamil, July 17, 1788, File No. 2312; Don Joseph Pontalba v. Don Josef Cultida, 2 mar. 1790, legajo 26; Pontalba vs. Don Luis Lalanna Daprement, Doc. #2310, File No. 168, Spanish Judicial Records, La. Hist. Ctr. Occasionally, Almonester is the judge.
8. Pontalba à Miró, 21, 26 avril, 12, 15, 31 mai, 14 juillet, 3, 12 août, 9 nov. 1792. Miró a Pontalba, 8 marzo, 24 mayo, 17 junio 1792. Miró-Pontalba correspondence is in La. Hist. Ctr. Miró left New Orleans on Dec. 30, 1791.

9. Pontalba à Miró, 10 avril, 6 oct. 1792.

10. *Ibid.*, 17 juin, 8 nov., 12 mai 1792.

11. *Ibid.*, 10 avril, 12 mai 1792.

12. Miró a Pontalba, 17 junio 1792; julio 1792. Pontalba á Miró, 26 avril 1792.

13. Pontalba à Miró, 6 juin, 22 juillet, 20 août, 5 sept. 1792; 31 mai 1794; Tin-Tin: 15 mai, 15 juin, 5 sept. 1792.

14. Aside from the accusation that Miró had taken a rake-off from Kentucky imports, the most damaging charge was that he had arrogated to himself a higher salary than he was entitled to; both charges were eventually judged false. Miró a Pontalba, 17 junio, 3 ago. 1792. Pontalba à Miró, 26 avril, 11, 15 mai, 14, 15, 18 juin, 5 sept., 6 oct. 1792; 31 mars 1794; Almonester: 7 mai 1792.

15. Pontalba à Miró, 26 avril, 11, 15 mai, 15 juin, 16 juillet, 5 sept. 1792.

16. Miró a Pontalba, 27 oct., 26 dic. 1792. Miró was in fact made field marshal on Oct. 10, 1793; Edouard de Pontalba à J. W. Cruzat, 19 sept. 1907, Spec. Coll., Manuscripts, H-T.

17. Miró a Pontalba, 24 sept., 17 junio, 28 sept., 27 oct., 28 nov. 1792. A translation of the *obra* is in *Publications of the Louisiana Historical Society*, IX (1916), 80–85.

18. Miró a Pontalba, julio 1792. The royal wardrobe mistress was the grandmother of one of Miró's nephews; see also 17 junio, 22 ago., 26 dic. 1792.

19. *Ibid.*, 26 dic. 1792.

20. *Ibid.*, 17 junio, julio 1792. In his official dispatches, Miró showed himself to be both competent and humane, as in Miró to las Casas, Dec. 30, 1790, Despatches.

21. See, for example, his irritation at friends in New Orleans such as Gayoso who failed to write, Miró a Pontalba, julio 1792. Miró was born in 1744, Pontalba in 1754.

22. Pontalba à Miró, 7, 31 mai, 3 août 1792.

23. Miró a Pontalba, 17 junio, 28 sept. 1792. Pontalba à Miró, 10 avril, 8, 9 mai 1792. There are indications that Carondelet did try to advance Pontalba to Colonel of the Regiment of the Militia of the German Coast, but was thwarted by superiors; *AGI Catálogo*, SD #2566, No. 2700. Pontalba's superiors frequently commented on his enthusiasm; only Governor Gayoso tempered his praise with the observation that his ambition was "extreme." AGI, Hojas de Servícios, dic. 1797, microfilm in Historic New Orleans Collection.

24. Carondelet to las Casas, April 4, 1792, Despatches. Carondelet became particularly indebted to Pontalba during the Pointe Coupée revolt, when Pontalba warned the governor of an alleged assassination plot against him; Carondelet to las Casas, April 4, 1792; "Confidential," July 30, 1795. Carondelet did not criticize Pontalba's equivocal actions during the 1794 fire, when two of the three men who were lost in the firefighting were under Pontalba's command, June 18, Dec. 28, 1794, Despatches; AGS, Hojas de Servícios Militares de America, 1785–1815, junio 1792, dic. 1796, ms. in Latin Amer. Lib., H-T.

25. Letters to His Wife, May 13, 1796.

26. Carondelet a Acuna, 23 nov. 1792, *AGI Catálogo*, SD #2561, No. 2628.

27. Records and Deliberations of the Cabildo, Nov. 6, 1795, WPA trans., microfilm, Louisiana Collection, New Orleans Public Library. The report upheld a charge made by Almonester's enemies that he had not properly supervised the slaughterhouse.

28. Miró died on June 4, 1795, at Mondragon (Guipuzcoa) while occupying the post of Commandante General de los puntos de Elosua, Musquaichu Villareal y Vergara. Edouard de Pontalba à J. W. Cruzat, 6 oct. 1902, Spec. Coll., Manuscripts, H-T.

29. Letters to His Wife, Feb. 24, 1796, letter diary in La. Hist. Ctr.

30. *Ibid.*, Feb. 25, 26, 28, Mar. 7, 25, 1796.

31. *Ibid.*, Mar. 3, 8, 13, 18, Apr. 19, 1796.

32. *Ibid.*, Mar. 5, July 10, 1796.

33. Letters to His Wife, Feb. 26, May 21, Mar. 12, 1796.

34. *Ibid.*, Feb. 27, May 21, June 8, 9, Sept. 19, Oct. 13, 1796. The Pontalbas had relatives everywhere, thanks to Mme. de Miró. The d'Aunoys lived across the yard from Pontalba and routinely fed him during his wife's absence.

35. Letters to His Wife, Oct. 4, July 16, 1796; Juana Macarty v. Bartolomé Lafont, 31 oct. 1796, ms. in La. Hist. Ctr. Barthélemy Lafon, a native of France, was a prominent architect in the city.

36. Letters to His Wife, July 16, 20, 1796. Pontalba expressed the fear that "after I leave him he is doomed to become prey to those who can wring their own advantages from him."

37. *Ibid.*, May, 19, June 18, Oct. 1, 1796.

38. *Ibid.*, Oct. 8, 14, 21, 23 (editor's note), 1796.

39. Letters to His Wife, April 18, May 10, June 11, 1796.

40. *Ibid.*, Mar. 1, 3, 8, 11, Sept. 8, 1796.

41. *Ibid.*, Mar. 26, Apr. 23, 28, 30, May 10, June 15, Sept. 15, Oct. 20, 1796.

42. *Ibid.*, June 15, Sept. 15, 19, Oct. 12, 20, Nov. 2, 1796.

43. *Ibid.*, Oct. 11, 15, 16, 1796.

44. *Ibid.*, cream of tartar: July 16, Sept. 15; quinine: Oct. 2, 3, 29, 1796.

45. *Ibid.*, exhalations: Sept. 11; garlic: Sept. 15, Oct. 30, 1796.

46. *Ibid.*, Oct. 7, 9, 15, 28, 1796.

47. *Ibid.*, Apr. 23, 1796; see also June 17, 1796.

48. *Ibid.*, Mar. 19, May 18, July 14, 19, 1796. He saw *The Honest Criminal* and was disappointed in the performance.

49. *Ibid.*, May 16, July 4, 1796.

50. *Ibid.*, Sept. 8, 1796.

51. *Ibid.*

52. *Ibid.*, Feb. 26, Mar. 11, 30, May 3, 1796.

53. Pontalba à Miró, 22 juillet 1792, La. Hist. Ctr. The wise rule was actually the Crown's.

54. *Ibid.*, 12 may 1792. The owner was a M. Tretonai.

55. *Ibid.*, 4 nov. 1792. Another "disagreeable affair" involved Pontalba's kinsman Robin, who was accused by his blacks of having them whipped on a plank containing long spikes. "The Baron assured Robin," Pontalba wrote, that the investigation "would soon be over and the result would not be damaging to him," 3 août 1792.

56. Spanish Document #2806, 7 feb. 1780, in La. Hist. Ctr.; for a summary of the trial see Henry Dart, "The Trial of Mary Glass," *LHQ*, VI (1923), 591–654. The execution took place in 1781.

57. Letters to His Wife, Augustin: May 4, 9; Lucille: July 10; Jeanette: May 9, 1796.

58. *Ibid.*, Lucille: May 4; slave with dysentery: May 12; pregnant slave: July 17; whipped slave: Mar. 12, 1796.

59. *Ibid.*, coachman: Mar. 20; Father: Mar. 8, 1796.

60. *Ibid.*, Oct. 25, 1796. See also Feb. 25, Sept. 11, 1796.

61. Letters to His Wife, Mar. 8, 20, Oct. 6, 24, 25, 1796. The Tremoulet Hotel was eventually located in Madame Castillon's house, the mansion she left when she and Micael

moved to France. It was this hotel that Benjamin Latrobe described as being filthy; he too commented on the Tremoulets' cruelty.

62. Ton-Ton's mother, Jeanne Françoise, one of the heiresses of the legendary Macarty wealth, married again, to Mauricio Conway, a nephew of Governor O'Reilly. The Pontalbas were on sufficiently good terms with Conway that Pontalba regularly reported on the health of his stepfather-in-law to Miró, and expressed some regret when Conway died. Pontalba à Miró, 10 juin, 9 sept., 1792, La. Hist. Ctr.

63. Letters to His Wife, Mar. 1, 1796.

64. *Ibid.*, June 5, July 9, 11, 1796.

65. *Ibid.*, July 15, 1796.

66. *Ibid.*, Apr. 20, June 25, July 10, 14, 17, 18, Sept. 7, 23, Oct. 16, 22, 1796.

67. *Ibid.*, Sept. 13, 1796.

68. *Ibid.*, Sept. 14, 1796.

69. *Ibid.*, Mar. 1, 2, 20, 1796.

70. *Ibid.*, Mar. 1, 2, 18, 20, 21, 1796.

71. *Ibid.*, June 12, 21, July 26, 1796.

72. *Ibid.*, Mar. 3; pralines: Sept. 25; courier: July 11, 1796. Pralines are brown sugar candies containing many pecans. They are crisp and look like large cookies. In New Orleans there is a brisk commerce in pralines, which are bought by tourists as gifts to take home. But it is doubtful whether there were any for Ton-Ton to purchase in Madrid in 1796.

73. Letters to His Wife, June 7, 1796.

74. *AGI Catálogo*, SD #32565, No. 5441, 16 dic. 1795; Edouard de Pontalba à J. W. Cruzat, 26 mai 1906, Spec. Coll., Manuscripts, H-T.

75. Edouard de Pontalba à J. W. Cruzat, 26 mai 1906; Pontalba to the First Consul [Napoleon], Paris, 12th Vendemaire, Year 11 of the French Republic [Oct. 3, 1802], in Pontalba Family Papers; Spec. Coll., Manuscripts, H-T. For a partial list of the numerous "memoirs" on Louisiana, see Abraham P. Nasatir and Gary Elwyn Monell, *French Consuls in the United States: A Calendar of Their Correspondence in the Archives Nationales* (Washington, D.C., 1967), for the years 1797–1812.

76. The most accessible source for reading the memoir is Alcée Fortier's *History of Louisiana* (New York, 1904), II, 185–215. In it, Pontalba offered a description of Louisiana to support his conclusion that the colony would be an advantageous French possession. The Mississippi River should be kept open to trade from the United States, at least until the colony could defend itself, he advised, since American traders would invade the colony with or without permission in order to get their goods to the mouth of the river. He recommended buying tobacco from the northern states, shipping it down to New Orleans, and reloading it for sale to Europe; this had, in fact, been Miró's practice. He thought the cultivation of sugar cane ought to be encouraged.

77. Pontalba to First Consul, [Oct. 3, 1802]. In "Notes to Documents," Pontalba Family Papers, Spec. Coll., Manuscripts, H-T, Edouard de Pontalba explains the rank as similar to chief of staff; it was an honorary title, since the commission "bore no designation of Corps."

78. Pontalba to First Consul, [Oct. 3, 1802]. Dr. Dow to Thomas Urquhart, July 8, 1802; for this letter I am indebted to Mr. and Mrs. Kenneth Trist Urquhart.

79. Mont-l'Évêque had been the residence of the bishops (*évêques*) of Senlis in medieval times. The final *s* in Senlis is sounded.

80. "Index aux Documents," Pontalba Family Papers, Spec. Coll., Manscripts, H-T. Pontalba's older brother, Louis Léon Delfau, already carried an assortment of curious titles, including Marquis of Pontalba. The family did well under Napoleon and managed to keep its honors and estates even after the restoration of the old nobility.

81. Letter of Appointment, 26 Brumaire, Year XIII [Nov. 17, 1804], and portrait, *ibid*. The court appointment was made before Napoleon's actual coronation on Dec. 22, 1804.

82. F. B. Goodrich, *The Court of Napoleon* (New York, 1857), 163 ff.

83. Ney explained that Célestin was not only a relative but "an only son." Letter of Appointment, Minister of War to Célestin de Pontalba, Sept. 11, 1809; Marshal Ney to the Minister of War, Nov. 12, 1809, Apr. 3, 1811, Pontalba Family Papers, Spec. Coll., Manuscripts, H-T. A glass Célestin was holding shattered, so that shards were lodged in his hand.

84. Decree for promotion signed by Napoleon June 22, 1811; Ney to the Minister of War, Apr. 3, 1811, Sept. 10, 1812, *ibid*. Ney refers to Célestin's detainment by the English, but naval records do not confirm the incident.

85. Pontalba to Ney, July 11, 1814, *ibid*. The letter to Laselve de St. Avid was on the order of a letter of introduction, although Ney's wife was St. Avid's cousin (as was Pontalba), and it was through his connection to St. Avid that Célestin got the position of aide to Ney, and Pontalba procured his barony. See also the portion of Proceedings of Marshal Ney . . . Court Martial, Pontalba Family Papers, La. Hist. Ctr.; Henri Welschinger, *Le Maréchal Ney, 1815* (Paris, 1893), 48; New Orleans *Times Democrat*, Jan. 17, 1892. Harold Kurtz in *The Trial of Marshal Ney* (New York, 1957), 229, asserts that the Royalists wanted Ney to escape to America; Ney was not prevented from taking out two passports, one in his own name.

IV. THE WIDOW

1. Records and Deliberations of the Cabildo, May 18, Dec. 3, 1798, Oct. 18, 1799, Jan. 30, 1801, WPA trans., microfilm, Louisiana Collection, New Orleans Public Library.

2. "Proceedings Instituted by Bishop Luis Peñalver y Cardenas vs. Widow Almonester, 1799–1801," WPA trans. of ms. in La. Coll., NOPL, 90, 55.

3. Records and Deliberations, July 31, 1801; Doña Luisa Delaronde, Viuda, vs. Estevan Griffin, 15 julio 1803, Spanish Document #4369, Louisiana Historical Center.

4. Funeral Records of St. Louis Cathedral, Book II, #642, ms., Archives of the Archdiocese of New Orleans.

5. Pierre Clément de Laussat, *Memoirs of My Life*, trans. Agnes Josephine Pastwa, ed. Robert D. Bush (Baton Rouge, 1978), II, 81; Claiborne to Casa Calvo, June 5, 1804, in Dunbar Rowland, ed., *Official Letter Books of W. C. C. Claiborne, 1801–1816* (Jackson, Miss., 1917), I, 193.

6. Laussat, *Memoirs*, II, 99; Ashe quoted in John F. McDermott, ed., *The Spanish in the Mississippi Valley, 1762–1804* (Urbana, Ill., 1974), 225. Almonester's succession established his assets at 129,351 pesos, according to the Peñalver suit, p. 56 (Almonester's succession documents have been lost). This was a low estimate, which allowed Louison to buy the existing property of her daughters and replace it with new houses. It was Louison's constructions, not Almonester's, that made Micael a rich bride. Almonester's Bayou Road property did not yet have the value it would acquire in later years. Louison may have been

quite right in her remonstration that Almonester had depleted much of his wealth in benefactions by the time he died.

7. 5 nov. 1799, Spanish Doc. #3825, No. 10; 13 feb. 1800, Spanish Doc. #3865; suit: 14 jan. 1802, Spanish Doc. #4142, all in La. Hist. Ctr. Sale of slaves: Sept. 22, 28, 1798; mortgages: Aug. 27, Nov. 29, 1798, June 5, 1799, Records of Pedro Pedesclaux, New Orleans Notarial Archives and La. Hist. Ctr. Castillon also purchased slaves during this period. See also Digest of the Acts of the Cabildo, 1769–1803, Jan. 9, 1801, in NOPL; and Stanley Faye, "Consuls of Spain in New Orleans, 1804–1821," *LHQ*, XXI (1938), 678.

8. Claiborne to James Madison, Mar. 16, 1804, in Rowland, ed., *Letter Books of Claiborne*, I, 47–48.

9. Faye, "Consuls of Spain," 677.

10. John Duffy, ed., *The Rudolph Matas History of Medicine in Louisiana* (Baton Rouge, 1958), I, 263–64 n197.

11. Letter from Onis to Pizarro, Nov. 22, 1818, in Stanley Faye, "The Great Stroke of Pierre Lafitte," *LHQ*, XXI (1940), 739.

12. Letters of Baron Joseph X. Pontalba to His Wife, Mar. 2, May 12, 14, June 10, 1796, ms. letter diary in Pontalba Family Papers, WPA trans., La. Hist. Ctr.

13. Inventory of the Estate of J. B. Castillon, Aug. 13, 1809, Wills and Successions of Carlos Ximenes, La. Coll., NOPL.

14. *Ibid.*, section on "Slaves."

15. *Ibid.*, advertisement near the end of the succession. For descriptions of the sugar plantation, see *Louisiana Courier*, Aug. 10, 1809. Included in the $20,000 Louison collected from Almonester's debtors was $5,000 from M. Sigur, which was to worry Pontalba when he thought Louison was hiding her assets from him, along with $7,000 from Orué.

16. Castillon Inventory, tableau of distributions.

17. Duffy, ed., *History of Medicine*, I, 421, 423.

18. "Constitution for the New Charity Hospital of New Orleans, 1793," WPA trans., La. Hist. Ctr., 23.

19. Records of Michel de Armas, NONA; Records of New Orleans City Council, Sept. 20, 1809, La. Coll., NOPL. Mother and daughter renounced their rights to the part of their residence on the plaza which had been pledged for the hospital's support; the council in turn sold back that part of the house to Madame Castillon for $20,000.

20. Floor plan in Samuel Wilson, Jr., ed., *Impressions Respecting New Orleans by Benjamin H. B. Latrobe* (New York, 1951), 23.

21. Castillon Inventory, "La chambre de Mlle. Michaelle."

22. Quoted in Edouard de Pontalba à J. W. Cruzat, 18 juin 1904, Correspondance de Baron Edouard de Pontalba, 1904–1914, in Cruzat Family Papers, Special Collections, Manuscripts Section, Howard-Tilton Library at Tulane University.

23. "Court Action Between the Baron and Baroness de Pontalba," Tribunal of Senlis, May 11, 1835, WPA trans., typescript in La. Hist. Ctr. Micael's lawyer contended in turn that before her marriage she was "sought by all the important men in New Orleans."

24. Edouard de Pontalba à J. W. Cruzat, 18 juin 1904, Cruzat Family Papers, Spec. Coll., Manuscripts, H-T.

25. Jan., 1811, "Court Action," 75.

26. Guizot à M. de Remusat, Paris, 18 oct., 13 nov. 1826, in Madame de Witt, ed., *Lettres de M. Guizot à sa Famille et à ses Amis* (Paris, 1884).

27. *Le Moniteur de la Louisiane*, 26 oct. 1811.

V. Mont l' Évêque

1. Micael, Célestin, and their mothers landed in France on July 1, 1812, Pontalba Family Papers, WPA trans., Louisiana Historical Center. For travel time between Senlis and Paris, see Eugen Weber, *Peasants into Frenchmen: The Modernization of Rural France, 1870–1914* (Stanford, 1976), 199, 200*n*, 204; François-Yves Besard, *Souvenirs d'un Nonagénaire* (Paris, 1880), 22.

2. Eugène Miller, *Senlis et ses Environs* (Senlis, 1896), 103 ff., 150–53, 188, 304. Pontalba put down 63,000 francs on a mortgage of 138,371 francs for Mont-l'Évêque, Bureau Hypothéques de Senlis, v. 44, No. 55, 7 fév. 1807. He purchased significant additions to the property in years following 1814. His wife and son continued to add neighboring lands to the estate, as did Micael herself after she gained control of it in 1864. The most detailed information about Mont-l'Évêque, the *majorat*, chain of title, and additions is in Records of A. L. Massion, Étude XXXIV/1333, "Inventaire aprés le décés de Mme. la Baronne de Pontalba," 30 avril 1874, III, coté cinquième, and VI, annexes, Archives Nationales, Paris, hereafter cited as AN. For a short summary in a New Orleans source, see Pont. v. Pont., Eastern District, Docket #2856, April, 1839, Document M, p. 81, Louisiana Supreme Court Records, Department of Archives and Manuscripts, Earl K. Long Library at the University of New Orleans.

3. "Court Action Between the Baron and Baroness de Pontalba," Tribunal of Senlis, May 11, 1835, WPA trans., La. Hist. Ctr., 90. This is a partial version in English of the trial reported in full in the *Gazette des Tribunaux,* 10–14 oct. 1835.

4. Françoise de Macarty, who died at Mont-l'Évêque in 1813. Micael's mother lived at 9 rue Taitbout in 1812.

5. "Court Action," 10, 79. The Pontalbas also claimed that they added diamonds worth $50,000 to Micael's trousseau. Possibly that was true. According to her estate inventory, Micael died with more diamonds than she was born with.

6. Pont. v. Pont., Eastern District, Docket #2129, June, 1831, pp. 8–11, Supreme Court Records, UNO.

7. "Court Action," 79.

8. Mme. Castillon à St. Avid, 30 avril 1811: "I have built a house which cost me 80,000 piasters and which will give me 1,200 a month." Pont. v. Pont., Docket #2856, Document F, p. 50.

9. The dowry given in 1817 by the duc de Bourbon to his mistress, the future baronesse de Feuchères, was a permanent yearly income of 7,200 francs ($1,440), which the bridegroom's parents were required to match. The bride was represented as the natural daughter of an Italian prince. Mme. Daloz, another natural daughter of another Italian prince, received a dowry of 800,000 francs ($160,000) in the form of rental real estate, Eugène Dupin, ed., *Plaidoyers de Philippe Dupin* (Paris, 1868), I, 307; Louis Blanc, *The History of Ten Years: 1830–1840* (New York, 1845), I, 284 ff; Claire Goldberg Moses, *French Feminism in the Nineteenth Century* (Albany, N.Y., 1984), 248.

10. An entire section of French law was devoted to dotal settlements where each party brought equivalent donations; André Raison, *Les Donations entre Époux* (Paris, 1978). See especially H. D. Lewis, "The Legal Status of Women in the Nineteenth Century in France," *Journal of European Studies,* X (June, 1980), 181.

11. *Code civil*, article 1549: "*Le mari seul a l'administration des biens dotaux pendant le mariage*"; quoted in Lewis, "Legal Status of Women," 187 (italics his). For Louisiana, see

Pont. v. Pont., Docket #2856, April, 1839, "Petition of plaintiff," p. 6, and "Judgement" by the lower court magistrate, Supreme Court Records, UNO; "Court Action," 79, 86. Neither husband nor wife could alienate the dowry; it was supposed to be maintained as it was in the beginning of the marriage.

12. *Code civil*, article 1428: "Le mari a l'administration de tous les biens personnels de la femme. . . . Il ne peut aliener les immeubles de sa femme sans son consentement," quoted in Lewis, "Legal Status of Women," 187. A wife could handle her own inheritance only if it came to her through a will stipulating that the money or property was solely for her use, a will such as Mme. Castillon would eventually make; however, it is worth noting that a French court discussing Mme. Castillon's will showed some uncertainty as to whether such a provision was necessary in order for Micael to administer her inheritance: "Court Action," 17, 79, 96, 97; Pont. v. Pont., Docket #2856, "Judgement," 156.

13. Records of L. H. Breton, Ét. XIV/685, "Donation entre vifs par M. et Mme. de Pontalba à leur fils," 9 avril 1818. Records of A. J. Fourchy, Ét. LVII/692, "Donation," 15 avril 1822; "Quittance," 24 jan. 1823, Répertoires d'Études, hereafter cited as RE, AN. Pont. v. Pont., Docket #2856, pp. 52, 45, 81–88. Joseph Pontalba v. Joshua Veasley, Docket #4487, Mar., 1822, Rare Manuscripts, New Orleans Public Library.

14. Pont. v. Pont., Docket #2856, Document S, No. 2, pp. 146–47; "Petition of Plaintiff," Mar. 29, 1834; Document D, p. 44.

15. *Ibid.*, Document J, pp. 59–69; "Court Action," 10–12, 81–83; Edouard de Pontalba à J. W. Cruzat, 20 oct. 1902, 10 avril 1908, Correspondance de Baron Edouard de Pontalba, 1904–1914, in Cruzat Family Papers, Special Collections, Manuscripts Section, Howard-Tilton Library at Tulane University.

16. Records of L. H. Breton, Ét. XIV/622, "Vente," 5–6 mars 1816; XIV/624, 642, 643, "Bail," 11–12 août 1816; 3 mars 1819; 23 août 1820. Records of Constant-Amédée Moquard, Ét. LXVIII/1130, 7 juin, 12 déc. 1861; 8 sept. 1870 (Place Vendôme). Records of Breton, Ét. XIV, "Vente," 14 juillet 1819; "Bail," 29–30 juillet 1819; 6 jan. 1820; 11 juillet, 16–20 sept. 1821; 27 mars, 26 sept. 1822; 10 mai, 14, 30 juillet 1823, RE, AN. There may have been other leases, the records for which are now lost, which could reflect an even greater profit.

17. However, in his will, made before Micael's birth, Almonester designated his wife his "universal legatee." Will of Don Andrés Almonester, Spanish Doc. #3166, Aug. 20, 1794, WPA trans., La. Hist. Ctr.

18. He was mistaken. In France the widow's remarriage affected her inheritance and position as tutrix; in Louisiana it did not. He averred that the sum repaid by the city for the Cabildo was $32,000; the actual amount was $28,000, Pont. v. Pont., Docket #2856, Document J; Edouard de Pontalba à J. W. Cruzat, 20 oct. 1902, Spec. Coll., Manuscripts, H-T. Mme. Castillon replied that she had left the Cabildo money out of the inventory because at the time she received the payments, she expected to incur new expenses in completing the building.

19. Edouard de Pontalba à J. W. Cruzat, 20 oct. 1902, Spec. Coll., Manuscripts, H-T. After Almonester's death an auction was held of the houses Mme. Almonester owned jointly with her daughters, with the result that she herself purchased all the property at low appraisals. She thus bought the property from her minor children and gave them little in return, on the face of it. Governor Claiborne confirmed the sale because he feared the wooden houses were likely to be destroyed by fire before the children came of age; but he made an express provision that the houses had to be restored to their full value if they lasted until the estate passed to them. In this way the children's interests were protected

and Louison was able to afford improvements on the houses, so that when Micael inherited her father's property, it was worth a great deal more than at the time of his death, Pont. v. Pont., Docket #2856, Document J, and "Judgement," pp. 61–68, 160–61.

20. "Court Action," 10.

21. Arthur Chuquet, ed., *Recollections of Baron de Frénilly* (New York, 1909), 202.

22. Pont. v. Pont., Docket #2856; Records of L. H. Breton, Ét. XIV/632, "Acception de donation . . . ," 9 déc. 1817, Série M. C., RE, AN.

23. Date of the signing was Mar. 12, 1814, Pont. v. Pont., Docket #2856, "Judgement," pp. 158–59; the "Donation" to Célestin was ratified 9 avril 1818, Records of L. H. Breton, Ét. XIV/632; Records of A. J. Fourchy, Ét. LVIII/692, 15 avril 1822, AN.

24. I am indebted to Baron Henri de Pontalba, Mayor of Mont-l'Évêque, for showing me the "Registre de l'État Civile de Mont-l'Évêque 1813 à 1822," ms. in mayor's office, and searching with me for documentary evidence of this little boy's existence. For Castillon house in Mont-l'Évêque, see Pont. v. Pont., Docket #2856, Document P, p. 95.

25. The second floor rented for 2,500 francs a year in her house at 343 St.-Honoré, whereas an apartment on the third floor rented for 1,000 francs a year, and the fourth floor for 700 francs, Records of L. H. Breton, Ét. XIV/644, 647, 23 août 1820; 29–30 juillet 1819; 6 jan. 1820. Note that in Honoré de Balzac's *Père Goriot*, the old man moves to a higher floor of Madame Vauquer's boardinghouse with each decline of his fortunes.

26. Henry Tuckley, *In Sunny France* (New York, 1894), 163.

27. Pont. v. Pont., Docket #2856, Document D. Napoleon's decree of Mar. 1, 1808, instituted the graded titles of prince, duke, baron, count, and chevalier. Prosecutors of the major law courts might be named barons, as well as archbishops and bishops. Pontalba also claimed a title handed down from his grandfather, "Appointment of Knight . . . ," Aug. 1, 1759, Pontalba Family Papers, La. Hist. Ctr.

28. Marcel Proust, *Du coté de chez Swann*, 4th ed. (Paris, 1919), 112.

29. Marshal Macdonald, who loyally served Napoleon until the emperor's first abdication (and who was a friend of Micael) was given the Order of St. Louis by the restored monarchy, as was Horace Sebastiani, who fought for Napoleon at Waterloo.

30. Records of A. J. Fourchy, Ét. LVIII/741, "Inventaire après le décès de M. le Baron de Pontalba," 9 nov. 1834, AN.

31. *Ibid.*, Ét. LVIII/806, "Échange entre M. et Mme. Pontalba et M. et Mme. Dupré," 14 mai 1823. The house on rue de Provence was purchased from A. L. Trouard, a captain of the militia in New Orleans and a friend of Pontalba.

32. *Ibid.*, "Dépôt de titres de propriété du domaine de Migneaux par M. de Pontalba," 21 fev. 1851. Records of Charles A. F. Berçeon, Ét. LVIII, "Bail pour M. de Pontalba à M. et Mme. Brémond," 18 juin 1842. Records of A. J. Fourchy, Ét. LVIII, "Quittance," 8 jan. 1836; "Bail," 5, 6 mars 1838; 31 mars, 24 avril 1841; 17 oct., 18 nov. 1846; 21 nov. 1849.

33. Berçeon, Ét. II, No. 8/1140, "Bail," 23, 27 fév., 3 mars 1837; 3 sept. 1839; 3 fév. 1842; 9 juin 1843; 9 juillet 1879. The yearly rent in 1879 amounted to 55,000 francs.

34. *Ibid.*, 10 juin 1865; 4 mai 1868 (Argenteuil); Ét. II, "Bail," 14 sept. 1877; 16 déc. 1878; 30 déc. 1878; 28 oct. 1881; 5 juillet 1883; 23 nov. 1883; 11 mars 1886; 14 sept. 1886 (St. Honoré). Records of L. H. Breton, Ét. XIV, "Donation," 9 dec. 1817 (du Houssaie). This house was also purchased from the Trouards. Célestin sold it in 1838, Registre 132, 3ième Chambre (1843), 8–9 nov. 1840, Cour Royale de Paris, Archives de Paris, Annexe at Villemoisin sur l'Orgue; Pont. v. Pont., Docket #2856, Document S, pp. 134, 137. *Hôtel* was a fashionable term for a large residence.

35. "Court Action," 13–15. The pleadings paraphrase or quote Célestin—the attorney referred to Célestin's "own words" in describing the note. The incident took place in July, 1815 or 1816.

36. *Ibid.*, 80: "Soon, it was no longer sufficient for Mme. de Pontalba to have become the idol of her husband's paternal household," said Pontalba's lawyer. "She wanted to become the sovereign mistress over one adorned with her own livery. She wanted it with a will already emancipated at eighteen, one already endowed with tireless energy, yes, she wanted it to the point of her steadfastly discouraging the most earnest attempts of all people to please her."

37. Comtesse d'Armaille, *Quand On Savait Vivre Heureux* (Paris, 1934), 209–10; *French Home Life* (New York, 1874), 57 (reprints from early editions of *Blackwood's* magazine).

38. René Marquis de Belleval, *Souvenirs de ma Jeunesse* (Paris, 1895), 45.

39. Pont. v. Pont, Docket #2856, Document D, p. 46; Records of L. H. Breton, 9 avril 1818.

40. In her letters Micael mentioned seeing Céleste Livaudais, Pierre Duverges, Alcée Labranche, and ladies of the Péchaud, Marigny, Soniat, and Claiborne families.

41. Robert Burnand, in *La Vie Quotidienne en France en 1830* (Paris, 1943), assures us that the typical Parisian woman bathed only once a month; but typical women are hard to find anywhere. William L. Langer, in *Political and Social Upheaval, 1832–52* (New York, 1969), 192, refers to an often-quoted statistic showing that the water supply of Paris was sufficient for only two baths per person per year.

42. "Registre de l'État Civile de Mont-l'Évêque 1813 à 1822." She died May 12.

43. Pont. v. Pont., Docket #2856, Madame Castillon's Will, Document O, p. 91. She further added, "It is well understood that this Will will not derogate in any way the right of my daughter to collect the remainder of my succession as my sole heir." The cost of each sheet (70 centimes) and a three-page description of the will is included in the document package to preclude falsification.

44. Pont. v. Pont., Docket #2856, Documents O and P; "Court Action," 17.

45. Pont. v. Pont., Docket #2856, Document P, p. 97; "Court Action," 22.

46. Pont. v. Pont., Docket #2856, Document P, pp. 96–105. Micael and Célestin each received property supposedly worth 786,212 francs and 89 centimes. All sums are converted to dollars. The equivalent in French money was five francs to one dollar in the 1820s, according to those court documents that recorded the transactions in both currencies. See also Judge Maurian's remarks as to the true value of Célestin's portion in "Judgement," Supreme Court Records, UNO.

47. Pont. v. Pont., Docket #2856, Document P; legal papers of the nineteenth century often reflected the emotional attitude of the signatories, since their wording was not as standardized as in modern documents.

48. Abrogated in 1816 during the post-Napoleonic reaction, divorce was not reinstated in France until 1885. The grounds for divorce under Napoleonic law now became the grounds for legal separation (the wife's adultery or, more rarely, extreme cruelty on either side.) A *cour de cassation* on Aug. 9, 1826, stated: "Le mari dont la femme refuse d'habiter avec lui peut l'y contraindre *manu militari*" (Lewis' italics), Lewis, "Legal Status of Women," 180–81, 187. See also Moses, *French Feminism*, 19, 257.

49. *Code civil*, articles 384, 374, 375 (italics mine). For a discussion of how the courts interpreted these laws, see the "Affaire Daloz," in Dupin, ed., *Plaidoyers*, I, 249–400.

50. *Code civil*, article 230. The court stretched this provision in one instance at least to grant a separation to a woman whose husband used her money to support a second wife and the children from this bigamous union, *Gazette des Tribunaux*, 8 juillet 1831.

51. Pont. v. Pont., Docket #2856, Document D, p. 45, and Document P, pp. 96–105; Dupin, ed., *Plaidoyers*, II, 43–45.

52. Records of Breton, Ét. XIV, "Vente," 24 juin 1823; XIV/13, 14, "Substitution," 12 août 1823, AN. The 1825 purchase does not appear in inventories of the elder Pontalba's holdings. Célestin later sued the tenants in his own name, Pontalba v. Domingon, *et al.*, Docket #2951, May, 1837, Supreme Court Records, UNO.

53. Dupin, ed., *Plaidoyers*, II, 43.

54. "Court Action," 111.

55. *Ibid.* 22. A member of the Chamber of Deputies until the end of the Bourbon Restoration in 1830, Persil supported the July Monarchy. He was the general prosecutor in Paris, twice minister of justice, and was appointed a peer in 1839. In 1852 he became one of Louis Napoleon's councillors of state and was appointed to the Senate in 1864.

VI. We All Live Here

1. The American Faubourg St. Mary (or Ste. Marie, as the Creoles called it) ranged over Magazine Street and St. Charles Avenue. Condé, or Chartres, with its slave auctions and boutiques, was the retail center of town; Royal Street was a main artery. Records of the New Orleans City Council, Dec. 12, 1821, June 12, 1819, microfilm in Louisiana Collection, New Orleans Public Library.

2. Samuel Wilson, Jr., ed., *Impressions Respecting New Orleans by Benjamin Henry Boneval Latrobe* (New York, 1951), 22–24; Records of the City Council, Sept. 25, 1830, NOPL.

3. Records of L. T. Caire, Mar. 10, 1828, New Orleans Notarial Archives; Pont. v. Pont., Docket #2129, Feb. 2, 1831, Louisiana Supreme Court Records, Department of Archives and Manuscripts, Earl K. Long Library at the University of New Orleans. On Feb. 1, 1828, before Célestin had returned to France, a fire destroyed the Government House and damaged Micaela's houses, including the just-renovated mansion. Célestin spent only $57,000 to renovate the property on both sides of the square, indicating that the cottages on the Place d'Armes must have been small dwellings which commanded high rents because of their central location.

4. She arrived on the 330-ton ship *Helvetia*, which crossed Harvé de Grace directly to New Orleans; the servants were listed as "Baptiste" and "Pauline." "Passenger Lists of Vessels Arriving at N. O., 1820–1902," Mar. 8–Dec. 28, 1830, List Nos. 44–250, NOPL.

5. Pont. v. Pont., Docket #2129, Feb. 2, 1831, Supreme Court Records, UNO.

6. Quoted in *Gazette des Tribunaux*, 12 oct. 1835; all italics here and later are in the original. Desuauneaux was a notary whose office was at 95 rue Richelieu in Paris.

7. Micael's mother still owed $52,000 on the original $130,000 dowry when in 1814 the elder Pontalba, by threatening to challenge Almonester's succession, forced her to add the entire left side of the Place d'Armes to the dowry. Mme. Castillon surrendered the French Quarter property in lieu of the $52,000, even though the lots were worth a great deal more. Now that the property might be returned, Micael correctly foresaw that Célestin would demand the amount originally promised in the dowry, even though he collected rents during the years he possessed the property that far exceeded $52,000. Pont.

v. Pont., Docket #2856, pp. 45, 151; "Court Action Between the Baron and Baroness de Pontalba," Tribunal of Senlis, May 11, 1835, WPA trans., typescript in Louisiana Historical Center, 103–104. This is a version, not complete, of the trial, which is reported in its entirety in *Gazette des Tribunaux*, 10–14 oct. 1835. The English version is cited whenever it seems adequate, especially in reporting the pleadings of Célestin's attorney, where the WPA translation is particularly good. The *Gazette* is cited mainly for Hennequin's remarks, or where the translated text is incomplete.

8. Charles Gayarré, *History of Louisiana*, 3rd ed. (New Orleans, 1885), 80. In 1827 the grounds for divorce had just been narrowed. Moreau Lislet was Micael's New Orleans attorney, one of the state's most prominent lawyers; he had been on hand for Castillon's inventory in 1809.

9. Sebastiani à Pontalba, Paris, 23 juin 1831, quoted in *Gazette des Tribunaux*, 14 oct. 1835; "M. de Pontalba fils est français," Pontalba Family Papers, La. Hist. Ctr. Sebastiani had been a general under Napoleon, a member of the Chamber of Deputies under the Restoration, minister of foreign affairs during the early years of the July Monarchy, and was to become a marshal of France in 1840. For an account of the murder that discusses him, see Ernest Daudet, ed., *Journal de Victor de Balabine* (Paris, 1914), 310–12.

10. Micael de Pontalba à Victoire de Lino de Chalmet, New York, mai 1831; Saratoga, 25 juillet 1831; Micael de Pontalba à Azélie Chalmet, Philadelphia, 1831, Letters of Micaela, Alfred, and Gaston de Pontalba, Special Collections, Manuscripts Section, Howard-Tilton Library at Tulane University.

11. Micael à Victoire, Saratoga, 25 juillet 1831; Micael à Azélie, Philadelphia, 1831, *ibid*. Jackson sent Edward Livingston, a former Louisiana senator. The plantation site of the Battle of New Orleans in the town of Chalmette has been restored with markers on the battleground, a museum, and some Andrew Jackson memorabilia.

12. Micael à Victoire, Saratoga, 25 juillet 1831.

13. There was a lively debate about Guillemin's age in the separation trial between the Pontalbas in 1836, Eugène Dupin, ed., *Plaidoyers de Philippe Dupin* (Paris, 1868), I, 14. Guillemin's wife, Caroline Pieray, died in 1817, according to Burial Records, Historic New Orleans Collection.

14. *Gazette des Tribunaux*, 14–15 oct. 1835.

15. Dupin, ed., *Plaidoyers*, I, 15.

16. Micael à Victoire, mai 1831. Her misspelling should not be taken as an indication of her closeness, or lack of it, to Guillemin. She also misspelled the name of the street where she lived in Paris, du Houssaie.

17. Aug. 8, 1831, quoted in "Court Action," 97; *Gazette des Tribunaux*, 14 oct. 1835. "Banker" was a loose term used to describe an agent who held money on deposit for someone else. The Pontalbas were occasionally described as bankers, meaning that the elder Pontalba kept money on account for shippers and accepted drafts on these accounts from various merchants. Small banking operations could be combined with shipping, lending, stock brokering, real estate management, or notarial work.

18. Micael à Victoire, Saratoga, mai 1831. Micael wrote: " . . . nous dinons à table d'autre." We assume she meant *table d'hôte* rather than *tables des autres*.

19. "La femme adultère sera condamnée par le même jugement, et sur la requisition du ministère public, à la reclusion dans une maison de correction, pour en temps determiné qui ne pourra être moindre de trois mois, ni exéder deux années." Quoted by H. D.

Lewis, "The Legal Status of Women in Nineteenth-Century France," *Journal of European Studies*, X (June, 1980).

20. Alexis de Tocqueville, *Journey to America*, trans. George Lawrence (New Haven, 1959), 103 ff. and 380 ff. The synopsis of Guillemin's interview is taken from the translated text and also from Tocqueville's notes that appear at the end of the book in French.

21. *Ibid.*, 383.

22. Eugène Ney, "Visite Récente à l'Île de Cuba," *Revue des Deux Mondes* (Jan., 1831), 425–50.

23. Micael sailed, or perhaps floated, since the boat was weighed down with cargo, on the *Brez Locorro* from Havana, with a Captain Torres, on March 12, 1832. U.S. Bureau of Customs, "Supp. Index to passenger lists of vessels arriving at Atlantic and Gulf Coast ports, 1820–1874," La. Coll., NOPL.

24. Pont. v. Pont., Docket #2856, Documents M, P, and O. The division of Micael's inheritance, that is, turning half of it over to Célestin, was valid in his view because Madame Castillon's will had specified that Micael was to receive her mother's property in France. This statement implied (to Célestin) that the New Orleans property was not part of her inheritance. The Pontalbas maintained this interpretation even though the will expressly stated that "the present Will will not derogate in any way the right of my daughter to collect the rest of my succession as my only inheritor." For dotal law in Louisiana, see Arts. 105, 106, *Code of Practice in civil cases for the State of Louisiana* (New Orleans, 1824), 34.

25. He could impound her income at its source, but in France only. Célestin could not require that the United States authorities enforce French law regarding her property. Once she received the New Orleans rents in France, he could legally take them away from her.

26. Micael à Victoire, Paris, 29–30 juillet 1832.

27. *Gazette des Tribunaux*, 10 oct. 1835.

28. Pont. v. Pont., Docket #2856, "Supplemental answer, April 18th 1834," 27; Documents M and N; *Gazette des Tribunaux*, 10 oct. 1835.

29. For some interesting comments about Hennequin, see Archibald Young, *An Historical Sketch of the French Bar: From its Origins to the Present Day* (1869; rpr. Littleton, Colo., 1987), 150–55; Rudolphe d'Apponyi, *Vingt-Cinq Ans à Paris* (Paris, 1913), II, 88.

30. George Sand à Pierre Acollas, Bourges, 16 juillet 1836, in George Lubin, ed., *George Sand: Correspondance* (Paris, 1966), II, 487. Hennequin was Sand's landlord when she lived at 19 du quai Malaquais; he died in 1840.

31. In his pleadings before a tribunal in 1835, Hennequin quoted her as giving the unlikely reply: "I never asked for anything else . . . he left me in Paris; if now he is calling me back, I won't hesitate to go." *Gazette des Tribunaux*, 10, 12 oct. 1835. Micael wrote on June 7, informing her husband that she was ready to resume their conjugal life and would arrive on the twelfth.

32. *Ibid.*; Micael à Victoire, Paris, 29 juillet 1832.

33. Micael à toutes mes cousines, Paris, 17 nov. 1833.

34. *Gazette des Tribunaux*, 10 oct. 1835.

35. Micael à Victoire, Paris, 29–30 juillet 1832.

36. Records of A. J. Fourchy, Étude LVIII/729, "Obligation," 15 oct., 23, 30 nov., 6 déc. 1831, Répertoires d'Études, Archives Nationales, Paris. The loans were made from Mssrs. Duchatelet, Luxeuil, Branville, Veron, and Mansard.

37. *Gazette des Tribunaux*, 10 oct. 1835.

38. *Ibid.*, 10–14 oct. 1835; Micael à Victoire, Paris, 29–30 juillet 1832; Micael described *"les rires sardoniques"* between father and son when she challenged the seating arrangements. Dupin, ed., *Plaidoyers*, II, 35.

39. *Gazette des Tribunaux*, 10 oct. 1835; Micael à Victoire, Paris, 29–30 juillet 1832.

40. Micael à Victoire, Paris, 29–30 juillet 1832.

41. *Gazette des Tribunaux*, 10, 12 oct. 1835; Micael à Victoire, Paris, 29–30 juillet 1832.

42. Micael à Victoire, 29–30 juillet 1832. For French dismay at English hospitals refusing to admit epileptics, see *Le Constitutionnel*, 24 oct. 1834.

43. Micael à Azélie, Paris, 16 sept. 1832. The friend was M. de la Croix.

44. *Gazette des Tribunaux*, 10, 12 oct. 1835.

45. Judgment reprinted *ibid.*, 14 oct. 1835.

46. *Ibid.*, 10–14 oct. 1835; Micael à Victoire, Paris, 26 nov. 1833.

47. Micael à toutes mes cousines, Paris, 17 nov. 1833. See judge's remarks preceding trial in Pont. v. Pont., Docket #2856.

48. Records of C. A. F. Berçeon, "Report of Dr. Marjolin," 23 jan. 1833, RE, AN.

49. Micael à Victoire, 29–30 juillet; Micael à Azélie, 16 sept. 1832. The Théatre du Gymnase on the boulevard Bonne-Nouvelle opened in 1820. Popular with both the old aristocracy and the wealthy bourgeoisie, the house was usually sold out long in advance of performances. It specialized in comedies that gently satirized all segments of society. *Le Chapéron* was a one-act, vaudeville-style comedy by Eugène Scribe and P. Duport which opened on June 2, 1832.

50. Micael à Azélie, Paris, 29 avril 1833.

51. Micael à Victoire, 26 nov. 1833. The Burthes and Livaudais were among those who allegedly refused to see Pontalba. Thomas and David Urquhart had collected rent for Pontalba in 1815–16. St. Avid collected Micael's rents in New Orleans. Noel Barthelémy LeBreton was one of her attorneys. In 1833 Micael was visited by "the Heurquoites ladies," as she spelled "Urquhart."

52. Micael à Azélie, 18 sept. 1832.

53. Micael à Azélie, 27 août 1834, 26 nov. 1833.

54. For details of the judicial system, see Peter Herzog, *Civil Procedure in France* (The Hague, 1967), 86–168, 283–84.

55. Micael à Victoire, Paris, 26 nov. 1833; Micael à Azélie, Paris, 27 août 1834. Maurian's first wife was a cousin of Zoe's husband; his second wife was Zoe's elder sister Céleste; however, he married Céleste some years after writing his judgment on Micael's case.

56. Micael à Azélie, 29 avril 1833, 27 août 1834; Micael à toutes mes cousines, 17 nov.; Micael à Victoire, 26 nov. 1833.

57. Micael à Azélie, 27 août 1834. Three thousand dollars was 15,000 francs. Note that the protagonist of Flaubert's *A Sentimental Education* considered 15,000 francs a year a decent inheritance which would allow him to present himself in bourgeois circles.

58. Notebooks and Sketches of Gaston de Pontalba, Graphics Collection, Louisiana Historical Center.

59. *Mémoires du Général Marquis Alphonse d'Hautpoul* (Paris, 1906), 29–65.

60. "Court Action," 116–44.

61. *Ibid.*; Will of Joseph Xavier Delfau, baron de Pontalba, Jan. 19, 1835, typescript trans. in Pontalba Family Papers, WPA trans., La. Hist. Ctr. The second revision was in

reaction to the Champs-Élysées incident described below. Micael apparently knew nothing about the revisions at this time.

62. Henri Boucher, *Souvenirs d'un Parisian pendant le Seconde République 1831–1852* (Paris, 1906), 53.

63. Micael à Azélie, 27 août 1834.

64. Duchesse d'Elchingen à son mari, 1834, Dossier 4; Napoléon Ney à sa mère, 1834, Dossier 4 (6), Les Archives du Maréchal Ney, AN.

65. Micael à Azélie, Paris, nov. 1833; août 1834.

66. The undated instructions are all that remain of the letter in the Howard-Tilton collection.

67. Duc d'Elchingen à Edgard Vatry, 1 juillet 1850, Dossier 6, Ney Archives, AN.

68. Duchesse d'Elchingen à son mari, 14 août 1833, Dossier 3; Duchesse d'Elchingen à sa belle mère, 1849, Dossier 22.

69. Micael à toutes mes cousines, 17 nov. 1833.

70. The incident occurred on July 7, 1834. Célestin and his friends failed to appear for the first trial in August and were sentenced in default to one month in prison and a fine. Célestin then produced a doctor's certification that they had been absent from the trial because of the illness of one of the defendants. The retrial took place on Sept. 15, 1834. *Gazette des Tribunaux*, 31 août, 14, 15 sept. 1834.

71. *Ibid.*, 12 oct. 1835.

72. This note is dated only "the 19th." Probably it was actually written on the eighteenth of October, 1834; Micael, writing hurriedly, simply put down the wrong date.

73. Monsieur Dupoux [writing for Micael] à Victoire de Lino de Chalmet, Paris, 12 nov. 1834, Letters of Micaela . . . de Pontalba, Spec. Coll., Manuscripts, H-T; *Gazette des Tribunaux*, 10, 12 oct. 1835. Letters d'Edgard, comte Ney à sa mère, Dossier 13; de Napoléon, prince de la Moskowa, Dossier 4 (6); de la duchesse d'Elchingen, 9 nov. 1834; d'Aloys, duc d'Elchingen, Dossier 10, Ney Archives, AN.

74. *Le Figaro*, 24 oct. 1834: ". . . [elle] avait obtenu de son mari un rapprochement qui irrita très vivement son beau-père." Similar reports in *Le Constitutionnel*, 24 oct. 1834; *Journal des Débats*, 23 oct. 1834. Hennequin gives Micael's version of the meeting in *Gazette des Tribunaux*, 10 oct. 1835.

75. *Journal de l'Oise*, 25, 27 oct. 1834.

76. *Gazette des Tribunaux*, 10 oct. 1835. Dupoux à Victoire, Letters of Micaela . . . de Pontalba, Spec. Coll., Manuscripts, H-T.

77. Duc d'Elchingen à sa mère, 22, 28 oct. 1834, Ney Archives, AN. What makes Marjolin's version doubtful is that he also reported that old Pontalba killed himself at once, whereas it appears that Pontalba stopped to rewrite his will.

78. The letters of the Ney family refer confidently to Pontalba's having blown out his brains. However, the court trials seem to indicate that what was blown away was his heart.

79. Dueling guns used musket balls, round rather than bullet-shaped, a little smaller in size than a child's marble. Because their velocity was slower than that of modern bullets discharged from modern weapons, these balls could have penetrated a lung without causing it to collapse. For these and other medical observations in this chapter, I am indebted to Herbert Marks, M. D., of New Orleans, and his collection of rare medical books on the subject of guns and injuries in the nineteenth century.

80. Dupoux à Victoire, Letters of Micaela . . . de Pontalba, Spec. Coll., Manuscripts, H-T; *Gazette des Tribunaux*, 10–14 oct. 1835. Tavernier and Polmier from Senlis attended

her. Doctors from Paris who signed the medical report were Marjolin, Adélon, Dumeril, Fougier, Lisfranc, and Magendie, all familiar names to the rich and sick.

81. *Gazette des Tribunaux*, 3 juin 1835. Faucher's remark found its way into the newspaper *La Quotidienne* and led to his dismissal.

82. *Ibid.*, 12 oct. 1835. Duc d'Elchingen (Aloys) à sa mère, 22 oct. 1834, Ney Archives, AN.

83. *Gazette des Tribunaux*, 10 oct. 1835, deposition of Dr. Tavernier of Senlis, a friend of Célestin, but presumably a man as careful of the truth as any of the other doctors.

84. Napoléon Ney à sa mère, 1834, Dossier 4 (6), Ney Archives, AN.

85. Duc d'Elchingen à sa mère, 4 nov. 1834, *ibid.*

86. Madame de Witt, ed., *Lettres de M. Guizot à sa Famille et à ses Amis* (Paris, 1884), 87.

87. *Gazette des Tribunaux*, 10 oct. 1835; Dupoux à Victoire, 12 nov. 1834, Letters of Micaela . . . de Pontalba, Spec. Coll., Manuscripts, H-T.

VII. A Separation of Body and Belongings

1. Monsieur Dupoux à Victoire de Lino de Chalmet, Paris, 12 nov. 1834, in Letters of Micael, Alfred, and Gaston de Pontalba, Special Collections, Manuscripts Section, Howard-Tilton Library at Tulane University. Dupoux lived in Micael's house.

2. *Journal des Débats*, 23, 26 oct. 1834.

3. See *Le Constitutionnel*, 23–26 oct. 1834. Stendhal considered using the Pontalba history as the basis for some story; he kept several newspaper accounts of the shooting and collected a dossier of biographical information about members of the family. To a friend Stendhal remarked, "I know the husband and the wife. Who was the indirect author-hero of all this mess?" Stendhal à Mme. Jules Gaulthier, Cività-Vecchia, 8 nov. 1834, in *Correspondance de Stendhal, 1800–1842* (Paris, 1908), IV, 132.

4. Prince de la Moskowa à sa mère, 3 nov. 1834, Dossier 4 (6), Les Archives du Maréchal Ney, Archives Nationales, Paris.

5. Duc d'Elchingen à sa mère, 28 oct. 1834, *ibid.*

6. Lettres d'Edgard, comte Ney à sa mère, (n.d.), Dossier 13, *ibid.*

7. Will of Joseph Xavier Delfau, baron de Pontalba, Jan. 19, 1835, typescript trans. in Pontalba Family Papers, Louisiana Historical Center. The will was inspected and signed in New Orleans by Judge Charles Maurian. It reached him two months after he rendered his decision on Micael's property; see *L'Abeille de la Nouvelle Orléans* (New Orleans *Bee*), 25 jan. 1835.

8. Pontalba left the endowment to the incorporated town of Mont-l'Évêque. The school was to be supported by leases on fourteen stores in New Orleans worth 100,000 francs, property that Pontalba had in fact signed over to his son several years previously in lieu of cash to match Micael's dowry. For the eventual negation of the will (Micael on behalf of her husband and children paid 100,000 francs to the town in return for their refusing the bequest), see Edouard de Pontalba à J. W. Cruzat, 10 avril 1908, Correspondance de Baron Edouard de Pontalba, 1904–1914, in Cruzat Family Papers, Spec. Coll., Manuscripts, H-T.

9. Pont. v. Pont, Docket #2856, Louisiana Supreme Court Records, Department of Archives and Manuscripts, Earl K. Long Library at the University of New Orleans. The foregoing comments are taken from Maurian's judgment, rendered in November, 1834,

which begins on p. 159 of the Supreme Court documents dated April, 1839. Micael had won the return of her property by the decision of Judge Pitot in 1831; Célestin appealed that judgment (Docket #2920) but also instituted his own suit (Docket #2856).

10. Victoire and Azélie would have already learned of the incident from Micael's letter, which was apparently the source of the news story. In 1838 Maurian ruled against Micael in a case involving a large sum; Pontalba v. the Phoenix Assurance of London, Docket #11.212, Oct. 29, 1838, Records of the Third Judicial Court 1835–42, New Orleans Public Library. Maurian, who lived at the corner of Burgundy and Barracks Streets, spent a long life on the bench and died with great honors in January, 1858.

11. Like much else that occurred during the marriage, the account of the attempted visit is given in the separation trial of May, 1835, but the exact date of the incident is not recorded. *Gazette des Tribunaux*, 12 oct. 1835.

12. Prince de la Moskowa à sa mère, 1834, Dossier 4 (6), Ney Archives, AN.

13. According to the report of several doctors, she could not bear to have anything touch one of the fingers which, though mutilated, was not removed. *Gazette des Tribunaux*, 12 oct. 1835.

14. Micael à ses cousines, Paris, 8 juillet 1835, Letters of Micaela . . . de Pontalba, Spec. Coll., Manuscripts, H-T.

15. Edgard, comte Ney à sa mère, (n.d.), Dossier 13, Ney Archives, AN.

16. *Gazette des Tribunaux*, 12 oct. 1835.

17. Micael à Azélie, Paris, 16 août 1851, Letters of Micaela . . . de Pontalba, Spec. Coll., Manuscripts, H-T. Leeches were applied in order to remove what was thought to be contaminated blood close to a wound. After the initial bite, the leech injected a secretion that prevented clotting so that it could suck out blood. According to reliable medical opinion, the procedure was not painful; the Humphrey Bogart hero in *The African Queen* had to look down to realize that his body had become host to a number of leeches.

18. *Gazette des Tribunaux*, 12 oct. 1835. Célestin responded to Hennequin's petition by insisting that Micael live with him before regaining her rents. He offered her a "temporary residence," so termed in his answer to the court, a hôtel that had formerly belonged to his father at 348 rue St.-Honoré in Paris. Hennequin, on February 14, protested against this solution.

19. "Séparation de corps et biens" is sometimes translated as "bed and board separation," the English term for the legal arrangement. The system of filing complaints and rebuttals was essentially the one used in Louisiana to try the two cases of the absentee Pontalba spouses. Judge Maurian made his decision without hearing testimony or taking depositions from either Célestin or Micael.

20. Henri Robert, *Un Avocat de 1830* (Paris, 1930), 87.

21. The records included pretrial hearings, as well as hearings of petitions that one side or the other may have presented to the court but which the Senlis tribunal decided did not merit a trial. Hennequin's speech is quoted in full in *Gazette des Tribunaux*, 10, 12 oct. Duval's speech is also given in its entirety 12, 14 oct. 1835.

22. Augustin Challamel, *Souvenirs d'un Hugolâtre* (Paris, 1885), 80.

23. *Gazette des Tribunaux*, 12 oct. 1835.

24. Four hundred sixty separations were granted in France in 1837; of these, sixty-two were in the Department of the Seine, which contains Paris. The number of separations steadily increased: 590 in 1838, 684 in 1842, 756 in 1850. Whether the plaintiff in each action was a husband or wife is not indicated. S. Ledermann, "Les divorces et les séparations de

corps en France," *Population* (April–June, 1948), 338. Micael's tribunal was presided over by a M. Jeury.

25. See the sketches by Honoré Daumier satirizing judges, appearing in the 1830s in *Charivari*.

26. Micael à Victoire, 21 mai 1835, Letters of Micaela . . . de Pontalba, Spec. Coll., Manuscripts, H-T.

27. Dorothy McBride Stetson, *Women's Rights in France* (New York, 1980), 83 ff. The courts in France found, for example, that a husband had the right to sell anything belonging to his wife that was movable; Adeline Daumard, *Le Bourgeoisie Parisienne de 1815 à 1848* (Paris, 1906), 109. Many of the same legal restrictions applied to wives in Louisiana as well, right up through the middle of the twentieth century; but Louisiana law unequivocally recognized a wife's right to control her inherited property. *Code of Practice in civil cases for the State of Louisiana* (New Orleans, 1824), 34.

28. Micael à Victoire, 21 mai 1835. For the exclusion of women from public life, see R. Cubain, *Trait des droits des femmes en matière civile et commerciale* (Paris, 1842), 370.

29. Quotation is from the doctors' report read by Hennequin.

30. Pierre-Sophie-Léon Duval was born in Marseilles in 1804 and attended the Collège de Ste.-Barbe. His clients included Giulia Grisi, Émile Girardin, Mlle. Rachel, and Augustine Duverger. He died at Blanville in 1878 without biographers.

31. "Court Action Between the Baron and Baroness de Pontalba," Tribunal of Senlis, May 11, 1835, WPA trans., typescript in La. Hist. Ctr., provides an excellent, though not quite complete, rendition of Duval's pleadings. For Hennequin's pleadings we cite the French text given in *Gazette des Tribunaux*.

32. Quoted in Eugène Dupin, ed., *Plaidoyers de Philippe Dupin* (Paris, 1868), II, 16–17. Duval compared her to *femmes perdues*, who were lost, clearly, because they were loose.

33. *Gazette des Tribunaux*, 14 oct. 1835.

34. *Ibid*. "At fifteen, pretty and rich, you will realize that she does not lack *amoreux*," Mme. Castillon à Xavier de Pontalba, 22 jan. 1811, ms. in New Orleans Notarial Archives. I am indebted to Sally Reeves for bringing to my attention the location of the original document.

35. Registre 122, 2ième Chambre, Cour Royale de Paris, 8, 9 nov. 1840, Archives de Paris.

36. *Gazette des Tribunaux*, 14 oct. 1835; "Court Action," 98.

37. *Gazette des Tribunaux*, 14 oct. 1835; "Court Action," 106.

38. He quoted a fragment of one of her letters to young Célestin in which she allegedly advised the boy to "wait a little longer" before making his escape. The letter reached the school after Célestin had already gone and so was forwarded to Mont-l'Évêque. In a later suit Micael's new lawyer Dupin insisted that the letter had nothing to do with any escape plans and had been quoted out of context. Dupin, ed., *Plaidoyers*, II, 20.

39. Nickname for the Théâtre-Italien.

40. One cannot, however, be certain that her right to spend her own money would have been more than a technicality to the judges, even if they had clearly understood that she was not depriving the Pontalbas of their personal resources. French law and society seem to have had no clear conception of a woman's private property, just as our own society and legal system are reluctant to concede that a married man may have resources to which his wife and children are denied lawful access.

41. In this Duval was entirely correct. If we follow Micael's letters to her aunt from Paris in the summer of 1832, it appears that she had a pattern of remaining at the château only a week or two before escaping to Paris for a week. In August she abandoned even the appearance of commuting when, after an alarming convulsive seizure, she decided to remain in Paris no matter what the consequences.

42. *Gazette des Tribunaux*, 14 oct. 1835; "Court Action," 184. There is significant divergence between the judgment reported in the *Gazette* and the "Judgement" in the WPA translation. The version that has found its way into the Pontalba Family Papers is one in which Célestin altered the wording.

43. Dupin, ed., *Plaidoyers*, II, 4.

44. Micael à Azélie, Paris, 21 mai 1835; Micael à ses cousines, 8 juillet 1835, Letters of Micaela . . . de Pontalba, Spec. Coll., Manuscripts, H-T.

45. Dupin, ed., *Plaidoyers*, II, 30.

46. Micael à Azélie, 6 avril 1836.

47. Thinking of the Pontalba trial, George Sand was inspired to inquire of Hennequin whether she too might qualify for a separation on the grounds that her husband had subjected her to public opprobrium. She also had one interview with Philippe Dupin.

48. He was born Oct. 7, 1795. It was common practice for the Chamber of Peers to hire lawyers to plead certain issues before the large assembly. Both Hennequin and Dupin had given many speeches before the chamber. Philippe Dupin's brother, André-Marie Dupin, called Dupin the Eldest, was one of the three lawyers who defended Marshal Ney in 1815. Born in 1783, Dupin the Eldest was a judge, president of the Chamber of Deputies from 1832 to 1840, and an admirer of Hennequin. Baron Charles Dupin, born in 1784, was a statistician, engineer, and a member of the Chamber of Peers. Philippe Dupin won a separation in another well-known trial called the Daloz Affair, in which, however, he represented the husband. He died in 1846. See Archibald Young's remarks about the family in *An Historical Sketch of the French Bar* (1869; rpr. Littleton, Colo., 1987), 165 ff.

49. Anatole Bérard des Glajeux, *Souvenirs d'un Président d'Assises (1880–1890)* (Paris, 1892), 117.

50. Dupin, ed., *Plaidoyers*, I, xxiii–xxxix. The duc de Broglie remarked that the Dupins belonged to "a group of arrogant and vulgar plebians," *Souvenirs, 1785–1870* (Paris, 1886), 57.

51. Lawyers were immune from prosecution for statements made during pleadings.

52. Dupin, ed., *Plaidoyers*, II, 41. Henry Fielding was himself a magistrate and a consistent exponent of the idea that life in high society was dull and socialites were shameless.

53. Micael à Azélie, Paris, 6 avril 1836.

54. The appellate court upheld Judge Pitot's decision to return the administration of Micael's property to her; however, the court agreed with Célestin's contention that she had never made "amicable demand" on him for the return of her rents, and therefore condemned her to pay Célestin's court costs and his legal fees. Micael appealed the part of the judgment relating to Célestin's costs. She won in the Louisiana Supreme Court—but not until 1839, Pont. v. Pont., Docket #2129, Supreme Court Records, UNO. Célestin did not drop his countersuit against her until April 29, 1839, just as it was about to be argued before the Louisiana Supreme Court; this was the same suit that had been adjudicated in the lower courts before Judge Maurian, Pont. v. Pont., Docket #2856.

55. The contract that governed their separation was made on June 15, 1836. According to its terms, the five lawsuits still pending between them were to be withdrawn. Célestin

admitted that both sides of the Place d'Armes were hers, along with her mother's property on rue St.-Honoré and Place Vendôme. He was to have no claim whatever on the property she was planning to buy on 41–43 St.-Honoré. He would return to her 9,943 francs which his agent had collected in rents from her houses in France. Célestin gave back to Micael the Bayou Road property he had appropriated, including 152,000 francs to compensate her for the part of that property he had sold. She received a total of 326,250 francs from the division of their community property. In return, she abandoned to him the house on rue du Houssaie and all of Mont-l'Évêque, with one exception: she wanted back the fruitwood bed, her bed, which he had taken out of her bedroom. Since he had apparently sold the bed already, he had to compensate her for it. He gave her in advance the authorization needed by a separated wife to sell her property and to make certain intended purchases, including a country house in France which she never got around to buying. As for the children, it was costing about 24,000 francs a year to keep the younger boys in a boarding school run by G. Charles Davilliers and Company. It is not clear who had been paying their expenses, but it was agreed that after the separation those expenses would be borne equally by Célestin and Micael. On reaching twenty-one, each of the boys would get an allowance of 8,000 francs a year which Célestin and Micael would provide equally; however, Micael made the provision that she would stop her part of the allowance to any one of her sons who married without her consent. Célestin II had been receiving 15,000 francs a year from Micael during his sojourn in America. Records of Ch. A. F. Berçeon, Étude LVIII/747, "Transaction entre M. le Baron et Mme. la Baronne de Pontalba," 16 juin 1836, Archives Nationales, Paris.

VIII. HOME ALONE

1. Micael à Azélie Chalmet, 6 avril 1836, Letters of Micaela, Alfred, and Gaston de Pontalba, Special Collections, Manuscripts Section, Howard-Tilton Library at Tulane University.

2. Louis Philippe's reign lasted until the somewhat stronger upheaval of 1848 established a republic in France with Louis Napoleon as president. In 1852 Louis Napoleon abrogated the republic, declaring France to be an empire with himself at its head. This empire ended in 1870 when France was defeated in the Franco-Prussian War and Napoleon III abdicated. The new republic, the Third Republic, lasted until the German occupation of 1940.

3. The ball was given by the comtesse de Flavigny. Frederick Artz, *France Under the Bourbon Restoration* (Cambridge, Mass., 1931), 257.

4. Servants' entrances came into general use about 1837, but among many people the new custom did not catch on for several more years.

5. On the interaction between levels of society, see René de Belleval, *Souvenirs de ma Jeunesse* (Paris, 1895), 52. In the Place Vendôme, the location of one of Micael's houses, a second-floor apartment such as Micael might occupy rented for 600 francs ($120); an attic apartment went for 40 francs (eight dollars).

6. Micael à Victoire, 29–30 juillet 1832; Micael à Azélie, 27 août 1834, Letters of Micaela . . . de Pontalba, Spec. Coll., Manuscripts, H-T.

7. Micael à Azélie, 27 août 1834. One thinks immediately of Eugène Delacroix; however, she mentions her friend traveling to New Orleans, whereas the painter is not known to have visited Louisiana.

8. Micael à Victoire, 21 mai 1835; Prosper Mérimée, *Correspondance Générale*, ed. Maurice Parturier (Toulouse, 1956), IV, 345.

9. Augustin Challamel, *Souvenirs d'un Hugolâtre* (Paris, 1885), 84, 288; *Le Moniteur universel*, 9 avril 1848.

10. Giulia Grisi (1811–1869), Giovanni Rubini (1806–1868), Antonio Tamburini (1800–1876), Luigi Lablache (1794–1858). "At Madame de Pontalba's the first place belonged to music, at Mme. de Rumford's, to politics. . . . The Baroness de Pontalba drew the great stars of Italian opera to her concerts, Rubini, la Grisi, Lablache, Tamburini. . . ." Louis Allard, *Esquisses Parisiennes* (Montreal, 1943), 83. Allard gives no source for this information.

11. *Ibid.*, 94; Rudolphe d'Apponyi, *Vingt-Cinq Ans à Paris* (Paris, 1913), 88.

12. Roughly a million for each, depending on which suburbs are included. Micael's circle of friends included the comtesses Valmy and Daubisson, the duchesse de Ventadour, the wife of Napoleon's Marshal Macdonald, the poet Jules Canonge, Mme. Dumésnil, Mme. de Rumford, and the Péreire bankers.

13. Charles de Franqueville, *Souvenirs Intimes sur la Vie de Mon Père* (Paris, 1878), 224.

14. Micael à Victoire, 29–30 juillet 1832.

15. Micael à Azélie, 6 avril 1836.

16. "Souvenirs rédigés par Mme. Gamot . . . 6 au 7 décembre 1815," s.d.; Duchesse d'Alrantès à Balincourt, Paris, 7 déc. 1815, Les Archives du Maréchal Ney, Archives Nationales, Paris.

17. Napoléon Ney à sa mère, 3 nov. 1834, Dossier 4, *ibid.*

18. "Mariage de M. le Prince de la Moskowa avec Mlle. Laffitte," notarial act by A. Batardy, 22 jan. 1828, *ibid.* See also Léon's letters to his mother, oct.–déc. 1834, Dossier 4.

19. Paul Duchon, ed., *Mémoires de Laffitte* (Paris, n.d.).

20. Charles Bousfield, trans., *Memoirs of Count Horace de Viel Castel* (London, 1888), II, 24.

21. Fontainebleau, s.d., Lettres d'Edgard, comte Ney (1812–82), Dossier 19, Ney Archives, AN.

22. Lettres de Michel-Louis Félix Ney, dit Aloys, 1833–54, Dossier 6, *ibid.*

23. Charles Boucher, *Mémoires* (Paris, 1908), II, 177, 483; Comtesse d'Armaille, *Quand On Savait Vivre Heureux* (Paris, 1934), 2, 3; Duchesse de Dino, *Chronique de 1831 à 1862* (Paris, 1909), II, 540.

24. Lettres de la duchesse d'Elchingen à son mari (1833–53), 14 août 1834, Dossier 4, Ney Archives, AN.

25. *Ibid.* 19 sept. 1834.

26. *Ibid.*, 26 nov. 1834.

27. *Ibid.* Versailles, 12 nov. 1835, Dossier 5.

28. *Ibid.*, 26 nov. 1835.

29. Lettres de la duchesse d'Elchingen à sa belle-mère, 9 oct. 1834, Dossier 21, *ibid.*

30. Lettres de la duchesse d'Elchingen à son mari, 7 jan. 1851, Dossier 23, *ibid.*

31. The princesse de la Moskowa was the daughter of a banker, Pierre Auguié, originally of Figeac, like the family Pontalba. She was a cousin of Joseph Xavier. Her mother was Adélaïde Genest, who had been first lady of the bedchamber to Queen Marie-Antoinette. Dossier 28, *ibid.*

32. Aloys' death certificate in the Ney Archives is dated July 14, 1854, 8:40 P.M. The "darling daughter," Louise-Hélène d'Elchingen (1842–1893), was to become the princess Bibesco.

33. "Inventaire après le décès de Mme. la duchesse d'Elchingen," Ney Archives, AN. She died June 30, 1889, at Versailles, leaving paintings, sketches, books on history, literature, science, poetry, and travel, and a modest estate.

34. Micael à Victoire, juillet 1835, Letters of Micaela . . . de Pontalba, Spec. Coll., Manuscripts, H-T.

35. 41, 43, 45 rue St.-Honoré. For contemporary reactions to the size of the mansion, see M. Audiganne, *Paris Dans Sa Splendeur* (Paris, 1861), III, 9.

36. *Le Figaro*, 27 fev. 1859; Charles Simond, *Paris Pendant l'Année 1859* (Paris, 1900), II; *Almanach Imperial, 1860* (Paris, 1868), 18. Louis Napoleon had three residences, including the Hôtel Sebastiani or Choiseau-Praslin, scene of the Praslin murder. The government purchased and completely renovated the infamous house for his use.

37. One noticeable difference was the elimination of several columns on the front; the Rothschilds' architect was Félix Langlais (1827–1889).

38. Some of the panels were made by Gabriel-Germain Boffrand and G.-M. Oppenordt during Louis XV's regency. Paintings by Jean Restout, Jean Dumont, Carle Van Loo, and Jean-Baptiste Oudry had been set in the panels in 1742. For an uncritical and somewhat inaccurate discussion of the Rothschild changes to the Hôtel Pontalba, see Bruno Pons, *Les Grands Décors Français* (Paris, 1995).

39. Marie Galbraith, ed., *The American Ambassador's Residence in Paris* (Paris, 1985). This is a commemorative booklet written under the aegis of the ambassador's wife who lived in the house immediately after the renovations were completed and supervised the decoration. "A Parigi, per l'Ambasciata Americana," *Domus*, No. 528 (Nov., 1973), provides blueprint details of the renovation.

40. Robert Hughes, "The Beaux-Arts Tradition Reconsidered," *Horizon*, XVII (Winter, 1976), 65–71.

41. Ville de Paris, Cadastre de 1862, rue du Faubourg St.-Honoré, Série D1P4416, Archives de Paris.

42. Records of Charles St.-Ange Berçeon, Étude II/1000, "Vente par le mandatoire de M. le duc d'Havré à Madame de Pontalba," 17 déc. 1838; "Ratification," 8 mars 1840; "Quittance à Mme. de Pontalba" (she was represented by Alfred), 2 juillet 1840; see also "Quittance 15, 16 juin 1836 par de Boisgelin à Mme. de Pontalba," 5, 6 déc. 1836; and "Vente par M. Armand Céleste Comte de Durfort à Mme. de Pontalba," 15 juillet 1839, Archives Nationales, Paris. The Hôtel d'Havré at 86 rue de Lille was near the Quai d'Orsay. The duc d'Havré may have been getting on in years when he signed the "Quittance" declaring Micael's debt to him fulfilled, for he seems to have signed his name with a blackened broom handle instead of a pen.

43. "Visconti présente à Napoléon III les plans d'achèvement du Louvre," by Jean-Baptiste Ange Tissier (1814–1876). The prince de la Moskowa stands behind the emperor to the right, looking away from Visconti; Moskowa was at that time a royal secretary.

44. "Note Adressée à Mssrs. les Experts, par Madame la Baronne de Pontalba," n.p., n.d., 2, ms. in Spec. Coll., Manuscripts, H-T. Visconti had designed the Gaillon Fountain in 1824. In 1825 he was named architect of the royal library; none of his many designs for the restoration of that building was executed. Also in 1825 he designed a house for Mlle. Mars in the artists' quarter on rue Tour des Dames. All Paris and several army officers had pressed their affections on Mlle. Mars, and her house was well received. Visconti restored the Hôtel Forbin-Jauson in 1831, and constructed the Louvois Fountain from 1835–39.

Within the next few years he constructed the Molière Fountain (1842) and the fountain of Saint-Sulpice (begun in 1843) and collaborated on a fountain in Bordeaux.

45. "Entrée des Cendres de Napoléon Ier à Paris," 15 déc. 1840, lithograph by E. Guérard, reproduced in Audiganne, *Paris Dans Sa Splendeur,* III.

46. To be admitted to the Invalides, a veteran had to be over sixty with thirty years of service, or he had to have lost at least one limb. Though begun by Visconti in 1843, the mausoleum was not completed for another decade. The architect who finished the tomb was J.-F. Bouchet, an admirer of Visconti who faithfully executed his design. See Visconti's catalogue for the tomb, *Tombeau de Napoléon Ier dans le dôme des Invalides* (Paris, 1853), in which he is of course not critical of the emperor.

47. Christiane Aulanier, *Le Nouveau Louvre de Napoléon III* (Paris, n.d.), 14.

48. "Note Adressée à Mssrs. les Experts," 3.

49. *Ibid.*, 3–5.

50. The late Comte Hervé du Périer de Larson of Paris, a direct descendant of Visconti, kindly allowed me complete access, at some inconvenience to himself, to his private collection of Visconti's papers; these include many of the plans for the Hôtel Pontalba.

51. "Note Adressée à Mssrs. les Experts," 5.

52. *Ibid.*, 7, 9.

53. Audiences, Tribunal de Commerce, 15 fév. 1841 (D2U332027), Archives de Paris, Annexe (at Villemoison, near Paris). Commercial court is a section of the French judiciary that hears disputes arising from business dealings.

54. "Note Adressée à Mssrs. les Experts," 10.

55. See the case involving Micael, Leroy, Texier, and Benois, 28 oct. 1841, and Baronne de Pontalba c. Vivenel, 18 mai 1843, Tribunal de Commerce, Archives de Paris, Annexe at Villemoison.

56. The date of completion is uncertain. In 1851 Gaston, writing to Eugène Rochereau, remarked, "I wish we had you with us on this [construction]," which may indicate either that Micael was planning another building or that substantial building was still going on in the Hôtel Pontalba. However, Micael and her sons were living in the house in the 1840s; Gaston à Eugène Rochereau, E. Pascagoula [?], Letters of Micaela . . . de Pontalba, Spec. Coll., Manuscripts, H-T.

57. Tencé c. de Pontalba et Vivenel, 23 avril 1842, Tribunal Civil de la Seine; 26 déc. 1842, Cour d'Appel; 20 nov. 1843, Cour d'Appel; Registre 131 (1843), 2ième Chambre, Archives de la Seine (D1U9, 131), Archives de Paris.

58. Records of Ch. St.-Ange Berçeon, Ét. II/1101, "Mainlevée par M. Mignon," 18 juin 1863, AN. To see what Micael actually paid for masonry, one of the largest expenses in the building, see Tencé c. de Pontalba et Vivenel, 23 avril 1842, Tribunal Civil.

59. David Van Zanten, *Designing Paris* (New York, 1987), 116–17, shows that some architects received 20 percent on government assignments and 40 percent on private commissions, which Van Zanten believes was standard. However, Visconti's papers show that on another large project similar to Micael's, his commission was only 5 percent, Collection of du Périer de Larsan, Paris.

60. Guy Thullier, *La Vie Quotidienne dans les Ministères au XIXe siècle* (Paris, 1976), 55; Pierre Guiral, *La Vie Quotidienne en France à l'âge d'or du capitalisme, 1852–1879* (Paris, 1976), 165; Joanna Richardson, *La Vie Parisienne* (London, 1971), 248.

61. Prince Napoleon (son of Napoleon I's brother Jerome and brother of Princesse Mathilde) attested to the expense of a society wedding when he petitioned the state treasury

to help him defray the cost of his nuptials, Bousfield, trans., *Memoirs of Viel Castel*, II, 147. The funeral was that of the duc de Modina Coeli, *La Gazette de France*, 9 jan. 1873.

62. Guiral, *La Vie Quotidienne*, 22–23; Bousfield, trans., *Memoirs of Viel Castel*, II, 221; Guy Thullier, *Bureaucratie et Bureaucrates en France au XIXe siècle* (Geneva, 1980), 73.

63. Pierre Bléton, *La Vie Sociale sous le Second Empire* (Paris, 1963), 65–66.

64. Being Jewish was something of a social handicap in Micael's day and became more of one with the passing decades. Education was not a social consideration. Micael could not write three sentences together without a misspelling; her husband, who completed his academic schooling at thirteen, was probably no more literate, though he could accurately compute the difference between his income and hers.

65. "Note Adressée à Mssrs. les Experts," 7.

66. Micael à mes cousines, 8 juillet 1835; 6 avril 1836, Letters of Micaela . . . de Pontalba, Spec. Coll., Manuscripts, H-T.

67. Micael à Azélie, 3 sept. 1842.

68. Micael à Azélie, 26 juillet 1846.

69. Micael à Azélie, 3 sept. 1842.

70. *Journal des Débats*, 22, 23, 24 fév. 1848.

71. Edouard de Pontalba à J. W. Cruzat, Valgenceuse, 20 oct. 1909, Correspondance de Baron Edouard de Pontalba, 1904–1914, in Cruzat Family Papers, Spec. Coll., Manuscripts, H-T.

IX. NEW ORLEANS IN 1850

1. Pontalba v. Felice David, f.w.c. [free woman of color], Third District, Docket #15.860, May 24, 1843, New Orleans Public Library. See also Pont. v. Joseph Vento, #12.589, Mar. 20, 1840, for $250 for three months' rent; Pont. v. Ramon Planas, #15.265, Nov. 8, 1842, for eight months' rent at $400 a month from two houses on the corner of Levee and St. Ann Streets; Pont. v. Lacroix Frères, #15.3114, Nov. 22, 1842, for $300 for three months' rent for a store between St. Peter and Jefferson Streets; Pont. v. Juan Presas, #15.921, June 20, 1843, for $870 owed for a house at the corner of Levée and St. Ann.

2. Ladies of the night: Journal of the Minutes of the Council of the First Municipality, Aug. 6, 1849; licensing beggars: Feb. 17, 1851; street paving: April 23, Oct. 1, 1849, Louisiana Collection, NOPL. There was no standard method for paying for street improvement; the costs might be borne by the city, by the property owners, or by both.

3. William Kernion Dart, "Walt Whitman in New Orleans," *Publications of the Louisiana Historical Association*, I (1914), 97–108, original ms. for this article is in Louisiana Historical Center; Micael à Azélie Chalmet, Paris, 1842, Letters of Micaela . . . de Pontalba, Special Collections, Manuscripts Section, Howard-Tilton Library at Tulane University.

4. *Daily Delta*, May 2, 1851.

5. Council Minutes, First Municipality, Sept. 7, 1846, Jan. 15, 1852, June 7, 1853.

6. L. H. Pilie, Surveyor, to Council, *ibid.*, Dec. 29, 1851. Such amenities as garbage boats and street signs were paid for out of taxes on slaves and real estate and by municipal bonds.

7. New York *Times*, Aug. 2, 1854. For general antipathy to dogs, see *L'Orléanais*, Mar. 6, May 29, 1849; Oct. 12, 1850; *Daily Picayune*, May 30, 1844; Mar. 5, 1852; Council Minutes, Second Municipality, June 23, 1846.

8. *Daily Picayune*, Sept. 14, Oct. 12, 1842; Sept. 14, Oct. 20, Nov. 3, 1847; May 28, 1854.

9. *L'Orléanais*, June 24, 1848; Jan. 18 and March, 1848 (continual coverage); May 4, June 1, 1849; Aug. 27, 1853; May 24, June 29, Aug. 5, 1854.

10. Ronald Vern Jackson, ed., *Mortality Schedule: Louisiana, 1850* (Bountiful, Utah, n.d.). This interesting resource is found together with the census records in Goverment Documents, H-T.

11. See random issues of the *Daily Crescent*, *L'Orléanais*, and the *New Orleans Bee*, 1849–50.

12. Inventory for a Partition, Oct. 21, 1853, Records of P. C. Cuvellier; Acts of Procuration, May 12 and 16, and Act of Sale, June 6, 1848, Records of Theodore Guyol; Act of Sale, April 29, 1853, Records of Robert J. Ker, all in New Orleans Notarial Archives. To get an idea of the value of this parcel, we may note that 59 of the squares, 1,282 lots, sold for $125,000.

13. For example: Micael acquired clear title to one parcel of 80 square blocks through a compromise with the heirs of Chalon in 1848. She gave 21 of the squares to her lawyer in lieu of a fee; she sold the remaining 59 to Edward Durell in 1853. Durell defaulted after two years, having paid out about $115,000. The sheriff auctioned off the repossessed property. Micael herself bought back five-sixths of it; most of the remainder, 96 lots, were bought by Patrick B. O'Brien, who paid cash but sued Micael when he discovered that he was responsible for paying for the drainage of the land. That suit was finally settled in her favor in 1858 by the Louisiana Supreme Court. As for the five-sixths of the sale that came back to Micael, she had to first settle a claim by the N.O. Canal and Banking Co. Then she sold her 19 squares, together with 11 squares from another parcel, for about $100,000.

14. Of these lawsuits, four were particularly significant: 1) Joseph Kenton v. Micaela Leonarda, N.O., Eastern District, Docket #3511, Feb., 1842, in La. Sup. Ct.; the case went to U.S. Sup. Ct. in Jan., 1850, 1 *Rob.* 344, p. 191; 2) Theodore Nicolet and Samuel Moore v. Mrs. Pontalba, Docket #3512, Dec. 27, 1836; 3) Mme. de Pontalba v. the Mayor, Aldermen, and Inhabitants of N.O., Docket #1936, Jan. 30, 1849, Louisiana Supreme Court Records, Department of Archives and Manuscripts, Earl K. Long Library at the University of New Orleans; 4) Mme. de Pontalba v. Chalon Heirs, Third District, #1750, Dec. 14, 1848, and Heirs of Chalon v. Mme. M. L. de Pontalba, #7662, Oct. 26, 1855, NOPL.

15. Kenton v. Micaela Leonarda, Docket #3511, Supreme Court Records, UNO.

16. "Partage Between Mme. de Pontalba and the Heirs of Chalon/Desruisseaux," Dec. 28, 1848, Records of Jules Mossy; "Inventory for a Partition," Oct. 21, 1853, Records of P. C. Cuvellier; "Partage, Mme. de Pontalba and Louis Janin," Dec. 30, 1848, Records of Jules Mossy, NONA; Mme. de Pontalba v. T. B. Blanchard, Second District, #6784, Oct. 21, 1853, NOPL (suit petitions for an inventory of land that parties have already agreed to divide).

17. Pontalba *et al.* v. Copland *et al.*, La. Sup. Ct., reported in 3 *La. Ann.* #86, pp. 73–76. A copy of the appeal is in Spec. Coll., Manuscripts, H-T.

18. Kenton v. Micaela Leonarda, Docket #3511, Supreme Court Records, UNO, "Petition for a re-hearing." The petition implied that the lower court judge had not taken the time to read all the material in the case, "435 Closely written pages, besides a number of other detached documents and some 10 or 12 plans."

19. 1 *Rob.* 339, New Orleans, Feb., 1842.

20. Mme. de Pontalba v. the Mayor, Aldermen, Docket #1936, Supreme Court Records, UNO; Municipality No. 1 v. Mrs. de Pontalba, Third District, #1936, Jan. 30, 1849, NOPL. The land, according to a survey by d'Hemecourt on Dec. 22, 1836, was Sq. 10, between Johnson, Galvez, Ursuline, and St. Philip Streets.

21. Mme. Baronne de Pontalba à Eugène et Albin Rochereau et William T. Hepp, Paris, Mar. 3, 1853, Records of Robert J. Ker, NONA.

22. An interesting study is Leon C. Soulé, "The Creole-American Struggle in New Orleans Politics, 1850–1862" (M. A. thesis, Tulane University, 1955), in La. Coll., H-T.

23. Robert C. Reinders, *End of an Era: New Orleans, 1850–1860* (New Orleans, 1964), 27.

24. Seventh Census, 1850, "Annual Statistics of New Orleans," Government Documents, H-T; *De Bow's Review*, X (1851), 446–49.

25. "Passenger Lists of Steamships Arriving in New York, 1848–1850," microfilm, New York Public Library. Ships arriving from Europe in 1848 were filled with Irish farmers escaping the potato famine.

26. Louisiana bank notes had *DIX* (TEN) printed on their backs, in deference to French spenders. Traders referred to such cash as "dixies," and Louisiana as "Dixie Land." The term was eventually applied to the whole South.

27. *L'Orléanais*, Sept. 14, 22, 1850; *Daily Crescent*, April 8, 1850.

28. 1840 Combined Tax Registry for New Orleans, microfilm, H-T. I am indebted to Lawrence Powell for bringing this document to my attention.

29. Council Minutes, First Municipality, Dec. 4, 1846; Oct. 12, 1839; Dec. 16, 1844, La. Coll., NOPL.

30. *Daily Crescent*, Feb. 9, 1850.

31. *L'Orléanais*, Oct. 18, 1850.

32. The suburb is not to be confused with the city of Lafayette, 110 miles west of New Orleans.

33. *Daily Crescent*, April 9, 10, 25–27, 1855; May 24, Oct. 26, 31, 1853; Mar. 16, 1854; Mar., 1855 *passim*.

34. 1840 Combined Tax Registry for New Orleans.

35. *Daily Crescent*, Jan. 24, 1850.

36. *Ibid.*, Oct. 9, 1849.

37. Council Minutes, Third Municipality, April 4, 1846, offers a comparative list of the municipality's revenues over a period of several years.

38. Council Minutes, Second Municipality, July 7, 1846.

39. Council Minutes, First Municipality, Oct. 5, 1849; Nov. 28, 1850.

40. *Ibid.*, Oct. 1, 1849; Oct. 25, 1851; Aug. 6., 1849.

41. Records of P. C. Cuvellier, Feb. 2, 1852, NONA; Council Minutes, First Municipality, Oct. 5, 1849; Feb. 3, 17, Mar. 10, Oct. 6, 1851. On Feb. 18, 1853, he was still petitioning for his fee.

42. Council Minutes, First Municipality, Oct. 14, 1850. French mansard roofs and dormer windows were added to the Cabildo and Presbytere in 1847, a little earlier than the other renovations to the square.

43. Félix de Courmont, *Le Taenarion: Satires Périodiques* (New Orleans, 1846). I am indebted to Wayne Everard for bringing to my attention this curious document from the La. Coll., NOPL; translation is mine and is assuredly not worse than the original. Courmont was an attorney born in the Antilles who studied law in France; he came to New Or-

leans some time between 1835–41 and began writing *Le Taenarion* in 1846. The periodical appeared twice a month for five months, an effort that must have left him little time for law. His satires, including an operetta he wrote protesting U.S. involvement in the Mexican War, got him into trouble, apparently; he suddenly left New Orleans for France in 1847. See Edward Larocque Tinker, *Les Écrits de Langue Française en Louisiane au XIX*ᵉ *Siècle* (Paris, 1932), 93–94.

44. Council Minutes, First Municipality, Aug. 28, Apr. 30, 1849.

45. Drawing in Graphics Collection, La. Hist. Ctr. After a few hurricanes, it was decided that the spires had to be closed. The beautiful grillwork was then covered with blue slate. See also "Contract . . . with John Patrick Kernion," Mar. 12, June 22, 1849; April 5, 1850, Records of Joseph Cuvellier, NONA; "Contract . . . with J. N. B. de Pouilly," n.d., La. Hist. Ctr; Council Minutes, First Municipality, Mar. 28, 1848, La. Coll., NOPL.

46. *Daily Picayune*, May 17, 1874.

47. *Daily Delta*, Dec. 8, 1850.

X. BUILDING

1. *Louisiana Courier*, Oct. 12, 1850. Number 5 now comprises several apartments, with the addresses 520–524 St. Peter Street.

2. Samuel Stewart v. Mme. de Pontalba, Second District, Docket #4194, Dec. 20, 1851, Rare Manuscripts, in New Orleans Public Library for the present, but the records are disintegrating rapidly. Penmanship is so difficult in many of the documents as to render much of the testimony unreadable.

3. *Ibid.*, Testimony of Allen Hill and Henry Howard, 19–20. Many years after the completion of the buildings, Howard listed the Pontalba Buildings first among constructions that had been executed "from my designs and specifications. . . ." Edwin L. Jewell, *Jewell's Crescent City Illustrated* (New Orleans, 1873). That claim is not borne out by any document concerning the construction of the Pontalbas. For Gallier's sketch, see Leonard V. Huber and Samuel Wilson, Jr., *Baroness Pontalba's Buildings*, 4th ed. (New Orleans, 1979), 37–38.

4. Pierre-François-Henri Labrouste (1801–1875) designed a seminary in Rennes; the Hôtels Fould, Vilgruy, and Thouret in Paris and the Hôtel Rouvenat in Neuilly-sur-Seine; the Clugny Tomb in Fontenay-aux-Roses; the administrative offices of the Paris-Lyon-Méditerranée Railroad; the Thouret Tomb in Montmartre Cemetery; and several tombs in Montparnasse Cemetery. See Henri Delaborde, *Notice sur la vie et les ouvrages de M. Henri Labrouste* (Paris, 1878).

5. I am indebted to Madame Claudine de Vaulchier, curator of the Académie d'Architecture, Paris, for her substantial assistance and knowledge of Labrouste's work.

6. Nottoway Plantation, White Castle, La.; the Carrollton Courthouse Building, which has been used in recent years as a New Orleans public school; and St. Elizabeth's Home, to name a few.

7. Stewart v. Pontalba, Rare Mss., NOPL.

8. In *Jewell's Crescent City*, Howard is described as having studied with James Dakin in 1849, the time of his encounter with Micael. Edwin Jewell, the author, was Howard's good friend.

9. Stewart v. Pontalba, Testimony of H. Lathrop and Henry Howard, 17 ff. The contractor solved the problem of the incline after some experimentation by building up the

foundation on one side thirteen inches above the curb. Even so, the building is (impercep-tibly) lopsided.

10. *Ibid.*

11. "Building Contract Between Mme. de Pontalba and Mr. Stewart," June 7, July 20, 1849, records of L. T. Caire, New Orleans Notarial Archives. See Vieux Carré Survey, in Historic New Orleans Collection, the museum's compendium of documents relating to certain pieces of property in the Old Quarter.

12. "The floors throughout the building (except the ground floors) shall be made of the best quality of cypress planks grooved and tongued at the joints, 5 inches wide, and 1 1/4 inches thick without sap knots or other defects, perfectly dry, and secret nailed, the heads tongued, and the surface planed smooth after being nailed down. The lower floors shall be of the first quality cypress planks 1 1/2 inches thick, with square points, nailed down upon cedar sleepers 2 inches by 4 inches laid upon a pavement of bricks laid with sharp sand and hydraulic cement, and covered with charcoal dust," "Building Contract Between Mme. de Pontalba and Mr. Stewart." The document reflects a surer knowledge of building than of English syntax, suggesting that Stewart himself probably wrote it. Stewart was given all the bricks and other materials from the demolition of the old build-ings.

13. "Building Contract, Samuel Stewart and agents of Mrs. M. L. A. de Pontalba," Jan. 6, 1852, records of A. Ducatel, NONA. The contract was obviously filed with the no-tary some time after it was made.

14. Stewart v. Pontalba, Testimony of Allen Hill and Joseph Jewell, Rare Mss., NOPL.

15. Samuel Stewart to Joseph Jewell, N.O., Sept. 10, 1849, in Stewart v. Pontalba, *ibid.*

16. Minard Lafever, *Beauties of Modern Architecture* (New York, 1845[?]), Plate 21, "De-sign for a Centre Flower."

17. Notebooks of Gaston de Pontalba, Graphics Collection, Louisiana Historical Cen-ter.

18. W. A. Tallen to Samuel Stewart, N.O., Sept. 25, 1849, in Stewart v. Pontalba, Rare Mss., NOPL. Stewart owned slaves who possibly worked on the building.

19. *Ibid.*, Testimony of Joseph Jewell.

20. *Ibid.*

21. Stewart v. Pontalba, Testimony of Howard.

22. *Ibid.*

23. Stewart v. Pontalba, Testimony of Lathrop. The injunction indicates that Micael was having trouble with the workers going ahead with work before she could approve what they had done.

24. *Ibid.*, Second testimony of Richard Rice.

25. Micael à Azélie Chalmet, Pascagoula, juillet 1849, Letters of Micaela, Alfred, and Gaston de Pontalba, Special Collections, Manuscripts Section, Howard-Tilton Library at Tulane University.

26. Stewart v. Pontalba, Testimony of Joseph Jewell; Supplemental Answer of Mrs. de Pontalba, May 2, 1851, Rare Mss., NOPL. In fairness to Micael, the gutters put in by Stew-art seem too small and shallow, judging by Jewell's description, and may have been badly installed.

27. *Ibid.*, Testimony of Richard Rice; Petition of Samuel Stewart.

28. *Ibid.*, Petition of Samuel Stewart, "Extra Work on the Above Buildings."

29. *Ibid.*, Testimony of Rice.

30. "Agreement between Samuel Stewart and Mrs. de Pontalba," Jan. 6, 1852; "Release of Privilege," Nov. 30, 1852, Records of A. Ducatel, NONA.

31. Stewart v. Pontalba, Testimony of Jewell, Rice, Allen Hill, and Talen.

32. *Ibid.*, List of Extra Charges.

33. *Ibid.*, Testimony of Allen Hill. I am indebted to Rena Wilson for sharing her information about her grandfather, Samuel Stewart.

34. W. A. Tallen to Samuel Stewart, N.O., Sept. 25, 1849, *ibid.*

35. Wrought iron is hammered with tools, as opposed to cast iron, which is formed in a mold.

36. For this and many other observations regarding the architectural value of the Pontalbas, I am indebted to Vaughn Glasgow of the Louisiana Historical Center, who has generously shared his knowledge of the buildings and his esthetic insights.

37. While she lived in New Orleans, Micael most frequently used the surname "Almonester de Pontalba." That form appears on notarial and court records.

38. Graphics Coll., La. Hist. Ctr.; Council Minutes, First Municipality, Dec. 4, 1846, Feb. 17, 1851, La. Coll., NOPL. The trees in Jackson Square were replaced, and the view of the houses facing each other is again obstructed by greenery.

39. City Hall (now Gallier Hall), designed in the Classic Revival style by James Gallier, Jr., was finished in 1850.

40. Turkeys were sold live. During the holiday season, they were herded up Camp Street on the way to market from one of the boat landings. Eliza Ripley, *Social Life in Old New Orleans* (New York, 1912), 160.

41. Notebooks of Gaston de Pontalba, Graphics Coll., La. Hist. Ctr.

42. S. A. Stockdale to Dr. Ross Johnson, N.O., July 27, 1858, "U.S. Customs House Correspondence, 1834–1912," typescript, La. Hist. Ctr.

43. W. C. Flanders to Cuthbert Bullett, N.O., July 7, 1863, *ibid.* See also letter of May 31, 1865, concerning proposed quarantines of ships carrying cases of Russian plague, Asiatic cholera, and smallpox. For other diseases, see Sept. 18, 1872, July 6, 1875, and Jan. 20, 1877.

44. John Duffy, *Sword of Pestilence: The New Orleans Yellow Fever Epidemic of 1853* (Baton Rouge, 1966), 19. The worst offenders were the St. Charles, Verandah, and City Hotels. The practice was still going on in the 1870s. See James Casey to Benjamin Flanders, N.O., July 25, 1872, in "Customs House Correspondence," La. Hist. Ctr.

45. John Duffy, ed., *Parson Clapp of the Strangers' Church of New Orleans* (Baton Rouge, 1957), 108–109.

46. *Ibid.*, 97.

47. Gaston de Pontalba à Azélie Chalmet, E. Pascagoula, 1848, Letters of Micaela . . . de Pontalba, Spec. Coll., Manuscripts, H-T.

48. *Ibid.*

49. Gaston à Azélie, 5 août 1847, avril 1849. Gaston wrote that his mother would take the train from the lake at 6:30 A.M.

50. Gaston à Azélie, 13 juillet 1849.

51. U.S. Censuses, 1830, 1840, 1850, Louisiana, City of New Orleans, microfilm, NOPL.

52. Gaston à Azélie, n.d.

53. Gaston à Azélie, 26 août 1850.

54. Gaston à Azélie, jeudi, 5 sept. 1850. Eliza Ripley remarked that no one except those in mourning wore black and that even old people went about in bright colors, *Social Life*, 60. Nisida, the wife of Commodore Rousseau, was Azélie's sister's daughter, that is, one of the fifteen second cousins provided to Micael by her fertile first cousin Victoire. Nisida died childless in 1878.

55. Gaston à Célestin de Pontalba, E. Pascagoula, 21 sept. 1849, Letters of Micaela . . . de Pontalba, Spec. Coll., Manuscripts, H-T.

56. In fact, Micael borrowed 180,000 francs, using her house on Place Vendôme as collateral. When she got back to France, she obtained a release from that mortgage and instead put up the Hôtel Pontalba as security, Records of Ch. St.-Ange Berçeon, Étude II/1131, "Translation d'hypothèque," 2 mai 1863, Répertoires d'Études, Archives Nationales, Paris.

57. Gaston à Azélie, 26 août 1850.

58. *Ibid.*, E. Pascagoula, avril 1849.

59. Alfred à Azélie, Mobile, 5 sept. 1849, 22 juillet, 1849, Letters of Micaela . . . de Pontalba, Spec. Coll., Manuscripts, H-T.

60. Zachaniel (no surname) to Decius Beebe, N.O., Aug. 22, 1853, in Beebe Family Papers, La. Hist. Ctr.

61. Gaston à Eugène Rochereau, E. Pascagoula, juin 1849, Letters of Micaela . . . de Pontalba, Spec. Coll., Manuscripts, H-T. John Duffy, in his study of the New Orleans yellow fever epidemic of 1853, commented that blistering, or the placing of vesicatories, fulfilled the principal medical requirement of the day: "In the first place, it was excruciatingly painful to the patient; in the second place, since the wound was almost certain to become infected and superation ensue, both the patient and the physician could see in the formation of pus that the blisters were drawing poison from the system." *Sword of Pestilence*, 151.

62. Duffy, *Sword of Pestilence*, 151. See also Dr. W. G. Austin's letter to his daughter (n. d.) describing his yellow fever treatment, in George Smith Collection, La. Hist. Ctr.

63. John Duffy, *The Tulane University Medical Center: One Hundred Years of Medical Education* (Baton Rouge, 1984), 37.

64. Alfred à Azélie, Mobile, 5 sept. 1849.

65. Gaston à Eugène Rochereau, 1850 [?].

66. Gaston à Azélie, oct. 1850.

67. *Louisiana Courier*, Sept. 28, 1850. Until she moved in, applications were taken by another of her agents, Judah P. Benjamin, at 51 Canal Street. Benjamin would later become part of the Confederate government.

68. Council Minutes, First Municipality, Mar. 19, 1851, La. Coll., NOPL. The council did at least try to keep the market clear of rotten fish and meat.

69. In New York the crowds would not let her carriage pass. People climbed on the roof of the carriage and sat on the wheels as the hapless driver first whipped the horses and then lashed at the crowd; Lind intervened. She had a much-delayed journey to her lodgings. See account in New Orleans *Weekly Delta*, Sept. 16, 1850. See also C. C. Rosenberg, *Jenny Lind's Tour of America and Cuba* (New York, 1851).

70. *Republican*, April 4, 1875.

71. The steamer was the *Falcon*. *Daily Delta*, Feb. 2, 1851.

72. *Daily Picayune*, Feb. 2, 1851.

73. *Ibid.*; see also New Orleans *Commercial Bulletin*, Feb. 2, 1851; New Orleans *Bee*, Feb. 2, 1851.

74. *Daily Picayune*, Feb. 2, 1851.

75. *Daily Delta*, Jan. 31, Feb. 6, 1851.

76. *Daily Picayune*, Mar. 12, 1851.

77. *Daily Delta*, Feb. 5, 16, 1851. The Vieux Carré fire department was not responsible for putting out fires in the Second Municipality, but in such an emergency they might have sent reinforcements.

78. Its successor was the famed French Opera House.

79. Henry Kmen, *Music in New Orleans* (New Orleans, 1966), 138, 196.

80. *Republican*, Apr. 4, 1875.

81. Ripley, *Social Life*, 65; Opera ticket for Tues., Dec. 19, 1865, in Miscellaneous Collection, La. Hist. Ctr.

82. Quoted by Robert C. Reinders, *End of an Era: New Orleans, 1850–1860* (New Orleans, 1964), 187. For another reaction to her voice, see New Orleans *Commercial Bulletin*, Feb. 3, 1851.

83. *Daily Delta*, Feb. 12, 1851.

84. *Daily Picayune*, May 17, 1874.

85. *Daily Delta*, Feb. 16, 1851. On one page containing twenty-three short articles in all, nine were either articles about Jenny Lind or advertisements for products that used her name.

86. *Ibid.*, Mar. 13, 18, 19, 1851; *Daily Picayune*, Feb. 8, 1852.

87. *Daily Delta*, Feb. 19, 20, 1851.

88. Marie Louise Hoffman, "The St. Vincent's Hotel" (M.A. thesis, Tulane University, 1933).

89. Gaston à Azélie, aboard the steamer *Washington*, 2 mai [?] 1851. Gaston also mentioned Micael missing her cousins Heloise and Malvina.

90. *Ibid.*

91. Notebooks of Gaston de Pontalba, Graphics Coll., La. Hist. Ctr.

92. Gaston à Azélie, 2 mai [?] 1851.

XI. THE WAR IS OVER

1. Micael à Azélie Chalmet, Paris, 16 août 1852, Letters of Micaela, Alfred, and Gaston de Pontalba, Special Collections, Manuscripts Section, Howard-Tilton Library at Tulane University.

2. Gaston à Azélie, Paris, 21 avril 1852, *ibid*.

3. Célestin's house is now the site of a church, St.-Honoré d'Eylau. He gave complete legal control of his assets to Micael. Notar. Records of Charles St.-Ange Berçeon, Étude II, "Procuration," and "Autorisation," 30 avril 1852, Archives Nationales, Paris.

4. Célestin was due to inherit more than half of Mont-l'Éveque, along with all of Migneaux and Mme. de Miró's stores in New Orleans, all left to him by his grandmother in her haphazard will. In exchange for taking over all of Mont-l'Éveque, he ceded part interest in the New Orleans property to his brothers, without their consent, Records of A. J. Fourchy, Ét. LVIII/763, "Pacte de Famille," 11 déc. 1845, in "Inventaire après le décès de Mme. la Baronne [Louise] de Pontalba," 1 avril 1840, AN.

5. Célestin's manipulation of his father's assets is revealed in Records of Ch. St.-Ange Berçeon, "Mainlévée," 21 jan. 1850; "Décharge," 25 juin 1851, 30 avril 1852, Répertoire d'Études, Archives Nationales. Records of Fourchy, Ét. LVIII/22, "Dépot," 31 jan. 1850;

"Procès verbal d'Enchère," 28 déc. 1850, 31 jan. 1851 (Migneaux); "Vente," and "Dépôt," 21 fév. 1851; "Quittance," 20–31 oct., 7 nov. 1851, 8 juillet, 28 oct., 4 nov. 1852. The Paris exchanges are explained in Records of Fourchy, Ét. LVIII/807, "Vente," 31 oct. 1851, and Ét. LVIII/22, "Adjudication," 2 fév. 1851, all in AN, and *L'Union de Seine-et-Oise*, 23 avril 1851.

6. "Pacte de Famille," 24 sept. 1851, passed before Victor Chartier of Senlis, is explained in old Célestin's sale of Migneaux: Records of Fourchy, Ét. LVIII/809, "Vente," 32 oct. 1851, and "Quittance," 31 déc. 1851, 1 sept., 12 fév., 4 nov., 19 mai 1852. See also Records of Berçeon, "Pacte," 10 août 1855. For Célestin's power of attorney to his sons: Records of Berçeon, "Procuration," 30 avril 1852, 5 mars 1854. For Micael's mortgage: Records of Berçeon, Ét. II/1131, "Translation d'Hypothèque," 25–30 déc. 1851; Ét. II/1101, "Mainlévée," 8 mai 1856, 2 mai, 18 juin 1863, 28 nov. 1864, all in AN.

7. "De Pontalba c. Préfet de l'Oise," Cour de Cassation, 17 déc. 1861, in *Journal du Palais* (Paris, 1861), 820. See also an eighty-six-month case in which a neighbor wanted Micael to tear down a yard wall because it blocked her sunlight, "Mattier c. de Pontalba," Cour de Cassation, juin 1850, in A. Dalloz, *Jurisprudence Générale* (Paris, 1861), VI, 820.

8. I am indebted to the late Countess Paul de Leusse of Mont-l'Évêque for showing me this and several other family portraits from her private collection.

9. Gaston à Azélie, 21 avril 1852, Letters of Micaela . . . de Pontalba, Spec. Coll., Manuscripts, H-T. Gaston also wrote of Albin Michel and his wife, who were close friends. "We were crestfallen," he continued, "to learn of the ruin of our poor cousin Marigny. What a frightful disaster and how we pity his wife, whose kindness, patience, courage, and devotion deserved a better reward. What will become of her? Will she go live with Mme. Sentimana [Sémana] and how will she stand such a cruel blow?"

10. Micael à Azélie, 16 sept. 1851.

11. Records of Berçeon, Ét. II/1104, 1122, "Contrat de Mariage," 24 mars 1859; see especially "Acceptation d'emploi," 11 mai 1859, attached to the contract; "Inventaire . . . de Mme. de Pontalba," 7 mai 1862, all in AN. The inventory, taken at old Célestin's house, shows that the residence was large and comfortable.

12. Records of Berçeon, Ét. II/1130, "Mariage," "Consentement," 30 déc. 1863.

13. Records of Joseph Cuvellier, Dec., 1844, and Feb., 1850; Records of L. T. Caire, Jan.–Dec., 1855, Aug. 2, Dec. 3, 1856; Records of Joseph Lisbony, June 14, 1856, also containing "Pacte de Famille," New Orleans Notarial Archives.

14. Mirès purchased *Journal des Chemins de Fer*, founded the *Conseiller du Peuple*, and bought the Bonapartist *Le Pays* and *Le Constitutionnel*.

15. Jules Mirès, *À Mes Juges* (Paris, 1864), 171 ff.

16. Records of Berçeon, "Mainlévée de Pontalba au profit de Mme. de Pontalba par . . . Crédit Mobilier," 21 juin 1858, RE, AN.

17. *Réponse de M. de Pontalba à l'écrit de M. Mirès intitulé "À Mes Juges"* (Paris, 1861), 15 ff.

18. Mirès accompanied Pontalba to Marseilles but remained in the suburbs, out of sight. Pontalba conferred with him every night.

19. Graphics Collection, Louisiana Historical Center.

20. Mirès, *À Mes Juges*, 196–200, gives a copy of the contract.

21. See the account by Mirès' chief prosecutor at the trial: Ernest Picard, *Mon Journal* (Paris, 1892), 69 ff.

22. *Ibid.*, 70–71. Documents bear out Mirès' contention. For two random examples, see Records of Constant Amédée Moquard, Ét. LXVIII/17, "Mainlévée, Mirès . . . au

profit de S. A. J. Mgr. le Prince Napoléon, d'hypothèque . . . ," 15 oct. 1860; "Quittance, Mirès . . . au prince Napoléon François Lucien Charles Murat de 100,000f," 4 juin 1861, AN.

23. Mérimée à la Comtesse de Montijo, Paris, août 1861, in Prosper Mérimée, *Correspondance Générale*, ed. Maurice Parturier, IV (Toulouse, 1956), 344 ff; Louis Bouihet à Flaubert, Paris, 13 juillet 1861, in Maria Luisa Cappello, ed., *Lettres à Gustave Flaubert* (Paris, 1996), 318. I am indebted to Harry Redman, Jr., for bringing this letter to my attention.

24. Picard, *Mon Journal*, 69.

25. Records of Berçeon, Ét. II/1131, "Transaction entre les liquidateurs . . . et . . . de Pontalba," 5 fév. 1864. See also Records of Fourchy, Ét. LVIII/846, "Quittance . . . de 1,075,000 francs," 17 jan. 1861, AN.

26. Records of Berçeon, Ét. II/1136, 1140, "Vente . . . à Mme. la Baronne de Pontalba," 3–4 jan. 1865; "Mainlévée," 25–26 nov. 1871, 17 juin 1865, including her husband's transfer to her of the *majorat*.

27. Records of Moquard, Ét. LXVIII/1130, "Vente," 7 juin 1861; "Quittance à Valoir," 12 déc. 1861; "Mainlévée," 14 sept. 1867; "Mainlévée définitive," 8 sept. 1871, AN.

28. Records of Fourchy, Ét. LVIII/746, 771, "Réquisition de certificat," 22 jan. 1836; "Bail," 3 mars 1837; "Ratification," 8 fév. 1840; "Bail," 23 nov., 18 jan., 18 juin 1843. Compare with Records of Berçeon, Ét. II/1115, "Bail," 23–29 fév. 1861, 13 avril 1864, 10 juin 1865, 1 juillet 1867, 22 avril 1870, 13 nov. 1871, 31 jan., 24 mai, 8 juin, 7 août, 30 oct. 1872, 8 août, 20 nov. 1873, 23 juillet 1874, and for rue Argenteuil, 4 mai 1868.

29. Records of Augustin-Louis Massion, Ét. XXXIV/1333, "Côté Cinquième," starting with "Échange avec P. R. Matière et L. Dabois," in "Inventaire après le décès de Mme. la Baronne de Pontalba, 30 avril 1874," AN.

30. *Ibid.*, "Côté Cinquième, Titres de propriété de la Terre de Mont-l'Évêque," starting with "Adjudication J. B. L. Lavoisière." See also Records of Berçeon, Ét. II/1132, 1134, "Bail," 13 août 1864.

31. "Bail Meignan," "Bail de chasse," "Bail Leclerc," all under "Côté vingt troisième" of "Inventaire, 30 avril 1874," *ibid.*

32. Records of Fourchy, Ét. LVIII/850, "Procuration . . . de Pontalba," 5, 6 août 1864. For information on the smelter's location and success, I am indebted to Joseph Papineau of Ontonagon, Michigan, for sharing his research on the now vanished smelter.

33. *La Presse*, Dec., 1866.

34. Johanna Richardson, *La Vie Parisienne* (London, 1971), 85.

35. Gustave Claudin, *Mes Souvenirs* (Paris, 1884), 160.

36. Charles Simond, *Paris de 1800 à 1900* (Paris, 1901), III, 24. This is a collection of reprints from Paris newspapers.

37. Micael mentioned to Azélie in 1852 that her closest friend in Paris was Mme. de Lévis. The Lévis accompanied the Bourbon heir-apparent into exile during the Napoleonic years. Célestin *fils* was friendly with the ardent royalist duc de Lévis.

38. Records of Massion, Ét. XXXIV/1333, "Inventaire après le décès de Mme. la Baronne de Pontalba, 30 avril 1874."

39. Based on the figures Moquard reported as the concierge's monthly wage, *ibid.*

40. Laure Adler, *La Vie Quotidienne dans les Maisons Closes, 1830–1930* (Paris, 1992).

41. Blanche de Pontalba à Henri de Pontalba, Mont-l'Évêque, 6 mai 1864. I am deeply indebted to Count Adrien Balny d'Avricourt of Paris, a direct descendant of Micael, who

kindly provided me with a handwritten copy of the original from the Maricourt Papers collected by André de Maricourt.

42. Records of Fourchy, Ét. LVIII/839, "Dépôt," et "Mariage . . . ," 30 avril 1864.

43. Grillades are marinated strips of meat, sauteed and then simmered in water.

44. Records of Fourchy, Ét. LVIII/859, "Contrat de Mariage," 14 mai 1864. Edouard's son, Célestin Félix George, was born at Senlis on Mar. 1, 1865; he died at the age of fifteen. Louise gave birth to Michaelle de Maricourt on Mar. 4, 1865, on Cyprus.

45. *Tägliche Deutsche Zeitung*, Mar. 24, April 17, 1857; "Pontalba Building Residents (1851–1861)," ms., La. Hist. Ctr; leases for Mar. 30–31, Records of A. Ducatel, NONA.

46. *Daily Picayune*, Dec. 4, 1866. Including promissory notes, Micael was owed $8,000–$9,000 at her death. Lafitte, Dufilho, & Co., agents, v. Wm. Fernandez, Docket #17.369, Aug. 30, 1866; v. John Slemmer, Docket #17.378, Dec. 4, 1865; v. M. Riley, Docket #17.372, Dec. 4, 1865; v. A. Boube, Docket #17.373, Dec. 3, 1865, all in 6th District, Docket F, microfilm in Louisiana Collection, New Orleans Public Library.

47. Of that amount $548 was back rent owed from previous months. Records of Massion, "Inventaire."

48. D. W. Brogan, *The Development of Modern France* (New York, 1940), 34; see also articles in London *Spectator* throughout 1871.

49. An excellent study of the uprising is Robert Tombs, *The War Against Paris, 1871* (Cambridge, Eng., 1981).

50. Ernest Alfred Vizitelly, *My Adventures in the Commune* (London, 1914), 186. Vizitelly was a journalist from England who remained in Paris largely unmolested by any side during the siege and civil war. His colorful reports cannot be verified; however, his descriptions of the Communards show the kind of information provided to English readers concerning the uprising.

51. Statistics for troops and casualties vary widely even in the government's own reports. The numbers offered by Tombs, *War Against Paris*, 12–30 *passim*, seem as reasonable as any and have been used throughout this account.

52. Ernest Legouvé, *Soixante Ans de Souvenirs* (Paris, 1887), II. For a complete list of damaged public buildings, see M. Denormandie, *Notes et Souvenirs* (Paris, 1895), 383–84.

53. "De Pontalba c. Préfet de l'Oise," 27 juin 1873, in A. Dalloz, *Jurisprudence Générale* (Paris, 1874), IV, 428.

54. Records of Massion, Ét. XXXIV/1337, "Consentement à exécution du testament de Mme. la Baronne de Pontalba" (contains will), 26 août 1874; "Holograph Will . . . ," in "Succession of M. L. A. Pontalba," Aug. 7, 1874, 2nd District Court, Docket #37.182, La. Coll., NOPL. The translation by J. S. Ware differs from the Massion will in the disposition of Micael's residence, and appears to be some version of the will that was later superceded. Micael chose as her executors her notaries, Berçeon and Moquard. When she deposited the will in their office, she paid their executors' fees in advance.

55. "Order of court putting Heirs in possession of Madame de Pontalba's succession," Jan. 13, 1875, Records of Conveyances, Book 103, p. 578, in Civil District Court, New Orleans.

56. An interesting detail of Micael's succession is that a "public administrator" in New Orleans, E. T. Parker, petitioned the 2nd District Court to name him "administrator and determinor" of her New Orleans properties. William Miltenberger, Micael's local agent, then came forward to oppose Parker's petition and was himself eventually named "authorized agent" of her children, "Succession of M. L. A. Pontalba," La. Coll., NOPL. Louise's

son Michael and Edouard's daughter Jeanne, who were Micael's godchildren, each received 100,000 francs. Louise and Edouard each had another child. These two youngsters were given 50,000 francs each.

57. "Acte de décès d'Almonaster Michael," numéro 579, Archives de Paris. For this document I am indebted to Madame Edmée Chanay.

58. The incident is recorded in the section near "Cloture" in Records of Massion, "Inventaire."

59. "Order of Court . . . succession of Gaston de Pontalba," 1876, Records of Conveyances, Civil District Court, New Orleans; Records of Berçeon, Ét. II, "Inventaire . . . Gaston Célestin Delfau," 19 nov., 16, 30 déc. 1875, 28 sept., 7 oct., 1876, AN. Gaston also left money to his brother Célestin's children.

60. Records of Berçeon, Ét. II, "Inventaire . . . d'Alfred C. D. de Pontalba," 17 fév. 1877; "Procuration," 31 jan., 15 fév. 1877; "État . . . de Pontalba," 9 juillet 1879; for leases: "Bail," 14 sept. 1877; 16, 30 déc. 1878; 28 oct. 1881. Michel's tutorship ended in 1881. 256 and 350 St.-Honoré continued to be highly profitable rental properties for many more years.

61. When Mont-l'Évêque was the home of the bishops of Senlis, the two estates had been joined.

62. Célestin married Marie Claire de Barneville. One of their children died in infancy. After Célestin's death, his widow married Léon Soyer and lived until about 1918.

63. Records of Moquard, Ét. LXVIII/17, Numéro 1279, "Certificat de vie," 31 mai 1875; Records of Berçeon, Ét. II, "Inventaire après le décés . . . ," 26 août 1878; Death certificate of J. X. C. de Pontalba in Pontalba Family Papers, La. Hist. Ctr.

64. The philanthropist was William Ratcliffe Irby who, when he was only eighteen, lost his father, mother, and brother to yellow fever, all within eleven days in 1878. Irby made his fortune in tobacco; he committed suicide in 1926. I am indebted to Gayle Smith for sharing her research on Irby.

Bibliography

The documents that form the basis of this work are contained in a confusing array of colonial archives, family papers, court cases, notarial acts, and municipal records. The most critical of the manuscripts are subsumed in broad collections whose names would provide no guide for the researcher attempting to survey the sources of this biography. Therefore, the primary documents will be annotated and arranged by subject in this bibliography. Most of the secondary materials, however, need no explanation beyond a simple listing.

MANUSCRIPTS AND DOCUMENTS

Documents for the Spanish colonial period in Louisiana are plentiful and obtainable because of the Crown's long tradition of detailed, well-organized record keeping in the colonies. Louisiana libraries have taken pains to preserve and catalog colonial documents; consequently, these are often the most accessible of the manuscript holdings. A good place to start in the documents is with the communications between the colonial officials in New Orleans and the royal administrators. The section of Seville's Archivo General de Indias that deals with Louisiana can be found on microfilm in the Historic New Orleans Collection. Before attacking the immense archive, however, one should make use of one of the excellent summaries available, such as José de la Peña y Camara, *et al.*, eds., *Catálogo de Documentos del Archivo General de Indias (Sección V. Gobierno-Audiencia de Santo Domingo) sobre la época española de Luisiana* (2 vols.; New Orleans, 1968), containing six thousand entries organized by *legajos*. A very useful but specific aid to research in the archive is Albert J. Robichaux, Jr.'s *Louisiana Census and Militia Lists, 1770–1789* (New Orleans, 1973), the first of his two volumes of translations from the Papeles Procedentes de Cuba; the original census and lists made by the Spanish government were written in French. Since a high proportion of colonists served in the army or militia in one capacity or another, it is worthwhile to look at another set of communications, the military service records prepared for the viceregal administrators; these are found in Archivo General de Simancas, Hojas de Servícios Militares de America, 1785–1815, in the Latin American Library of Howard-Tilton Memorial Library at Tulane University. Despatches of the Spanish Governors of Louisiana, a typescript in both Howard-Tilton and the Louisiana Historical Center, is a fascinating collection of letters addressed mainly to the governors' superiors, the captains-general of Cuba. Like many of the manuscripts used in this study, the despatches were compiled and translated by the Work Projects Administration in the Survey of Federal Archives in Louisiana. To follow the correspondence of the governor through the transfer of Louisiana to the United States, see Dunbar Rowland, ed., *Official Letter Books of W. C. C. Claiborne, 1801–1816* (6 vols.; Jackson, Miss., 1917). Dunbar Rowland and E. C. Sanders, eds., *Mississippi*

Provincial Archives, rev. ed. Patricia Kay Galloway (Baton Rouge, 1984), is useful for studying the background of relations between the Indians and the colonial administrators.

The day-to-day administration of New Orleans can be seen nowhere so clearly as in the voluminous Records and Deliberations of the New Orleans Cabildo, 1763–1803, and in Acts of the Cabildo, 1769–1803. The original Spanish manuscripts and the WPA translations are on microfilm in the New Orleans Public Library; they include all of the orders of the governors and significant communications from the Crown, along with minutes of the meetings of the town council. The *cabildo* records are essential for tracing Almonester's career and the history of Charity Hospital; the New Orleans City Council Records are similarly necessary for following the disputes between the widow Almonester and the city. Other critical documents regarding Almonester are "Constitution for the New Charity Hospital of New Orleans, 1793," WPA translation in the Louisiana Historical Center, and "Inventory and Delivery of the Effects and Utensils of the Charity Hospital, April 17, 1801," manuscript in Howard-Tilton. For a comparison of Charity Hospital with other medical facilities in the Spanish colonies, see *Constitutiones y ordenazas para el régimen y gobierno del Hospital Real y General de los Indios de esta Nueva España (1778)*, Vol. B-1 of *Documenta Novae Hispaniae* (20 vols.; Windsor, Ontario, 1980).

For an examination of Spain's commercial policies, see "Regulations and Royal Tariffs for the Free Commerce of Spain to Louisiana, the Indies, and Her Other Possessions, 1788," WPA-translated typescript in the Louisiana Historical Center, keeping in mind that the regulations were constantly changed, stretched, or ignored in practice; for an idea of the reality of trade with Louisiana, see the Diego de Gardoquí Papers and the Robert Smith and Nicholas Low Papers, 1782–1811, both collections in Howard-Tilton.

Useful miscellaneous manuscripts from the Spanish period are "Plan Showing the Location of the Fire–March 21, 1788," and Will of Andrés Almonester, WPA translations in the Louisiana Historical Center; "Mayor's Office: Spanish Census of New Orleans," microfilm in the New Orleans Public Library; "Droit de Levée du Baron de Carondelet, 28 juin 1792," in the Louisiana Historical Center; and "Auto de buen Gobierno de Don Manuel Gayoso de Lemos, 1798," in Howard-Tilton. Daily life in colonial New Orleans is reflected in merchandise accounts of Don Josef Reynes and Don Pedro Ancil (1797–1798), and Joseph Vidal (1799), and in the letters of Nathanial Cox, all in the John Smith Collection, Louisiana Historical Center.

By far the most valuable documents for comparing the wealth and tastes of New Orleanians are estate inventories, which also give considerable information about slaves. "Inventory of the Estate of J.-B. Castillon" (Aug. 13, 1809), in Wills and Successions of Carlos Ximenes, New Orleans Public Library, was used extensively. See also "Intestate Succession of Carlos Favre d'Aunoy, Oct. 10, 1780" and "Proceedings Related to the Estate of Francisco Maria de Reggio, Oct. 5, 1787," both WPA translations in the Louisiana Historical Center. For other inventories and specific conveyances of property and slaves, see Records of Michel de Armas, Pedro Pedesclaux, J. B. Garic, L. Mazange, and Andrés Almonester, in the New Orleans Notarial Archives, Civil Court Building.

The complicated intermarriages of Louisiana families, including the de la Rondes, Pontalbas, and Almonesters, are clarified in Emile Ducros, "Genealogical Papers Series, 1946," manuscript in Cruzat Family Papers, Howard-Tilton. Sooner or later, every researcher in this area turns to the Funeral Records and Sacramental Registers of the Archives of the Archdiocese of New Orleans, and the burial records in the Historic New Orleans Collection. These have been recently compiled under the supervision of Earl C. Woods, published in succession as *Sacramental Records of the Roman Catholic Church of the Archdiocese of New Orleans* (10 vols. to date; New Orleans, 1987–   ).

Several letter collections have been used exhaustively in this study. Correspondance du Gouverneur Don Estevan Miró à son neveu Joseph Delfau de Pontalba (in Spanish, though the title is in French), 1791–1794, and Pontalba's side of the correspondence (in French) are both in the Louisiana Historical Center, the location of Pontalba's later, more important letter diary, Letters of Joseph X. Pontalba to His Wife, 1796, translated by the WPA. It should be noted that there are several major Pontalba repositories in New Orleans, the Pontalba Family Papers and Miró Papers in the Louisiana Historical Center, and Pontalba documents contained in a number of collections in Howard-Tilton, including the Cruzat Family Papers, the Pontalba Family Papers, and Letters of Micaela, Alfred, and Gaston de Pontalba. The Pontalba document collections in the Louisiana Historical Center and Howard-Tilton overlap but are by no means identical. Micael's letters to her aunt and cousins are only in Howard-Tilton, which also contains Correspondance de Baron Edouard de Pontalba, 1904–1914, from the Cruzat Family Papers. Also worthwhile are the collected letters of Julian Poydras, "Private and Commercial Correspondence of an Indigo and Cotton Planter, 1794–1800," in the Louisiana Historical Center.

The original documents concerning the 1811 slave revolt of St. Charles and St. John the Baptist parishes are in a volume of uncataloged manuscripts, "1810–1811, Original Acts, Judge Pierre B. St. Martin, St. Charles Parish Records of Commandants, Judges and Recorders, 1734–1871," housed in the St. Charles Parish Courthouse, Hahnville, Louisiana.

Micaela's life in France is outlined in her many court trials, cited below, and her letters. The property conveyances of all the Pontalbas and Madame Castillon, along with their debts, rental income for any given period, temporary separations, and "family pacts" can be laboriously but precisely reconstructed using notarial records in Paris. First, the Répertoires d'Études, a chronological description of all acts of a particular notary, must be consulted. Often the *répertoires* are not indexed, so one must search the gist year by year, through all the notary's clients, to find acts passed for the Pontalbas or Madame Castillon. However, the répertoires summarize each notarial act so that one can distinguish routine proxies or, let us say, simple receipts for payments from significant documents. The notarial documents themselves are contained in each notary's *études*, collections covering successive periods of three or four months of his work. Since a researcher is permitted to consult only a few études per day, it is necessary to first scan the répertoires and narrow the search. The records for notaries working in Paris in Micael's day are generally found in the Archives Nationales and, occasionally, the Archives de Paris; records for Senlis notaries are theoretically in either Senlis or Beauvais, but few of these have actually survived from the first half of the nineteenth century. For Madame Castillon's life in Paris, the notary to be researched is L. H. Breton who, along with Victor Chartier and Auguste Guibourg of Senlis, also handled the affairs of the Pontalbas during the early years of

Micael and Célestin's marriage. From the 1830s on, A. J. Fourchy's records contain the Pontalba documents, including the extremely valuable succession papers of the elder Pontalbas and Madame de Miró. Charles A. F. Berçeon was one of Micael's chief notaries during the years when she was disengaging from Célestin and building the Hôtel Pontalba; details of her purchase of the Havré mansion as well as her purchases of 41, 43, and 45 rue St.-Honoré are contained in his records. In her later years, Micael used Charles St.-Ange Berçeon and C. A. Moquard, from whose records the Mirès affair can be traced, as well as young Célestin's copper-smelting debacle, and Alfred's two marriages. However, Micael's estate inventory, that most useful of all her documents, was registered under the notary A.-L. Massion, an associate of Moquard. "Inventaire après le décès de Mme. la Baronne de Pontalba, 30 avril 1874," aside from being an amazing list of Micael's possessions, is the single most comprehensive source of information about Mont-l'Évêque—the *majorat*, chain of title, and additions to the property and château.

Plans for the Hôtel Pontalba, along with dozens of useful miscellaneous documents, were found in the architect L.-T.-J. Visconti's papers, in the private collection of the late Count Hervé du Périer de Larson. Micael's "Note Adressé à Mssrs. les Experts," summarizing her objections to Visconti, is among the manuscripts in the Howard-Tilton Library in New Orleans.

A single source provided nearly all of the information about the Ney family: Les Archives du Maréchal Ney in the Archives Nationales, Paris, contains hundreds and hundreds of letters that various members of the family sent to each other, as well as some official correspondence concerning the execution of Marshal Ney. Included are the letters of the duchesse d'Elchingen to her husband and the letters of the Ney sons to their mother.

Miscellaneous manuscripts dealing with Micael's married life include the birth and death records of some of her children in the Registre de l'État Civile de Mont-l'Évêque, 1813 à 1822, in the town of Mont-l'Évêque; civil registers in Senlis; and passenger lists of vessels arriving in New Orleans (1820–1902) and New York (1848–1850) in the New Orleans and New York public libraries. To locate official letters of François Guillemin in the Archives Nationales, consult Abraham P. Nasatir and Gary Elwyn Monell, *French Consuls in the United States, A Calendar of Their Correspondence in the Archives Nationales* (Washington, D.C., 1967), where one also meets the dozens of memoirs on Louisiana submitted to Napoleon. Useful also was "Ville de Paris, Cadastre de 1862," rue du Faubourg St.-Honoré, in the Archives de Paris. Blanche de Pontalba's letter to her son came from a private collection of the Maricourt family.

For an assessment of Micael's wealth, property, and business interests in New Orleans after the draining of Bayou Road, the essential records are those of Orleans Parish Probate Court in the New Orleans Public Library, especially the New Orleans inventories made for her succession and those of her sons. See also the records of Edward Barnett, Felix Grima, Theodore Guyol, and Jules Mossy in the New Orleans Notarial Archives. The notarial records are generally indexed but are by no means complete for New Orleans, since many years are missing altogether. These records contain important documents concerning partitions and exchanges of Micael's property during the 1840s and 1850s, as well as letters to her agents. The Combined Tax Registry for 1840 and 1850 is on microfilm in the New Orleans Public Library. To judge the immensity of Micael's holdings and trace the individual buyers of her property, see the Conveyance Records of New Orleans in the Civil Court Building, where a dismaying number of Micael's sales are recorded for the years 1836–1860.

The important manuscripts for the chapters on New Orleans during the construction of the Pontalba Buildings are the journals of the minutes of the three municipalities, respectively, on microfilm in the New Orleans Public Library, but not translated when in French. Miscellaneous documents include the sixth and seventh censuses of the United States, and construction contracts filed with P. C. Cuvellier, L. T. Caire, Joseph Lisbony, and A. Ducatel, New Orleans Notarial Archives. See also "WPA Plans by Weiss, *et al.*," July 21, 1936; "Contract: Church Wardens with J. N. P. de Pouilly," 1849; and "Building Contract with Pierre and Raymond Pelanne," Feb. 14, 1851, in the C. L. Thompson Collection, all in the Louisiana Historical Center. Other relevant and interesting manuscripts are the letters of John McDonogh in Howard-Tilton. Walt Whitman's first draft for his articles on New Orleans which appeared in the *Daily Picayune*, and the drawings of Gaston de Pontalba in the Graphics Collection, are both in the Louisiana Historical Center, where one also finds a useful record of the names and occupations of Micael's tenants, "Pontalba Building Residents, 1851–1861." The Vieux Carré Survey in the Historic New Orleans Collection is the museum's collection of documents relating to certain sites in the Old Quarter.

For yellow fever in New Orleans and life during the Civil War, see "U.S. Customs House Correspondence, 1848–58"; the Beebe Family Papers; and "John C. Dunlap, Miscellaneous Papers, 1841–1862" in the George Smith Collection, all in the Louisiana Historical Center.

JUDICIAL RECORDS

Both civil and criminal court proceedings in New Orleans during the Spanish period can be found in the Spanish Judicial Records in the Louisiana Historical Center. The collection is particularly thorough for the years 1788–1791, in cases judged by Almonester, and also includes a number of cases in which Almonester or Pontalba were parties to a suit. The manuscripts are still sturdy but the cases, despite preservation efforts, are often illegible due to deterioration of the ink; however, many cases were summarized by the WPA during the 1930s in typescript volumes available at the desk. See also Laura Porteous' "Index to Judicial Records of Louisiana," in the early volumes of *Louisiana Historical Quarterly*. For Madame Almonester's struggles to avoid completing Almonester's charitable projects, see "Proceedings Instituted by Bishop Luis Peñalver y Cardeñas vs. Widow Almonester, 1799–1801," WPA translation in the Louisiana Historical Center and the New Orleans Public Library.

Micael's two major separation trials, in 1835 and 1836, took place in France. The pleadings of lawyers for both sides appeared in *Gazette des Tribuneaux, Journal de Jurisprudence et des Débats Judiciares*, which, like several similar publications, served as a juridical reporting service as well as a newspaper. A WPA translation of part of the 1835 trial only, "Court Action Between the Baron and Baroness de Pontalba," May 11,

1835, is included in the Pontalba Family Papers in the Louisiana Historical Center and Howard-Tilton. A number of documents filed during these French trials are included in two Louisiana proceedings, which were interrelated suits for property separation tried in New Orleans: Pontalba v. Pontalba, Docket #2129 (1831), and #2856 (1839), in Louisiana Supreme Court Records, Earl K. Long Library, University of New Orleans. Micael's other Supreme Court cases are useful for sorting out the complicated title disputes and partitions of the Bayou Road property. These cases are: Nicolet/Moore vs. Pontalba, 1836; Kenton vs. Michaela Leonarda, 1842; O'Brien vs. Pontalba, 1858; and Pontalba vs. Mayor, Aldermen, *et al.*, 1849. The United States Supreme Court record of Pontalba vs. Copland, 1848, is not in New Orleans, but a summary appears in *3 La. Ann.* #86. The U.S. Supreme Court decision in Kenton v. Michaela Leonarda is reported in I *Rob.* 344. See also Pontalba vs. Phoenix Assurance Co., 1842.

Micael's important lower-court cases run from 1838 to 1859 in the First, Second, Third, Fourth, and Sixth Judicial Districts, and in Parish Court, all in the New Orleans Public Library. Suits that turn up in the 1860s are minor cases involving, for example, delinquent renters.

The main source of information for the construction of the Pontalba Buildings remains the fragile court record in manuscript, Samuel Stewart vs. Mme. de Pontalba, Second District, Dec. 20, 1851, in the New Orleans Public Library's rare manuscripts.

Micael's lawsuits in France with contractors, tenants, and so on, are summarized in various repositories of the Archives de Paris, where fragments of some cases can still be found. The cases surrounding the construction of the Hôtel Pontalba are located in an annex of the Archives in the town of Villemoison-sur-l'Orgue. There are no indexes to the cases meticulously filed in Villemoison. Alone with endless rows of identical binders, one proceeds year by year through the enormous archive of manuscripts, many of which disintegrate on contact, looking for the Pontalba name. The extant cases involving Micael are Pontalba c. Salles, 1841, 1843, Tribunal de Commerce; and Tencé c. Pontalba et Vivenel, Tribunal Civil de la Seine, 1842, Cour d'Appel, 1842, 1843. Some cases involving the elder Pontalbas are also in Villemoison: Pontalba c. Odier, 1840, and St. Avid c. Heriteurs de Trouard, 1840, both in the section Tribunal Civil de la Seine, where the separation trial of the prince and the princesse de la Moskowa, 1845, can also be perused.

The Paris repository of the Archives de Paris has a court calendar, but here the researcher is permitted to consult the archives only a few hours on certain weekdays and is allowed a limited number of documents each day. Nevertheless, one eventually finds several of Micaela's minor cases: Pontalba c. Corbasière, 1842; Lesieur c. Pontalba, 1843; and Ville de Paris c. Pontalba, 1843. Printed reports of other cases involving Micael can be found in *Journal du Palais*, *Gazette du Palais*, *Recueil Sirey*, and *Recueil Dalloz*, 2ᵉ série, all specialized legal publications.

NEW ORLEANS NEWSPAPERS

Commercial Bulletin, 1851
Courier de la Louisiane, 1809, 1850
Daily Crescent, 1849–50, 1853–55

Daily Delta, Weekly Delta, 1850–51
Daily Picayune, 1842–47, 1851–52, 1874
Era, 1864
L'Abeille de la Nouvelle Orléans, 1835, 1849–51
Le Moniteur de la Louisiane, 1802–1803, 1811
L'Orléanais, 1849–50, 1853–54
Republican, 1875
Tägliche Deutsche Zeitung, 1847–52, 1857
Times Democrat, 1892
Times-Picayune, 1912–36

FRENCH NEWSPAPERS

Charivari, 1832
Gazette des Tribunaux, 1834–36
Journal des Débats, 1834, 1848
La Gazette de France, 1873
La Presse, 1866
Le Constitutionnel, 1834
Le Figaro, 1834
Le Journal de l'Oise, 1834
Le Moniteur Universel, 1811–15
Le Pays, 1849

OTHER NEWSPAPERS

Christian Science Monitor, 1974–76
London *Chronicle*, 1870–71
New York *Times*, 1848–52

BOOKS

Agulhon, Maurice. *La Vie Sociale en Provence Interieure au Lendemain de la Revolution.* Paris, 1970.
Almanach Imperial, 1860. Paris, 1868.
Arvin, N. C. *Eugène Scribe and the French Theater: 1815–1860.* Cambridge, Eng., 1924.
Audiganne, M. *Paris Dans Sa Splendeur.* 4 vols. Paris, 1861.
Aulanier, Christiane. *Le Nouveau Louvre de Napoléon III.* Paris, n.d.
Bannon, J. F. *The Spanish Borderlands Frontier, 1513–1821.* Albuquerque, 1963.
Bauchal, Charles. *Nouveau Dictionnaire des Architectes Français.* Paris, 1887.
Baudier, Roger. *The Catholic Church in Louisiana.* New Orleans, 1931.
Bawr, Madame de. *Mes Souvenirs.* Paris, 1853.
Becker, George, trans. *Paris Under Siege, 1870–1871: From the Goncourt Journal.* New York, 1969.
Belleval, René Marquis de. *Souvenirs de ma Jeunesse.* Paris, 1895.
Bérard des Glajeux, Anatole. *Souvenirs d'un President d'Assises (1880–1890).* Paris, 1892.
Berquin-Duvallon, [?]. *Vue de la Colonie Espagnole du Mississipi.* Paris, 1803.
Bertaut, Jules. *Le Faubourg St.-Germaine sous l'Empire et la Restauration.* Paris, 1949.

Bertier de Sauvigny, Guillaume. *The Bourbon Restoration*. Philadelphia, 1966.

Bésard, François-Yves. *Souvenirs d'un Nonagénaire*. Paris, 1880.

Blanc, Louis. *The History of Ten Years, 1830–1840*. 2 vols. New York, 1845.

Bléton, Pierre. *La Vie Sociale sous le Second Empire*. Paris, 1963.

Boucher, Charles. *Mémoires*. 2 vols. Paris, 1908.

Boucher, Henri. *Souvenirs d'un Parisien pendant la Seconde République, 1831–1852*. Paris, 1906.

Bousfield, Charles, trans. *Memoirs of Count Horace de Viel Castel*. 4 vols. London, 1888.

Brault, Elie. *Les Architectes par leurs Oeuvres*. Paris, n.d.

Broglie, Duc de. *Souvenirs, 1785–1870*. Paris, 1886.

Bruns, J. Edgar. *Archbishop Antoine Blanc Memorial*. New Orleans, 1981.

Burnand, Robert. *La Vie Quotidienne en France en 1830*. Paris, 1943.

Burson, Caroline M. *The Stewardship of Don Esteban Miró, 1782–92*. New Orleans, 1940.

Carter, Hodding, ed. *The Past as Prelude: New Orleans, 1718-1968*. New Orleans, 1968.

Challamel, Augustin. *Souvenirs d'un Hugolâtre*. Paris, 1885.

Chuquet, Arthur, ed. *Recollections of Baron de Frénilly*. New York, 1909.

Clark, John G. *New Orleans, 1718–1812: An Economic History*. Baton Rouge, 1970.

Claudin, Gustave. *Mes Souvenirs*. Paris, 1884.

Code of Practice in Civil Cases for the State of Louisiana. New Orleans, 1824.

Coker, William S., and Robert R. Rea, eds. *Anglo-Spanish Confrontation on the Gulf Coast During the American Revolution*. Pensacola, 1982.

Coleman, James J., Jr. *Gilbert Antoine de St. Maxent: The Spanish-Frenchman of New Orleans*. New Orleans, 1968.

Coupérie, Pierre. *Paris Through the Ages*. New York, 1968.

Curtis, Nathaniel C. *New Orleans: Its Old Houses, Shops, and Public Buildings*. Philadelphia, 1933.

Daly, César. *L'Architecture Privée au XIXe Siècle sous Napoléon III*. 3 vols. Paris, 1864.

d'Apponyi, Rudolphe. *Vingt-Cinq Ans à Paris*. 4 vols. Paris, 1913.

d'Armaille, Comtesse. *Quand On Savait Vivre Heureux*. Paris, 1934.

Daudet, Ernest, ed. *Journal de Victor de Balabine*. Paris, 1914.

Daumard, Adéline. *Le Bourgeoisie Parisienne de 1815 à 1848*. Paris, 1906.

David, René. *The French Legal System*. New York, 1958.

Desmoulins, Evariste. *Histoire Complet du Procès du Maréchal Ney*. Paris, 1815.

d'Hautpoul, Alphonse. *Mémoires du Général Marquis Alphonse d'Hautpoul*. Paris, 1906.

Din, Gilbert C., and John E. Harkins. *The New Orleans Cabildo: Colonial Louisiana's First City Government, 1769–1803*. Baton Rouge, 1996.

Dino, Duchesse de. *Chronique de 1831 à 1862*. Paris, 1909.

Duffy, John. *Sword of Pestilence: The New Orleans Yellow Fever Epidemic of 1853*. Baton Rouge, 1966.

———. *The Tulane University Medical Center: One Hundred Years of Medical Education*. Baton Rouge, 1984.

———, ed. *Parson Clapp of the Strangers' Chruch of New Orleans*. Baton Rouge, 1957.

——, ed. *The Rudolph Matas History of Medicine in Louisiana.* Vol. I of 2 vols. Baton Rouge, 1958.

Dupeux, Georges. *La Société Française, 1789–1960.* Paris, 1964.

Dupin, Eugène, ed. *Plaidoyers de Philippe Dupin.* 2 vols. Paris, 1868.

Ellis, Geoffrey. *Beyond the Terror.* Cambridge, Eng., 1983.

Farat, H. *Persigny: Un Ministre de Napoléon III.* Paris, 1957.

Ferry, Jules. *Comptes Fantastiques d'Haussmann.* Paris, 1868.

Field, Rachel. *All This and Heaven Too.* New York, 1938. A novel, the basis for a Bette Davis movie about the Praslin affair.

Fortier, Alcée. *A History of Louisiana.* 4 vols. New York, 1904.

Fossier, Albert. *New Orleans, The Glamour Period: 1800–1840.* New Orleans, 1957.

Franqueville, Charles de. *Souvenirs Intimes sur la Vie de Mon Père.* Paris, 1878.

French Home Life (reprints from *Blackwood's* magazine). New York, 1874.

Galbraith, Marie, ed. *The American Ambassador's Residence in Paris.* Paris, 1985. The only copies of this useful commemorative brochure seem to be in the possession of private individuals and U.S. State Department officials.

Galignani, W. *Galignani's New Paris Guide for 1864.* London, 1864.

Gayarré, Charles. *History of Louisiana.* 3rd ed. 4 vols. New Orleans, 1883.

Gibson, Charles. *Spain in America.* New York, 1967.

Girard, L. *La Politique des Travaux Publics du Second Empire.* Paris, 1952.

Goncourt, Edmond de, and Jules de Goncourt. *Journal.* 6 vols. Monaco, 1903.

Goodrich, F. B. *The Court of Napoleon.* New York, 1857.

Guiral, Pierre. *La Vie Quotidienne en France à l'age d'or du capitalisme, 1852–1879.* Paris, 1976.

Hall, Abraham Oakey. *The Manhattaner in New Orleans.* New York, 1851.

Hargreaves-Mawdsley, W. N. *Spain Under the Bourbons, 1700–1833: A Collection of Documents.* Columbia, S.C., 1973.

Hautecoeur, L. *Histoire de Louvre.* Paris, 1928.

Hearn, Lafcadio [Wil H. Coleman]. *Historical Sketchbook and Guide to New Orleans and Environs.* New York, 1885.

Herzog, P. *Civil Procedure in France.* The Hague, 1967.

Hillebrand, Karl. *France and the French in the Second Half of the Nineteenth Century.* London, 1881.

Hirsch, Arnold R., and Joseph Logsdon, eds. *Creole New Orleans: Race and Americanization.* Baton Rouge, 1992.

Holtman, Robert B., ed. *Napoleon and America.* Pensacola, 1988. See especially the chapter "A Tale of Two Codes: The Code Napoleon and the Louisiana Civil Code."

Huber, Leonard V., and Samuel Wilson, Jr. *Baroness Pontalba's Buildings.* 4th ed. New Orleans, 1979.

——. *The Basilica on Jackson Square.* New Orleans, 1966.

Hull, Anthony. *Charles III and the Revival of Spain.* Washington, D.C., 1980.

Hutchins, Thomas. *Historical Narrative of Louisiana and West Florida.* Philadelphia, 1784.

Institute for Advanced Study. *Fertility and Family Structure in France.* Princeton, 1972.

Jacques, Annie. *La Carrière de l'Architecte au XIXᵉ Siècle.* Paris, 1986.

Jewell, Edwin. *Jewell's Crescent City Illustrated*. New Orleans, 1873.

Jordan, David P. *Transforming Paris: The Life and Labors of Baron Haussmann*. Chicago, 1995.

Kinnaird, Lawrence, ed. *Spain in the Mississippi Valley, 1765–1794*. 3 vols. Washington, D.C., 1946–49.

Kmen, Henry. *Music in New Orleans*. New Orleans, 1966.

Kurtz, Harold. *The Trial of Marshal Ney: His Last Years and Death*. New York, 1957.

Lafever, Minard. *Beauties of Modern Architecture*. New York, 1845[?].

Lane, Adolphe. *Dictionnaire des Architectes Français*. 2 vols. Paris, 1872.

Laussat, Pierre Clément de. *Memoirs of My Life*. Translated by Agnes-Josephine Pastwa. Edited by Robert D. Bush, 2 vols. Baton Rouge, 1978.

Legouvé, Ernest. *Soixante Ans de Souvenirs*. 2 vols. Paris, 1887.

Lewis, Gwynne, *et al*. *Beyond the Terror*. Cambridge, Eng., 1983.

Leys, M. D. R. *Between Two Empires*. London, 1955.

Lubin, George, ed. *Georges Sand: Correspondance*. 4 vols. Paris, 1966.

Lynch, John. *Spanish Colonial Administration, 1782–1810*. London, 1958.

McDermott, John F. *The Spanish in the Mississippi Valley, 1762–1804*. Urbana, 1974. See especially Samuel Wilson, Jr.'s essay on Almonester's benefactions.

McMurtrie, Douglas. *Early Printing in New Orleans*. New Orleans, 1929.

Martin, Benjamin F. *Crime and Criminal Justice Under the Third Republic: The Shame of Marianne*. Baton Rouge, 1990.

Martin, F. X. *History of Louisiana*. New Orleans, 1882.

Menière, Prosper. *Journal*. Paris, 1903.

Mérimée, Prosper. *Correspondance Générale*. Edited by Maurice Parturier. 4 vols. Toulouse, 1956.

Michel, François. *Stendahl Fichier*. 4 vols. Boston, 1964.

Miller, Eugène. *Senlis et ses Environs*. Senlis, 1896.

Mirès, Jules. *À Mes Juges, Ma Vie et Mes Affaires*. Paris, 1861. The only copy I could locate of this interesting book is in the Bibliothèque Nationale in Paris.

Moses, Claire Goldberg. *French Feminism in the Nineteenth Century*. Albany, 1984.

Nasatir, A. P. *Borderland in Retreat*. Albuquerque, 1976.

——. *Spanish War Vessels on the Mississippi, 1792–1796*. New Haven, 1968.

Parry, J. H. *The Sale of Public Office in the Spanish Indies Under the Hapsburgs*. Berkeley, 1953.

Picard, Ernest. *Mon Journal*. Paris, 1892.

Pittman, Philip. *The Present State of the European Settlements on the Mississippi*. Facsimile edition by Joseph G. Tregle, Jr. Gainesville, Fla., 1973.

Pontalba, Célestin de. *Réponse de M. de Pontalba à l'Écrit de M. Mirès Intitulé "À Mes Juges."* Paris, 1861. The only copy I could locate of this book is in the Bibliothèque Nationale in Paris.

Ponteuil, Félix. *Les Institutions de la France de 1814 à 1879*. Paris, 1966.

Price, Roger. *A Social History of 19th-Century France*. London, 1987.

Raison, André. *Les Donations entre Époux*. Paris, 1978.

Reinders, Robert. *End of an Era: New Orleans, 1850–1860*. New Orleans, 1964.

Richardson, Johanna. *Princess Mathilde*. London, 1979.

——. *La Vie Parisienne*. London, 1971.

Ripley, Eliza. *Social Life in Old New Orleans*. New York, 1912.

Robert, Henri. *Un Avocat de 1830.* Paris, 1930.

Robertson, J. A., ed. *Louisiana Under the Rule of France, Spain, and the United States (1785–1807).* Cleveland, 1911.

Robin, C. C. *Voyage to Louisiana, 1803–1805.* Translated by Stuart O. Landry, Jr. New Orleans, 1966.

Rodríguez, A. A. *La Pobalción de Luisiana Española, 1763–1803,* Madrid, 1979.

Rosenberg, C. C. *Jenny Lind's Tour of America and Cuba.* New York, 1851.

Salvaggio, John. *New Orleans' Charity Hospital: A Story of Physicians, Politics, and Poverty.* Baton Rouge, 1992.

Simond, Charles. *Paris de 1800 à 1900.* 3 vols. Paris, 1901.

——. *Paris Pendant l'Année 1859.* 4 vols. Paris, 1900.

Stendahl [Marie-Henri Beyle]. *Correspondance de Stendhal, 1800–1842.* 4 vols. Paris, 1908.

Stern, Daniel. *Mes Souvenirs.* Paris, 1877.

Stetson, Dorothy McBride. *Women's Rights in France.* New York, 1980.

Stoddard, Amos. *Sketches Historical and Descriptive of Louisiana.* Philadelphia, 1812.

Thullier, Guy. *La Vie Quotidienne dans les Ministères au XIXe siècle.* Paris, 1976.

Tombs, Robert. *The War Against Paris, 1871.* Cambridge, Eng., 1981.

Van Zanten, David. *Designing Paris.* New York, 1987.

Visconti, L.-T.-J. *Tombeau de Napoléon Ier dans le dôme des Invalides.* Paris, 1853. The only copy I was able to locate is in the Bibliothèque Nationale, Paris.

Vizetelly, Ernest Alfred. *My Adventures in the Commune.* London, 1914. A colorful account by an English journalist, to be read critically.

Welschinger, Henri. *Le Maréchal Ney, 1815.* Paris, 1893.

Williams, Roger L. *Gaslight and Shadow: The World of Napoleon III.* New York, 1957.

Wilson, Samuel, Jr. *The Cabildo.* New Orleans, 1961.

——. *Louisiana Purchase.* New Orleans, 1953.

——. ed., *Impressions Respecting New Orleans by Benjamin Henry Boneval Latrobe.* 1905; rpr. New York, 1951.

Witt, Madame de, ed. *Lettres de M. Guizot à sa Famille et à ses Amis.* Paris, 1884.

Young, Archibald. *An Historical Sketch of the French Bar: From its Origins to the Present Day.* 1869; rpr. Littleton, Colo., 1987.

Zolà, Émile. *Correspondance.* Edited by B. H. Bakker. Paris, 1978.

ARTICLES AND ESSAYS

Anderson, Susan. "An American Embassy." *Architectural Digest,* XXXVI (July, 1979), 130–36.

"A Parigi, per l'Ambasciata Americana." *Domus,* No. 528 (Nov., 1973), 87–98.

Barbet de Jouy, H. "J. F. Bouchet, Architecte." *Gazette de Beaux-Arts,* VI (1860), 173.

Beerman, Eric. "Colonel Andrés Almonester: Spanish Louisiana's First Philanthropist." New Orleans *Genesis,* XVIII (Sept., 1978), 389–94.

Bjork, D. J. "Documents Relating to the Establishment of Schools in Louisiana, 1771." *Mississippi Valley Historical Review,* XI (1925), 561–69.

Brasseaux, Carl A. "François-Louis Hector, Baron de Carondelet et Noyelles." In *The Louisiana Governors: From Iberville to Edwards,* edited by Joseph G. Dawson. Baton Rouge, 1990.

Brink, Florence. "Literary Travelers in Louisiana Between 1803 and 1860." *Louisiana Historical Quarterly*, XXI (April, 1948), 414.

"A Catholic Lady in 'Red' Paris." London *Spectator* (April, 1871), 62.

Dart, Henry. "Account of the Credit and Debit Funds of the City of New Orleans for the Year 1789." *Louisiana Historical Quarterly*, XIX (1936), 584–94.

Dart, William Kernion. "Walt Whitman in New Orleans." *Publications of the Louisiana Historical Association*, I (1914), 97–108.

"A Decree for Louisiana Issued by the Baron de Carondelet, June 1, 1795." *Louisiana Historical Quarterly*, XX (July, 1937), 590.

De Rojas, Lauro. "The Great Fire of 1788 in New Orleans." *Louisiana Historical Quarterly*, XXI (1940), 739.

Din, Gilbert C. "The Offices and Functions of the New Orleans Cabildo." *Louisiana History*, XXXVII (Winter, 1996), 5–30.

Faye, Stanley. "Consuls of Spain in New Orleans, 1804–1821." *Louisiana Historical Quarterly*, XXI (1938), 677–84.

——. "The Great Stroke of Pierre Lafitte." *Louisiana Historical Quarterly*, XXI (1940), 739.

Gramont, Sanche de. "Proust's Paris." *Horizon*, XIV, No. 4 (1972).

Holmes, J. D. "Dramatis Personae in Spanish Louisiana." *Louisiana Studies*, VI (Summer, 1967), 183.

Huber, Leonard V. "Heyday of the Floating Palace." *American Heritage*, VIII (Oct., 1957), 14–23.

Hughes, Robert. "The Beaux-Arts Tradition Reconsidered." *Horizon*, XVII (Winter, 1976), 65–71.

Kendall, John S. "The Foreign Language Press of New Orleans." *Louisiana Historical Quarterly*, XII (1929), 358–80.

Ledermann, S. "Les divorces et les separations de corps en France." *Population*, XVIII (April–June, 1948), 338.

Lewis, H. D. "The Legal Status of Women in Nineteenth-Century France." *Journal of European Studies*, X (June, 1980), 181–85.

Louisiana Scrapbook, LXX (July 11, 1937), 7; XXXIII (July 18, 1937), 118–40.

McCutcheon, Robert P. "Books and Booksellers in New Orleans, 1730–1830." *Louisiana Historical Quarterly*, XX (July, 1937), 607–11.

Nasatir, A. P. "Government Employees and Salaries in Spanish Louisiana." *Louisiana Historical Quarterly*, XXIX (Oct., 1946), 889.

O'Connor, Stella. "The Charity Hospital of Louisiana." *Louisiana Historical Quarterly*, XXXI (Jan., 1948), 12–28.

Porteous, Laura. "Torture in Spanish Criminal Procedure." *Louisiana Historical Quarterly*, VIII (Jan., 1925), 5–27.

——, trans. "Index to Spanish Judicial Records of Louisiana, XXXVIII." *Louisiana Historical Quarterly*, XV (Oct., 1932), 686–87.

——. trans. "A Regulation Concerning the General Police . . . 1795." *Louisiana Historical Quarterly*, VIII (Jan., 1925), 598.

——. trans. "Sanitary Conditions in New Orleans Under the Spanish Regime, 1799–1800." *Louisiana Historical Quarterly*, XV (Oct., 1932), 610–14.

Priestly, Herbert. "Spanish Colonial Municipalities." *Louisiana Historical Quarterly*, II (1922), 28.

Riley, Martin. "Development of Education in Louisiana." *Louisiana Historical Quarterly,* XIX (1936), 614–15.

Tregle. Joseph G., Jr. "Early New Orleans Society: A Reappraisal." *Journal of Southern History,* XVIII (Feb., 1952).

Whittington, G. P. "The Sibley Papers, Journal and Letters." *Louisiana Historical Quarterly,* X (1927), 474–501.

Wood, Minter, "Life in New Orleans in the Spanish Period." *Louisiana Historical Quarterly,* XXII (July, 1939), 642–737.

UNPUBLISHED WORKS

Fiehrer, Thomas Marc. "The Baron de Carondelet as Agent of Bourbon Reform," Ph.D. dissertation, Tulane University, 1977.

Soulé, Leon C. "The Creole-American Struggle in New Orleans Politics, 1850–1862." M.A. thesis, Tulane University, 1955.

Index